An Anglo-Saxon Cemetery at Collingbourne Ducis, Wiltshire

By Kirsten Egging Dinwiddy and Nick Stoodley

An Anglo-Saxon Cemetery at Collingbourne Ducis, Wiltshire

By Kirsten Egging Dinwiddy and Nick Stoodley

with contributions by Catherine Barnett, Eleanor Blakelock, Nicholas Cooke, Elizabeth McCormick, Jacqueline I. McKinley, Lorraine Mepham and Jacqui Watson

Illustrations by
Rob Goller, Nick Griffiths, S. E. James and Rob Read

Wessex Archaeology Report 37
2016

Published 2016 by Wessex Archaeology Ltd
Portway House, Old Sarum Park, Salisbury, SP4 6EB
www.wessexarch.co.uk

British Library Cataloguing in Publication Data
A catalogue record for this book is available from the British Library

ISBN 978-1-911137-00-9

Designed and typeset by Kenneth Lymer
Edited by Phil Andrews and Philippa Bradley
Cover design by Rob Goller

Printed by Lightning Source

Front cover
Gilded copper alloy bell-shaped brooch (grave 92, ON 221)

Back cover
Pair of gilded copper alloy saucer brooches (grave 69, ONs 163 and 164)
Gilded copper alloy keystone garnet disc brooch (unstratified, ON 140)
Pair of copper alloy equal-armed brooches (grave 64, ONs 5 and 6)
Artist's impression of a bed similar to that from grave 96 (S. E. James)

Wessex Archaeology Ltd is a company limited by guarantee registered in England, company number 1712772. It is also a Charity registered in England and Wales number 287786, and in Scotland, Scottish Charity number SC042630. Our registered office is at Portway House, Old Sarum Park, Salisbury, Wiltshire, SP4 6EB.

Contents

List of Figures

List of Plates

List of Tables

List of Contributors

Catherine Barnett
University of Reading (formerly Wessex Archaeology)

Eleanor Blakelock
Archaeomaterials (formerly Bradford University)

Nicholas Cooke
Wessex Archaeology

Kirsten Egging Dinwiddy
Wessex Archaeology

Nick Griffiths
Freelance illustrator

Rob Goller
Wessex Archaeology

S. E. James
Wessex Archaeology

Elizabeth McCormick
Formerly Archaeological Conservation and Technology Team, English Heritage

Jacqueline I. McKinley
Wessex Archaeology

Lorraine Mepham
Wessex Archaeology

Rob Read
Freelance illustrator

Nick Stoodley
Freelance archaeologist of the Anglo-Saxon period

Jacqui Watson
Formerly Head Conservator, English Heritage

Acknowledgements

Wessex Archaeology are grateful to Sarsen Housing Association and Persimmon Homes South Coast Limited for funding the main excavation, post-excavation and publication stages; Jude Barber and Jon Bentley are recognised for their support in this respect. The co-operation of Mr and Mrs Bainton of number 106, and Mr and Mrs Smith of 'Roxana', Cadley Road is duly acknowledged, as is the assistance provided by Sue Farr and Vanessa Clare (Wiltshire County Archaeological Service (WCAS)).

The archaeological fieldwork carried out between 2006 and 2009 was managed for Wessex Archaeology by Nick Truckle, the various stages being directed in the field by Kevin Ritchie, Steve Thompson, Phil Harding and Steve Tatler.

Conservation of most of the copper alloy finds was carried out by Lynn Wootten at Wessex Archaeology, with the remainder of the copper alloy and all of the ironwork conservation undertaken by Kelly Abbot, Sebastian Foxley, Beth Werrett and Helen Williams at the Wiltshire Council Conservation Laboratory, Chippenham. The x-radiography of the metalwork was undertaken by Angie Britten. Jessica Grimm identified the animal bone and Matt Leivers examined the flint.

Elizabeth McCormick undertook the XRF and investigational analysis of the metalwork and identification of the mineral-preserved organics whilst at English Heritage, and we are also grateful to Jacqui Watson, formerly of English Heritage, for her contribution on the bed burial. We were fortunate that Eleanor Blakelock was able to undertake analysis of the knives as part of her doctoral research at Bradford University and include a summary of that work here.

The post-excavation programme was managed by Jörn Schuster and Phil Andrews, and we are particularly grateful to Jacqueline I McKinley for commenting on an earlier draft of this report. The report was edited by Phil Andrews and Philippa Bradley. The site illustrations, distribution maps and grave plans are by Rob Goller, with the non-ferrous objects drawn by Nick Griffiths, the iron objects by Rob Read, and bed fittings by S. E. James.

This report was subject to revisions in 2015, but has not been substantially updated since it was prepared in 2011.

Abstract

The 2007 excavations at Collingbourne Ducis revealed almost the full extent of an Anglo-Saxon cemetery first recorded immediately to the west in 1974, providing one of the largest samples of burial remains from Anglo-Saxon Wiltshire. The cemetery lies 200 m to the north-east of a broadly contemporaneous settlement on lower lying ground next to the River Bourne.

Eighty-two inhumation graves and four cremation graves were recorded, in addition to the 33 inhumation graves discovered in 1974. The cemetery was in use between the late 5th and 7th centuries – delineated to the east by a coombe for the majority of its duration, when graves tended to focus around particular cemetery features such as the mortuary structures and earlier graves. There was an apparent shift to the south and east in the 7th century – when, for the first time, the area to the east of the coombe was utilised. Notable features here included a four-post structure and a rare example of a 'bed' burial. The cremation graves all lay to the west of the coombe, but most of a series of small pits containing redeposited cremation-related material were found to the east; some cut the fills of inhumation burials, whilst 'placed' cremation-related deposits were included in two inhumation burials. Similar material was also recovered from the mortuary structures. Study of the human bone assemblage has provided a glimpse into the lives of those living in a community on the western frontier of the Anglo-Saxon world, in the late 5th–7th century. The cemetery was probably used for several generations by most, if not all, members of the local community. Some individuals or groups might have originated outside the local area, possibly implied by mixed burial practices and the variety of grave goods. General health was notably poorer than that of some contemporaneous rural populations, and there is some evidence for infections such as tuberculosis and leprosy.

The grave goods include several burials with weapons and a diversity of jewellery assemblages, though none exhibit a particularly impressive range of wealth. Because virtually the entire cemetery appears to have been explored, however, reliable observations can be made about its establishment, layout and development. This is particularly significant for the 7th century, when the focus of burial shifted, and changes in mortuary strategy may have reflected changes to the structure of society and the emergence of large Anglo-Saxon kingdoms.

Zusammenfassung

Während der 2007 in Collingbourne Ducis durchgeführten Ausgrabungen wurde nahezu das gesamte Areal eines erstmals 1974 auf dem westlich angrenzenden Gelände untersuchten, angelsächsischen Gräberfelds erfasst, womit hier nun einer der umfangreichsten Bestattungsplätze des angelsächsischen Wiltshire vorliegt. Das Gräberfeld liegt 200 m nordöstlich einer mehr oder weniger gleichzeitigen Siedlung, die sich auf dem tiefer gelegenen Gelände entlang des Flusses Bourne befindet.

Es wurden 82 Körpergräber und vier Brandgräber untersucht, zusätzlich zu den 1974 entdeckten 33 Körpergräbern. Die Nutzung des Gräberfelds erstreckte sich vom späten 5. bis ins 7. Jahrhundert. Eine Senke bildete seine östliche Begrenzung über den größten Teil der Belegungsdauer, als sich die Gräber um bestimmte Gräberfeldbefunde wie z. B. Grabbauten und ältere Gräber konzentrierten. Im 7. Jahrhundert fand offensichtlich eine Verlagerung nach Süden und Osten statt – in diesem Zeitraum wurde auch erstmals der Bereich östlich der Senke genutzt. Unter den hervorzuhebenden Befunden finden sich u.a. eine Vier-Pfosten Struktur sowie ein seltenes Beispiel einer Bestattung in einem Bett. Die Brandgräber lagen allesamt westlich der Senke, aber der Großteil einer Reihe kleiner Gruben, die umgelagertes, mit Brandbestattungen in Verbindung zu bringendes Material enthielten, wurden östlich davon gefunden; einige schnitten die Verfüllungen von Körpergräbern, während zwei Körpergräber mit Brandbestattungen in Verbindung zu bringende, intentionelle Deponierungen enthielten. Vergleichbares Material wurde auch aus den Grabbauten geborgen.

Die Untersuchung des menschlichen Knochenmaterials erlaubt einen Einblick in die Lebensumstände von Individuen einer im westlichen Grenzbereich der angelsächsischen Welt existierenden Gemeinschaft während des späten 5. bis 7. Jahrhunderts. Das Gräberfeld wurde wahrscheinlich über mehrere Generationen von den meisten, wenn nicht gar allen Angehörigen der örtlichen Gemeinschaft genutzt. Einige Individuen oder Gruppen stammen vielleicht von außerhalb der engeren Umgebung, was sich durch gemischte Bestattungspraktiken und die Auswahl an Grabbeigaben andeutet. Im Vergleich zu einigen anderen zeitgleichen ländlichen Populationen war der allgemeine Gesundheitszustand merklich schlechter, so fanden sich u.a. Hinweise auf Infektionen wie Tuberkulose und Lepra.

Die Grabeigaben mehrerer Bestattungen umfassten Waffen sowie verschiedene Schmuckensembles, von denen aber keine ein besonders eindrucksvolles Ausmaß an Wohlstand zur Schau stellte. Da nahezu das gesamte Gräberfeld untersucht werden konnte, können jedoch verlässliche Aussagen zu seiner Gründung, räumlichen Anordnung und Entwicklung gemacht werden. Dies ist besonders für das 7. Jahrhundert von Bedeutung, als der Schwerpunkt der Bestattungen verlagert wurde und Veränderungen der Bestattungsweise möglicherweise als Niederschlag von Änderungen der Gesellschaftsstruktur und der Herausbildung großer angelsächsischer Königreiche zu werten sind.

Übersetzung: Jörn Schuster

Résumé

Les fouilles de 2007 à Collingbourne Ducis ont révélé la quasi-totalité d'un cimetière anglo-saxon, découvert en 1974 dans le terrain immédiatement à l'ouest, et fournissant un des exemples les mieux documentés des inhumations dans le Wiltshire anglo-saxon. Le cimetière se trouve à 200 m au nord-est d'un habitat en grande partie contemporain, sur une basse terrasse de la rivière Bourne.

Quatre-vingt-deux sépultures à inhumation et quatre fosses à crémation ont été enregistrés, en plus des 33 inhumations découvertes en 1974. Le cimetière a été utilisé de la fin du 5ème au 7ème siècle. Limitées à l'est par une cuvette pendant presque toute leur chronologie, les tombes ont eu tendance à se concentrer autour de certaines structures particulières, comme les structures funéraires et les tombes antérieures. On perçoit un déplacement apparent vers le sud et l'est dans le courant du 7ème siècle, quand, pour la première fois, la zone à l'est de la cuvette a pu être utilisée. Il y a là des structures remarquables, comme par exemple une structure à quatre poteaux et un rare exemple de sépulture en lit funéraire. Toutes les tombes à crémation se trouvaient à l'ouest de la cuvette, mais la plupart des petites fosses contenant des dépôts secondaires liés à des crémations ont été trouvés à l'est; certaines recoupent le remplissage de sépultures à inhumation, tandis que des dépôts liés à la crémation, «déposés» intentionnellement, ont été inclus dans deux sépultures à inhumation. Des traces similaires ont été également observées dans les structures funéraires. L'étude des restes humains a fourni un aperçu de la vie d'une population vivant à la frontière occidentale du monde anglo-saxon, de la fin du 5ème au 7ème siècle. Il est probable que le cimetière a été utilisé pendent plusieurs générations par la plupart, sinon tous les membres de la communauté locale. Certains individus ou groupes pourraient provenir de l'extérieur de la région, ce qu'indiquent peut-être les pratiques funéraires mixtes et la variété des objets funéraires. Il est frappant d'observer une santé générale moins bonne que celle de certaines populations rurales contemporaines : on a trouvé des preuves d'infections comme la tuberculose et la lèpre.

Les objets funéraires proviennent de plusieurs inhumations avec des armes et plusieurs séries d'objets de parure, mais aucun ne fait étalage d'un niveau de richesse particulièrement impressionnant. Parce que la quasi-totalité du cimetière semble avoir été exploré, des observations fiables peuvent être faites sur sa création, son aménagement et son évolution. Ce point est d'une importance particulière pour le 7ème siècle, lorsque se déplacent la majorité des inhumations : des changements dans la stratégie funéraire peuvent refléter des évolutions structurelles de la société et l'émergence de grands royaumes anglo-saxons.

Traduction: Jörn Schuster avec Michel Feugère

Preface

As a young boy I walked this land, my uncle owned it, looking for flints. Little did I know what lay beneath my feet. As a young man, setting out on a profession in archaeology, I took part in the initial excavations on the site. Little did I know the detailed story that that subsequent work might tell. But there was more than this; the personal bit. For much of that time I lived in Collingbourne. The men, women and children of this cemetery were the ancestors of 'my village'. Now the story of their lives can be told through their diet, age, illnesses, artefacts, art and contacts. Such stories are the record of inhabitants of ordinary English villages everywhere. What better way to look at their lives than through the bones of the people themselves.

Phil Harding
September 2011

Chapter 1
Introduction

Project Background

The cemetery was discovered in 1974 during groundworks for the Saxon Rise residential development (Gingell 1978; Fig. 1.1). Between 2006 and 2009, the land immediately to the east and south-east was subject to a programme of archaeological investigations ahead of housing construction and during minor works in adjacent gardens, and it is the results of these investigations which are presented here. The western limit of the cemetery was identified during the earlier excavations, whilst the most recent works confirmed its extent to the north, south and east. It is likely that the majority of the original cemetery features have been revealed and investigated.

Location, Topography and Geology

The site lay on the eastern side of the Wiltshire downland village of Collingbourne Ducis, between Marlborough and Amesbury (SU 2463 5419; Fig. 1.1). The village, situated in a valley on the eastern edge of Salisbury Plain, derives its name from the River Bourne – a tributary of the Avon – that runs 200 m to the west; the Upper Bourne river was previously known as the Coll. The Marlborough–Andover road (A338 and A346) passes north–south through the village and likely follows an early route along the Bourne Valley (Baggs *et al.* 1999; Kennet District Council (KDC) 2002, 1).

The site comprised two excavation areas, one of 4840 m² investigated in 2007 and a further 80 m² investigated in 2009. It was situated on a south-facing slope (140 m to 131 m above Ordnance Datum), mainly in an area of pasture and dense scrubland. Private gardens associated with residential developments bound the site to the south, east and west, the earliest of these having led to the initial investigation of the cemetery in 1974 (Gingell 1978). Arable farmland lay to the north.

The underlying natural deposits comprise heavily weathered, periglacially scarred Upper Cretaceous Chalk overlain by colluvial deposits up to 1 m thick towards the base of the slope and within the shallow central coombe (Fig. 1.2; Pl. 1.1). Soils are mapped as brown forest and grey-brown podsolic, and brown forest with redzinas (Geological Survey of Great Britain, sheet 283).

Plate 1.1 Central southern area of the site, with coombe to the right (from the north-west)

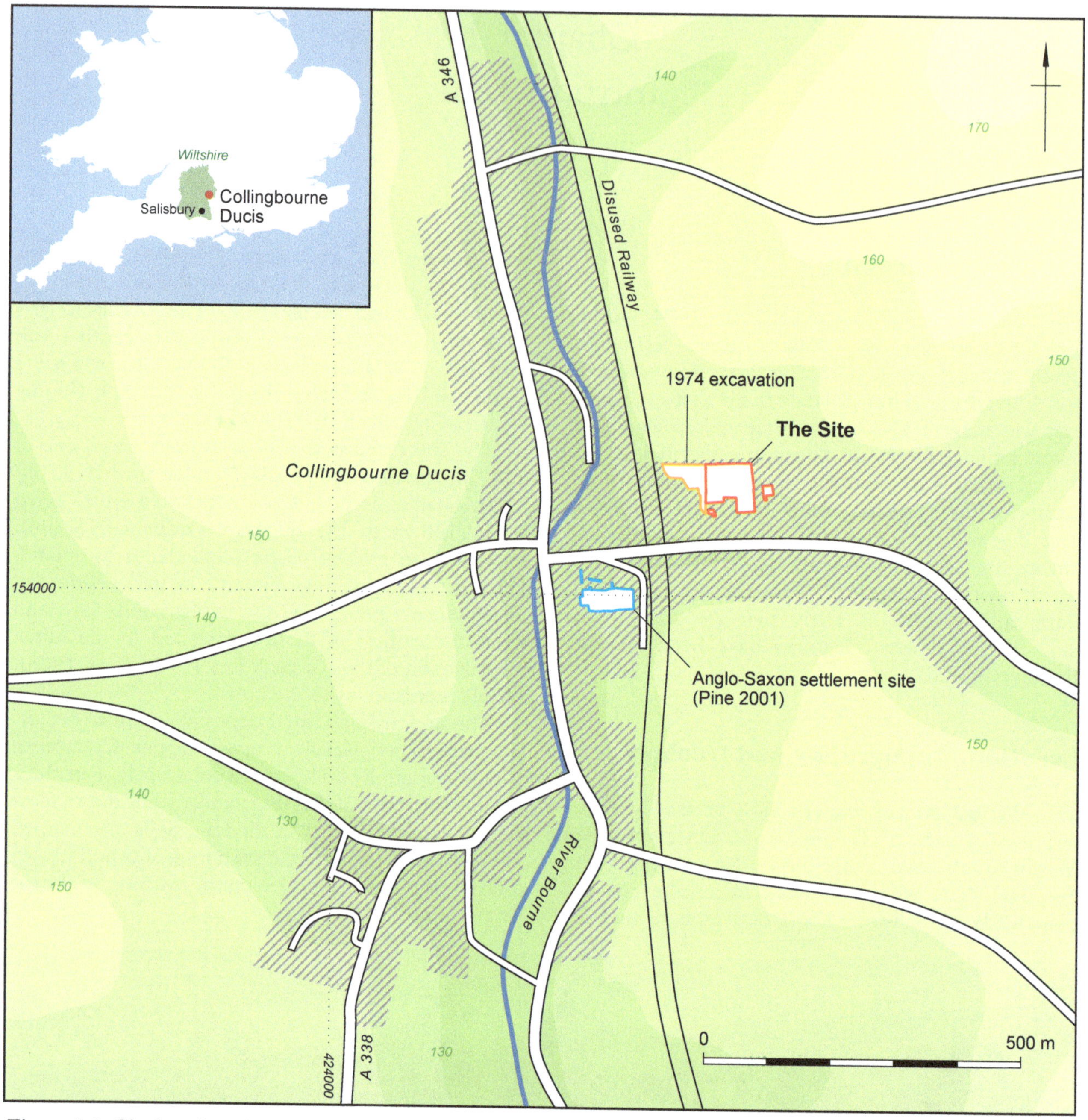

Figure 1.1 Site location plan

Archaeological and Historical Background

Collingbourne Ducis is located in a rich archaeological landscape that contains Salisbury Plain and the Stonehenge World Heritage Site to the west. The extensive and abundant archaeological remains demonstrate settlement and mortuary activity from the later prehistoric period onwards (Richards 1991; Fitzpatrick and Morris 1994; Cleal *et al.* 1995, Lawson 2000; McOmish *et al.* 2002; Brown *et al.* 2006; Fulford *et al.* 2006).

On Fairmile Down, only a few kilometres to the north-east of Collingbourne Ducis, is a well-preserved Neolithic long barrow – Scheduled Monument List Entry Number (SM No.) 1013051 – one of several such monuments recorded in the wider area. Sidbury Hill (SM No. 1010138), 4.5 km to the south-west at North Tidworth, is known to have been occupied during the Neolithic period (KDC 2002, 54; Castleden 1992, 212).

There is an abundance of Bronze Age barrows in the vicinity of Collingbourne Ducis, such as those at Wick Down 2 km to the east, and Hougoumont Farm 2 km to the south-west (SM No. 1012510 and 1009925 respectively). Such monuments sometimes provided a focus for later activity, as evidenced locally by slightly later secondary burials and settlement at

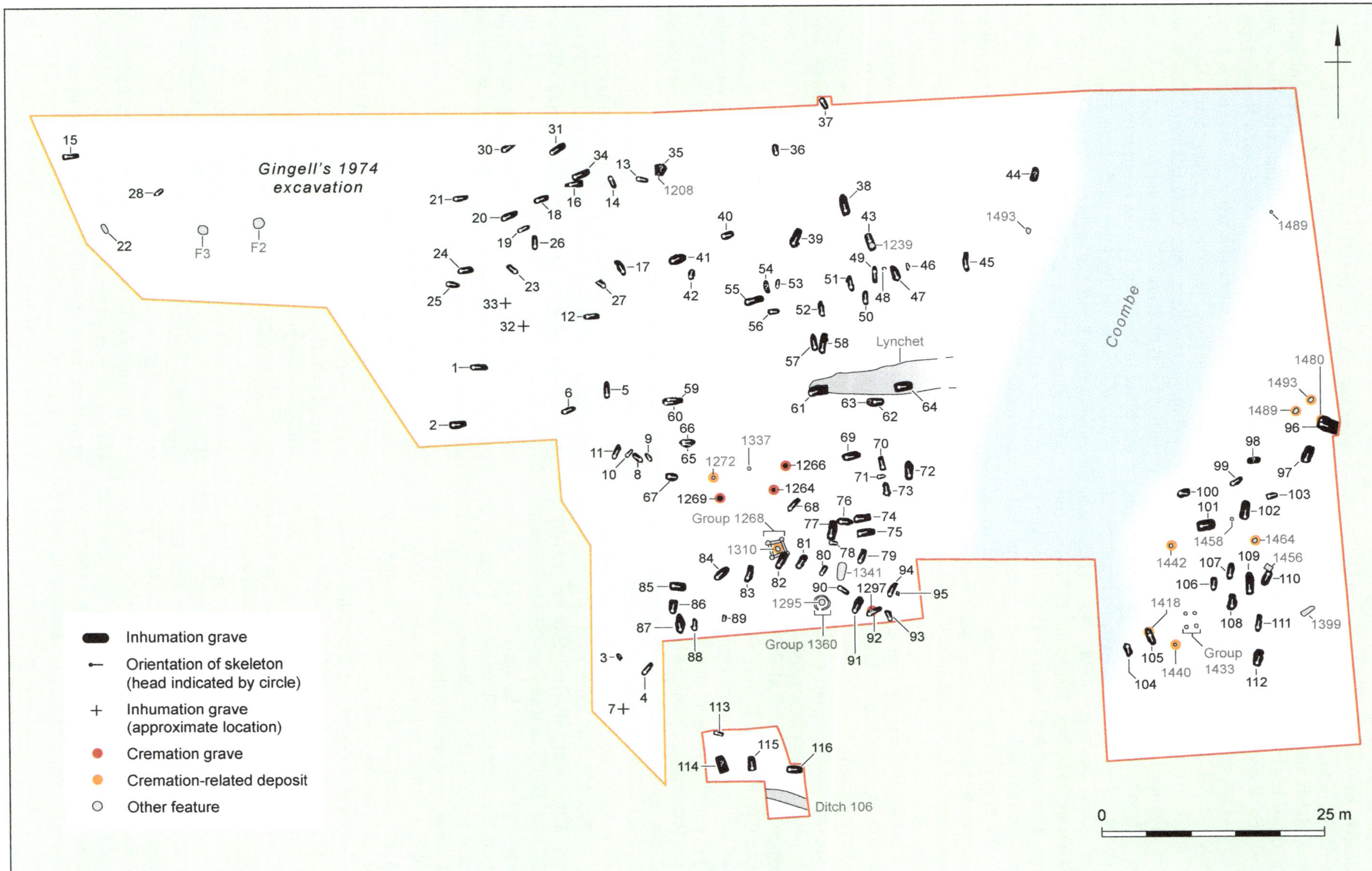

Figure 1.2 Cemetery plan: graves and other features

the extensive barrow cemetery at Snail Down, Salisbury Plain (SM No. 1009351; Thomas 2005), and the establishment of Anglo-Saxon cemeteries including those recorded on the Old Dairy site in Amesbury, and Barrow Clump (SM No. 1009697) near Figheldean; (Gingell 1978, 61; Wessex Archaeology 2013; Harding and Stoodley forthcoming). Extensive later prehistoric field systems have been identified in the village environs (Baggs *et al.* 1999, 2), and a number of large, later prehistoric enclosures are recorded to the west, for example at Godsbury near Burbage (SM No. 1004759), Everleigh Down (SM No. 1010066, 1009445) and Figheldean, Fittleton (Applebaum 1954). Substantial earthworks thought to be prehistoric territorial land-markers – the Wessex Linear Ditches – extend across Salisbury Plain and beyond; some form parts of the parish boundary of Collingbourne Kingston (Baggs *et al.* 1999, 1).

The substantial East Chisenbury Late Bronze Age/Early Iron Age midden (Wiltshire and Swindon Historic Environment Record No. MWI13881) is situated approximately 10 km to the west, perhaps indicating periodic, significant gatherings of peoples in the region (McOmish et al 2010; Tubb 2011). Prehistoric and Romano-British field systems and landscapes are recorded nearby at Figheldean (SM No. 107939), whilst the aforementioned Sidbury Hill features the remains of a bivallate Iron Age hillfort.

There are many examples of Romano-British settlement and other activity on Salisbury Plain, particularly on the spurs of higher ground (Bonney 1979, 46–7, fig. 4.5; McOmish *et al.* 2002, Fulford *et al.* 2006). Chisenbury Warren (SM No. 1010053; McOmish *et al.* 2002), a Romano-British settlement connected via a trackway to Lidbury Camp, lies a few kilometres to the west of Collingbourne Ducis.

Evidence suggests that in the post-Roman period much of what is now Wiltshire came under the control of the Saxon peoples, possibly those later known as the *Geurissae* of the Upper Thames Valley (Williams and Newman 2006).

The 'Conversion Period' (*c.* AD 600–850) was a time of upheaval featuring changes to the political landscape and the adoption of Christianity (Geake 1997, 24, 131–4), when social organisation became more rigid and stable. Changes in dress and weaponry were marked in the 7th century, followed by changes in burial customs. A move away from furnished burial in field cemeteries to unfurnished burials in churchyards occurred variably between the late 7th to late 9th centuries, and a distinct drop in the number of furnished graves (initially amongst the elite) is evident from the early 8th century (Geake 1997).

The name 'Collingbourne' is thought to be of Anglo-Saxon derivation, meaning 'stream of the dwellers on the [river] coll', or the stream of 'Cols/Cola's family or followers' (Ekwall 1991, 117; Mills 1991, 86–7). By the end of the 9th century the settlement, now known as Collingbourne Ducis, was well established. It was the subject of a Royal charter in AD 903 that distinguished it (*Colengaburn Minor*) from its larger neighbour '*Colengaburn Major*' – Collingbourne Kingston. Collingbourne Ducis was part of lands given to Winchester Minster by Edward the Elder in 903, but it soon returned to the crown. Wulfgar, made an Earl by Aethelstan in 938, and dying in 948, listed Collingbourne along with several other estates in his will, with Aughton, a small village to the north-west of Collingbourne Kingston, left to and named for his wife Aeffe (KDC 2002, 1).

In 1974 the construction of a housing estate immediately to the west of the site led to the discovery of 33 late 5th- to 7th-century graves (Fig. 1.1; Gingell 1978). The assemblage comprised the remains of a minimum of 31 individuals, including four infants, three juveniles, three subadult/adults and 19 adults (nine male, eight female), consistent with a 'normal' domestic population. Many of the burials were inclusive of grave goods such as weapons and personal items. The published demographic data for this material has been treated with caution as there have been subsequent advances in ageing and sexing techniques. However, the overall results, including the types, date and distribution of the metalwork, have been considered below.

Subsequent investigations beginning in 2006, comprising a ground penetrating radar survey (Stratascan 2006), an evaluation (Wessex Archaeology 2006) and two watching briefs (Wessex Archaeology 2009a; 2009b) confirmed that the cemetery continued to the east and south-east of the location of the 1974 excavation, into the area forming the focus of this report.

The cemetery is one of several broadly contemporaneous examples in the region. It lay approximately midway between those at Blacknall Field, Pewsey and Portway, Andover (Annable and Eagles 2010; Cook and Dacre 1985), with Market Lavington further to the west (Williams and Newman 2006), Aldbourne, near Marlborough to the north (Stoodley *et al.* 2012), and Winterbourne Gunner to the south (Musty and Stratton 1964). Others nearby include Old Dairy, Amesbury and Barrow Clump, Figheldean (Wessex Archaeology 2013; Stoodley forthcoming; Harding and Stoodley forthcoming).

Settlement evidence is, by contrast, relatively rare. However, part of an Anglo-Saxon rural settlement, including several sunken-featured buildings, was discovered in the centre of Collingbourne Ducis in 1998, 200 m to the south-west of the site, and on the eastern side of the River Bourne (Pine 2001; see Fig. 1.1). Although predominantly of 8th- to 10th-century date, one radiocarbon-dated structure provided evidence for 5th- to 7th-century occupation, contemporary with the cemetery. Several disc and saucer brooches have also been found in Collingbourne Kingston suggesting that another cemetery broadly contemporary with that at Collingbourne Ducis may lay a short distance upstream, perhaps related to a further settlement (Annable and Eagles 2010, 106).

By 1086 and the compilation of *Domesday*, Collingbourne's population numbered around 300–400 individuals (Wood 1986, 109), however the entry does not acknowledge the division between the two Collingbournes, with both described under the name 'Coleburne' (KDC 2002, 1). The village was for a brief period Collingbourne 'Earls', when John of Gaunt acquired the land; 'Ducis' was added when he was made Duke of Lancaster in the late 14th century (Ekwall 1991, 117; Mills 1991, 86–7).

In later centuries the local economy was principally agricultural and forestry-based and there is no reason to suppose the situation was any different in the Anglo-Saxon period. The downland provided reasonably fertile arable land, but was particularly suitable for pasture. Chute Forest, remnants of which still exist 2 km to the east, would have provided good opportunities for swine herding, nut harvesting and the procurement of other woodland resources (KDC 2002).

Methodology

All excavation and post-excavation procedures followed Wessex Archaeology's guidelines, which complied with all legislation (up to early 2009) and recommended standards current at the time. A full archive has been compiled and forms the foundation of the analysis and interpretation presented here. Specialist methodologies are summarised in the relevant sections.

The archive will be deposited at the Wiltshire Heritage Museum, Devizes, under site codes 62670, 62671, 71750 and 71830.

Chapter 2
The Cemetery

The evidence presented here comprises a summary of the results of the 2007 and 2009 excavations, with reference to earlier investigations where appropriate. Grave numbers were assigned in post-excavation in order to continue the sequence from the previous excavation.

Soil Sequence

The topsoil comprised an approximately 0.24 m deep dark brown clay loam with chalk inclusions. The underlying reddish brown silty clay subsoil (0.62 m to 0.98 m deep) extended across the entire site; this colluvial deposit was deepest downslope to the south and within the coombe (Fig. 1.2), and less substantial to the north-west (0.30–0.75 m deep; Gingell 1978, 61). The natural chalk bedrock was heavily weathered, broken-up by roots and striped with periglacial scars filled with reddish brown silty clay.

The Cemetery Features

The archaeological sequence was relatively uncomplicated with most features cut into the natural geology, or in one or two cases, into the edge of the upper fills of the coombe. There were a few examples of intercutting between cemetery features (see below). Erosion, agricultural activity, landscaping and geotechnical works were particularly detrimental to the state of the archaeological remains, whilst minor disturbance by root activity was common.

The excavated cemetery features included 82 inhumation graves (115 including those excavated in 1974; Gingell 1978), four cremation graves, several cremation-related deposits and two possible cenotaphs (Fig. 1.2). The remains of two post-built mortuary-related structures, a penannular ditch and a section of a possible southern boundary ditch were also recorded.

Inhumation Graves and Burials

Full details are in the *Grave Catalogue* (see below).

The coombe had a major influence on the layout of the cemetery, forming the eastern boundary for much of the period of use; it remained largely unused when the cemetery was extended to the east and south (Fig. 1.2). On the western side lay 98 inhumation graves, including the 33 found in 1974 (Gingell 1978). Clusters of graves may represent defined cemetery plots, some of which appear to have focused on earlier graves and/or mortuary structures (Stoodley, below). Seventeen further graves, including a rare example of a bed burial, lay to the east of the coombe (Pl. 2.1, and see Pl. 2.10. These, together with a few to the south of the western portion, form the latest group in the sequence.

Intercutting between graves was rare. Two examples (graves 59/60 and 65/66) indicate the deliberate re-use of earlier graves, yet little or no disturbance to the earlier burial remains had occurred. Grave 76 just clipped the foot end of grave 77, whilst grave 82 truncated part of a mortuary structure (group 1268, see below), representing the only direct stratigraphic relationship between the graves and other cemetery features.

Where observable, most graves were sub-rectangular in plan, usually with rounded ends (apsidal/sub-apsidal). Variations included distinctly narrowed foot-ends (graves 51, 52 and 71), and wide mid-sections (59 and 83) – in one case potentially related to the inclusion of a shield. The majority of graves had flat bases and straight, steep sides; a few examples of less steep or concave sides, and sloping or concave bases, were also recorded. Graves containing the remains of adults survived to depths of between 0.03 and 0.70 m (average 0.2 m), and were 1.49–2.92 m long and 0.52–1.56 m wide (mean 2.02 m and 0.87 m respectively). Graves for immature individuals were, unsurprisingly, smaller at 0.75–1.90 m long (mean 1.34 m), 0.20–1.10 m wide (mean 0.61 m), and 0.03–0.40 m deep (average 0.17 m). The ranges and averages change little when the data are combined with those from the previous excavation. There were no integral features such as steps or shelves within any of the graves.

Most graves were oriented south–north or west–east or minor variations thereof (46.6% and 37.3% respectively). Approximate north–south and south-west–north-east alignments were rare (5.1% and 4.2%), whilst no cases of east–west alignment were recorded. Determining factors for grave orientation can include the season, time of day, method of ascertaining north, cultural preferences and points of reference in the cemetery and wider landscape. See Stoodley (below) for further discussion.

The excavation revealed the remains of 82 *in situ* burials (83 individuals including an *in utero* foetus, excluding redeposited material) – see human bone report below for minimum number of individuals.

Most bodies had been placed in a supine position (69.5%), the majority with legs extended (82.5%). The remaining identifiable positions comprised flexed and on the side (19.5%), with equal proportions on the left and right. The 1974 excavation revealed similar patterns. The burial in grave 90 was the only one to have been made in a crouched position; it also followed one of the less frequently recorded alignments (approximately north–south).

No conclusive evidence for coffins was recorded, though a rare example of a bed burial was found in grave 96. The corpse of an adult female had been placed extended and supine (see Watson, Chapter 4 and *Grave Catalogue*, below). The substantial piece of charred split timber from a mature oak found in grave 77 may have been a piece of pyre structure rather than a coffin, which implies that the two mortuary rites were practiced contemporaneously (Barnett, Chapter 4). A similar deposit was noted by Gingell (1978).

Grave goods, comprising personal equipment, personal ornamentation and clothing, weapons and other items, were found in 64 graves (78% of the 82 graves excavated in 2007 and 2009). See the *Grave Catalogue*, below and Stoodley (Chapter 4) for details.

Personal equipment – knives, latchlifters and toilet implements – was recovered from 51 graves (18 male, 19 female, 14 immature). Knives were by far the most common grave good. Many were found at the waist, situated most frequently on the left side.

Jewellery (beads, brooches) and items associated with clothing (buckles) were recovered from 43 graves (12 male, 23 female, eight immature). In the majority of cases, their location indicated that the items were worn on the body at the time of burial, though some of the grave goods from grave 38 may have been contained within a purse or pouch.

Weapons, comprising shields, spears and a sword were found in 11 male graves. Shields were predominantly placed over the torso, whilst spears were found along the side of the grave. The sword was placed along the right side of the corpse (grave 59).

The burials made in graves 93 and 69 included parts of a bucket and a cup respectively. Single iron nails, potentially apotropaic in nature (see below) were seen in six graves, though there were no obvious patterns regarding location, age or sex.

Eight burials included small deposits of human bone, or single teeth – probably 'tokens' or *memento mori* (graves 40, 41, 74, 85, 96, 103, 105 and 111). In two graves small, probably bagged, cremation-related deposits were interred with the corpse(see McKinley, Chapter 3).

Cremation Graves and Cremation-related Deposits

Cremation-related material (including cremated bone and redeposited pyre debris) was recovered from a number of features across the site. Four cremation graves were recorded in the central-southern area of

Plate 2.1 South-eastern corner of the site (from the north-west)

the site, in an otherwise blank area between the clusters of inhumation graves (Fig. 1.2). Small quantities of cremated remains were recovered from a number of small pits, in two mortuary structures and a penannular ditch (see below). Others were deliberately placed in inhumation graves (see above), or accidentally incorporated into later features. McKinley discusses their context and nature (Chapter 3); details are in the *Grave Catalogue*.

The remains of the four cremation graves (three urned burials, one unurned) were heavily truncated (0.07–0.16 m deep), though the burial remains in grave 1269 lay protected in the base of the urn. Grave 1297 was cut into the backfill of inhumation grave 92. All were sub-circular in plan, measuring 0.23–0.59 m long, and 0.28–0.59 m wide. The two similarly-sized graves (1264 and 1266, urned) had moderate to steep sides and flat bases, whilst the sides and base of graves 1269 and 1297 were concave. The backfill around the urns contained very little cremated bone/pyre debris. The burial deposits consisted of dark, charcoal-rich silty-clay fills, with varying quantities of fuel ash and burnt bone.

Groups of up to four sub-circular pits, approximately 0.30 to 0.40 m in diameter and 0.06–0.20 m deep, were recorded in four areas – the north,

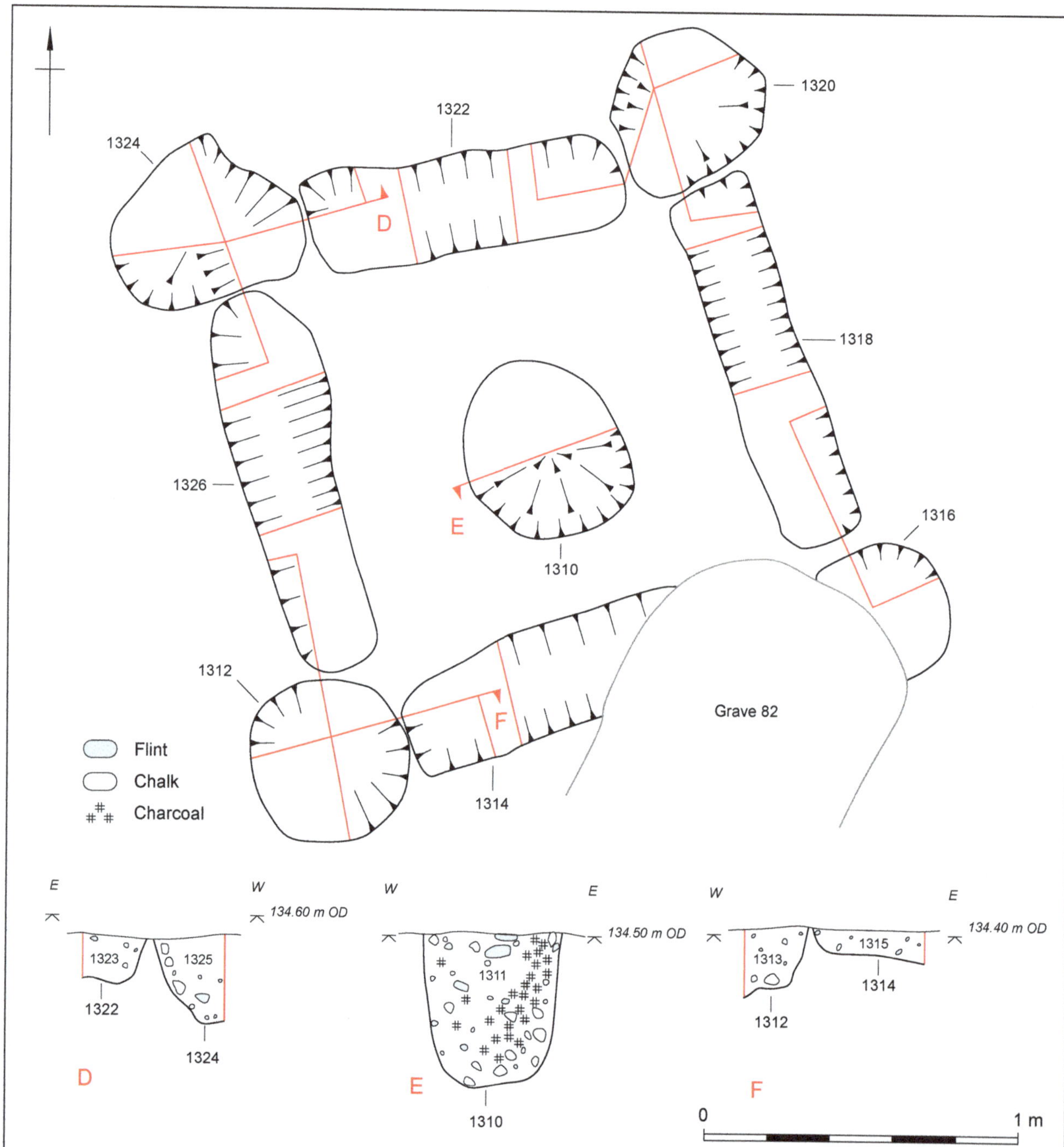

Figure 2.1 Plan and sections of structure 1268

central south, east and south-east (Fig. 1.2). Nearly all of them contained small quantities of redeposited cremated bone; a few pottery sherds were also recovered. Pits 1208, 1239 and 1480 were cut into the upper fills of inhumation graves 35, 43 and 96 respectively.

Other Cemetery Features

Two grave-like features (1341 and 1399; Fig. 1.2), and one from the 1974 excavation (grave 22), were devoid of human remains, suggesting that they may have been cenotaphs – a physical representation of mortuary rites undertaken in honour of someone whose body was not available for interment. A small iron stud was recovered from 1399, though this could have been residual.

Two four-post mortuary structures were identified in the southern portion of the cemetery, one either side of the coombe (Group 1268 and 1433; see Fig. 1.2). On the western side, square structure 1268 comprised four corner postholes (0.42–0.56 m diameter, 0.16–0.29 m deep), with four probable beam slots (1.08–1.20 m x 0.26–0.38 m, 0.12–0.19 m deep) forming the sides (Fig. 2.1; Pl. 2.2). Pit 1310 was situated within the enclosed 1.25 m^2 area, just off-centre. The circular cut (0.46 m diameter, 0.49 m deep) had steep sides and a concave base, and contained a single fill comprising dark greyish-brown silty clay, with pottery sherds, cremated bone and redeposited pyre debris ie, potentially the redeposited remains of an urned cremation burial (McKinley, below). The beam slots contained similar fills, including cremated bone. The south-east corner of the structure had been truncated by grave 82, dated to the 6th century, suggesting that 1268 was one of the earlier features of the cemetery.

Structure 1433 to the east of the coombe was represented by four small postholes, each around 0.40 m in diameter and 0.41–0.23 m deep, forming a 2 x 1.5 m rectangle. A single sherd of pottery and an iron strip were recovered from one of the postholes. The layout of the surrounding graves (Fig. 1.2) suggests that this structure was standing in the 7th century, and was potentially a focal feature.

Penannular ditch 1360 (5 m to the south-west of structure 1268) was 0.25 m wide, 0.17 m deep and 1.7 m in diameter, with a 0.4 m wide causeway to the south (Fig. 2.2; Pl. 2.3). It contained a small amount of cremated bone. Central pit 1295 was 0.65 m in diameter and 0.40 m deep with steeply sloping sides. The single fill was devoid of artefacts. The locations of the nearby graves suggest that it was still extant in the 6th century, possibly into the 7th.

A short section of ditch (106; 1.3 m wide, 0.3 m deep; Fig. 2.2) was recorded on the southern edge of the site, immediately south of graves 113–6. It had been heavily truncated by garden landscaping. It is possible that this demarcated the southern extent of the cemetery, but a lack of datable evidence precludes a more conclusive interpretation.

Plate 2.2 Structure 1268, cut by grave 82 (scale = 1 m; from the south-west)

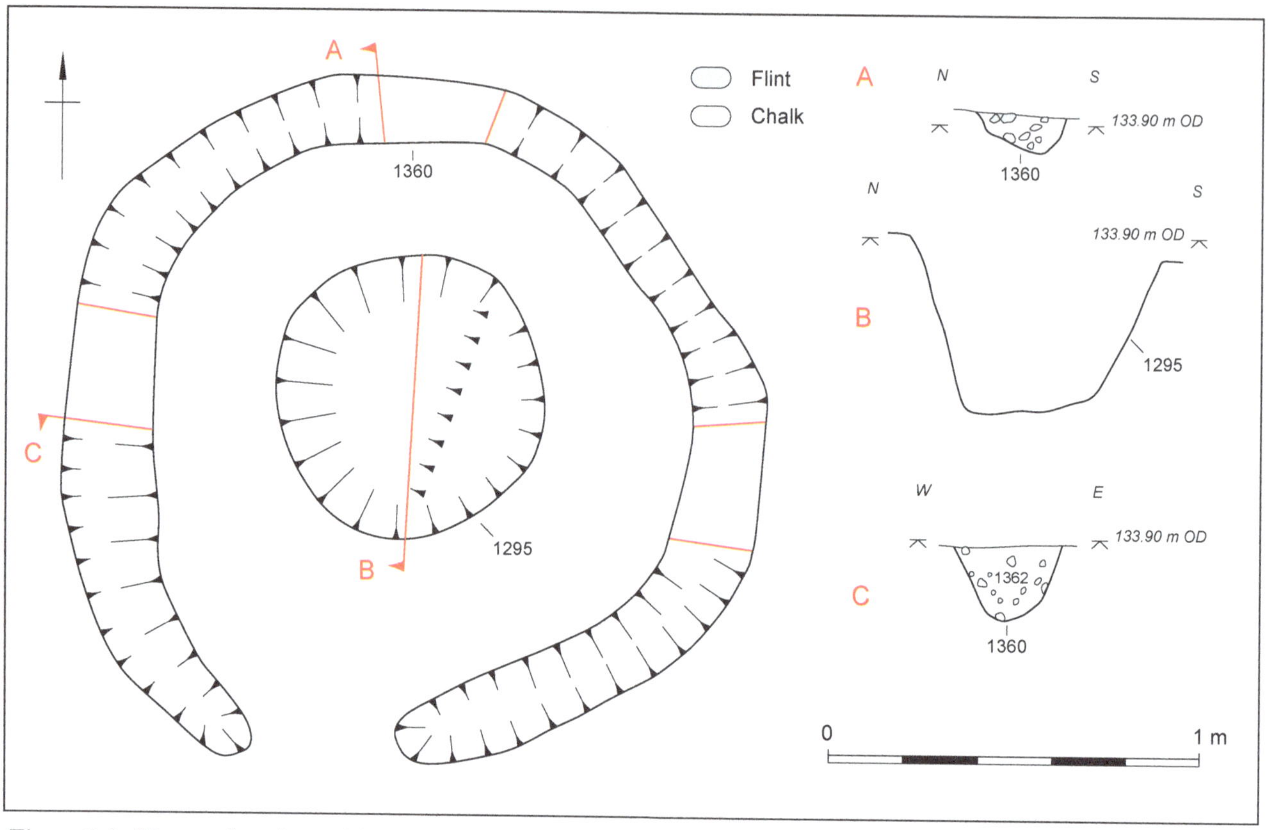

Figure 2.2 Plan and sections of feature 1360

Plate 2.3 Feature 1360 (scale = 1 m; from the south)

Grave Catalogue

The graves were all cut into the natural chalk and clay-with-flint geology. The fills of the inhumation graves were invariably pale greyish brown silty clay loam, with varying proportions of flint and chalk inclusions. There was no conclusive evidence for coffins. Any exceptions are detailed below.

For further details regarding mineral-replaced textile, the bed burial and knife structure see McCormick, Watson and Blakelock respectively (Chapter 4, and Appendices 1–2).

Key: s.a.u.l. – skull, axial, upper limbs, lower limbs (where not all elements recovered)

Graves 1–34: 1974 excavation (see Gingell 1978).

Grave 35: cut 1179 (burial 1181; fill 1180)
(not illustrated)
WSW–ENE unclear– oval/irregular, steep sides, flat base. 0.94 x 0.94 m, 0.27 m deep (base at 138.82 m OD – overcut by *c.* 0.07 m). Posture not discernible. Heavy root disturbance.
Human bone: *c.* 10% s.a.l. infant *c.* 2–3 yr.
Grave goods:
ON 32: iron pin (location unknown); fragmentary. ?knob or looped-headed. Surviving length 36 mm.
ON 33: iron knife, tip missing (location unknown); fragmentary. Tapering tang central to blade; curves gently up to back and down to blade; cutting edge resharpened. Type unidentified. Surviving length 78 mm; width 13 mm; thickness 5 mm.
Residual finds: 1 sherd pottery (Saxon, organic-tempered).

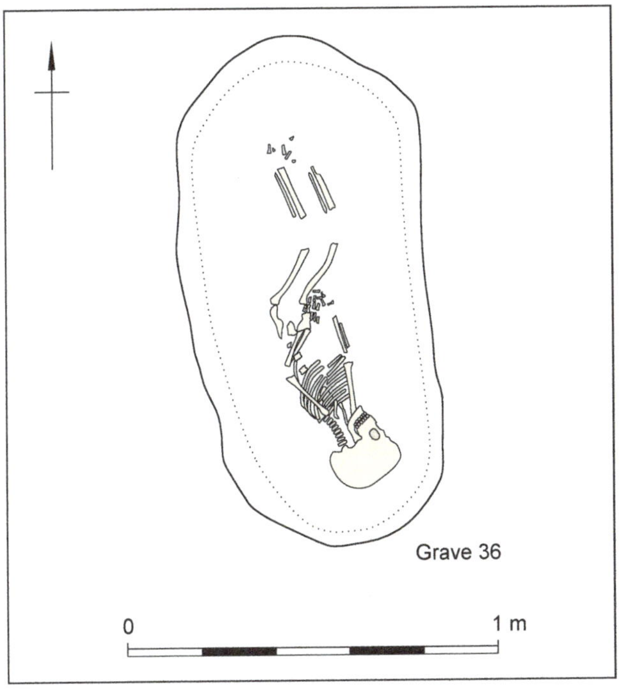

Figure 2.3 Grave 36

Grave 36: cut 1228 (burial 1129; fill 1230)
(Fig. 2.3)
S–N, sub-rectangular, rounded ends, moderately sloping concave sides and flat base. 1.36 x 0.66 m, 0.18 m deep (base at 138.93 m OD). Flexed on right side, hands in lap.
Human bone: *c.* 55% juvenile *c.* 5–8 yr. ???male.
Residual finds: flecks baked clay.

Grave 37: cut 1224 (burial 1225; fill 1226)
(Fig. 2.4)
NW–SE, sub-rectangular, rounded/irregular ends, steep sides, flat base. 1.4 x 0.64 m, 0.18 m deep (base at 139.18 m OD). Extended, supine. Root disturbance.
Human bone: *c.* 40% juvenile *c.* 5–8 yr.
Grave goods:
ON 68: iron knife, between lower left arm and waist, tip towards foot end. Tang central to blade, tapering with angular shoulder up to back of blade with a gentle slope to cutting edge. Back straight before curving down to tip; blade curves up to tip. Böhner Type A. Length 160 mm; width 20 mm; thickness 3 mm.

Grave 38: cut 1202 (burial 1203; fill 1204)
(Figs 2.5 and 2.6)
SSE–NNW, sub-rectangular, rounded foot end, steep sides, flat base. 2.45 x 1.00 m, 0.35 m deep (base at 137.72 m OD). Extended, supine, hands crossed over abdomen.
Human bone: *c.* 85% adult *c.* 25–35 yr. female.

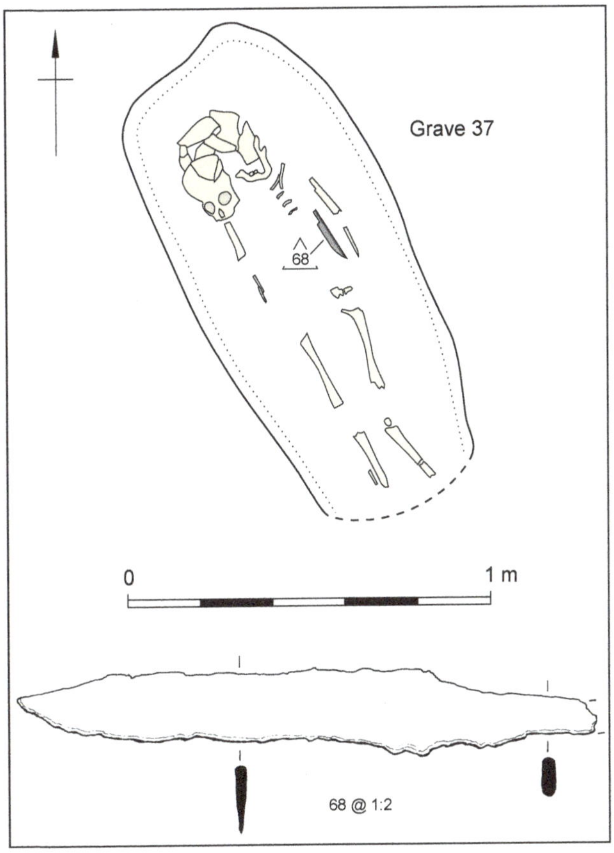

Figure 2.4 Grave 37 and iron knife

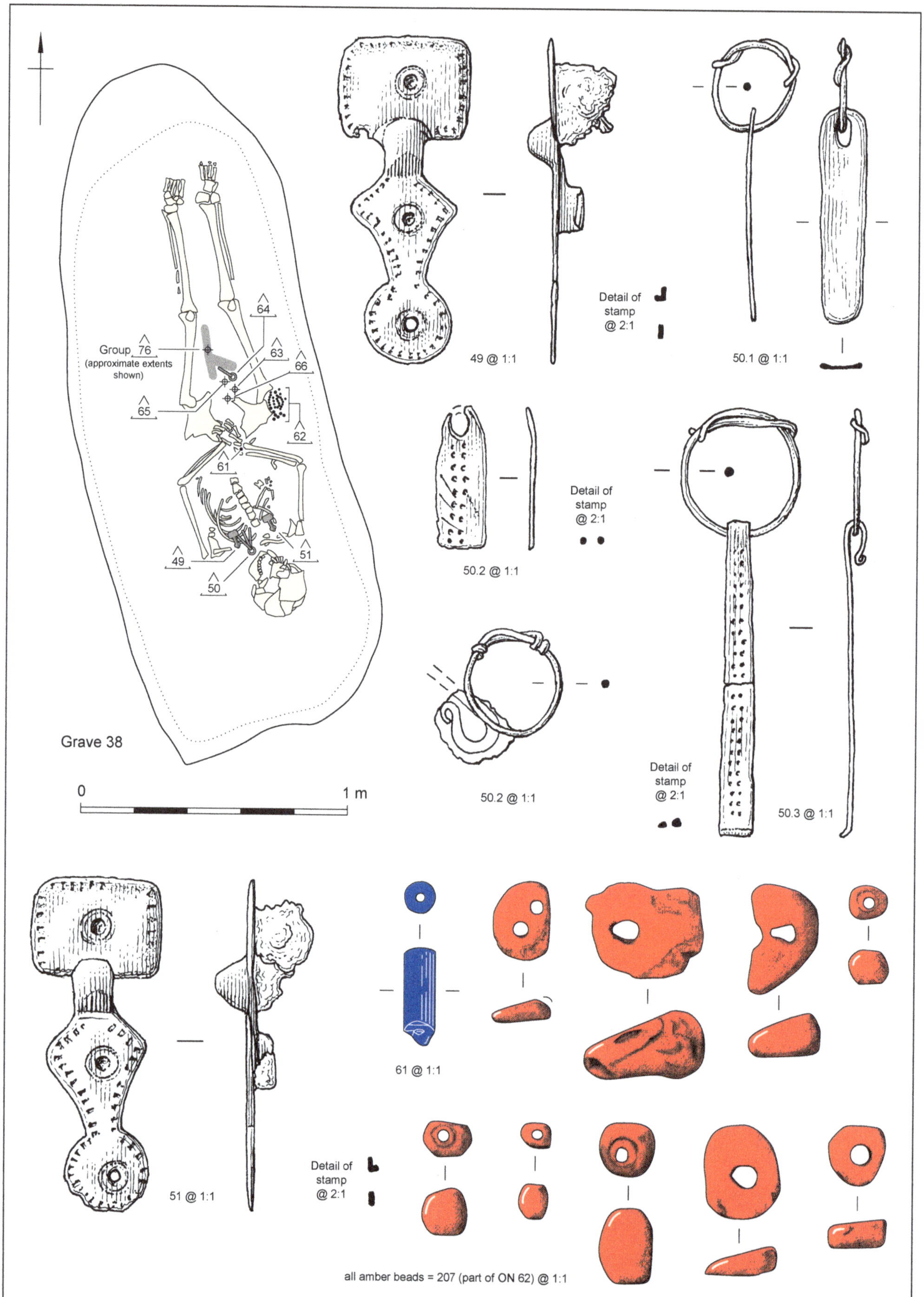

Figure 2.5 Grave 38 and selected grave goods

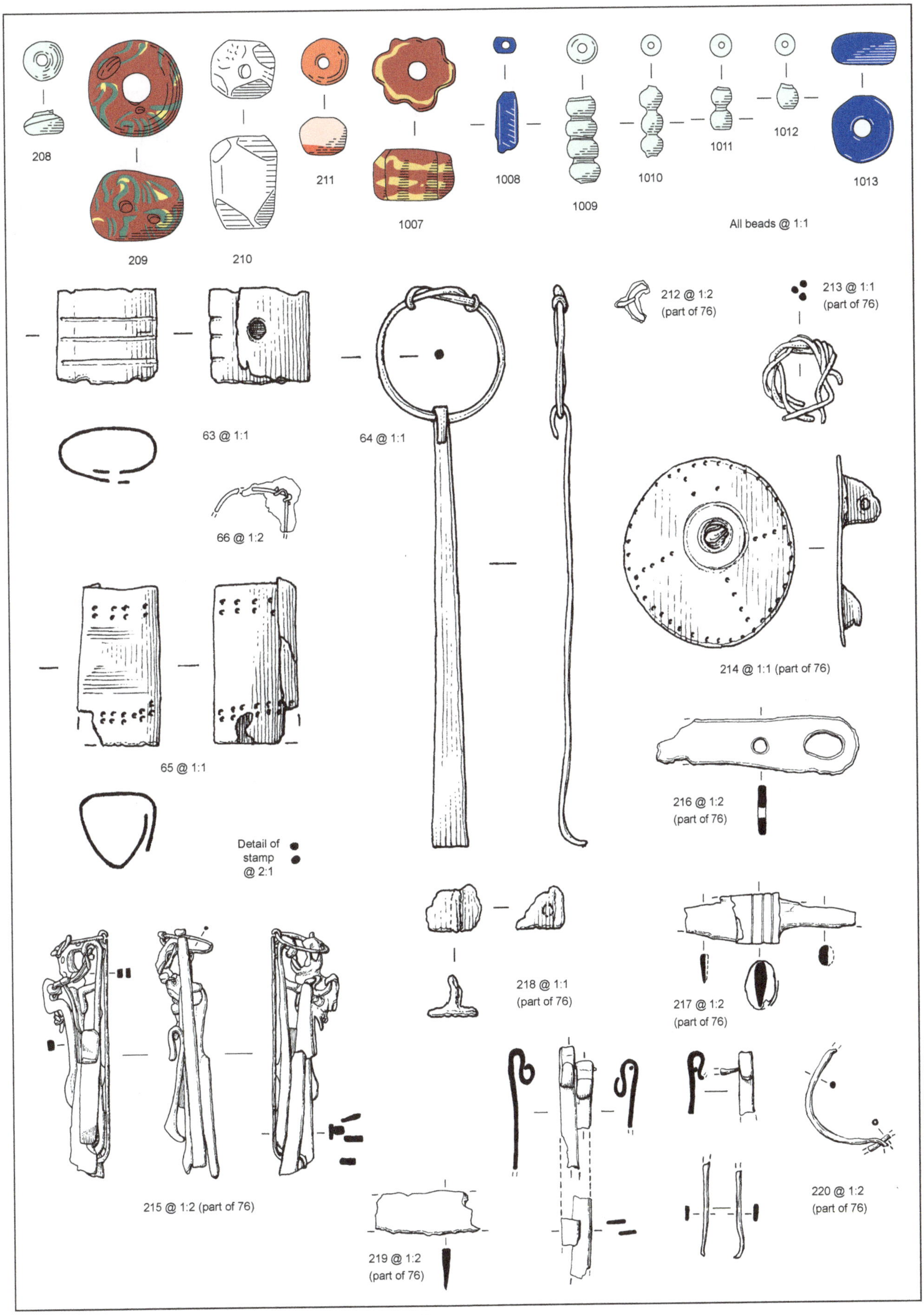

Figure 2.6 Grave 38 selected grave goods (continued)

Grave goods:

ON 49: copper alloy small-long brooch, over upper left chest/shoulder. Rectangular head-plate, damage to lower left corner; central punched dot surrounded by faint incised circle; border of punched stamps on three sides. Arched bow leading to flat foot which expands on either side forming (mismatched) sub-triangular lateral lobes. An off-centre punched dot is surrounded by a faint incised circle and the lobes have a border of small punched stamps extending to outline a sub-circular terminal with an off-centre perforated hole. Hinge with remains of iron pin and catch. Length 61 mm; width of head 25 mm. Leeds Type V.

ON 50: copper alloy implements and slip-knot rings, in area of upper left chest/lower neck. Location suggests the complex consists of necklace fittings, but no. 3 is a scraper.

1) Plain strip, ?spangle, attached to slip-knot wire ring; perforated head; gradually narrowing towards the terminal. Length 40 mm; width 9 mm; diameter of ring 12 mm.

2) Short strip with (broken) perforated head and separate slip-knot wire ring. Vertically-aligned double row of stamped dots; expands gradually towards terminal. Length 25 mm; width 10 mm; diameter of ring 19 mm.

3) Scraper (fragmentary), attached to slip-knot wire ring; top of shank recurved forming a looped head; shank expands gradually towards terminal which is bent at right angles. Decorated by vertically-aligned double row of stamped dots. Length 59 mm; width 6 mm; diameter of ring 24 mm.

ON 51: copper alloy small-long brooch over upper right chest. Rectangular head-plate with central punched dot surrounded by a faint incised circle; border of punched stamps on three sides. Arched bow leading to flat foot which expands on either side forming (mismatched) sub-triangular lateral lobes. Off-centre punched dot is surrounded by a faint incised circle. Lobes have a border of small punched stamps extending to outline a sub-circular terminal that an off-centre perforated hole. Hinge with remains of iron pin, catch broken. Length 61 mm; width of head 24 mm. Leeds Type V.

Chatelaine and ?pouch located between legs and extending down to knees:

ON 61: 3 glass beads (at right wrist). Medium, colour 7.7, shape L1.

ON 62: coloured glass bead group (in a ?pouch, against outside of right hip).

ON 207: 69 amber beads. 56 small and medium, shape AO1, 1 in 2 frags; 1 incomplete (including S. No 5126); 13 medium and large, 1 has 2 perforations; 2 frags (not illustrated).

ON 208: 2 glass beads. Medium, colour 9.1, shape A1.

ON 209: glass bead. Traffic Light? very degraded. Large, colour 2.1/5.1/?, poly P29. Shape B1.

ON 210: faceted quartz bead. Large.

ON 211: carnelian bead. Medium, shape A11.

ON 1007: glass bead. Three yellow stripes. Large, colour 2.1/5.1, poly P1a. Shape F1.

ON 1008: glass bead, wound. Medium, colour 7.7, shape G2.

ON 1009: 3 glass beads. Small, colour 9.1, shape M4.

ON 1010: 7 glass beads. Small, colour 9.1, shape M3.

ON 1011: 12 glass beads. Small, colour 9.1, shape M2.

ON 1012: 10 glass beads, some clearly from multiple segments. Small, colour 9.1, shape M1.

ON 1013: glass bead. Medium, colour 7.7, shape A1.

ON 63: copper alloy strip binding overlapped at ends and riveted together; three incised circumferential lines. In lap. Length 17 mm; width 9 mm.

ON 64: copper alloy scraper (fragmentary) threaded on wire slip-knot ring; top of shank tapered and recurved creating a looped head; shank expands gradually towards terminal which is bent at right angles. Incised vertically-aligned line down outer surface. In lap. Length 79 mm; width 6 mm; diameter of ring 25 mm.

ON 65: copper alloy strip binding overlapped at the ends. Damaged. Line of paired stamped dots on either edge. In lap. Length 30 mm; width 15 mm.

ON 66: iron L-shaped fragment (and separate tiny fragment), part of chatelaine/?pouched objects. Length 23 mm.

ON 76: copper alloy and iron objects (?in pouch between thighs):

ON 212: 2 pieces of iron twisted together.

ON 213: ring formed from ?2/3 twisted copper alloy strips. ?fragment of Roman bracelet. Diameter 15 mm.

ON 214: copper alloy disc brooch with ring and dot decoration. Diameter 35 mm; width 1 mm. Hinge obscured, catch-plate and remains of iron pin.

ON 215: iron latchlifters or (less likely) toilet set threaded onto copper alloy wire ring.

ON 216: ?small iron buckle and plate.

ON 217: knife (fragmentary) with ?remains of scabbard including a copper alloy fitting. Type unidentified. Length uncertain; width 16 mm; thickness 3 mm.

ON 218: copper alloy fragment. ?catch plate for ON 214.

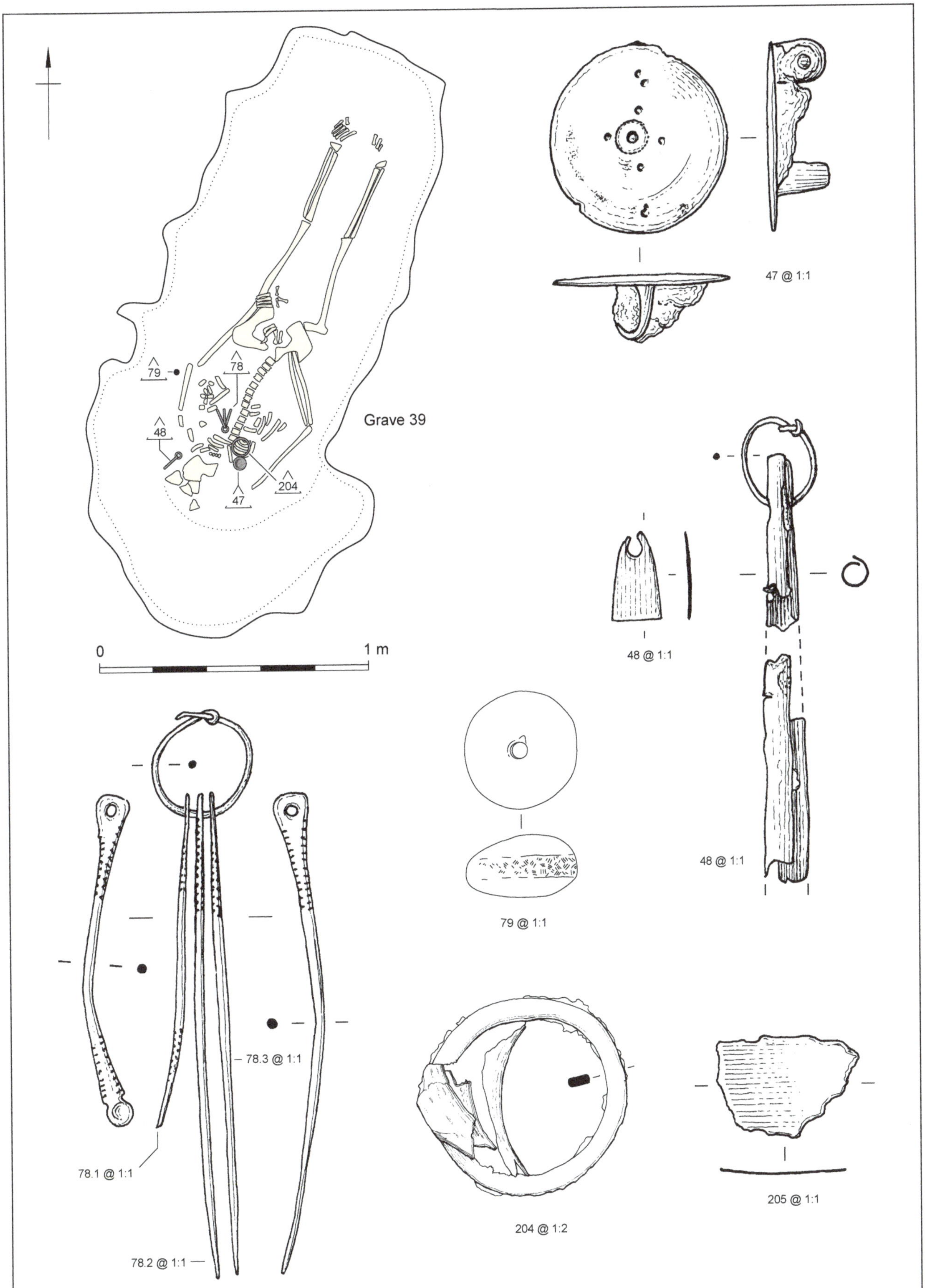

Figure 2.7 Grave 39 and selected grave goods

ON 219: knife (fragmentary). Type unidentified. Length uncertain; width 15 mm; thickness 3 mm.

ON 220: iron rods, ?chatelaine. 3 broken strips; tops of shanks recurved forming looped heads. Max surviving length 90 mm; width 6 mm; thickness 2 mm. Part of iron wire ring on to which the strips were threaded?

ON 237: four iron fragments; left upper chest. Largest is sub-rectangular. Length 17 mm, width 14 mm. Pin from ON 49 (not illustrated).

Grave 39: cut 1198 (burial 1199; fill 1200)
(Fig. 2.7)
SSW–NNE, sub-rectangular/irregular, irregular sides and base. 2.30 x 1.0 m, 0.08 m deep (base at 137.65 m OD). Extended, supine, hands on left abdomen/hip. Shallow, truncated.
Human bone: *c.* 70% adult *c.* 35–40 yr. female.

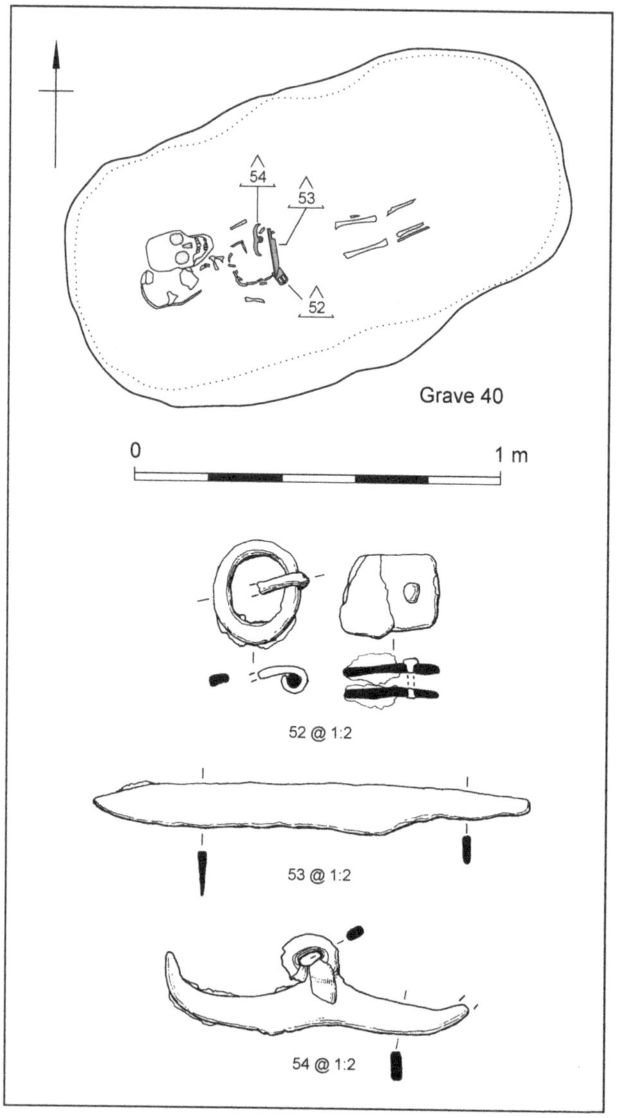

Figure 2.8 Grave 40 and grave goods

Grave goods:

ON 47: copper alloy disc brooch in right chest/shoulder area; damage to surface and rim; central punched dot surrounded by single concentric inscribed circle, surrounded by four punched dots. Single hinge and catch, remains of iron pin. Diameter 35 mm (sub-circular).

ON 48: copper alloy cosmetic brush (fragmentary), with attachment ring and separate triangular pierced spangle, to left of skull. Traces of tinning. Length 78 mm; diameter 9 mm; diameter of ring 11 mm; length of spangle 16 mm, width 10 mm. Probably *ex situ*, originally with ON 78.

ON 78: copper alloy toilet set joined by a slip-knot wire ring, over left chest:
1) ear-scoop; flat perforated lozenge-shaped head, circular-section (bent) shank becoming flattened at ends, shallow bowl. Two zones of crude notching on edges of shank ends.
2–3) Picks (bent) with circular-sectioned shanks tapering towards point, flattened towards head (pierced lozenge). Zone of notching on upper flat edge section of shanks. Length (1) 62 mm; length (2–3) 89 mm. Fragment of copper alloy plate: 23 mm x 18 mm.

ON 79: rock crystal bead, worn around circumference. Large, shape A03.

ON 204: iron ring (right chest area); rectangular section. A probable annular brooch (see also ON 206) and its pin or ?purse ring (see McCormick, Chapter 4). Diameter 72 mm; width of ring 7 mm.

ON 205: copper alloy fragment. Length 25 mm; width 19 mm.

ON 206: Two iron objects, right upper chest. ?related to ON 204. Iron plate with two rivet holes. Length 34 mm; width 15 mm. Fragmentary rod that widens at head and perforated (not illustrated). Diameter of head 12 mm; length 80 mm.

Grave 40: cut 1173 (burial 1174; fill 1175)
(Fig. 2.8)
WSW–ENE, sub-rectangular, rounded ends, steep sides, flat base. 1.40 x 0.75 m, 0.25 m deep (base at 137.89 m OD). Extended, supine.
Human bone: *c.* 40% infant *c.* 2–3 yr.
redep. (misnumbered?) a few frags. a.u. subadult/adult >16 yr.

Grave goods:

ON 52: simple iron buckle; circular with D-shaped section, fragmentary tongue; at right waist. Length 29 mm; width 24 mm. ON 234: ?remains of tongue. Length 20 mm; width 11 mm.

ON 53: iron knife, across waist, almost horizontal, tip to right. Tang of rectangular section in line with back; gentle curve down to blade which curves up to tip. Marked sharpening curve. Böhner Type B. Length 120 mm; width 14 mm; thickness 5 mm.

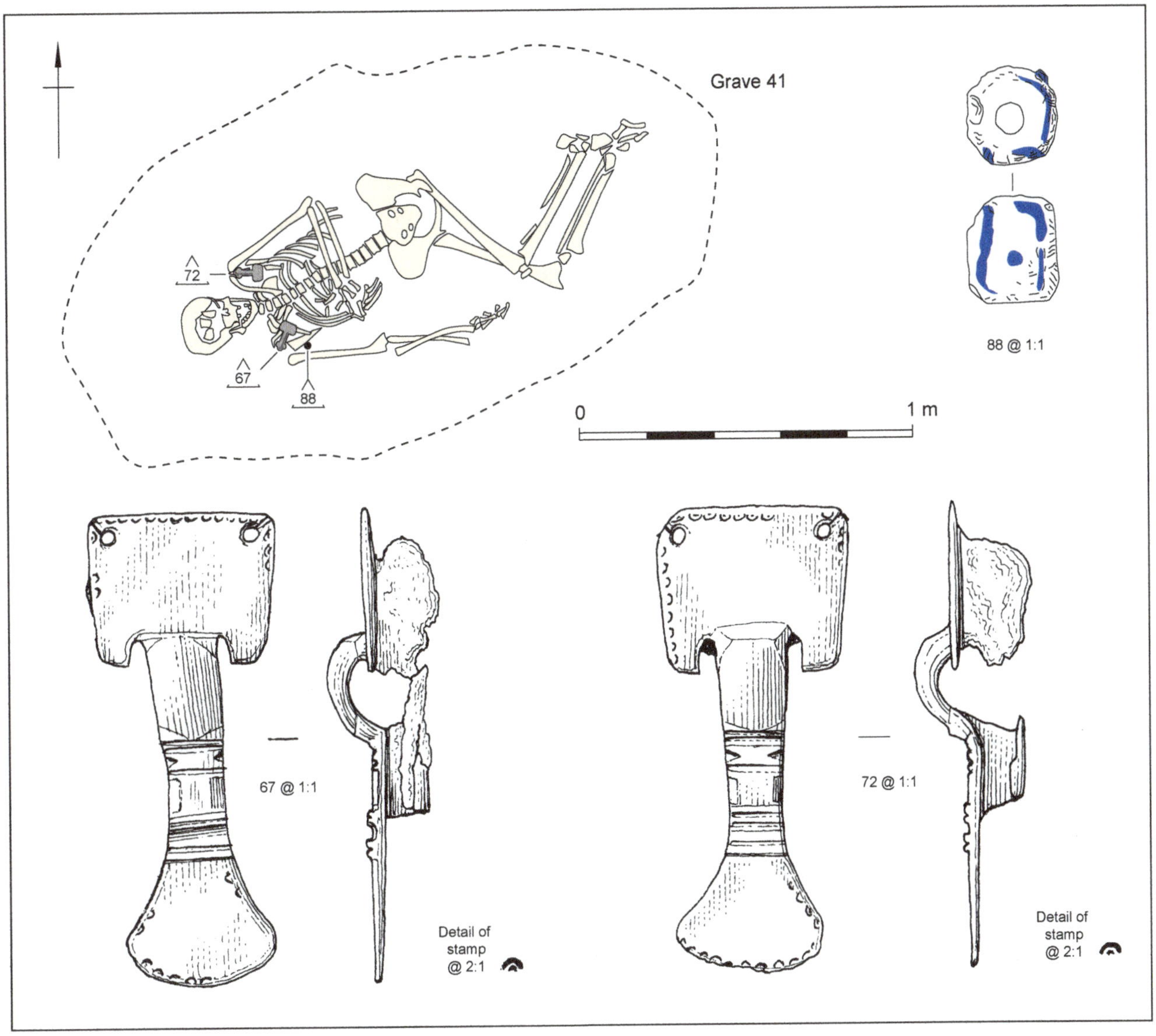

Figure 2.9 Grave 41 and grave goods

ON 54: iron pursemount; pair of crescentic arms and a centrally placed attachment buckle, over left lower chest, diagonal. Left arm complete, terminates in a point. Right arm broken off close to where it would have curved upward. Length 84 mm; width (from centre/buckle) 23 mm.

Grave 41: cut 1221 (burial 1222; fill 1223)

(Fig. 2.9)

WSW–ENE, unclear – sub-rectangular, rounded ends, steep sides, flat base. 2.06 x 1.15 m, 0.47 m deep (base at 137.58 m OD). Flexed, supine with legs to right side. Right arm straight and *c.* 20° from body, left hand on right ribs.

Human bone: *c.* 90% adult >45 yr. female

redep. 1 tooth, juvenile *c.* 6–8 yr.

Grave goods:

ON 67: copper alloy small-long brooch, on right shoulder diagonal. Trapezoidal head-plate notched on the lower edge to either side of the bow and with a circular perforation in each of the upper edge corners; faint crescentic punch marks probably outlining the top and sides. Incised line leading from each perforation to the corner. Arched bow with central ridge, with a moulding at the top and bottom creating faceted corners. This leads to a flat foot with single transverse band at the top and two paired transverse mouldings at the bottom before forming a crescentic terminal. Hinge and catch plate, iron pin. Length 67 mm; width of head 29 mm. Leeds Type III (e.i).

ON 72: copper alloy small-long brooch, on left shoulder diagonal. Trapezoidal head-plate notched on the lower edge to either side of the bow and with a circular perforation in each of the upper corners; crescentic punch marks around the periphery. An incised line leads from the perforation on the right hand side to the edge corner. Arched bow with central ridge, with a moulding at the top and bottom creating faceted corners. This leads to a flat foot with two transverse bands at the top and two paired transverse mouldings at the bottom before forming a crescentic terminal bordered by crescentic punches. Obscured hinge, catch plate, and remains of iron pin. Length 67 mm; width of head 29 mm. Leeds Type III (e.i).

ON 88: glass bead. Right armpit. Polychrome, badly degraded (trails and spots in blue?). Large, shape G1.

Residual finds: 1 sherd pottery (Romano-British).

Grave 42: cut 1189 (burial 1188; fill 1187)
(Fig. 2.10)
S–N, sub-rectangular, steep, concave sides, flat base. 1.22 x 0.75 m, 0.37 m deep (base at 137.48 m OD). Flexed on right side, hands probably in lap or in front of abdomen.
Human bone: *c.* 30% infant *c.* 1.5–2.5 yr.
Grave goods:

ON 37: 7 amber beads. 1 incomplete; 1 other chipped. Small, but different sizes. Shape A01. In front of chest.

ON 38: ?copper alloy ring (fragmentary) formed from a thin piece of folded metal, located at right waist. Length of longest fragment 12 mm; width 1 mm.

ON 39: iron knife (fragmentary) at left waist diagonal with tip to left. Tang central to blade. Blade angled up to back and curves gently down to blade; back may be slightly angled down to tip. Böhner Type ?C. Length 106 mm; width 15 mm; thickness 5 mm.

ON 40: heavy iron latchlifter of square section with a hooked bottom terminal and fragmentary attachment ring. Left waist/hip. Length (not including ring) 84 mm; width 11 mm.

ON 224: copper alloy (finger-) ring formed from a tapering strip of metal (location unknown); a border line runs around the wider part of the periphery of the ring and encloses possibly five punched dots each surrounded by an incised circle; the narrower part of the ring is decorated by hatching. Diameter 19 mm; height 5 mm.

Residual finds: 1 sherd pottery (Romano-British).

Grave 43: cut 1241 (burial 1242; fill 1243)
(Fig. 2.11)
SSE–NNW, sub-rectangular, moderately sloping sides, flat base. 1.98 x 0.80 m, 0.36 m deep (base at 137.27 m OD). Extended, supine, with left arms alongside, right slightly flexed with hand over right hip. Root disturbance.
Human bone: *c.* 95% adult *c.* 24–29 yr. female.
Grave goods:

ON 95: simple iron belt buckle, at centre of waist, by right hand. D-shaped with a circular section and fragmentary tongue. Length 19 mm; width 32 mm; surviving length of tongue 15 mm.

ON 96: iron knife, left waist inside left forearm, aligned diagonally with point to foot end. Triangular section tang in line with back; curves down to blade. Clear line where blade and tang meet. Back of knife and cutting edge curve to tip. Resharpened. Böhner Type B. Length 150 mm; width 14 mm; thickness 5 mm.

Residual finds: 1 sherd pottery (Saxon, sandy), charcoal flecks.

Grave 44: Cut 1486 (burial 1487; fill 1488)
(Fig. 2.12)
NNE–SSW (unclear), sub-rectangular, rounded ends, steep sides, irregular base. 1.66 x 0.78 m, 0.44 m deep (base at 137.46 m OD). Posture not discernible. Heavy root disturbance.
Human bone: 10 frags. s.u. adult >35 yr.

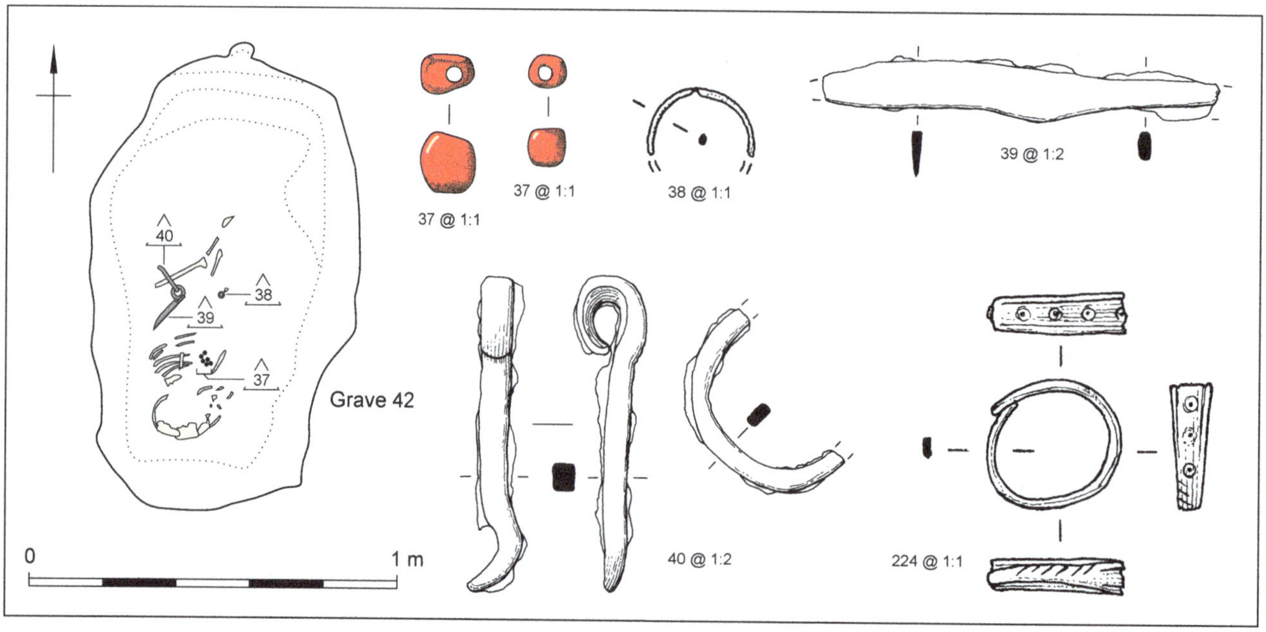

Figure 2.10 Grave 42 and grave goods

Grave goods:

ON 289: glass bead. Koch 20 Yellow. Medium, colour 2.1/5.1, poly P23a, shape D1.

ON 290: glass bead. Degraded. Medium, colour 7.6, shape G1 (not illustrated).

ON 291: two tiny copper alloy fragments, right edge of grave?. 1–2 mm² (not illustrated).

ON 292: glass bead. Koch 34 blue. Medium, colour 8.1/7.5a, poly P9, shape A1.

ON 293: glass bead. Medium, colour 7.7, shape G1.

ON 294: glass bead. Koch 20 white. Medium, colour 2.1/8.1, poly P23a, shape A1 (not illustrated).

ON 295: glass bead. Koch 34 white. Medium, colour 2.1/8.1, poly P9, shape A2 (not illustrated).

ON 296: glass bead. Very degraded, in 3 frags. Medium, shape B1 (not illustrated).

ON 297: glass bead. Koch 20, but marvered trail missing (not illustrated). Medium, colour 2.1/?, poly P23, shape D1.

ON 299: glass bead. Polychrome (Koch 27?). Medium, colour 8.1/7.5a, poly P10, shape B1.

ON 401: iron fragment right edge of grave? Length 6 mm (not illustrated).

ON 402: iron knife; tang central to blade with angular shoulder up to back of blade and gentle curve to cutting edge. Back straight before curving down to tip; blade curves up to tip. Böhner Type A. Length 162 mm; width 19 mm; thickness 5 mm.

Residual finds: 2 clinker (intrusive).

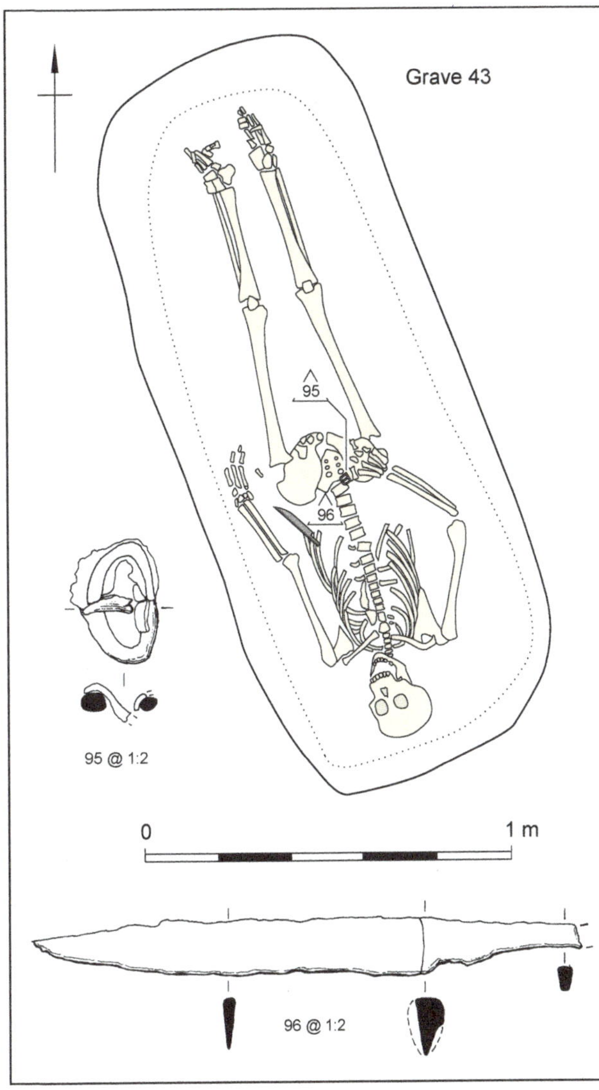

Figure 2.11 Grave 43 and grave goods

Grave 45: cut 1251 (burial 1249; fill 1251)

(Fig. 2.13)

S–N, sub-rectangular (curved) with rounded head end, moderately sloping sides, flat base (sloping to the S). 2.20 x 0.60 m, 0.22 m deep (base at 136.78 m OD). Extended, supine, right arm along side, left hand on right pelvis. Shallow, truncated, ? overdug to S.

Human bone: *c.* 85% adult *c.* 40–50 yr. male.

Grave goods:

ON 77: fragmentary iron spearhead, socket cleft for *c.* 50 mm, rivet *c.* 10 mm from end, right of skull, diagonal, tip towards head of grave. Angular parallel-sided blade, lozengiform section. Swanton Group G1. Length 324 mm; width 26 mm.

ON 89: iron knife, left of waist, diagonal, point out. Tang central to blade, tapering, with curved shoulder up to back of blade and angled down to cutting edge. Back straight before curving down to tip; blade curves up to tip. Böhner Type A. Length 116 mm; width 20 mm; thickness 5 mm.

ON 90: iron plate with slot in end, right waist. Possible buckle plate (X-ray shows two rivets, ?copper alloy/tinned). Length 24 mm; width 10 mm.

Residual finds: 2 sherds pottery (Romano-British).

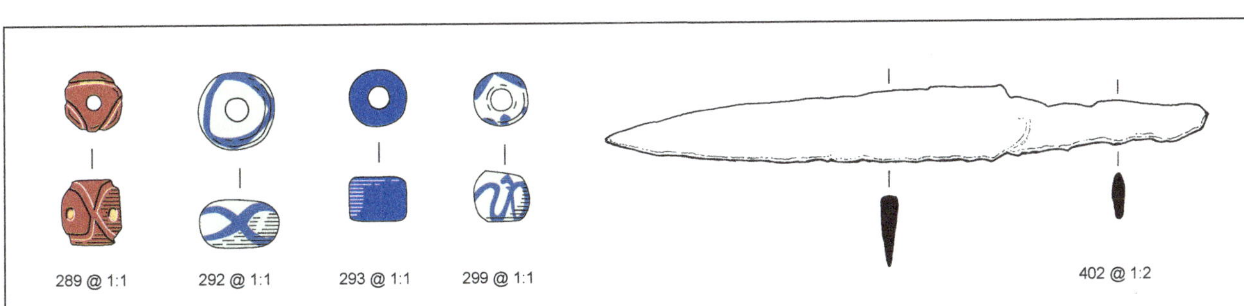

Figure 2.12 Selected finds from grave 44

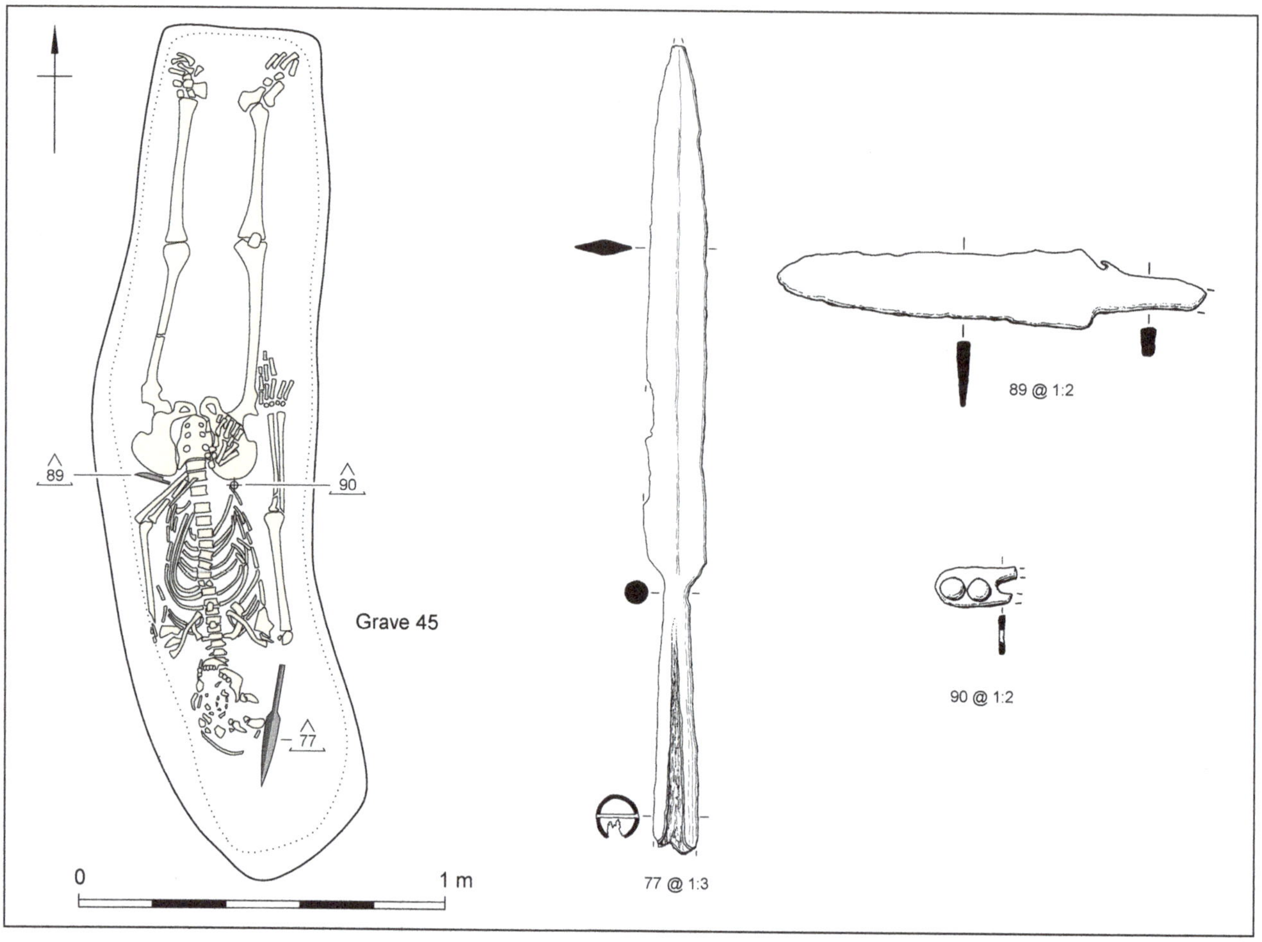

Figure 2.13 Grave 45 and grave goods

Grave 46: cut 1233 (burial 1234; fill 1235)
(not illustrated)
S–N, incomplete cut. Approximately 0.95 x 0.35 m, 0.05 m deep (base at 136.94 m OD). ?flexed or ?extended, supine. Very truncated.
Human bone: *c.* 10% a.u.l. subadult/adult >14 yr.

Grave 47: cut 1227 (burial 1231; fill 1232)
(Fig. 2.14)
SSE–NNW, sub-rectangular/irregular, shallow sides, uneven base. 1.91 x 0.92 m, 0.21 m deep (base at 136.98 m OD). Extended, supine with hands on/by respective femur. Ankles crossed right over left.
Human bone: *c.* 60% adult *c.* 24–29 yr. female.
Grave goods:
ON 80: probable iron toilet set (fragmentary), between upper left chest and arm. Consisting of 11 fragments and including several rods one with a disc head and another with a scoop and at least one ring.
ON 84: iron ring with pin, probable penannular brooch, on left shoulder. Oval shape with circular section. Pin wrapped around loop. Diameter 24 mm.
ON 86: simple iron buckle on left pelvis. D-shaped with circular section and iron tongue wrapped around loop. Length 18 mm; width 31 mm; length of tongue 22 mm.

Grave 48: cut 1236 (burial 1238; fill 1237)
(not illustrated)
NNW–SSE, incomplete, ?sub-rectangular, rounded head end. Very shallow unclear sides, flat base. Approximately 0.14 x 0.20 m, up to 0.03 m deep (base at 137.08 m OD). Posture not discernible. Heavily truncated, root disturbance.
Human bone: *c.* 5% s. neonate/infant.
Residual finds: 1 sherd pottery (late prehistoric).

Grave 49: cut 1246 (burial 1248; fill 1247)
(Fig. 2.15)
N–S, sub-rectangular, rounded ends, steep sides, uneven base. 1.90 x 0.50 m, 0.08 m deep (base at 137.07 m OD). Probably extended, supine.
Human bone: *c.* 15% s.l. juvenile *c.* 6–8 yr.
Grave goods:
ON 87: iron knife, lying diagonally over left chest/ abdomen, tip to left. Tapering tang of rectangular section central to blade, angled up to back of blade and gentle slope to cutting edge. Back straight before curving down to tip; blade curves up to tip. Resharpened. Rivet that would have helped to attach the handle located on tang near blade shoulder. Böhner Type A. Length 143 mm; width 18 mm; thickness 5 mm.

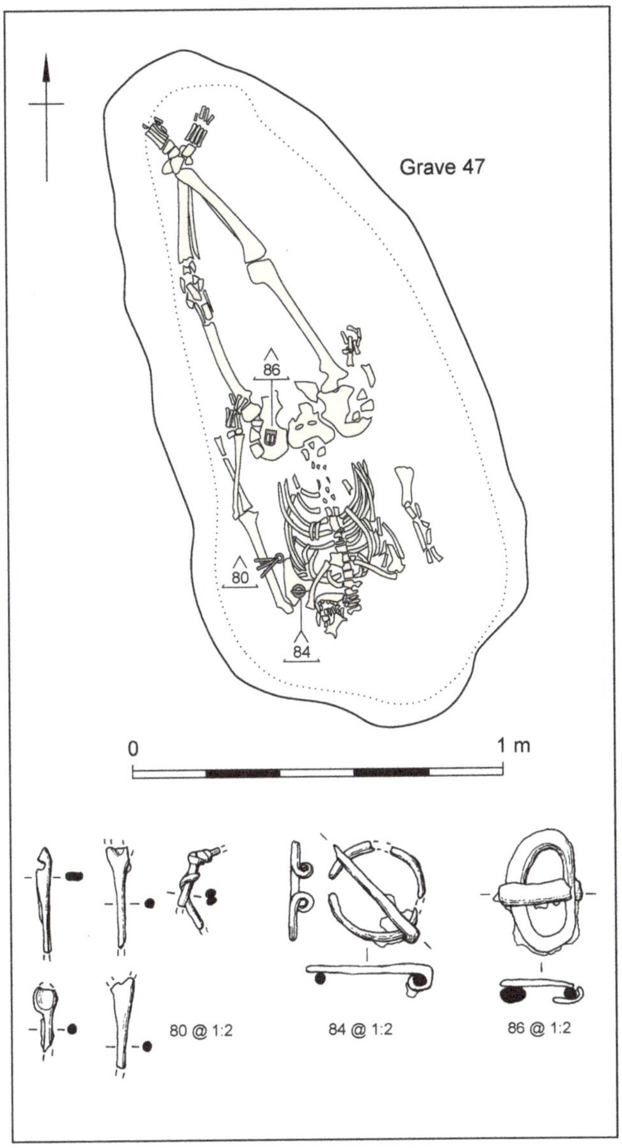

Figure 2.14 Grave 47 and grave goods

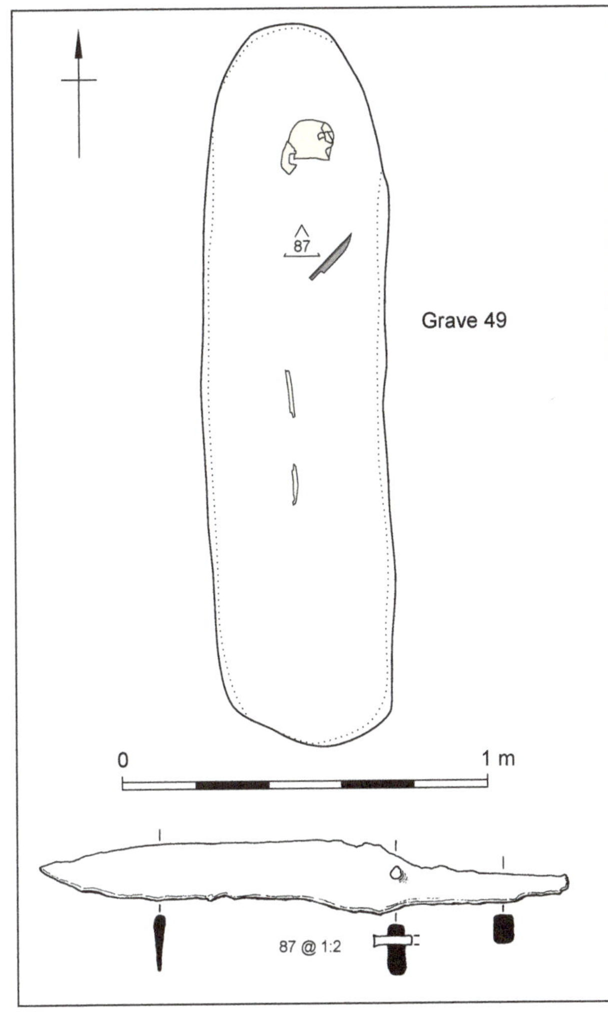

Figure 2.15 Grave 49 and iron knife

Residual finds: 2 sherds pottery (1 Romano-British; 1 Saxon, organic-tempered).

Grave 50: cut 1205 (burial 1206; fill 1207)

(Fig. 2.16)

S–N, sub-rectangular, rounded ends, steep, concave sides, flat base. 1.60 x 0.60 m, *c.* 0.05 m deep (base at 137.03 m OD). Extended, supine, left arm along side, right hand at left hip.

Human bone: *c.* 40% juvenile *c.* 4–6 yr.

Residual finds: 1 sherd pottery (Saxon, organic-tempered).

Grave 51: cut 1166 (burial 1167; fill 1168)

(Fig. 2.17)

SSW–NNE (burial more S–N), sub-rectangular, narrower foot end, shallow concave sides, undulating base. 2.0 x 0.6 m, 0.05 m deep (base at 137.09 m OD). Extended, supine, arms across abdomen. Fill darker than most, truncated.

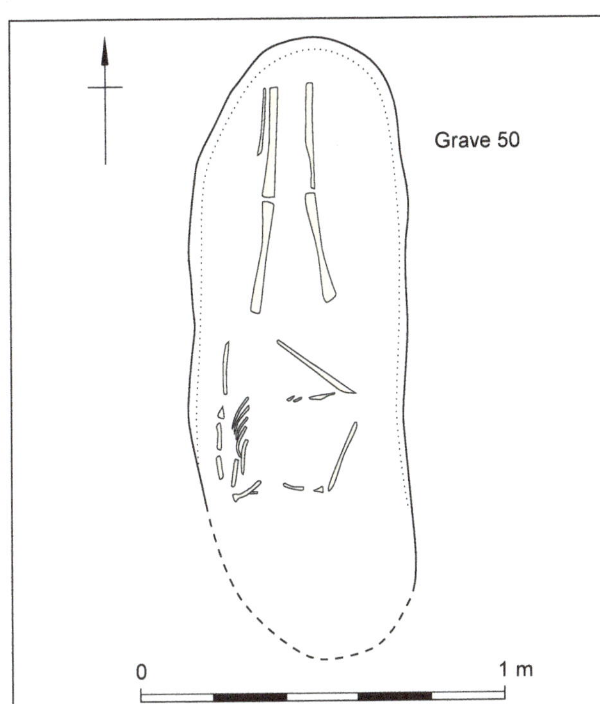

Figure 2.16 Grave 50

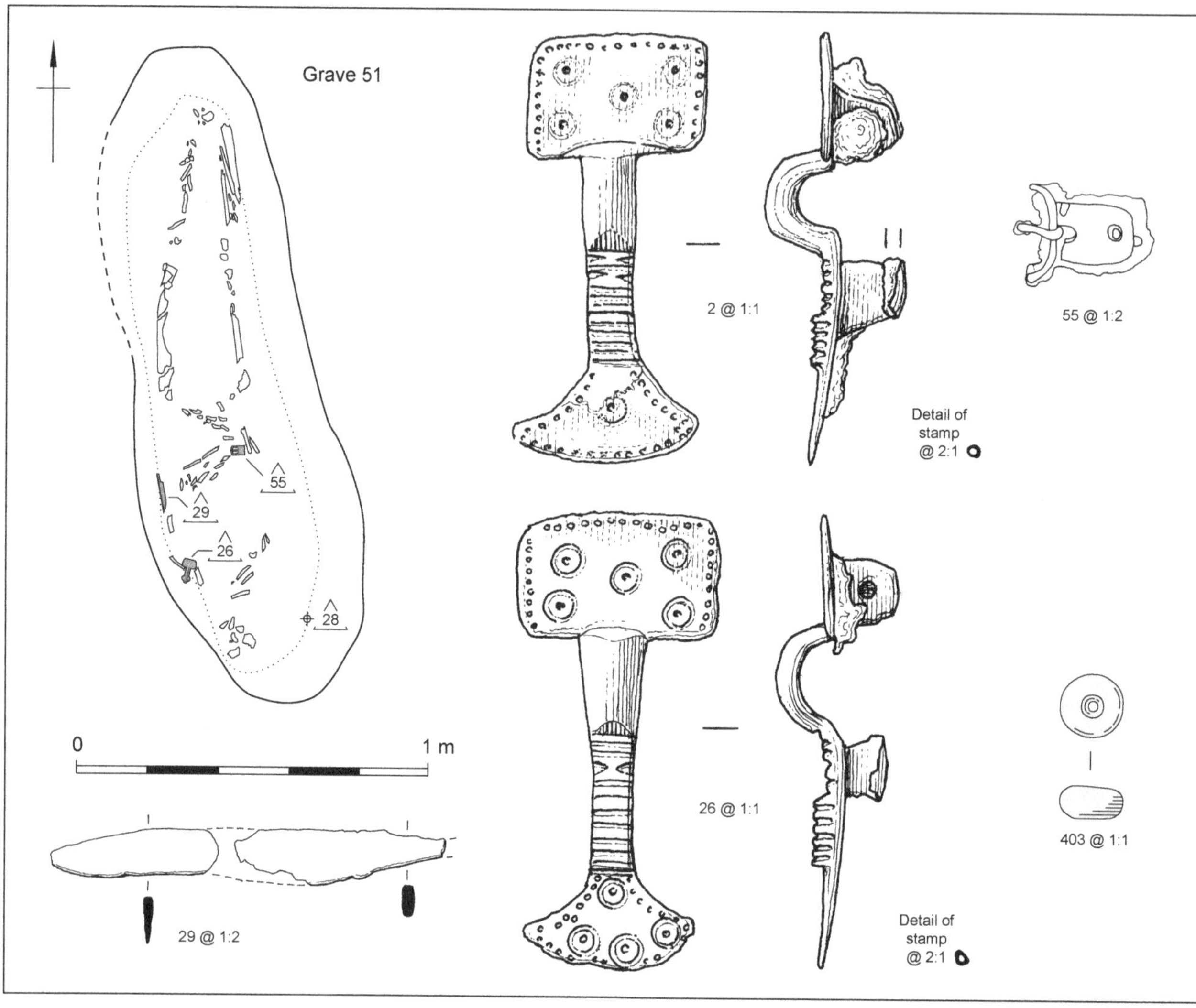

Figure 2.17 Grave 51 and selected grave goods

Human bone: *c.* 25% adult >45 yr. ??female.

Grave goods:

ON 2: copper alloy small-long brooch (location unknown). Rectangular head-plate with five stamped dots (very faint incised circle enclosing at least one); faint border of punched stamps on three sides. Acutely arched bow leading to foot exhibiting nine crudely executed transverse grooves. The foot expands into a wide crescentic terminal with a central punched dot and a border of punched stamps. Traces of tinning remain on the headplate and the terminal. Hinge and catch with remains of iron pin. Length 57 mm; width of head 26 mm. Leeds Type IV/I.

ON 26: copper alloy small-long brooch (not paired with ON 2), in left shoulder area, lying diagonally. Rectangular head-plate with five ring-and-dot motifs enclosed by a border of punched stamps on three sides. Arched bow with central ridge leading to foot exhibiting irregular transverse grooves and a series of bands. The foot expands into a asymmetrical triangular terminal bordered by irregular punched dots and enclosing four ring-and-dot motifs. Hinge and catch-plate, traces of an iron pin (probably ON 31). Length 64 mm; width of head 28 mm. Leeds Type IV/I.

ON 28: tiny iron fragment, edge of grave, to right of skull. Length 4 mm; width 5 mm (not illustrated).

ON 29: fragmentary iron knife, located to left of waist, outside left arm and aligned vertically with tip to head end of grave. Tapering rectangular-sectioned tang in line with back, gentle curve to cutting edge. Back slopes gently to tip; cutting edge curves up to tip. Böhner Type A. Length *c.* 107 mm; width 15 mm; thickness 5 mm.

ON 31: fragmentary iron (possible) pin; remains of a ?knob head and shank (location unknown) (not illustrated).

ON 55: fragmentary simple iron buckle with rectangular plate (inc. ON 56 part of loop), at right waist. Shape/section of loop unknown; rivet near end of plate and slot to accommodate tongue; fragmentary tongue wrapped around loop. Length 25 mm; width 17 mm. Length of plate 22 mm;

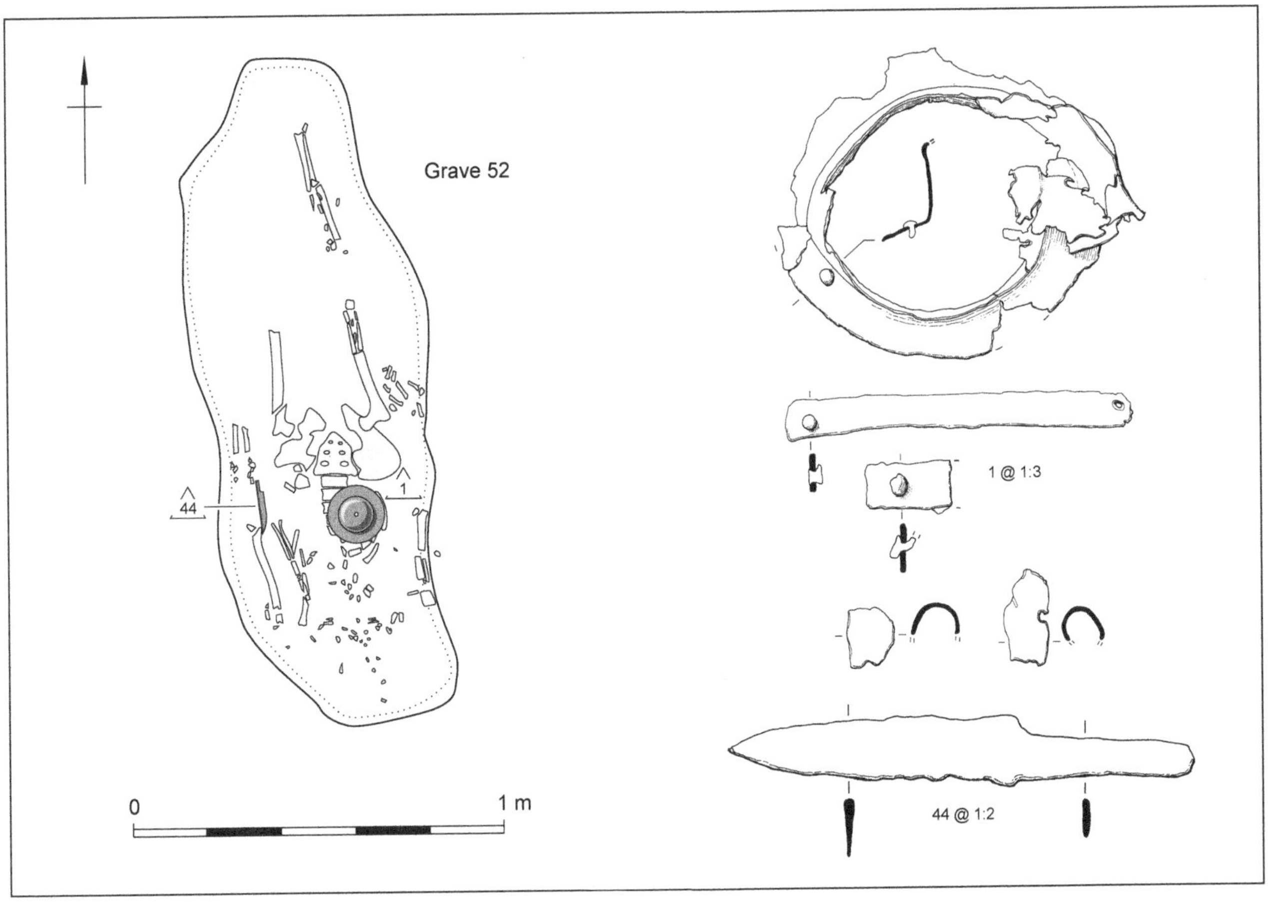

Figure 2.18 Grave 52 and selected grave goods

width 16 mm. Length of tongue 12 mm.

ON 232: three iron fragments (location unknown). Length of largest fragment 8 mm; width 7 mm (not illustrated).

ON 233: amber bead, frags only (location unknown; not illustrated).

ON 403: glass bead. Sample 5065 (grave base); degraded. Medium. Colour 8.1, shape A1.

Grave 52: cut 1193 (burial 1194; fill 1195)

(Fig. 2.18)

S–N, sub-rectangular, narrow foot section, concave sides, flat base. 1.79 x 0.52 m, 0.03 m deep (base at 137.07 m OD). Extended, supine, arms along sides.

Human bone: *c.* 30% a.u.l. adult >45 yr. male.

Grave goods:

ON 1: very fragmentary and distorted iron shield-boss and grip, right waist; only flange and lower section of neck and boss wall remaining. Straight walls, flange (25 mm width), number of rivets unknown. Possibly Dickinson and Härke Type 3 or very possibly Type 5.

ON 44: iron knife lying to left of waist inside left arm, vertical with tip to head end. Rectangular section tang central to blade; angular shoulder up to back of blade with a gentle slope to cutting edge. Back straight for most of its length but curves down to tip; blade curves up to tip. Böhner Type A. Length 125 mm; width 15 mm; thickness 4 mm.

ON 405: spear ferrule (found amongst the remains of the shield boss; not illustrated).

Residual finds: 1 sherd pottery (Romano-British).

Grave 53: cut 1190 (burial 1191; fill 1192)

(Fig. 2.19)

SSW–NNE, sub-rectangular with rounded ends, steep sides, flat base. 1.15 x 0.50 m, 0.28 m deep (base at 137.18 m OD). Flexed slightly on right side, hands crossed over pelvis. Notably tight grave; flint nodules against edge in NW corner.

Human bone: *c.* 60% juvenile *c.* 4–7 yr.

Grave goods:

ON 46: simple fragmentary iron buckle with fragmentary tongue wrapped around loop, at centre of waist. Oval loop of circular section. Length 21 mm; width 28 mm; surviving length of tongue 21 mm.

Residual finds: 1 sherd pottery (Romano-British), charcoal flecks.

Grave 54: cut 1184 (burial 1185; fill 1186)

(Fig. 2.20)

NNW–SSE, sub-rectangular, rounded ends, steep sides, flat base. 1.49 x 0.56 m, 0.25 m deep (base at 137.16 m OD). Posture not discernible.

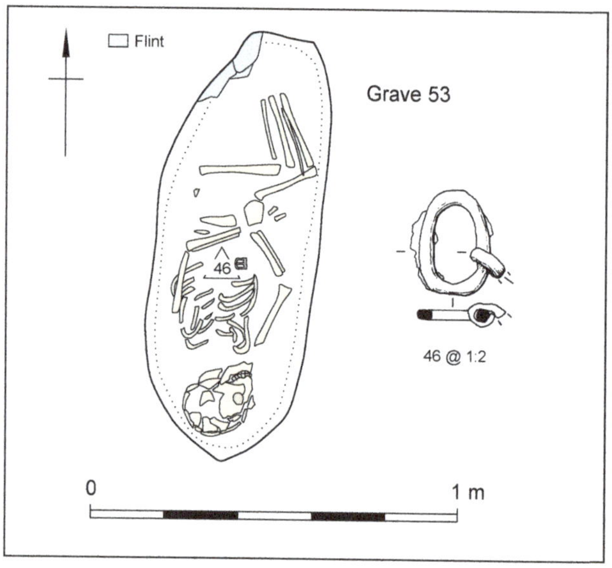

Figure 2.19 Grave 53 and iron buckle

Human bone: 2 teeth and a few unid frags. adult >45 yr. ??male.

Grave goods:

ON 34: iron knife with tip missing, probably located in waist area. Tang central to blade with rectangular section; shoulder sloping up to back of long blade and a very gentle slope to cutting edge. Back straight for most of its length before curving down to tip; blade appears to curve up to tip. Böhner Type A. Length 200 mm, width 14 mm; thickness 5 mm.

ON 35: iron circular fitting with attachment on reverse; *ex situ*; ?mount. Diameter 42 mm.

ON 41: iron object (SW of grave). Probable fragment of a pursemount/firesteel. Length 79 mm; width 19 mm.

Residual finds: ON 36: 1 sherd pottery (Romano-British).

Grave 55: cut 1176 (burial 1177; fill 1178)

(Fig. 2.21)

WSW–ENE, sub-rectangular, rounded ends, steep sides,

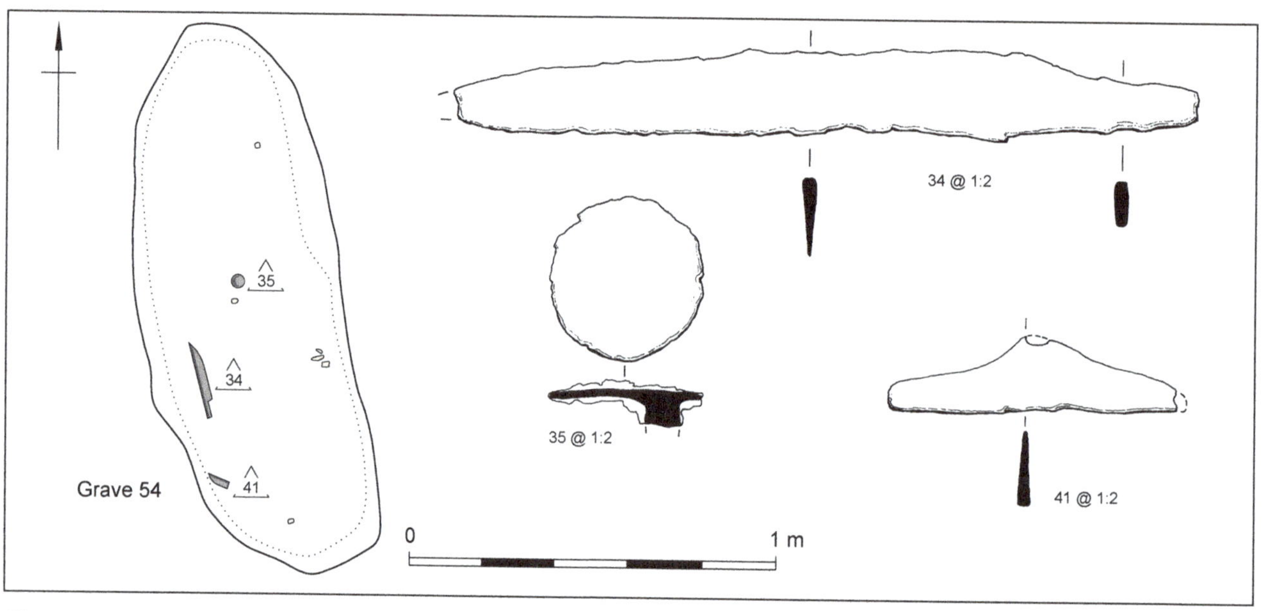

Figure 2.20 Grave 54 and grave goods

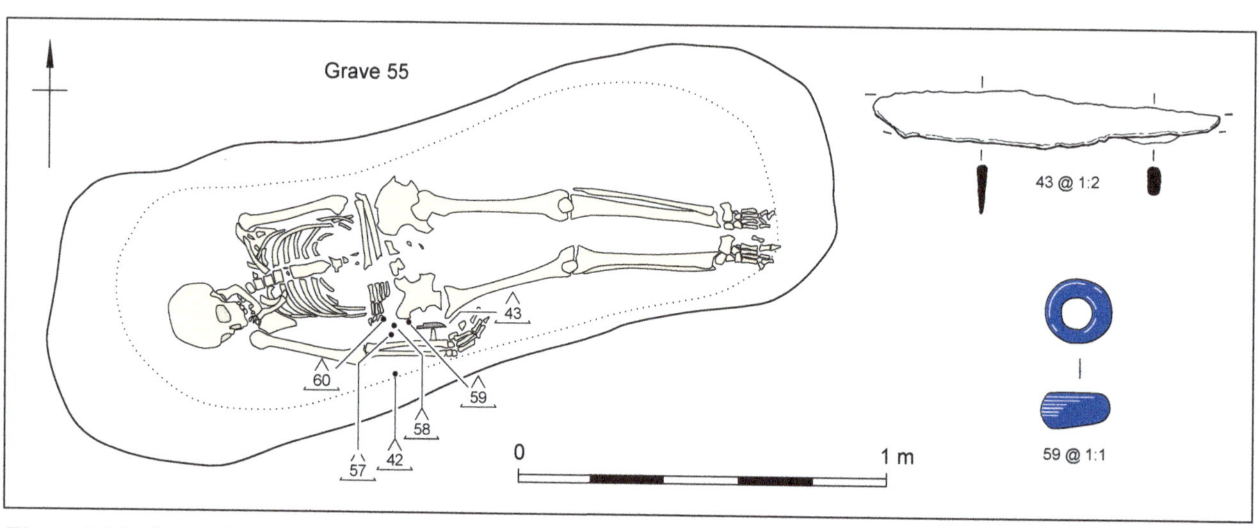

Figure 2.21 Grave 55 and selected grave goods

flat base. 2.19 x 0.81 m, 0.51 m deep (base at 136.79 m OD). Extended, supine, right arm along side, left hand at right elbow.

Human bone: *c.* 90% adult >40 yr. female.

Grave goods:

ON 43: fragmentary iron knife to right of hip, inside right arm, aligned vertically with point to ?foot end. Tang in line with back of knife; curves gently down to blade. Back and cutting edge may curve to point; unidentified type. Surviving length 94 mm; width 19 mm; thickness 6 mm.

ON 42: glass bead. Medium. Colour 7.7, shape A2. (not illustrated).

ON 57–59: 3 glass beads. Medium. Colour 7.7, shape A2. (ON 59 illustrated only)

ON 60: glass bead, wound. Medium. Colour 7.7, shape A2. (not illustrated).

Grave 56: cut 1196 (burial 1201; fill 1197)

(Fig. 2.22)

W–E, sub-rectangular, rounded foot end, moderately sloping sides, slightly concave base. 1.28 x 0.58 m, 0.22 m deep (base at 136.92 m OD). Extended, supine, arms along sides, right slightly splayed.

Human bone: *c.* 30% juvenile *c.* 4–6 yr.

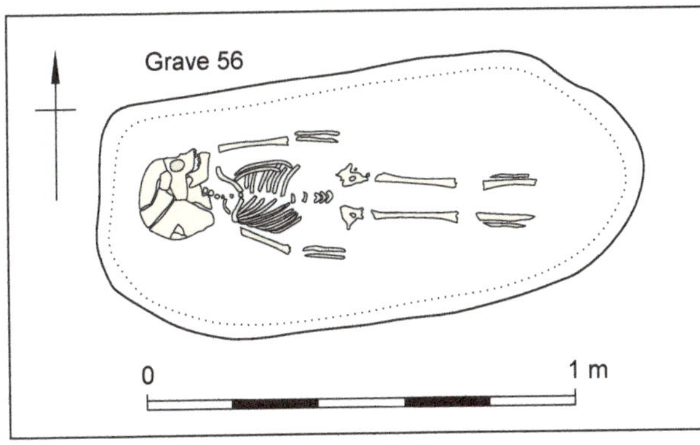

Figure 2.22 Grave 56

Residual finds:

ON 45: iron nail head with fragment of stocky shank, located approximately in the centre of the grave. Length 17 mm; width (head) 20 mm. (not illustrated).

Grave 57: cut 1215 (burial 1216; fill 1217)

(Fig. 2.23)

S–N, sub-rectangular, rounded ends, shallow sides, flat base. 1.97 x 0.67 m, 0.08 m deep (base at 136.50 m OD). Slightly flexed right leg, supine/slightly on right side. Right shoulder tilted down, right hand at left elbow, left hand

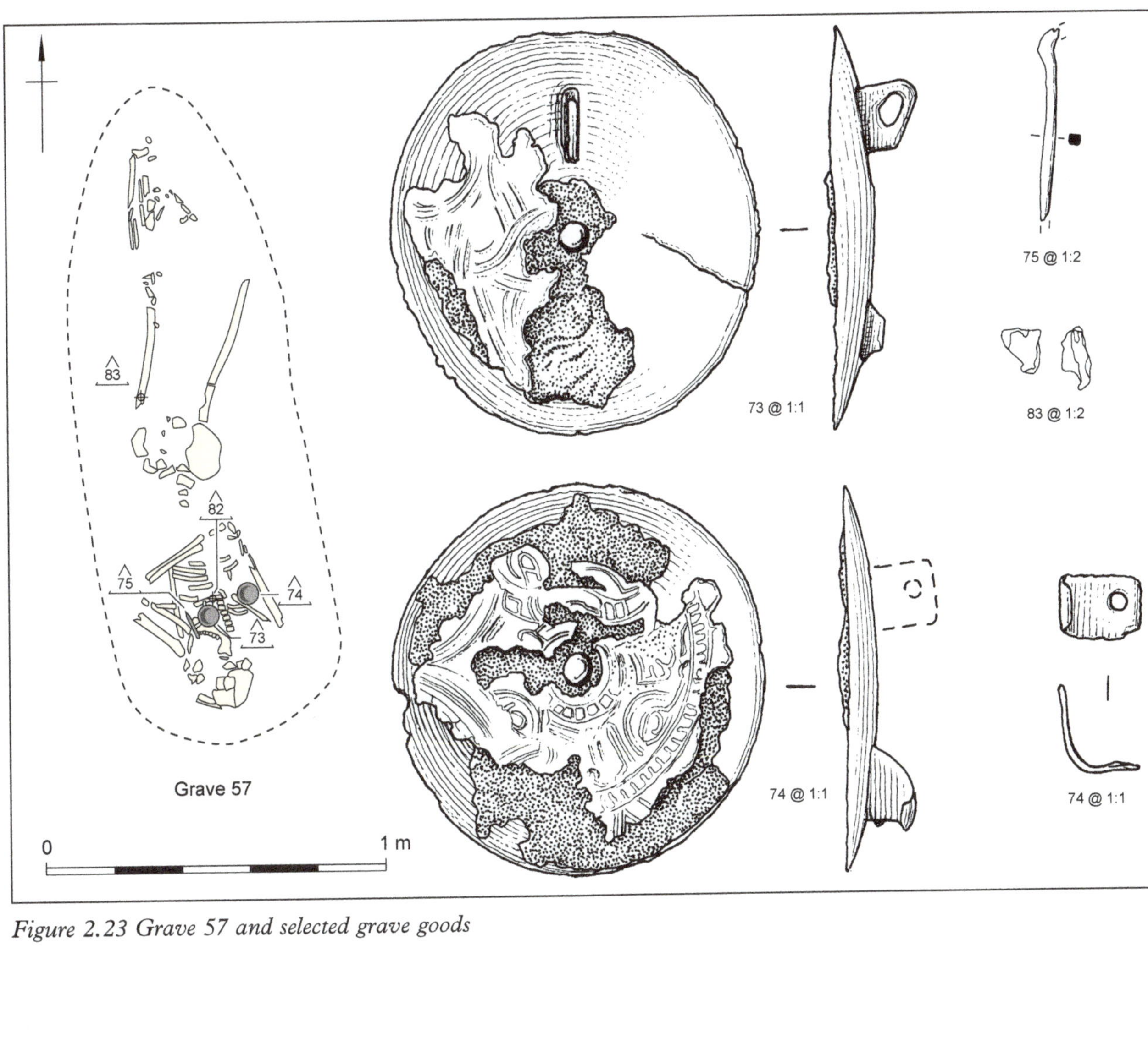

Figure 2.23 Grave 57 and selected grave goods

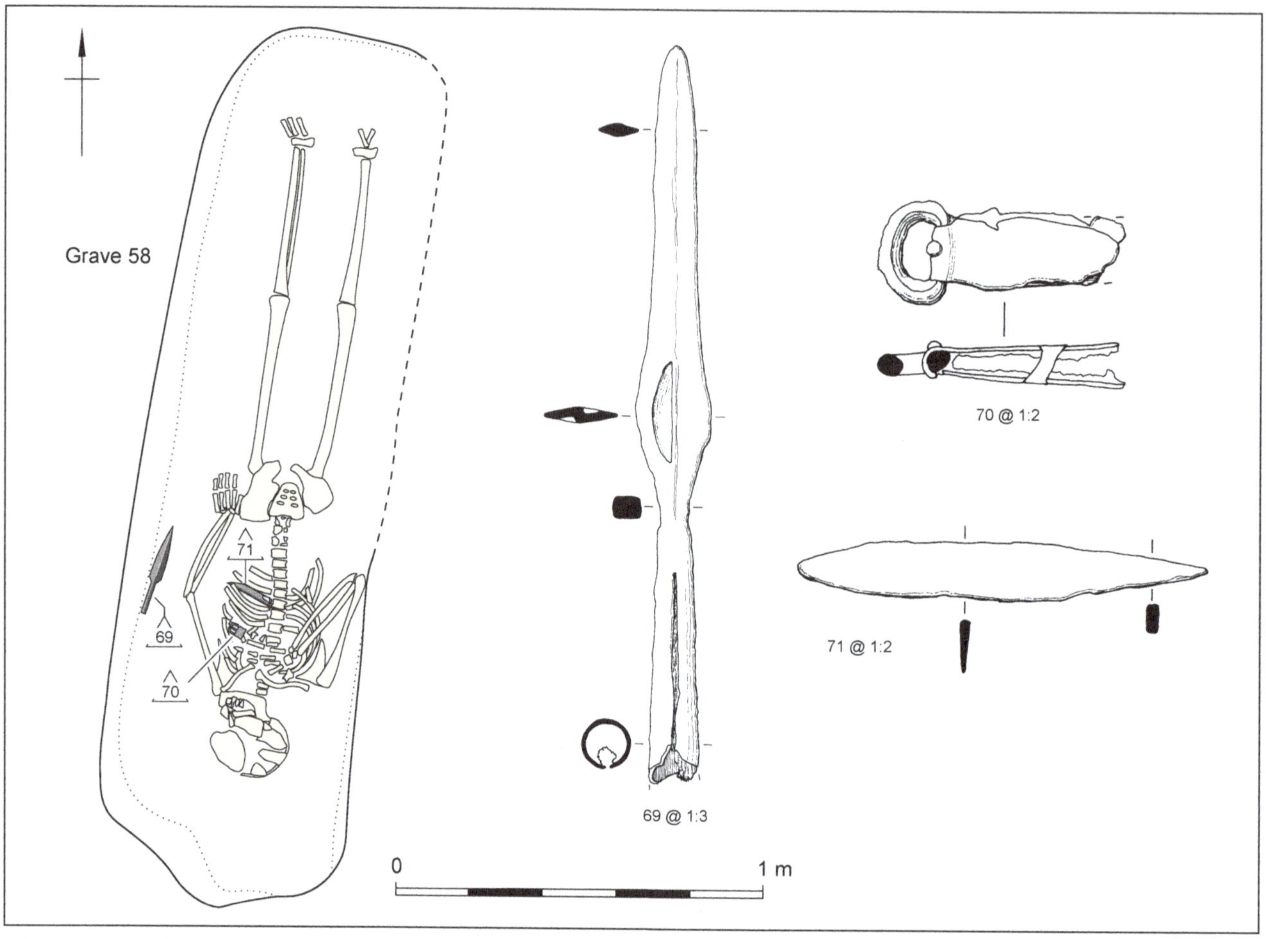

Figure 2.24 Grave 58 and grave goods

probably on right shoulder. Foot end disturbed by tree-throw hole.

Human bone: *c*. 40% adult >55 yr. female.

Grave goods:

ON 73: fragmentary copper alloy applied brooch; sub-circular back-plate into which the pin catch and hinge are slotted. Located over upper left chest. Very fragmentary face, gilt, central blue cabochon setting. Diameter 58 mm.

ON 74: fragmentary copper alloy applied brooch; sub-circular back-plate into which the pin catch is slotted, hinge separated. Located over upper right chest. Very fragmentary face, gilt, central red cabochon setting. Diameter 56 mm.

ON 75: fragmentary iron pin? to left of ON 73. Square section. Length 55 mm; diameter 4 mm.

ON 82: iron fragment; probable remains of brooch pin (ON 73). Length 9 mm; width 5 mm (not illustrated).

ON 83: two iron fragments, one a possible shank; located in the area of the waist.

Sample 5115: copper alloy pin catch and fragment of gilt copper alloy and possible pin. (location unknown; not illustrated).

Sample 5128: Fragment of leaded bronze brooch (location unknown; not illustrated).

Grave 58: cut 1214 (burial 1213; fill 1212)
(Fig. 2.24)

SSW–NNE, sub-rectangular, steep sides, flat base. 2.45 x 0.75 m, 0.40 m deep (base at 136.41 m OD). Extended, supine with left arm along side and right hand on chest.

Human bone: *c*. 90% adult >50 yr. male.

Grave goods:

ON 69: iron spearhead, socket cleft to *c*.70 mm, disturbed – at left elbow and alongside grave edge, tip to foot of grave. Angular, straight/concave-sided blade (X-ray shows slight concavity above blade angle), ?lozengiform section. Swanton Group E2/H2. Length 295 mm; width 28 mm.

ON 70: simple iron buckle with rectangular plate, located over left chest. Oval in outline with circular section; fragmentary tongue, wrapped around loop; slot in plate to accommodate tongue and rivet near terminal of plate. Possibly the fastener of a strap to which the knife was attached. Total length 66 mm; length of loop 22 mm; width 30 mm. Length of plate 47 mm; width 21 mm.

ON 71: iron knife lying horizontally just above left waist. Tapering tang central to blade, rectangular section; shoulder gently curving up to back of blade and down to cutting edge. Back straight for most its length before curving down to tip; blade curves up

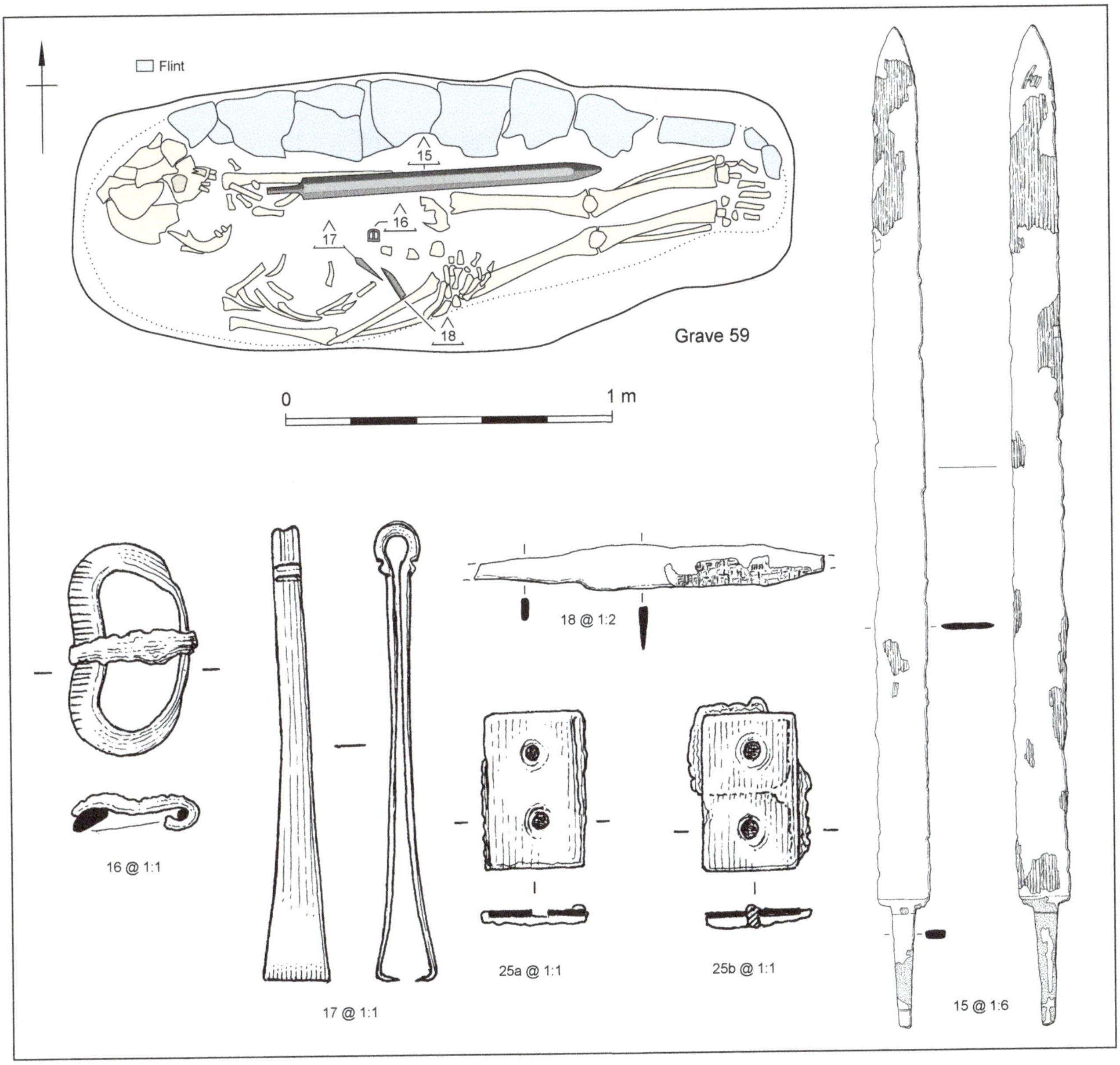

Figure 2.25 Grave 59 and selected grave goods

to tip. Böhner Type A. Length 110 mm; width 15 mm; thickness 4 mm.

Grave 59: cut 1150 (burial 1132; fill 1151)

(Fig. 2.25)

W–E, sub-rectangular, wider mid-portion, steep sides, flat base. 2.30 x 0.75 m, 0.70 m deep (base at 135.75 m OD). Extended, supine, right hand on right leg, left hand ?under sword. N edge lined with flint nodules. Fill cut by grave 60 – deliberate re-use, burial undisturbed.

Human bone: *c.* 70% adult >50 yr. male.

Grave goods:

ON 15: iron sword lying over left side, shoulder to knee, point to foot end. Parallel sided; Sword length 910 mm; blade width 48 mm; hilt without terminal bar of length 123 mm. Upper guard 21 mm, grip 89 mm, lower guard 13 mm, extending 6 mm over blade. Hilt material – horn. Scabbard – willow/poplar.

ON 16: copper alloy buckle loop, at centre waist. The loop is kidney-shaped in outline but narrows in the axis area forming a bar. It is decorated by zones of incised radial lines. The iron tongue is anchored around the loop. Length 19 mm; width 32 mm; length of tongue 20 mm.

ON 17: copper alloy tweezers, located to right of waist and probably suspended from the belt. Stout pair with thickened head formed into a loop; the head is delineated by a transverse groove on either side and a groove runs around the head. The plain arms expand and curve gradually outward towards the bottom; they are then sharply incurved forming the jaws. Length 68mm; width of jaws 10 mm.

ON 18: iron knife (end of tip missing), to right of waist

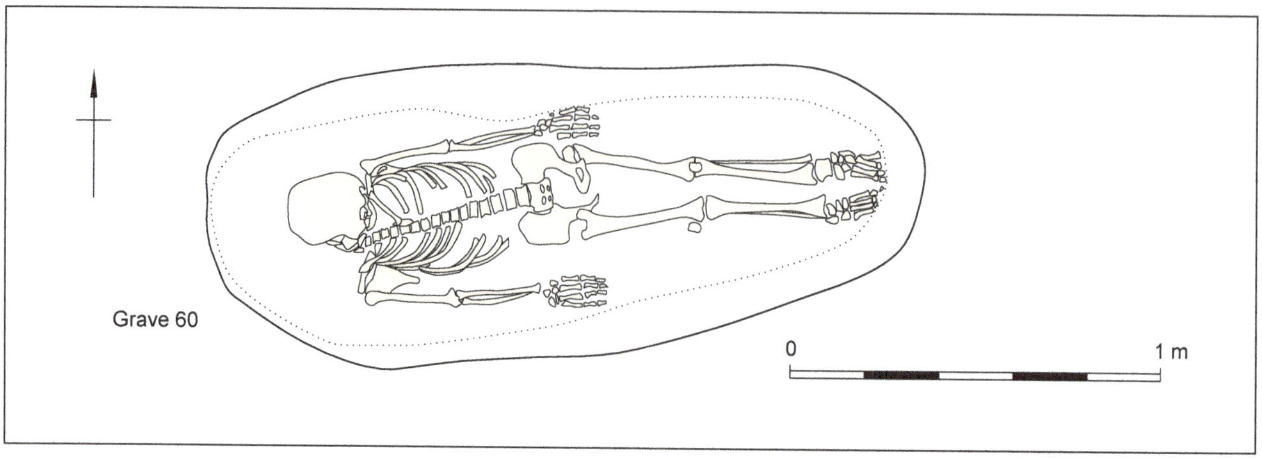

Figure 2.26 Grave 60

lying diagonally and partially under right arm. Tapering tang central to blade of rectangular section; with shoulder very gently sloping up to back of blade and gently sloping down to cutting edge. Back straight for most its length before curving down to tip; blade curves up to tip. Böhner Type A. Length 117 mm; width 14 mm; thickness 5 mm. Textile remains.

ON 25: pair of rectangular copper alloy fittings or clasp (location unknown); both with two rivet-holes.
a) Plate exhibits a lug situated along edge bent at right angles. Length 24 mm; width 20 mm.
b) Length 25 mm; width 17 mm.

ON 231: two iron fragments (location unknown), ?nail. Length of shank 19 mm; width 4 mm. Length of head 26 mm; width 11 mm (not illustrated).

Grave 60: cut 1103 (burial 1104; fill 1105)

(Fig. 2.26)

W–E, sub-rectangular, rounded ends, steep sides, flat base. 2.10 x 0.85 m, 0.55 m deep (base at 136.49 m OD). Extended, supine, arms along sides. Abundant large flint nodules in fill, ?deliberately placed (not illustrated). Cuts fill of grave 59. Deliberate re-use, underlying burial undisturbed

Human bone: *c.* 99% adult *c.* 35–45 yr. male.

Residual finds: 1 flint; 32 animal bone.

Grave 61: cut 1116 (burial 1117; fill 1118)

(Fig. 2.27)

WSW–ENE, sub-rectangular, rounded head end, moderately sloping sides, flat base. Oversized - 2.31 x 1.13 m, 0.27 m deep (base at 135.66 m OD). Supine, legs slightly flexed to right, hands on neck.

Human bone: *c.* 75% adult *c.* 45–55 yr. female.

Grave goods:

ON 8: copper alloy penannular brooch, by left ear. Circular-sectioned hoop, with transverse ribbing probably over the entire surface. The terminals are bent back on themselves possibly shaped into crude zoomorphic motifs. Adhering to the hoop are the possible remains of a pin loop. Diameter 28 mm; thickness of terminal 3 mm. Fowler Type E. ?associated with veil.

ON 10: copper alloy disc brooch located in the centre of the upper chest; damage to the outer rim. A small central stub is surrounded by six incised concentric circles; crescentic stamps around the edge. Faint traces of tinning on the obverse. Single hinge and catch, remains of iron pin. Diameter 33 mm. Textile preserved on the obverse.

ON 11: copper alloy disc brooch (paired with ON 10), left waist. A small central stub is surrounded by six incised concentric circles; crescentic stamps around the edge. Faint traces of tinning on the obverse. Single hinge (damaged) and catch (damaged). Diameter 33 mm.

ON 12: iron knife, found right of hip/elbow, vertically-aligned with tip to foot end. Tang central to blade of rectangular section, with shoulder very gently curving up to back of blade and down to cutting edge. Back straight for most its length; blade curves up to tip. Böhner Type B. Length 145 mm; width 16 mm; thickness 3 mm. Sharpening curve near tang end of blade.

ON 13: copper alloy pin/picker attached to a wire slip-knot ring, located to right of the skull. Expanded head, flattened and perforated; tapering shank of circular-shaped section. Under the perforation are two horizontally-aligned punched circles below which are three similar vertically-aligned motifs. Length 87 mm; diameter of ring 17 mm.

ON 14: copper alloy penannular brooch, lying to right ear/mandible. Rectangular-sectioned hoop, with transverse ribbing close to each terminal. The terminals are bent back on themselves forming a scroll at right angles to the hoop, each exhibiting a transverse inscribed line. Adhering to the hoop are the possible remains of a pin loop. Diameter 24 mm; thickness of terminal 2 mm. Fowler Type D4.

ON 404: glass bead, Sample 5013 (grave base); completely opaque. Medium. A1

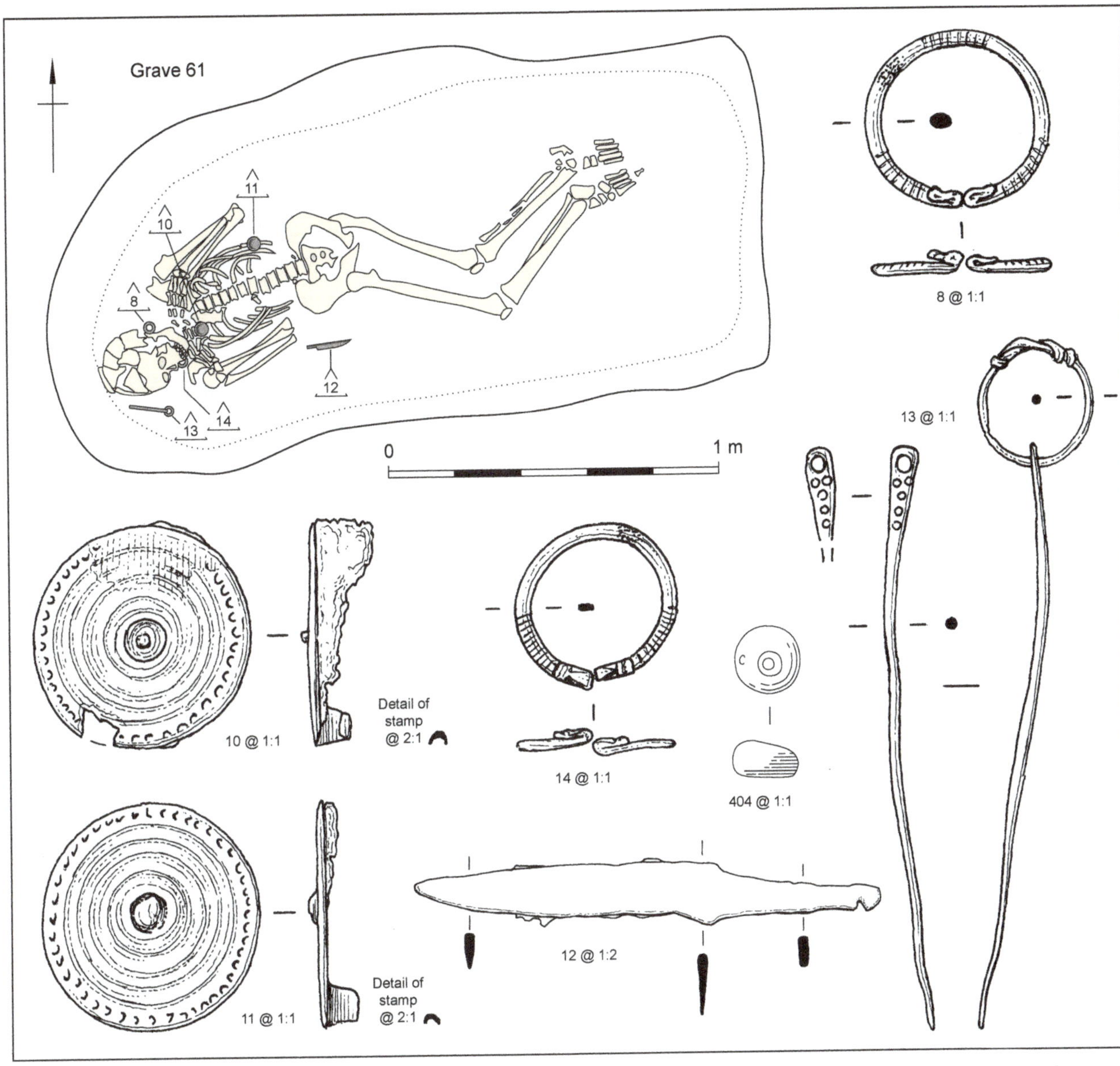

Figure 2.27 Grave 61 and grave goods

Grave 62: cut 1157 (burial 1158; fill 1159)
(Fig. 2.28)
W–E, sub-rectangular, rounded ends, moderately sloping sides, flat base. 1.94 x 0.96 m, 0.25 m deep (base at 135.39 m OD). Extended supine, arms by sides, hands over thighs. Skull removed by grave 63 (glass beads ON 27 and ON 30 may come from infant grave 63).
Human bone: *c.* 70% adult >55 yr. female.
c. 5% s.a. infant *c.* 1.5–3 yr. (=1161a).
Grave goods:
ON 19: copper alloy small-long brooch, over upper left chest, lying diagonally. Trapezoid head-plate with a border of stamped triangles containing dots. Gently arched bow with two faint incised transverse lines at the bottom and a moulding in front leading to a short and narrow foot exhibiting a pair of transverse grooves. The foot expands into a sub-triangular terminal with a pair of transverse stamped triangles containing dots and a border of similar motifs along the bottom edge. A largely obscured hinge and broken catch, remains of iron pin. Length 64 mm; width of head 22 mm. Leeds Type IV/II.
ON 20: copper alloy small-long brooch; at right shoulder lying diagonally. Rectangular head-plate with a border of stamped triangles containing dots. Gently arched bow extending to a foot with a pair of incised transverse lines at the top and another at the bottom, in between these are mouldings forming faceted corners. The foot expands into a sub-triangular terminal; at the top are three stamped triangles containing dots and along the bottom edge is a border of similar motifs. A largely obscured hinge and broken catch-plate, remains of iron pin. Length 63 mm; width of head 22 mm. Leeds Type IV/I.

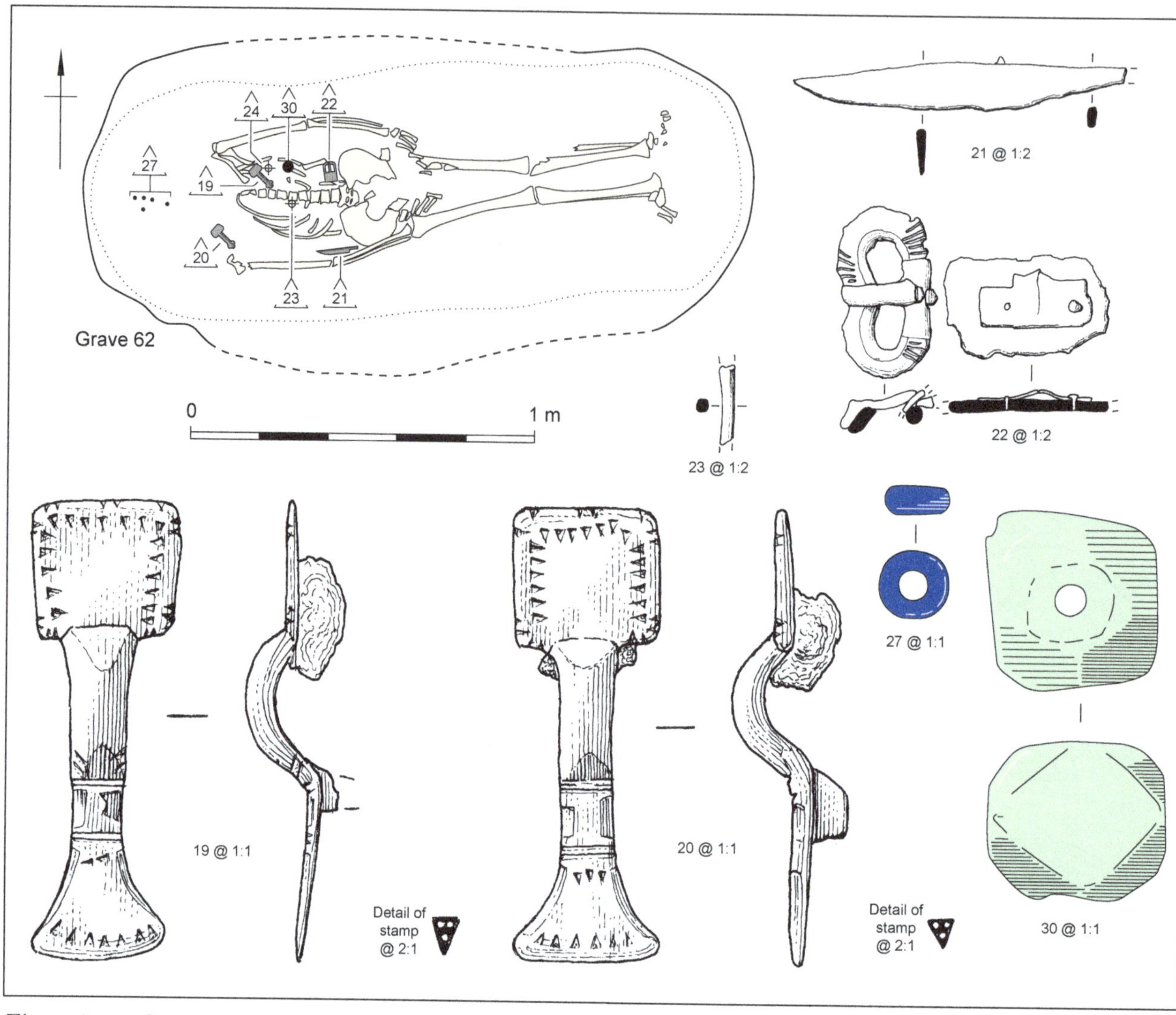

Figure 2.28 Grave 62 and selected grave goods

ON 21: iron knife, right of waist, inside right arm, lying vertically with tip to head end. Tang of rectangular section in line with back, gently sloping down to cutting edge. Back straight for most its length; blade curves up to tip. Böhner Type B. Length 95 mm; width 13 mm; thickness 5 mm.

ON 22: fragmentary iron buckle and plate, left waist. Kidney-shaped buckle loop; rectangular plate. Front of plate and buckle inlaid with copper alloy. Length of loop 27 mm; width 47 mm. Length of plate 47 mm; width 26 mm.

ON 23: shank of an iron ?pin, over centre of chest. Rectangular section. Length 21 mm; diameter 7 mm (not illustrated).

ON 24: tiny copper alloy pin-catch, adjacent to ON 19. Length 7 mm; width 7 mm. Probably belongs to ON 19. (not illustrated).

ON 27: 5 glass beads, 1 with degraded (opaque) surface. Medium. Colour 6.2, shape A2. Above skull area.

ON 30: glass bead, in 3 frags; biconical but with 4 flattened sides to give sub-square section. Large. Colour 6.2, shape C1. Left chest.

Grave 63: cut 1160 (burial 1161; fill 1162)

(Fig. 2.29)

WNW–ESE, incomplete, shallow, *c.* 0.25 x *c.* 0.20 m, *c.* 0.10 m deep (base at 135.82 m OD). Supine. Disturbed by animal burrowing. (Glass beads ON 27 and ON 30 (above) may belong here).

Human bone: *c.* 20% infant *c.* 1.5–3 yr.
9 frags. a. adult >55 yr. female (=1158a).

Grave 64: cut 1100 (burial 1101; fill 1102)

(Fig. 2.30)

WSW–ENE, sub-rectangular, steep sides, flat base. 1.90 x 1.01 m, 0.40 m deep (base at 135.27 m OD). Flexed on left side, hands at left shoulder.

Human bone: *c.* 95% adult *c.* 35–45 yr. female (=1106b, 1109 and 1110).

Grave goods:

ON 4: by the right hand, mid-chest area:

ON 200: iron pin, ?square-section with looped-head. Length 62 mm; diameter of head 11 mm.

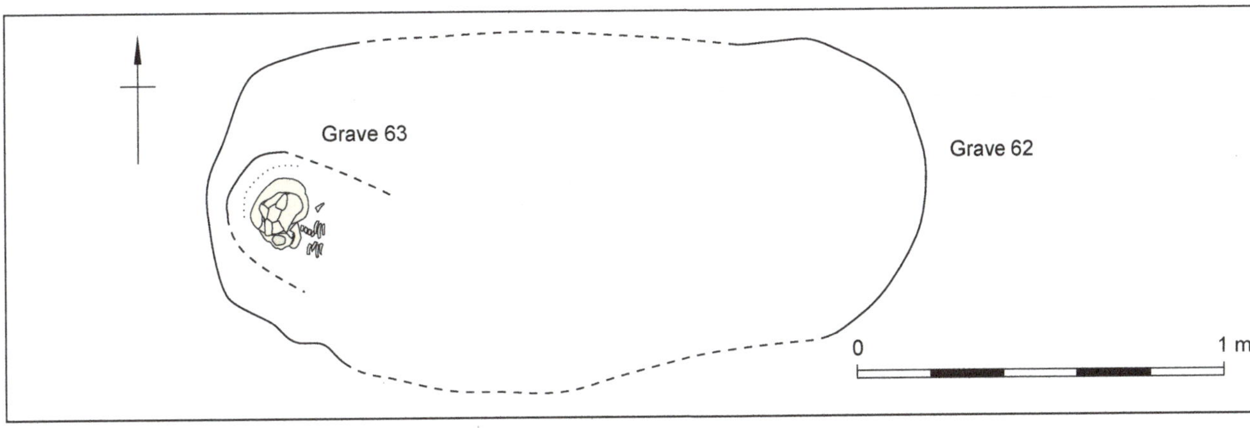

Figure 2.29 Grave 63

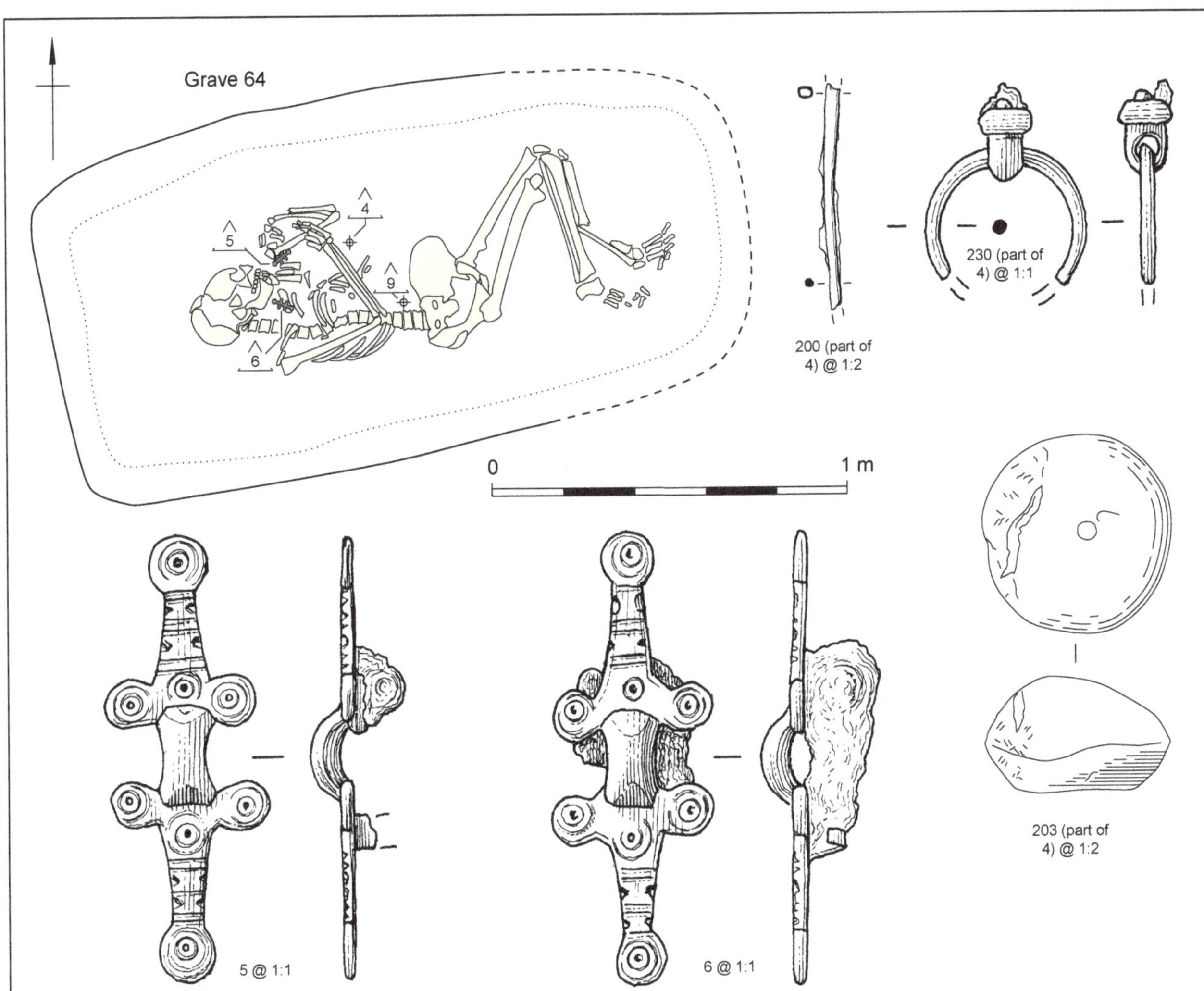

Figure 2.30 Grave 64 and selected grave goods

ON: 201: copper alloy coin; pierced. Very worn *nummus* AD 367–375 (see Cooke, Chapter 4; not illustrated).

ON: 202: copper alloy coin; pierced. Very worn *nummus*, AD 330–335 (see Cooke, Chapter 4; not illustrated).

ON 203: rock crystal; worn around circumference; shape slightly irregular. Large. A03

ON 230: fragmentary copper alloy ring (?fitting) threaded onto a loop; circular-sectioned hoop. Diameter of ring 23 mm; section 2 mm.

ON 5: copper alloy equal-armed brooch, left shoulder, diagonal. Central gently arched bow extending on either side forming a pair of small circular lappets before expanding into a flat foot. Each lappet

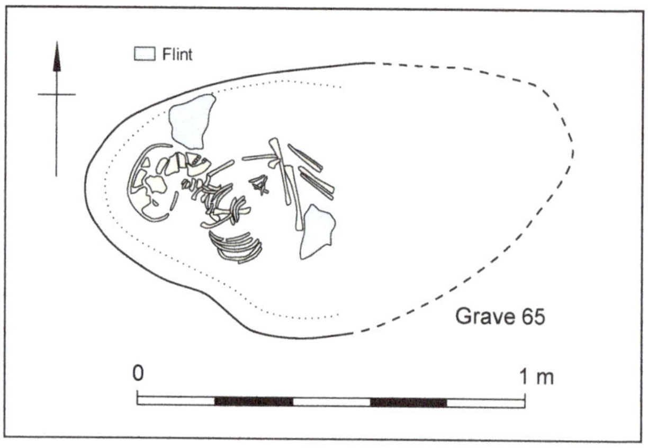

Figure 2.31 Grave 65

exhibits a pair of punches (three are off-centre) surrounded by a pair of incised circles. At the top of the foot and between each lappet is another stamped punch (one off-centre) encircled by a pair of incised circles. Each foot exhibits two pairs of transverse incised lines before forming a sub-circular terminal that is decorated with a stamped punch surrounded by a pair of circles. Traces of tinning survive at top of each terminal. Hinge obscured, damaged catch. Length 60 mm; width across lappets 22 mm.

ON 6: copper alloy equal-armed brooch, neck area, diagonal. Central gently arched bow extending on either side forming a pair of small circular lappets before expanding into a flat foot. Each lappet exhibits a pair of off centre punches surrounded by a pair of incised circles. At the top of the foot and between each lappet is another stamped punch encircled by a pair of incised circles. Each foot exhibits two pairs of transverse incised lines before forming a sub-circular terminal that is decorated with a stamped punch surrounded by a pair of circles. Traces of tinning survive at top of each terminal. Pin mechanism obscured. Length 63 mm; width across lappets 23 mm.

ON 9: two rectangular iron fragments, at waist. Possible fittings; location suggests blade or belt fitting. Both length 26 mm; width 21 mm (not illustrated).

Residual finds: 4 sherds pottery (2 Romano-British; 1 Saxon, organic-tempered; 1 medieval).

Grave 65: cut 1274 (burial 1275; fill 1276)

(Fig. 2.31)

W–E, incomplete oval, moderately sloping sides, flat base sloping to the east. 0.75 x 0.65 m, 0.09 m deep (overcut, base at 135.71 m OD). Flexed on left side, hands in lap. Large flint nodule between heels and hips, and in front of skull. Overlies grave 66. Abundant roots.

Human bone: *c.* 65% infant *c.* 2–4 yr.

Grave 66: cut 1291 (burial 1290; fill 1289)

(Fig. 2.32)

W–E, sub-rectangular, steep sides, concave base. 1.77 x 0.85 m, 0.28 m deep (base at 135.57 m OD). Slightly flexed, supine with legs turned to the left. Left arm along side, right hand between left pelvis and arm. Under grave 65.

Human bone: *c.* 85 % adult *c.* 25–40 yr. female.

Grave goods:

ON 123: iron knife, horizontally-aligned across abdomen, tip to right. Tang central to blade, with shoulder curving gently up to back of blade and angled down to cutting edge. Back curves down to tip; blade curves up to tip. Böhner Type A. Length 90 mm; width 14 mm; thickness 3 mm. Resharpening curve near tang end of blade.

Grave 67: cut 1335 (burial 1336; fill 1331)

(Fig. 2.33 – ON 138 only)

WNW–ESE, sub-rectangular, rounded ends, concave moderately sloping sides, flat base. 1.17 x 0.78 m, 0.16 m deep (base at 135.32 m OD). Posture not discernible. Skull ? on left side. Heavy bioturbation.

Human bone: *c.* 25% s.u.l. infant *c.* 3–4 yr.

Grave goods:

ON 138: fragmentary knife in location of probable waist area, lying horizontally, tip to ? Tip missing; tapering tang central to blade, with shoulder angled up to back of blade and gently down to cutting edge. Type unknown. Surviving length 88 mm; width 19 mm; thickness 3 mm. Resharpening curve near tang end of blade.

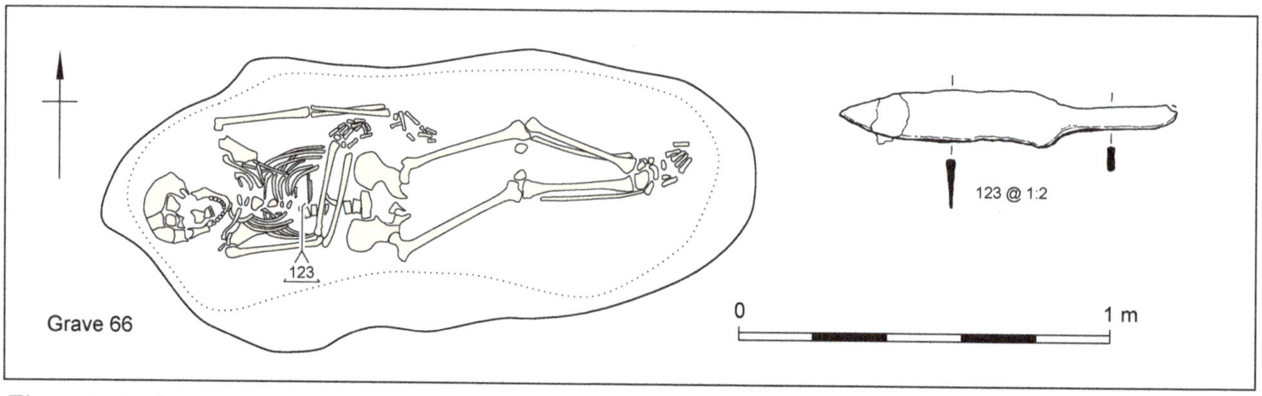

Figure 2.32 Grave 66 and iron knife

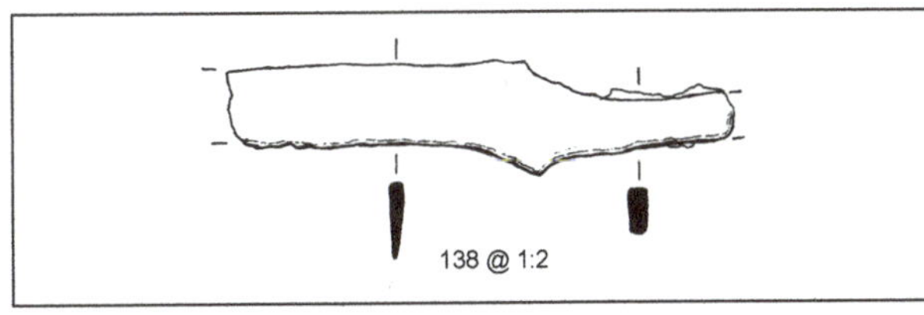

Figure 2.33 Knife from grave 67

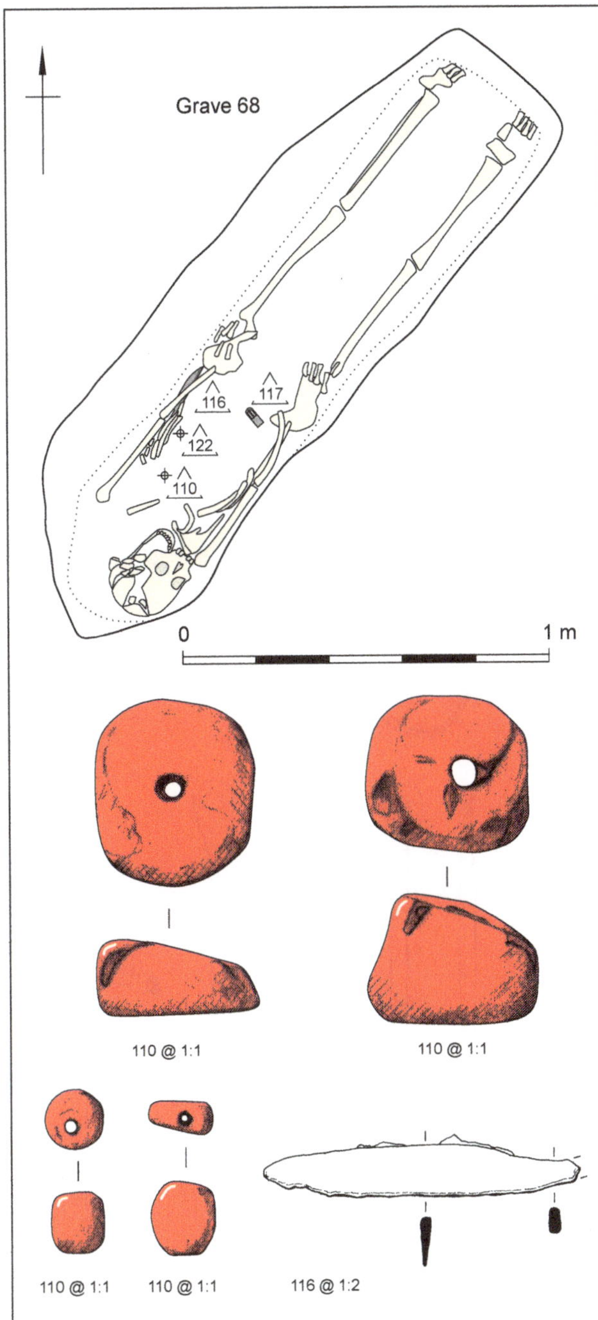

Figure 2.34 Grave 68 and selected grave goods

Grave 68: cut 1280 (burial 1281; fill 1282)
(Fig. 2.34)
SW–NE, sub-rectangular, rounded/pointed head end, vertical sides, flat base. 2.00 x 0.60 m, 0.30 m deep (base at 134.61 m OD). Extended supine, arms along sides, hands over respective hips. Tight fit.
Human bone: *c.* 85% adult *c.* 30–40 yr. female.
Grave goods:
ON 110:2 amber beads. Large, shape A04; 8 amber beads. Small to medium, shape A01. Left chest.
ON 116:iron knife under left forearm lying vertically with tip to foot end. Tapering tang of triangular section central to blade; shoulder curves up to back of blade and gently down to cutting edge. Back straight, blade curves up to tip. Böhner Type B. Length 89 mm; width 14 mm; thickness 4 mm.
ON 117:simple iron buckle, right waist, fragmentary tongue. Circular outline of oval section. Length 23 mm; width 34 mm. Length of tongue 18 mm (not illustrated).
ON 122:amber bead. Left abdomen. Large, shape A09 (not illustrated).
Residual finds: 2 animal bone; 4 sherds pottery (2 Romano-British; 2 Saxon, sandy), occasional charcoal flecks.

Grave 69: cut 1348 (burial 1347; fill 1346)
(Figs 2.35–6; Pl. 2.4)
WSW–ENE, sub-rectangular, rounded foot end, steep sides, flat base. 1.95 x 0.95 m, 0.26 m deep (base at 134.89 m OD). Extended supine with hands crossed over abdomen. Flints in upper part of fill, siltier towards base.
Human bone: *c.* 60% adult *c.* 30–45 yr. female.
Grave goods:
ON 162:iron buckle, identification uncertain, three fragments, one with rivet (possible plate, belt fitting; illustrated), lying left of pelvis, aligned vertically with tip to ?foot end. The largest fragment is length 20 mm, width 17 mm.
ON 163:saucer brooch, at left chest. Cast in one piece out of copper alloy with angular rim. Slight wear to the leading edge of the rim; the front is gilded but has worn away from much of the upper edges of the decoration but is preserved within the features. The decoration consists of a central ring-and-dot motif enclosed by seven running spirals. The extensions emanating from each spiral join with an outer plain ring, which is in turn enclosed by a ring of notched design. Hinge and catch with the remains of an iron pin. Diameter 42 mm, rim 5 mm high angled at *c.* 45˚. Dickinson Group 1.3.
ON 164:saucer brooch, at right upper chest close to shoulder (paired with ON 163). Cast in one piece out of copper alloy with angular rim. Slight wear to the leading edge of the rim; the front is gilded but worn away from much of the upper edges of the decoration but is preserved within the features. The decoration consists of a central ring-and-dot motif enclosed by seven running spirals. The extensions emanating from each spiral join with an outer plain ring, which is in turn enclosed by a ring of notched design. Hinge and catch with the

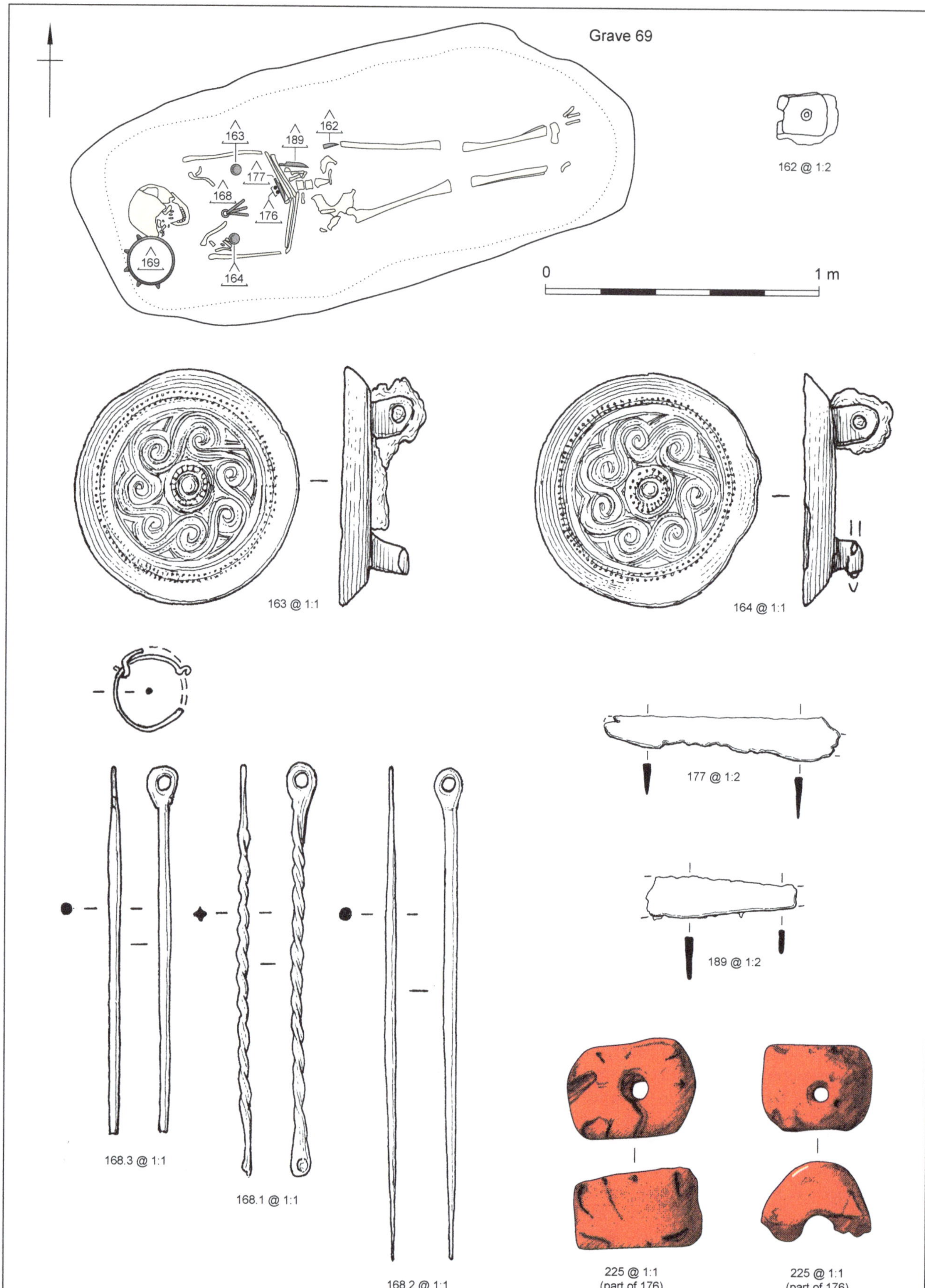

Figure 2.35 Grave 69 and selected grave goods

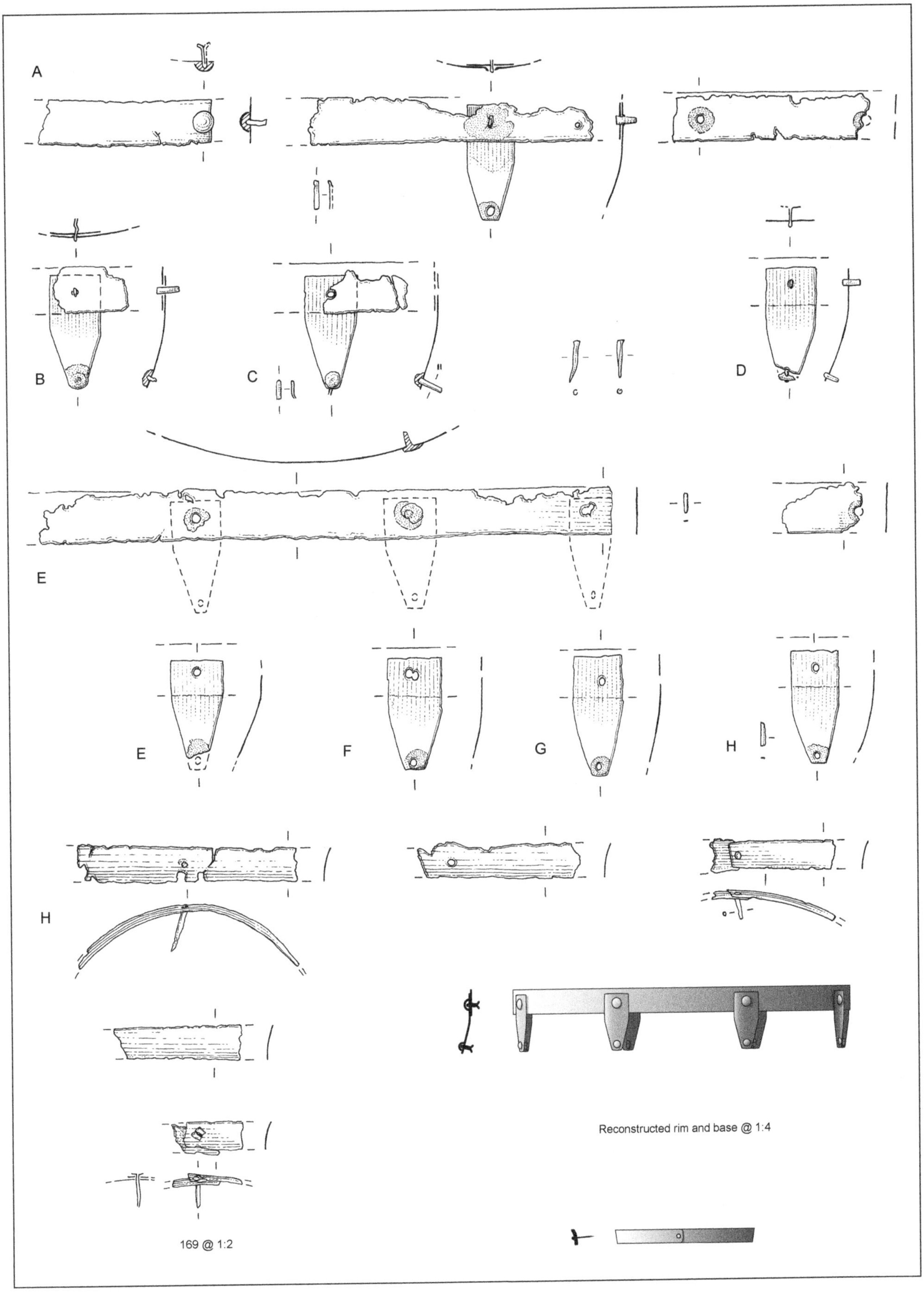

Figure 2.36 Grave 69 copper alloy fittings from bucket

Plate 2.4 Detail of grave 69, showing bucket ON 169 adjacent to skull (from the south)

remains of an iron pin. Diameter of 42 mm, rim 5 mm high which is angled at *c.* 45°. Dickinson Group 1.3.

ON 168: copper alloy toilet set with fragmentary wire ring, upper chest, centre. The set comprises:

1) ear scoop with a perforated circular head, writhen shank end and spoon-shaped bowl. Length 75 mm.

2–3) pair of picks.

2) Flattened, circular, pierced head; circular-sectioned shank tapering to a pointed tip. Length 89 mm.

3) Flattened, circular, pierced head; circular-sectioned shank tapering to a pointed tip (missing) (vertical line running down the length of the shaft: fracture?). Length 66 mm.

ON 169: copper alloy bucket fittings, against right side of skull and grave edge (Pl. 2.4). A group of fragmentary hoops and appliqués that originally furnished a stave-built wooden bucket. The appliqués would have decorated the upper rim of the vessel. The fittings, base and rivets are tinned. There appear to be no uprights.

A) Plain hoop fragment with appliqué attached by rivet and rivet hole at other end. Length of hoop 108 mm; width 17 mm. Length of appliqué 42 mm; width 18 mm. Tiny ?rivet fragment recurved. Length 10 mm; width 2 mm.

A: D–C) Plain hoop fragment with one complete rivet hole and the remains of a second on the edge of the fragment. Length 75 mm; width 17 mm.

A: G–H) Plain hoop fragment with remains of a rivet hole and rivet on one edge. Length 30 mm; width 17 mm.

B) Plain appliqué formed from tapering strip of metal, rivet at either end; fragment of hoop with rivet hole, plus tiny sheet fragment. Length of appliqué 42 mm; width 19 mm. Length of hoop 23 mm; width 17 mm.

C) Plain appliqué formed from tapering strip of metal, rivet at bottom, hole at top; fragment of hoop with rivet hole, plus tiny sheet fragment and rivet. Length of appliqué 49 mm; width 20 mm. Length of hoop 35 mm; width 15 mm.

D) Plain appliqué formed from tapering strip of metal, rivets at either end. Length 42 mm; width 20 mm.

E) Plain fragment of curved hoop with three rivet holes. One rivet has become separated; the middle hole has a rivet *in situ* while a fragmentary section of hoop is attached by a rivet through the third hole. A fragmentary triangular appliqué may also have been attached to this rivet. Length of loop 226 mm; width 19 mm. Length of shorter section 70 mm; width 17 mm. Length of appliqué 36 mm; width 19 mm.

F) Plain appliqué formed from tapering strip of metal, rivet holes at either end; the top hole has been double-punched. Length 41 mm; width 20 mm. Tiny strip of metal recurved, ?rivet. Length 11 mm; width 2 mm.

G) Plain appliqué formed from tapering strip of metal, rivet hole at either end. Length 45 mm; width 18 mm. Tiny strip of metal recurved, ?rivet. Length 10 mm; width 2 mm.

H) Plain appliqué formed from tapering strip of metal, rivet holes at either end. Length 42 mm; width 17 mm. Tiny strip of metal, ?rivet. Length 9 mm; width 2 mm.

'Base ring.' Six fragments of a plain loop; three have rivets *in situ*, in two cases joining sections of hoop, two have rivets holes.

i) Includes rivet. Length *c.* 88 mm; 13 mm.

ii) Includes rivet hole. Length 63 mm; width 13 mm.

iii) Includes rivet joining two pieces. Length 47 mm; width 11 mm.

iv) Length 48 mm; width 12 mm.

v) Includes rivet joining two pieces. Length 26 mm; width 10 mm.

vi) Includes rivet hole. Length 11 mm; width 12 mm.

'Fragments etc' remains of sheeting (n=3), rivets (two shanks, two heads and fragment of shank and head) and wood fragments.

ON 176: bead group:

ON 225: 2 amber beads. One large, shape A04; Other, broken and re-perforated through side, large, shape ?A02.

ON 226: glass bead. Medium, colour 7.7, shape A2 (not illustrated).

ON 1014: glass bead. Medium, colour 2.1, shape A1 (not illustrated).

ON 177: iron knife at centre of waist, alongside left forearm (handle under left elbow), diagonal, point to ?fragmentary tang central to blade, shoulder appears to be angled up to back of blade but slopes gently down to cutting edge. Back is straight for its length before gradually sloping down to meet the blade; blade curves up to tip. Böhner Type ?B. Length 76 mm; width 20 mm; thickness 3 mm.

ON 189: fragmentary iron knife, left waist, at left elbow (handle under left elbow), almost vertical with point to foot end. Tang central to blade, shoulder curves gently up to back of blade. Back apparently straight but no information about the tip is known. Type unknown. Surviving length 55 mm; width 15 mm; thickness 3 mm.

Residual finds: 1 sherd pottery (Romano-British).

Grave 70: cut 1372 (burial 1373; fill 1374)
(Fig. 2.37)
SSE–NNW, sub-rectangular, rounded foot end, steep sides, flat base. 1.64 x 0.64 m, 0.19 m deep (base at 134.72 m OD). Extended, slight turned to right, right arm along side, left hand on abdomen.
Human bone: *c.* 65% juvenile/subadult *c.* 12–14 yr.
Grave goods:

ON 187: fragmentary iron knife, left abdomen, aligned diagonally, tip? Type unknown. Surviving length 47 mm; width 17 mm; thickness 4 mm.

ON 188: simple iron buckle located right lower chest. D-shaped outline, circular section with intact tongue wrapped around the hoop. Length 24 mm; width 31 mm.

Grave 71: cut 1384 (burial 1385; fill 1386)
(Fig. 2.38)
WSW–ENE, sub-rectangular, rounded ends (narrower foot end), shallow concave sides, flat base. 0.75 x 0.35 m, 0.07 m deep (base at 134.69 m OD). Posture not discernible. Several flint nodules in east half of grave. ?disturbed.
Human bone: *c.* 5% s.a.u. infant *c.* 1–2 yr.
Grave goods:

ON 196: fragmentary iron knife, right side, midway down grave. Tang in line with back and curving gently down to cutting edge. Back curves down to blade. Evison Type 4. Surviving length 59 mm; width 11 mm; thickness 4 mm.

Grave 72: cut 1387 (burial 1388; fill 1389)
(Fig. 2.39)
S–N, sub-rectangular, rounded ends, steep sides, flat base.

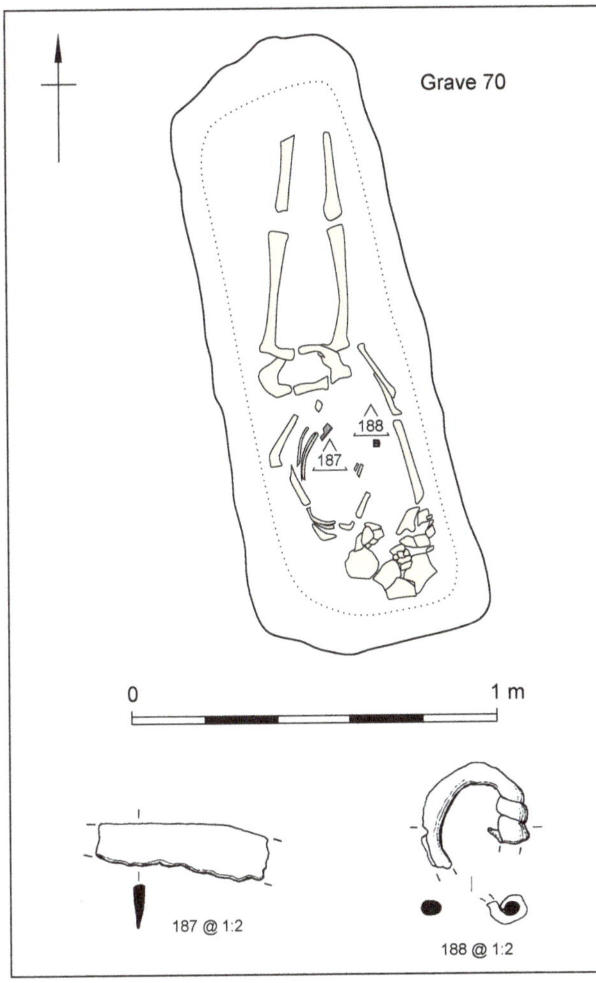

Figure 2.37 Grave 70 and grave goods

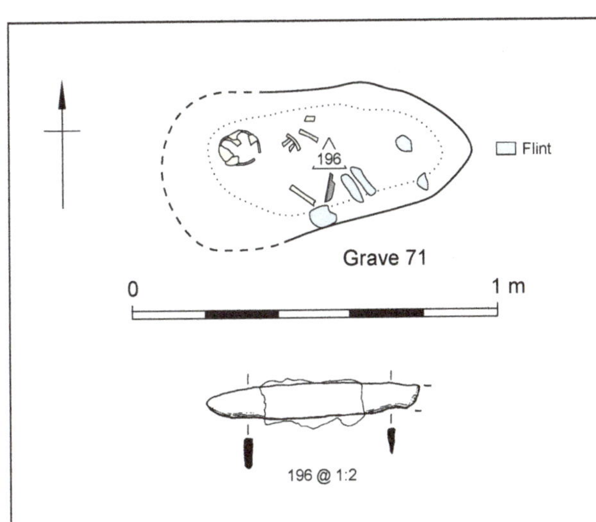

Figure 2.38 Grave 71 and iron knife

2.22 x 0.96 m, 0.23 m deep (base at 134.51 m OD). Supine, legs flexed on right side, ?slumped back. Right hand under left knee, left hand at left shoulder. 0.75 m space at head end of grave.
Human bone: *c.* 95% adult *c.* 30–40 yr. male.

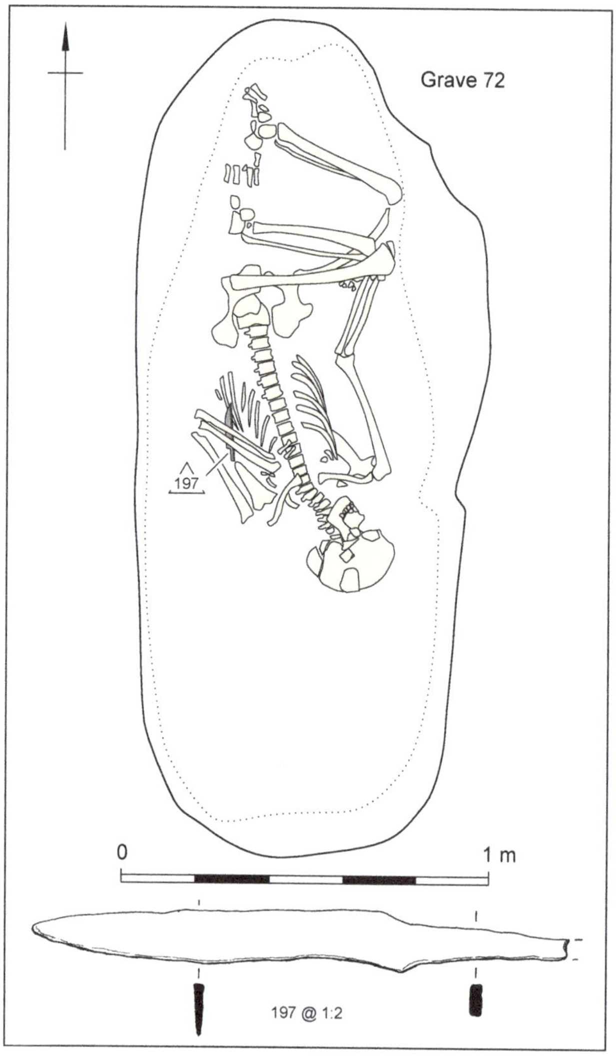

Figure 2.39 Grave 72 and iron knife

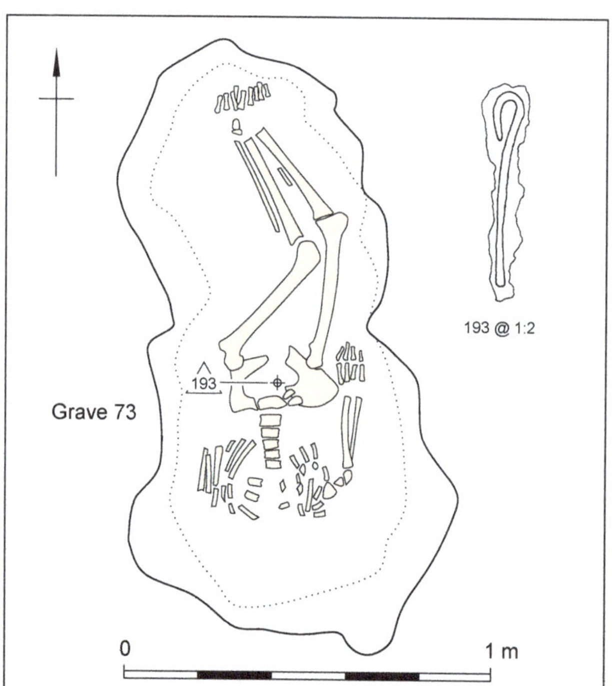

Figure 2.40 Grave 73 and fragmentary iron pin

Grave goods:

ON 197: fragmentary iron knife (end of tang missing), lying left of chest and under left forearm, tip towards feet. Tapering tang central to blade; shoulder curving gently up to back of blade and curving gently down to cutting edge. Back possibly straight; blade curves up to tip. Böhner Type A/B. Length 145 mm; width 15 mm; thickness 6 mm.

Grave 73: cut 1378 (burial 1379; fill 1380)

(Fig. 2.40)

S–N, irregular/sub-rectangular, convex steep sides, irregular base. 1.65 x 0.90 m, 0.23 m maximum depth (base at 134.51 m OD). Supine, legs flexed to right, right arm along side, left hand at left shoulder. Root disturbance.

Human bone: *c.* 45% a.u.l. adult *c.* 35–45 yr. ?female.

Grave goods:

ON 193: fragmentary iron pin of circular section with hooked end. Lower abdomen. Length *c.* 55 mm; diameter *c.* 5 mm.

Grave 74: cut 1355 (burial 1356; fill 1357)

(Fig. 2.41)

W–E, sub-rectangular, moderately sloping sides, flat base. 1.90 x 0.91 m, 0.09 m deep (base at 134.34 m OD). Extended supine, hands on respective hips.

Human bone: *c.* 95% adult *c.* 30–35 yr. female.
c. 45% foetus *c.* 32–36 weeks.
redep. 2 teeth infant/juvenile *c.* 2–8 yr.
a few frags. a. neonate/infant *c.* birth–1 yr.

Grave goods:

ON 170: copper alloy disc brooch exhibiting wear to the edge, on right clavicle close to neck. Central punched dot surrounded by one inscribed concentric circle and four fainter inscribed circles; enclosed by a ring of punched ring-and-dot motifs. Possible ring of stamped dots around the periphery. Single hinge and catch (broken – may have been broken in antiquity and repaired with separate catch) and remains of iron pin. Diameter 40 mm.

ON 171: bead group between ON 170 and 173
- ON 227: 3 amber beads. Large, shape A09; large, shape A04; medium, shape A01.
- ON 228: 6 glass beads. Medium, colour 7.7, shape A2.

ON 172: fragmentary iron rod/object, on left shoulder. Length 82 mm; diameter 9 mm (not illustrated).

ON 173: copper alloy disc brooch, exhibiting wear to the edge, left of jaw/neck area (paired with ON 170). Central punched dot surrounded by two concentric inscribed circles. Circle of ring-and-dots around the periphery. Two areas of ?tinning/solder on the reverse (repair to pin mechanism?). Detached hinge and remains of iron pin. Diameter 35 mm (sub-circular).

ON 174: glass bead, wound. Large, colour 6.2a, shape A1. Left upper arm.

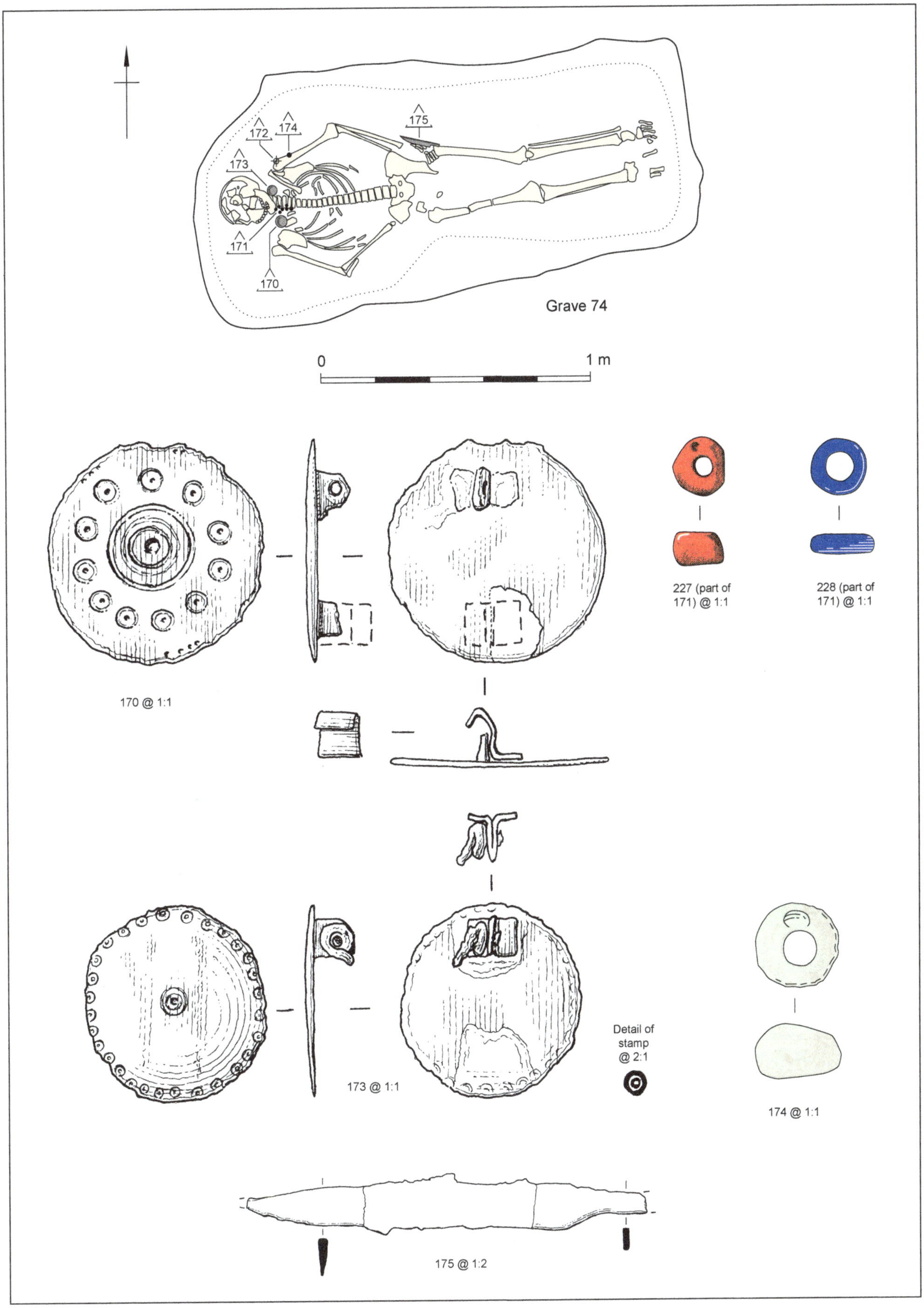

Figure 2.41 Grave 74 and selected grave goods

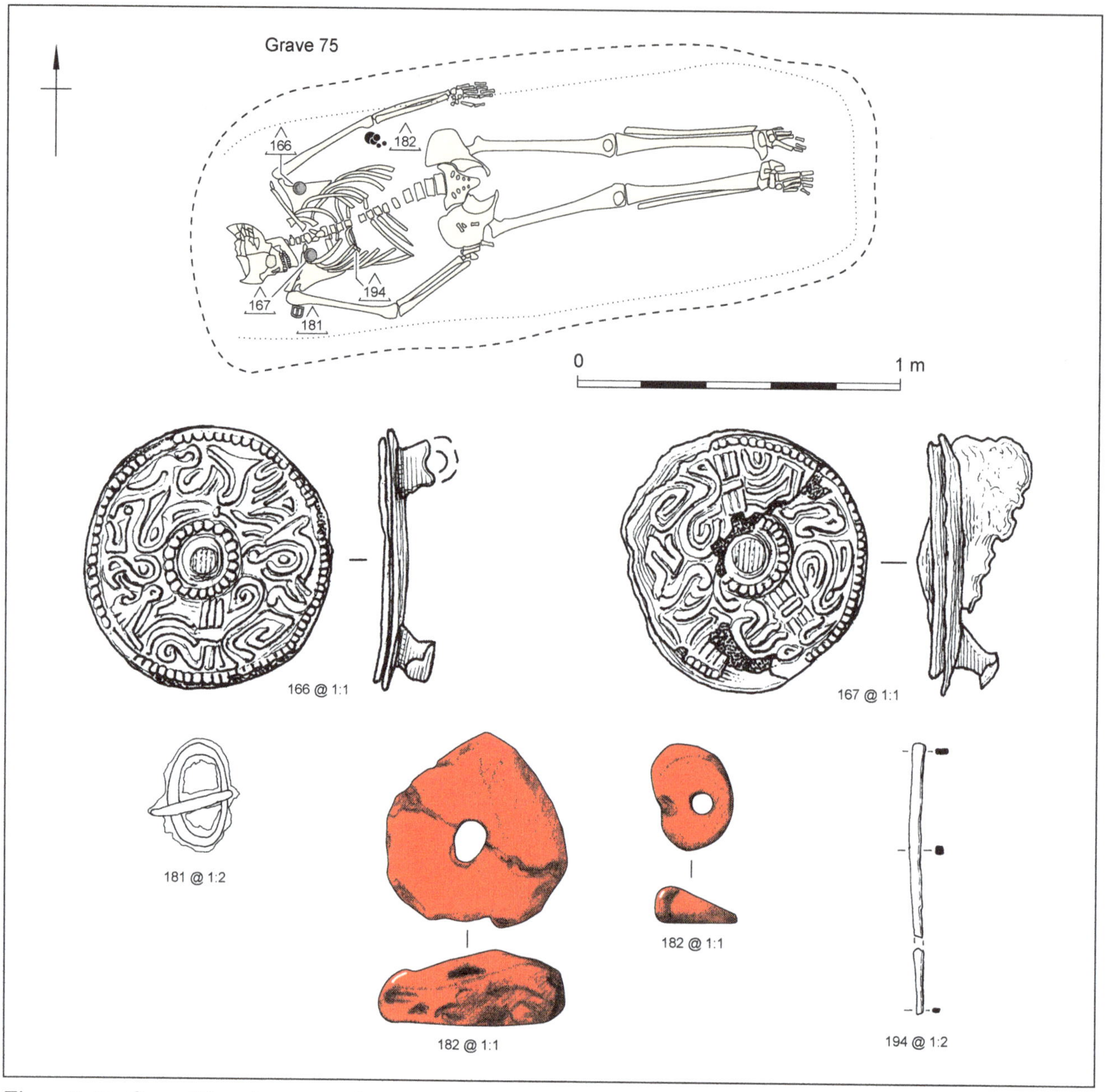

Figure 2.42 Grave 75 and grave goods

ON 175: iron knife, left hip, diagonal, point to head end. Tang central to blade, with shoulder curving gently up to back of blade and gently down to cutting edge. Back straight before curving down to tip; blade curves up to tip. Böhner Type A/C. Length 150 mm; width 16 mm; thickness 4 mm.

ON 1006: glass bead. Large, colour 7.5, shape F3 (not illustrated).

Grave 75: cut 1349 (burial 1350; fill 1351)

(Fig. 2.42)

W–E, sub-rectangular, steep concave sides, flat base. 2.00 x 0.86 m, 0.22 m deep (base at 134.16 m OD). Extended supine, right hand under hip, left hand outside hip. Frequent charcoal flecks and slight bioturbation. Top of skull truncated by geotechnical test pit.

Human bone: *c.* 95% adult >45 yr. female.

Grave goods:

ON 166: copper alloy applied brooch over left shoulder. Fragmentary face, zoomorphic motif. Hinge and catch-plate cast with back-plate, no pin. Diameter of back-plate 40 mm.

ON 167: copper alloy applied brooch, lying over right neck. Fragmentary face, zoomorphic motif. Hinge and catch-plate cast with back-plate; possible remains of pin. Diameter of back-plate 40 mm.

ON 181: simple iron buckle, located outside right shoulder. D-shaped in outline and section. Tongue intact and wrapped around loop. Length 25 mm; width 35 mm. Tongue length 28 mm.

ON 182: 6 amber beads, 12–30 mm. Large, shape A04; amber bead, frags of at least 1 more, shape ?A02.

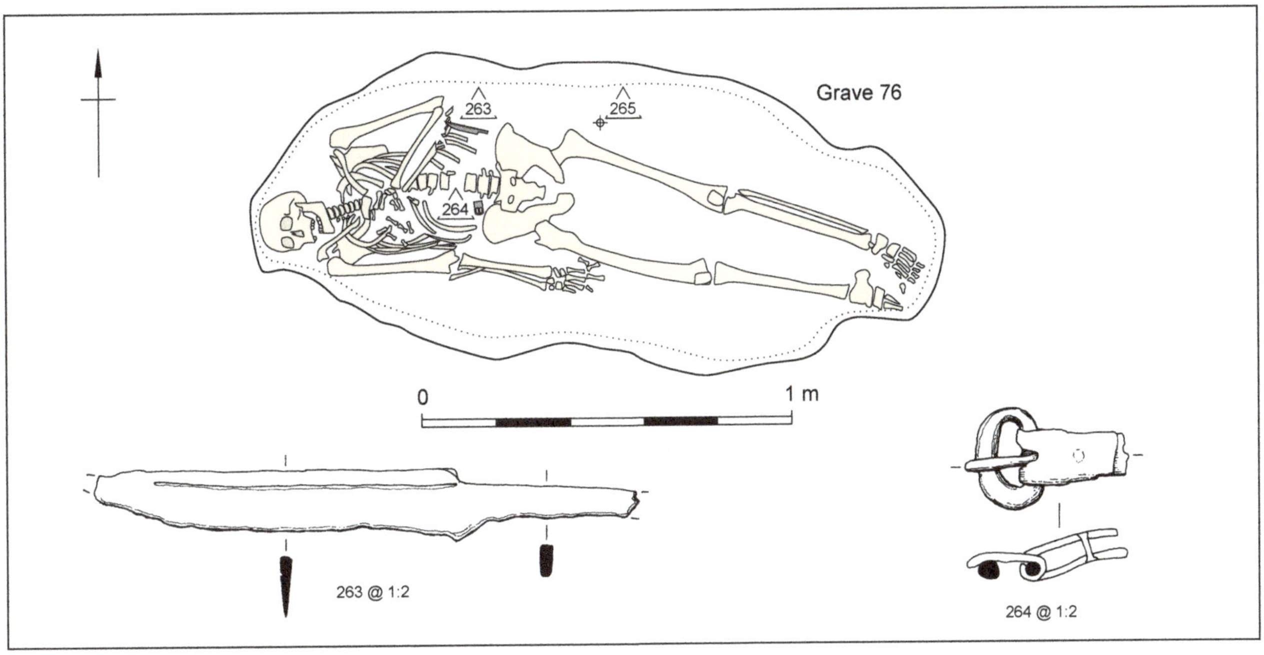

Figure 2.43 Grave 76 and selected grave goods

Between left elbow and waist

ON 194: long and thin iron pin at right chest. Length 90 mm; diameter 3 mm.

Grave 76: cut 1390 (burial 1391; fill 1392)

(Fig. 2.43)

W–E, irregular/sub-rectangular, moderately sloping sides, flat base. 1.90 x 0.80 m, 0.13 m deep (base at 134.35 m OD). Extended, supine, right arm along side, left hand on sternum.

Human bone: *c.* 95% adult >50 yr. male.

Grave goods:

ON 263: iron knife, left waist, partly under left forearm, vertical, tip towards head end. Tapering tang central to blade, shoulder curves up to back of blade and down to cutting edge. Back straight; blade curves up to tip. Böhner Type B. Length 141 mm; width 16 mm; thickness 4 mm.

ON 264: simple iron buckle, right of waist. With fragmentary riveted rectangular plate. Loop is D-shaped and circular in section; tongue is intact and wrapped around the loop. Length of loop 17 mm; width 29 mm. Plate length 24 mm; width 13 mm; length of tongue 21 mm.

ON 265: iron stud or pyrite? Outside left hip (not illustrated).

Grave 77: cut 1369 (burial 1370; fill 1371)

(Fig. 2.44; Pl. 2.5)

SSW–NNE, sub-rectangular, steep sides, flat base. 2.27 x 0.96 m, 0.25 m deep (base at 134.25 m OD). Extended supine, hands crossed over left abdomen. Oversized grave. Large charred split oak timber (1422; 1.75 x 0.27 x 0.08 m) along the right side of the grave.

Human bone: *c.* 90% adult *c.* 45–50 yr. male.

Grave goods:

ON 178: iron shield boss over right chest with straight walls and straight cone terminating in a small knob; flange (23 mm wide); four rivets remaining. Dickinson and Härke Type 3. Diameter 155 mm; height 73 mm. Largely complete grip, flanged end. Dickinson and Härke Type IA1. Length *c.* 120 mm.

ON 179: iron spearhead, left side head end, some way beyond skull, vertical with point to top of grave. Socket cleft for *c.* 55 mm. Angular blade with ?concavity above the blade-angle, lozengiform section. Swanton Group H1/2. Length 198 mm; width 24 mm.

ON 180: simple fragmentary iron buckle at right waist. Circular outline and section, fragmentary tongue. Length unknown (too fragmentary to reconstruct); width 30 mm.

ON 183: fragmentary iron shield stud to right of boss. Diameter 23 mm; thickness 1 mm.

ON 185: fragmentary iron nail (head and fragments of shank), between skull and spearhead. Not reconstructed.

ON 186: iron fragments, left pelvis. Possible pin. Length 26 mm; width 3 mm.

ON 190: iron knife, tip missing, left pelvis, aligned diagonally with tip to left. Broken tapering tang central to blade, shoulder curving gently up to back of blade and down to cutting edge. Back straight before curving gradually down to tip; blade curves up to tip. Böhner Type A/C. Length 116 mm; width 19 mm; thickness 3 mm.

ON 191: fragmentary iron shield stud, to left of boss. Diameter 26 mm; thickness 1 mm. Left chest.

ON 192: iron shield stud to left of boss (north of 191). Diameter 25 mm; thickness 1 mm. Left chest.

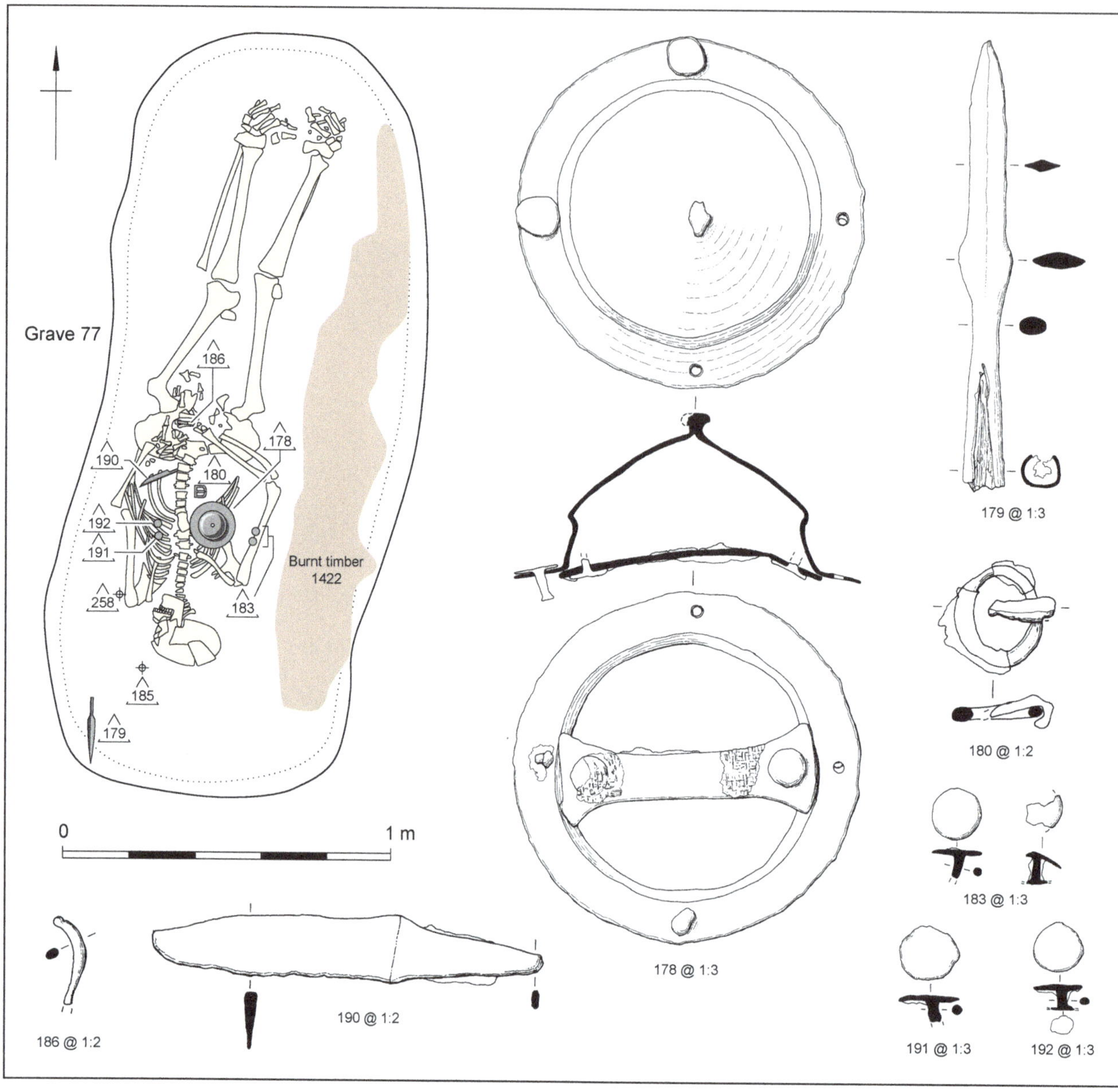

Figure 2.44 Grave 77 and selected grave goods

ON 258: iron ?nail head, outside left shoulder. Length 23 mm, diameter 14 mm (not illustrated).

Grave 78: cut 1393 (burial 1398; fill 1394)

(Fig. 2.45)

W–E, sub-rectangular, rounded ends, steep concave sides, concave base. 0.99 x 0.50 m, 0.24 m deep (base at 134.06 m OD). Flexed on left side, hands in lap/at abdomen. Medium flint nodule on right upper arm. Occasional charcoal flecks and bioturbation.

Human bone: *c.* 40% infant/ juvenile *c.* 4–5 yr. ???female.

Grave 79: cut 1301 (burial 1302; fill 1303)

(Fig. 2.46; Pl. 2.6)

SW–NE, sub-rectangular with rounded head end, concave moderately sloping sides, flat base. 1.67 x 0.70 m, 0.20 m deep (base at 134.07 m OD). Extended, supine with left arm along side, right hand over abdomen. Slightly oversized grave. Abundant flint nodules (? naturally occurring).

Human bone: *c.* 85% juvenile *c.* 10–12 yr.

Grave goods:

ON 136: iron knife lying at left waist, diagonal and pointing to right. Tang central to blade, shoulder angled up to back of blade and sharply angled down to cutting edge. Back straight; blade curves up to tip. Sharpening curve near tang end of blade. Böhner Type B. Length 151 mm; width 22 mm; thickness 6 mm.

Residual finds:

ON 131: unidentified iron object in area of upper body. Length 43 mm, width 25 mm.

1 sherd pottery (Saxon, organic-tempered).

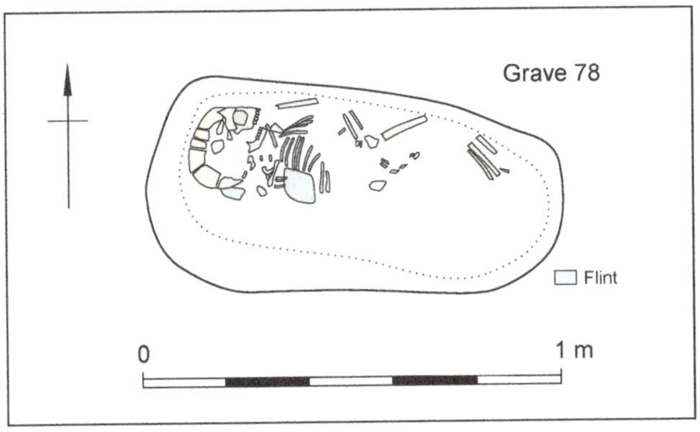

Figure 2.45 Grave 78

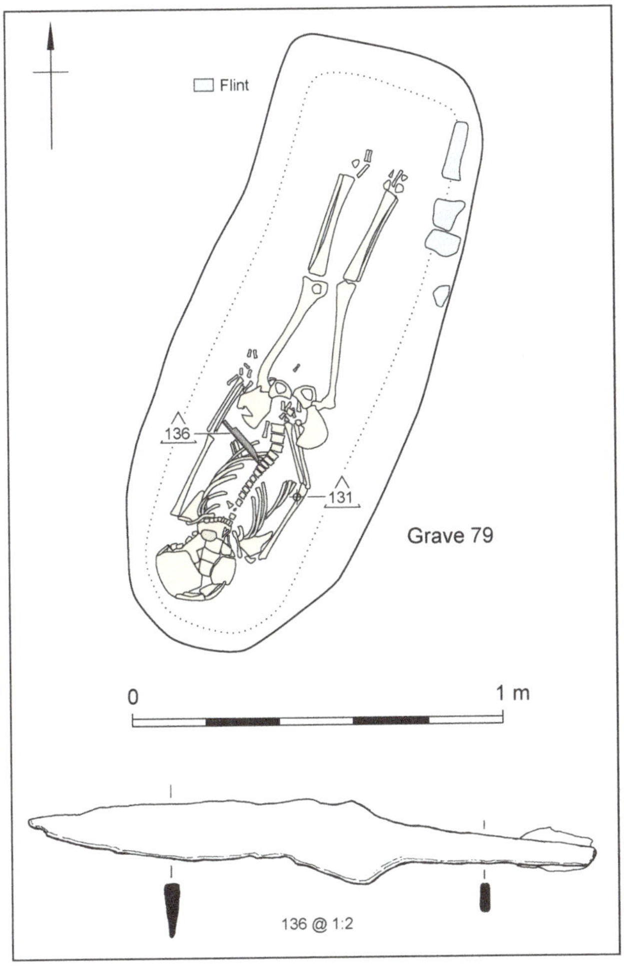

Figure 2.46 Grave 79 and iron knife

Grave 80: cut 1352 (burial 1353; fill 1354)
(Fig. 2.47)
SW–NE, sub-rectangular, rounded ends, steep sides, flat base. 1.83 x 0.74 m, 0.40 m deep (base at 133.77 m OD). Extended supine, right hand by right hip, left hand over abdomen. Medium flints ? deliberately placed over the burial.
Human bone: *c.* 80% subadult *c.* 12–15 yr.
Grave goods:
ON 184: fragmentary simple iron buckle in centre of waist. Circular outline and section. Length *c.* 33 mm; width 29 mm.

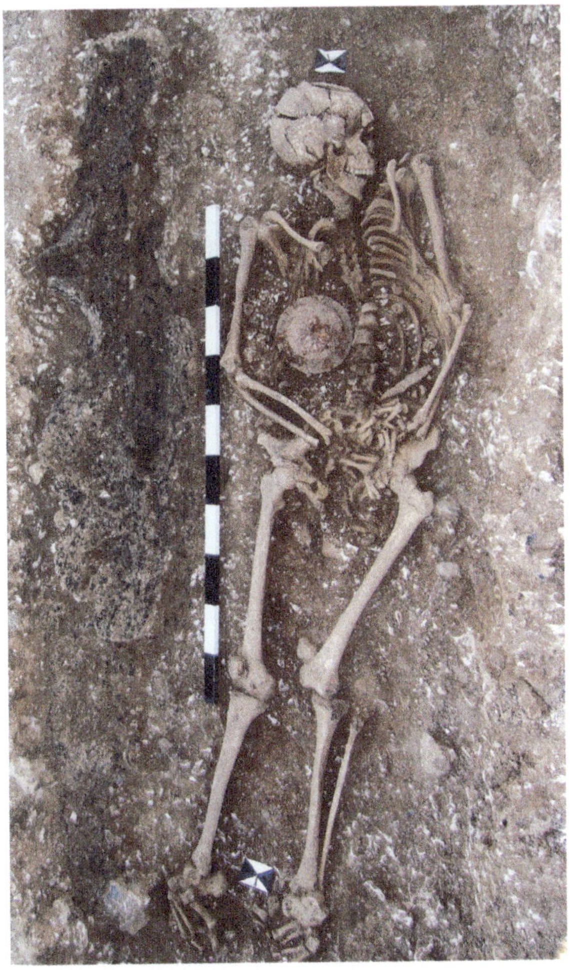

Plate 2.5 Grave 77 (scale = 1m; from the south)

Plate 2.6 Grave 79 (scale = 1m; from the north-west)

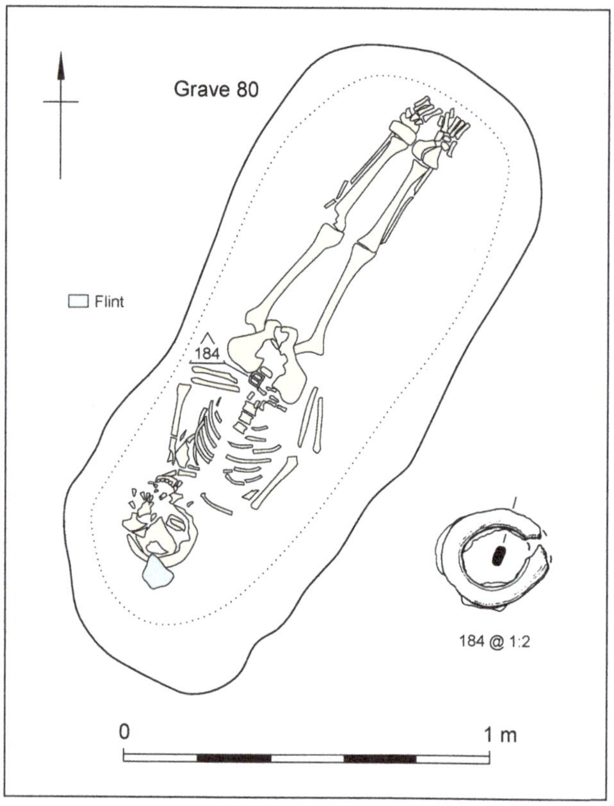

Figure 2.47 Grave 80 and fragmentary iron buckle

Grave 81: cut 1286 (burial 1288; fill 1287)
(Fig. 2.48)

SW–NE, sub-rectangular, rounded ends, steep sides, flat base. 1.85 x 0.74 m, 0.29 m deep (base at 134.06 m OD). Extended supine, slightly raised left side (ie, lying slightly on right side). Right arm along side, left hand over right pelvis.

Human bone: *c.* 99% adult *c.* 24–29 yr. female.

Grave goods:

ON 113: large iron pin with hooked end located over right chest. Length 83 mm; diameter *c.* 5 mm; diameter of head 19 mm.

ON 114: glass bead. RB glass vessel frag reused as bead (rim/footring). Large. With ON 113.

ON 115: copper alloy disc brooch at centre upper chest. Tinning surviving over about one third of the obverse. Double row of small punched dashes around the periphery. Single hinge and catch; remains of iron pin. Diameter 40 mm.

ON 120: iron knife (tip missing), under right pelvis, diagonal with point to head end. Tapering tang rectangular section central to blade; shoulder angled up to back of blade and sloping gently down to cutting edge. Back straight; blade curves up to tip. Böhner Type B. Possible remains of organic handle. Length 157 mm; width 26 mm; thickness 5 mm.

ON 121: simple iron buckle located right waist. Circular outline and section and intact tongue wrapped around loop. Length 25 mm; width 23 mm.

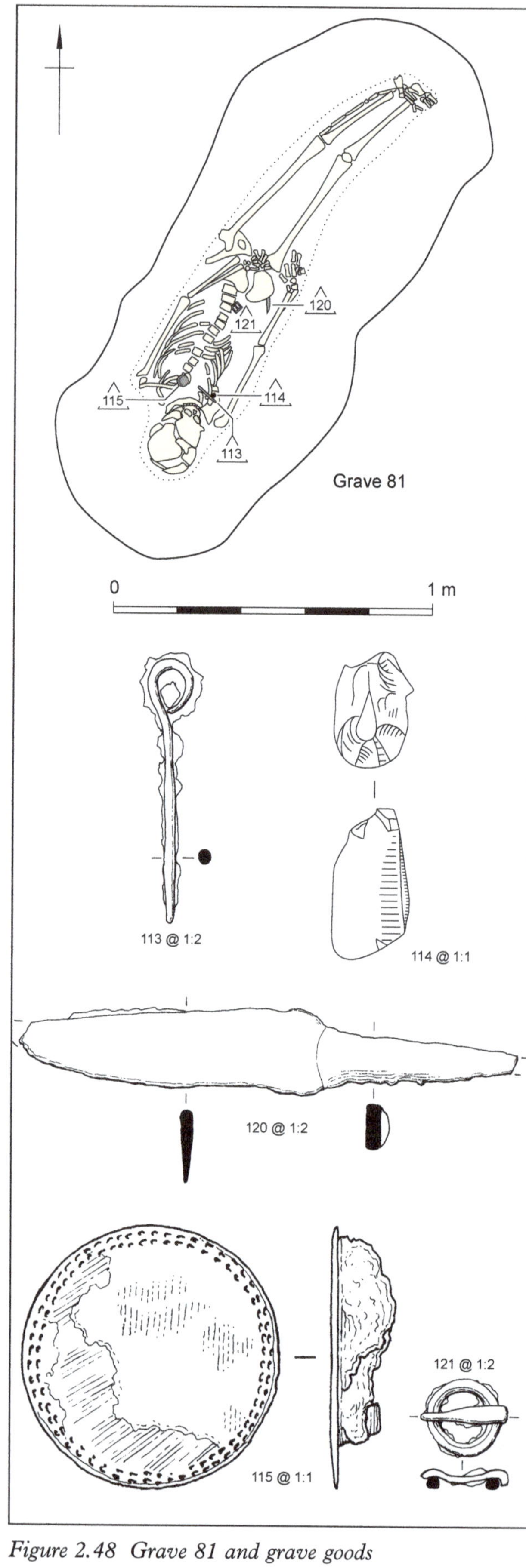

Figure 2.48 Grave 81 and grave goods

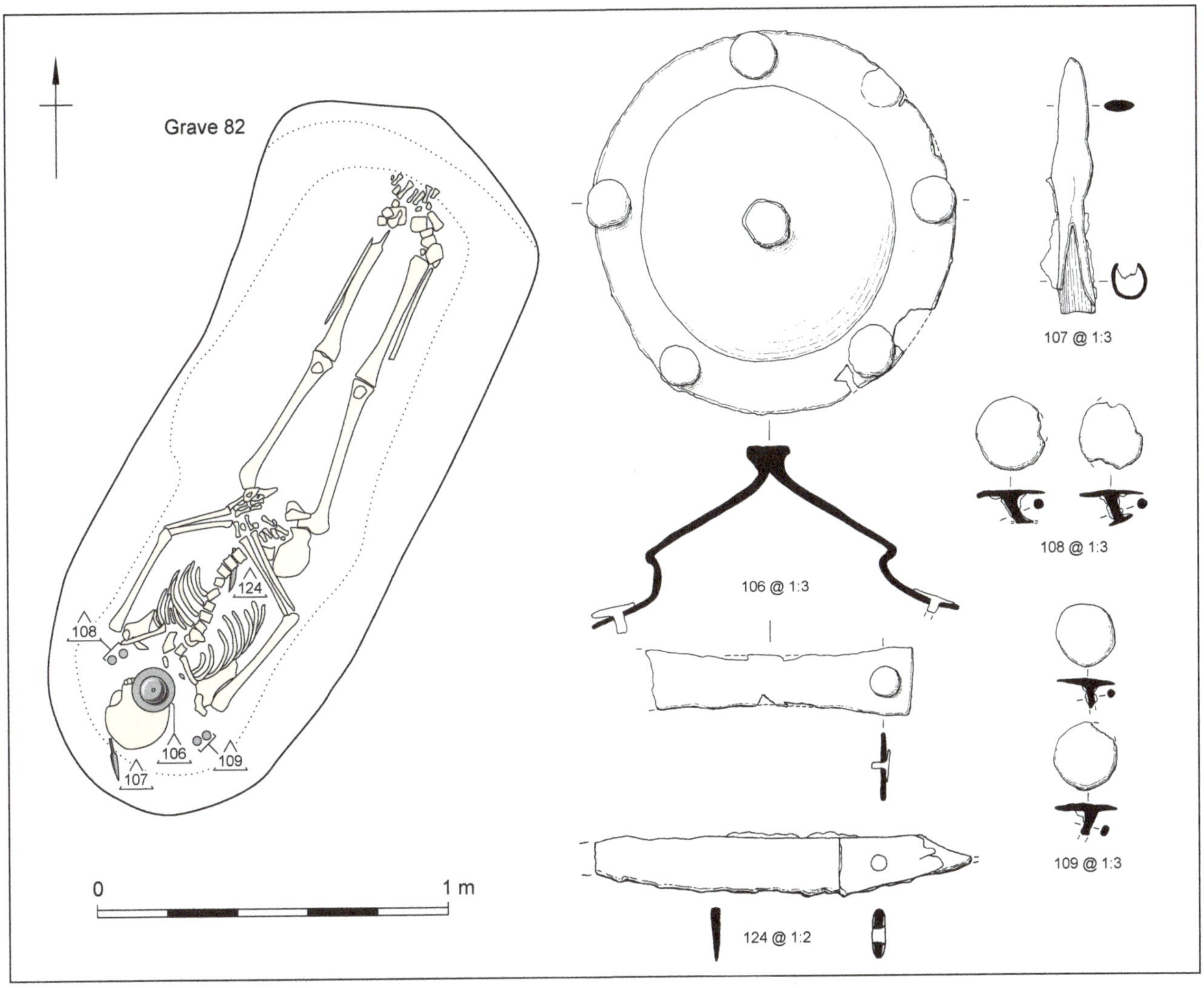

Figure 2.49 Grave 82 and selected grave goods

Grave 82: cut 1283 (burial 1284; fill 1285)
(Fig. 2.49)
SW–NE, sub-rectangular, rounded head end, steep sides, flat base. 2.12 x 0.83 m, 0.33 m deep (base at 134.05 m OD). Extended supine, hands crossed over abdomen. Cut 1268.
Human bone: *c.* 98% adult *c.* 24–29 yr. male.
Grave goods:
ON 106: iron shield boss lying over face. Concave walls and straight cone terminating in a narrow disc (diameter 18 mm); flange (35 mm width); five or six rivets remaining. Dickinson and Härke Type 1.1. Diameter 159 mm; height *c.* 70 mm. Dickinson and Härke Type Ia1 grip with one rivet *in situ*. Remains of wood on lower surface of grip and on lower surface of rim.
ON 107: iron spearhead located between skull and head end of grave, diagonal with point to head end. Socket cleft for most of length. Angular straight-sided blade with ?concavity above the blade-angle, lozengiform section. Swanton Group ?E1. Length 106 mm; width 19 mm.
ON 108–9: Four iron shield studs (ON 108 to left of boss, above left shoulder and ON 109 to right of boss, above right shoulder): each a pair of studs *c.* 30 mm in diameter.
ON 124: iron knife, behind lumbar region, diagonal, direction of tip unknown. Tip missing; tapering tang in line with back; shoulder curves down to cutting edge. Back straight and blade curves up to tip. Böhner Type B. Length 117 mm; width 15 mm; thickness 4 mm. Clear distinction between tang and blade.
Sample 5211: two iron fragments by skull, possible pin (not illustrated).
Residual finds: 1 flint; 2 sherds pottery (Romano-British).

Grave 83: cut 1260 (burial 1261; fill 1262)
(Fig. 2.50)
SSW–NNE, sub-rectangular (slight widening for shield), moderately sloping sides, flat base. 2.04 x 0.74 m, 0.20 m deep (base at 134.18 m OD). Extended, supine with right leg turned out. Both hands tucked up together at right shoulder.

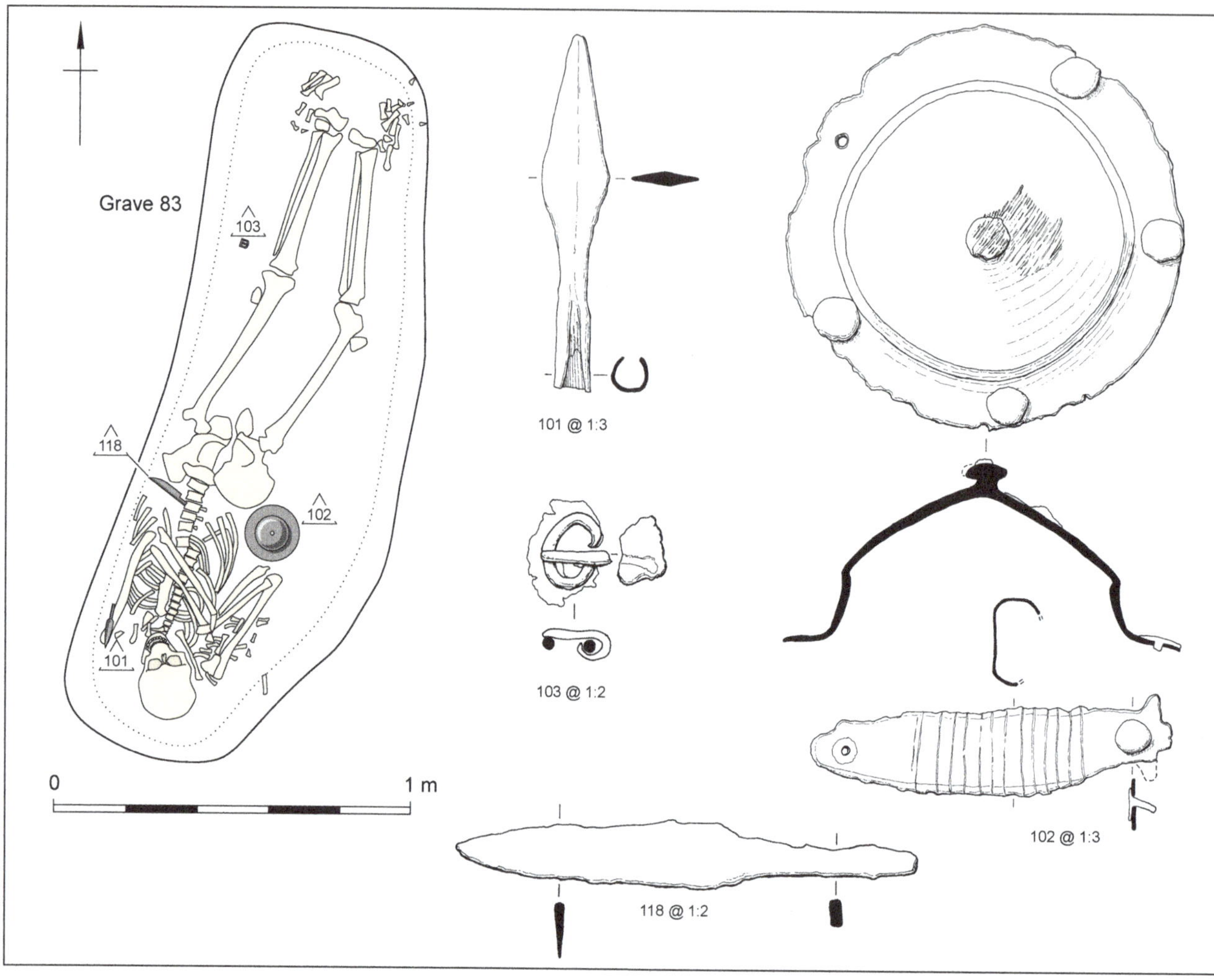

Figure 2.50 Grave 83 and grave goods

Human bone: *c.* 90% adult *c.* 24–29 yr. male.

Grave goods:

ON 101: iron spearhead, over left shoulder, vertical to head end. Socket cleft for length of *c.* 30 mm Angular straight-sided blade with marked concavity above the blade-angle, lozengiform section. Swanton Group E1. Length 144 mm; width 28 mm.

ON 102: iron shield boss, between right elbow and hip, right of abdomen. With straight walls and ?straight cone terminating in knob; flange of 20 mm width; 4 rivets remaining, Dickinson and Härke Type ?2. Diameter 165 mm; height 75 mm. Type II grip with wrapping and iron 'caps' for rivets?

ON 103: fragmentary simple iron buckle and associated rectangular plate to left of knee/shin. Circular loop, round section, tongue intact and wrapped around loop. Overall length 37 mm. Length of loop 20 mm; width 28 mm. Length of plate 18 mm; width 12 mm. Length of tongue 20 mm.

ON 118: iron knife, left waist, aligned diagonally to left. Tang of rectangular section, central to blade, with shoulder sloping gently up to back of blade and gently down to cutting edge. Back straight before curving down to tip; blade curves up to tip. Böhner Type A. Length 128 mm; width 16 mm; thickness 5 mm.

Grave 84: cut 1330 (burial 1329; fill 1328)

(Fig. 2.51)

SW–NE, sub-rectangular, rounded head end and wide mid-section, steep irregular sides, flat base. Slightly oversized, deep. 2.05 x 0.94 m, 0.46 m deep (base at 133.93 m OD). Supine, legs flexed to left. Left arm along side, hand under thigh, right hand at left shoulder.

Human bone: *c.* 90% adult >50 yr. male.

Grave goods:

ON 137: copper alloy disc brooch, located outside left shin. Central punched dot; notched around the periphery. Single hinge and catch (both fragmentary). Diameter 29 mm.

Residual finds: 1 sherd pottery (Saxon, sandy).

Grave 85: cut 1254 (burial 1255; fill 1256)

(Fig. 2.52)

W–E, sub-rectangular, moderately sloping sides, flat base. 1.79 x 0.93 m, 0.23 m deep (base at 134.20 m OD). Extended, supine, left arm along side, right hand at left elbow. Feet folded back.

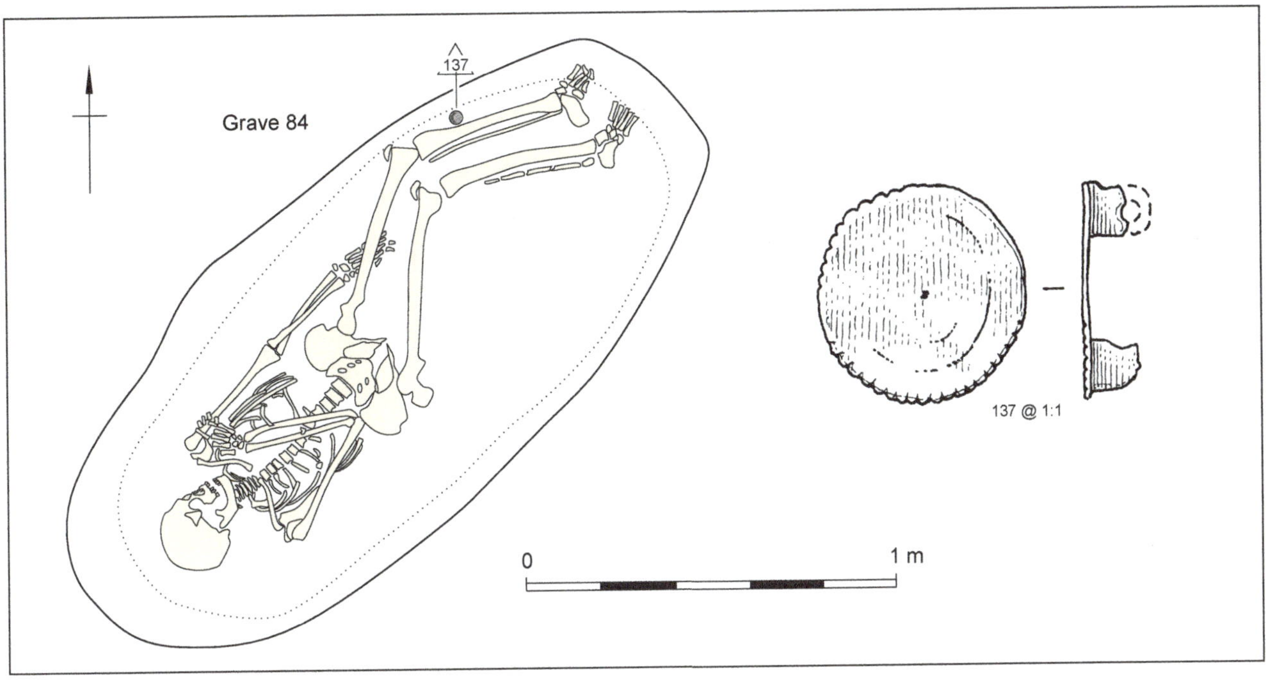

Figure 2.51 Grave 84 and copper alloy disc booch

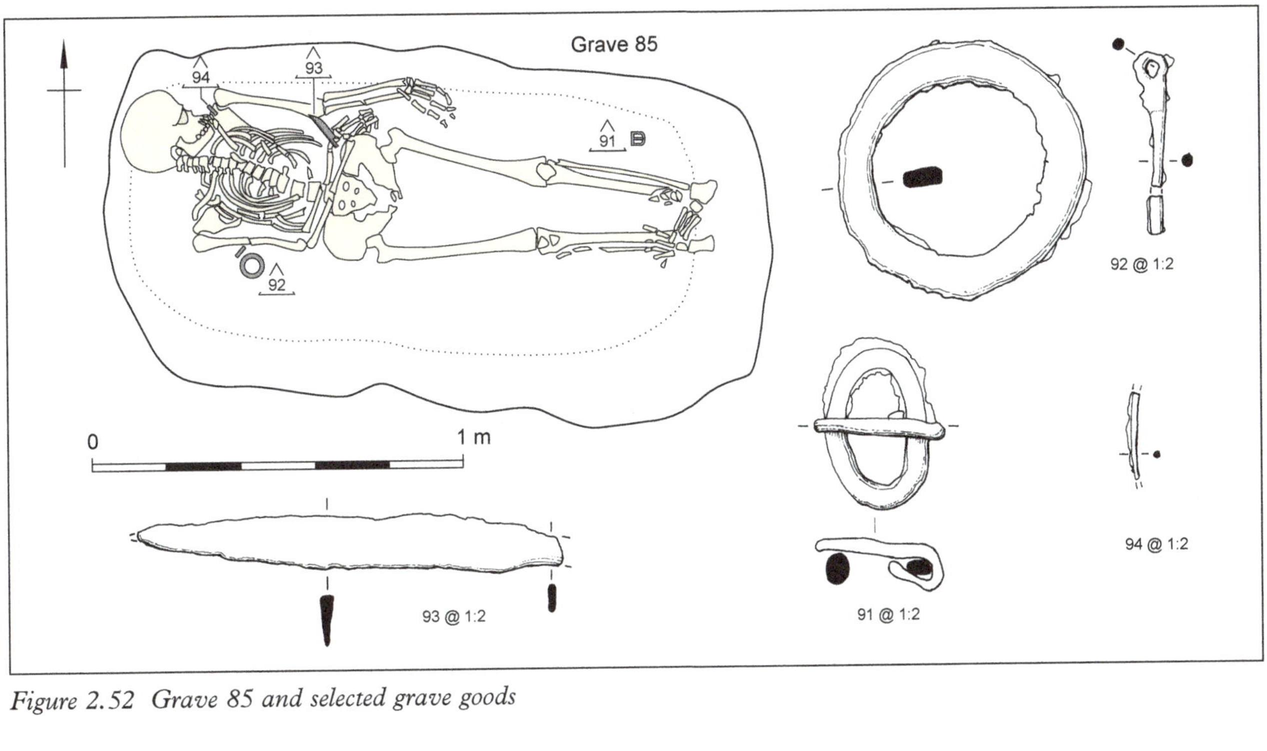

Figure 2.52 Grave 85 and selected grave goods

Human bone: *c.* 85% adult < 45 yr. female.
redep. 1 tooth. infant *c.* 1.5–4 yr.

Grave goods:

ON 91: large simple iron buckle, located outside left shin. D-shaped outline with oval section, tongue is intact and wrapped around the loop. Length 31 mm; width 45 mm. Length of tongue 45 mm.

ON 92: large iron (purse) ring, sub-circular of rectangular section, outside upper right arm. Diameter 68 mm; width of ring 10 mm. It was associated with 6 separate items, including a fragmentary pin of circular section with looped head; other items comprise small unidentified fragments. Length *c.* 53 mm; diameter 4 mm; width of head 11 mm.

ON 93: fragmentary iron knife, left waist, diagonal with tip to left, at left elbow. Tip missing. Tapering tang of triangular section in line with back of blade; curves gently down to cutting edge (object possibly corroded at tang and blade intersection). Back curving down to tip; blade curves up to tip. Böhner Type ?A. Length 114 mm; width 15 mm; thickness 5 mm.

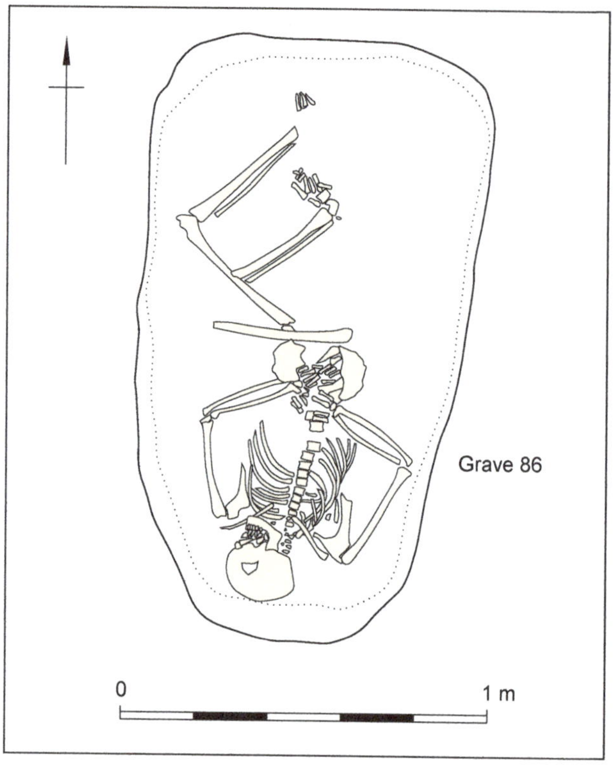

Figure 2.53 Grave 86

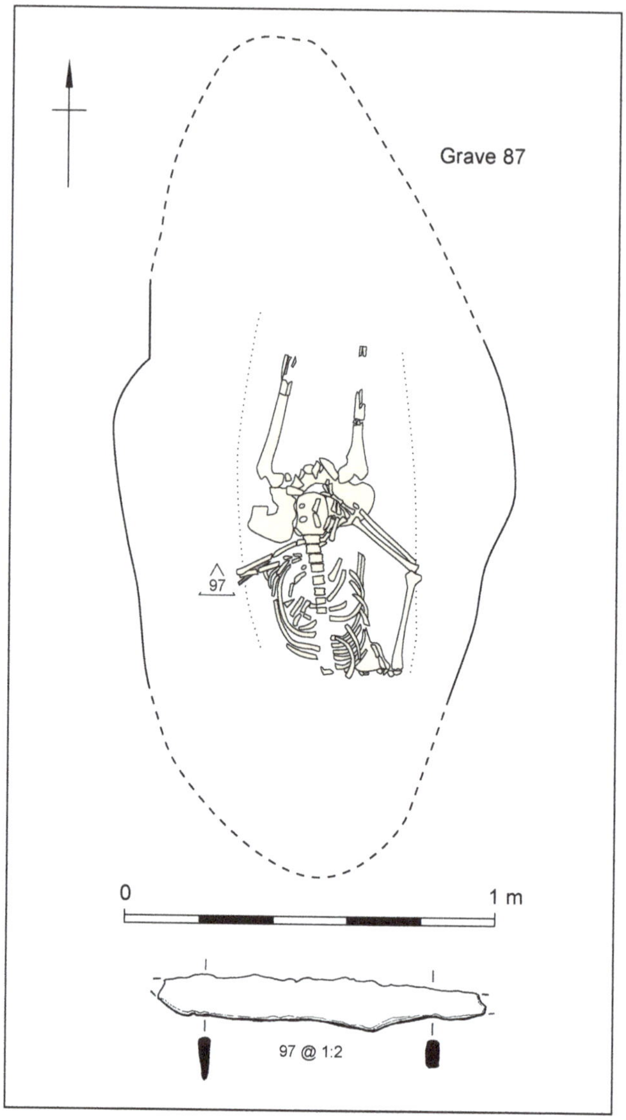

Figure 2.54 Grave 87 and fragmentary iron knife

ON 94: fragmentary iron pin of circular section, on left shoulder. Length 23 mm; diameter 4 mm.

ON 235: copper alloy purse fitting (?by ON 92); fragmentary binding/rim with rivet holes. ?Most complete example length 6 mm; width 8 mm (not illustrated).

Sample 5164: iron nail, square section (grave base). Length 29 mm; diameter 6 mm. (not illustrated)

Residual finds: ON 98: 1 animal bone.

Grave 86: cut 1375 (burial 1376; fill 1377)
(Fig. 2.53)
S–N, sub-rectangular, slightly wider foot end, steep sides, flat base. 1.60 x 0.94 m, 0.20 m deep (base at 133.87 m OD). Supine, legs flexed on left side, hands over abdomen.
Human bone: *c.* 90% adult *c.* 30–35 yr. female.

Grave 87: cut 1257 (burial 1259; fill 1258)
(Fig. 2.54)
S–N, incomplete, probably sub-rectangular; shallow, concave sides, concave base. Truncated to 1.0 x 1.1 m, 0.21 m deep (base at 133.97 m OD). Extended, supine with hands crossed over abdomen.
Human bone: *c.* 40% a.u.l. subadult *c.* 14–17 yr. male.
Grave goods:

ON 97: fragmentary knife, left of waist, under left arm, ?diagonal. Tip missing. Rectangular section tang in line with back of blade and angled down to cutting edge. Böhner Type ? Length 86 mm; width 13 mm; thickness 4 mm.

Residual finds: 3 sherds pottery (Saxon, organic-tempered).

Grave 88: cut 1304 (burial 1305; fill 1306)
(Fig. 2.55)
S–N, irregular, ?sub-rectangular, flat base. 1.39 x 0.71 m, 0.07 m deep (base at 133.80 m OD). Flexed on left side, hands over abdomen. Truncated.
Human bone: *c.* 65% juvenile *c.* 6–8 yr.
Grave goods:

ON 130: simple iron buckle with fragmentary tapering plate with rivet(s), centre waist. Sub-circular loop of rectangular section; fragmentary tongue wrapped around the loop. Length of loop 23 mm; width 25 mm. Length of plate 32 mm; width 15 mm.

ON 133: short stumpy iron knife, centre waist, diagonal, tip to head end. Fragmentary tang central to blade, with sharp angle to back of blade and sharp angle down to cutting edge. Back slopes gently to tip (may rise upwards just before tip); blade slopes up to tip. Böhner Type ?D. Length 92 mm; width 24 mm; thickness 4 mm. ?Rivet where tang joins blade. (not illustrated).

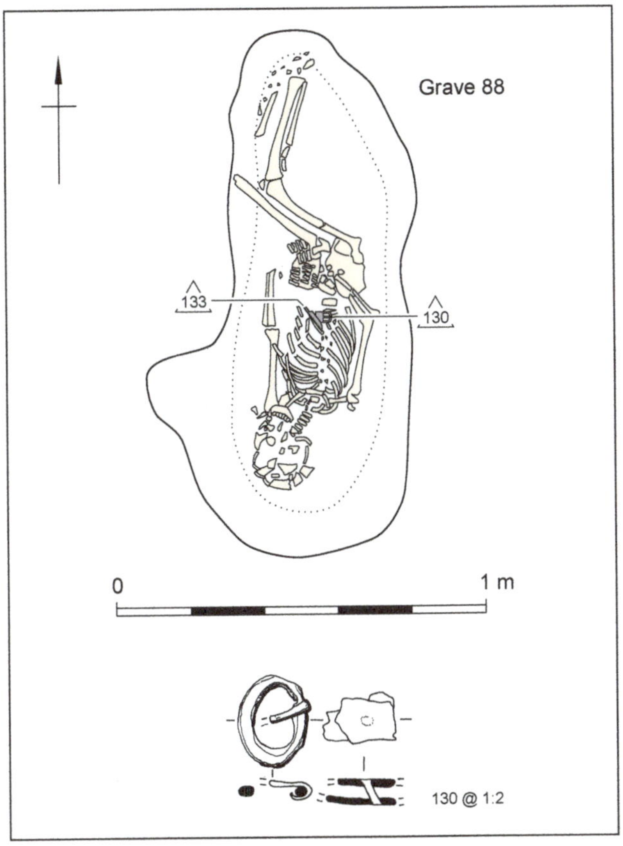

Figure 2.55 Grave 88 and iron buckle

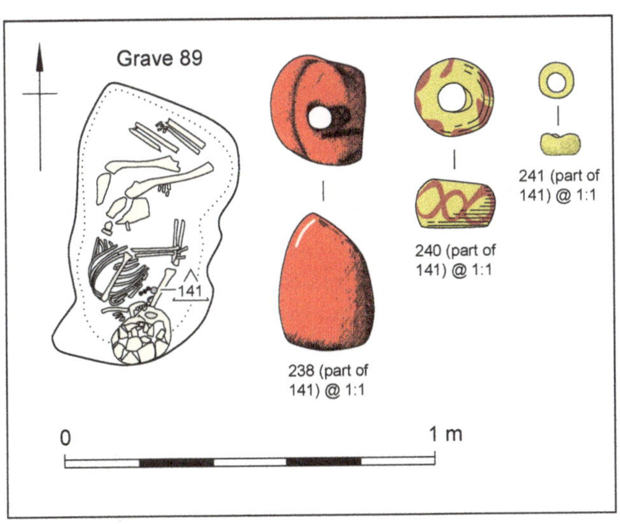

Figure 2.56 Grave 89 and selected grave goods

Grave 89: cut 1332 (burial 1333; fill 1334)

(Fig. 2.56)

S–N, sub-rectangular, rounded head end, steep concave sides, concave base. 0.88 x 0.50 m, 0.14 m deep (base at 133.73 m OD). Flexed on right side. Right arm straight, hand towards lap. Left hand over right elbow. Suggestion of organic deposits (not located).

Human bone: *c.* 55% juvenile *c.* 5–7 yr.

Grave goods:

ON 141: necklace group:

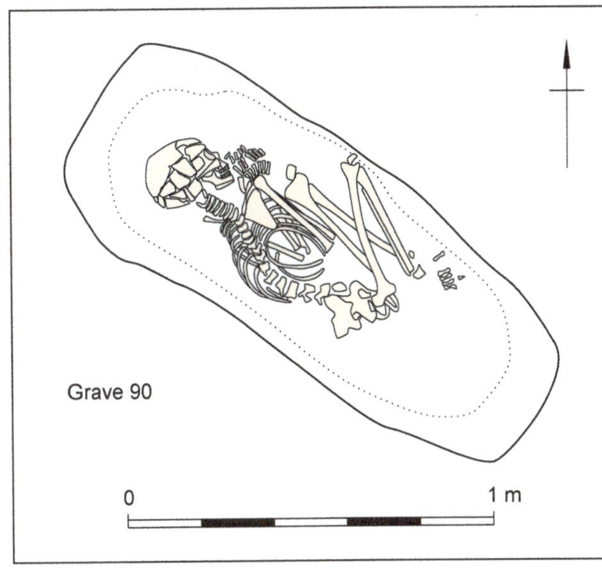

Figure 2.57 Grave 90

ON 238: amber bead. Large, shape A02

ON 239: copper alloy coin; damaged. Worn 4th-century *nummus* (see Cooke, Chapter 4; not illustrated)

ON 240: glass bead. Polychrome (Koch 34?). Medium, colour 5.1/2.1, poly P9, shape A2.

ON 241: glass bead, very degraded. Also 2 separate frags. Small, colour 5.1, shape A2.

Residual finds: 2 sherds pottery (Saxon, 1 sandy, 1 organic-tempered).

Grave 90: cut 1397 (burial 1396; fill 1395)

(Fig. 2.57)

NW–SE, sub-rectangular, steep sides, concave base. 1.46 x 0.55 m, 0.22 m deep (base at 133.59 m OD). Crouched on left side, knees to chest, hands together between skull and knees.

Human bone: *c.* 90% juvenile/ subadult *c.* 12–14 yr. ?female.

Grave 91: cut 1292 (burial 1293; fill 1294)

(Fig. 2.58; Pl. 2.7)

SW–NE, sub-rectangular, moderately sloping sides, flat base. 1.86 x 0.80 m, 0.25 m deep (base at 133.49 m OD). Flexed on right side, left shoulder slumped back. Right arm straight, hand towards knees, left hand on sternum. Slight animal disturbance.

Human bone: *c.* 98% adult >45 yr. male.

Grave goods:

ON 125: iron spearhead; approximately midway down right edge of grave, partially overlying right forearm, diagonal, point to head end. Socket cleft to 97 mm, rivet at 24 mm. Leaf-shaped long blade; lozengiform section. Swanton Group C3 (marked blade angle on one side?). Length 380 mm; width 58 mm.

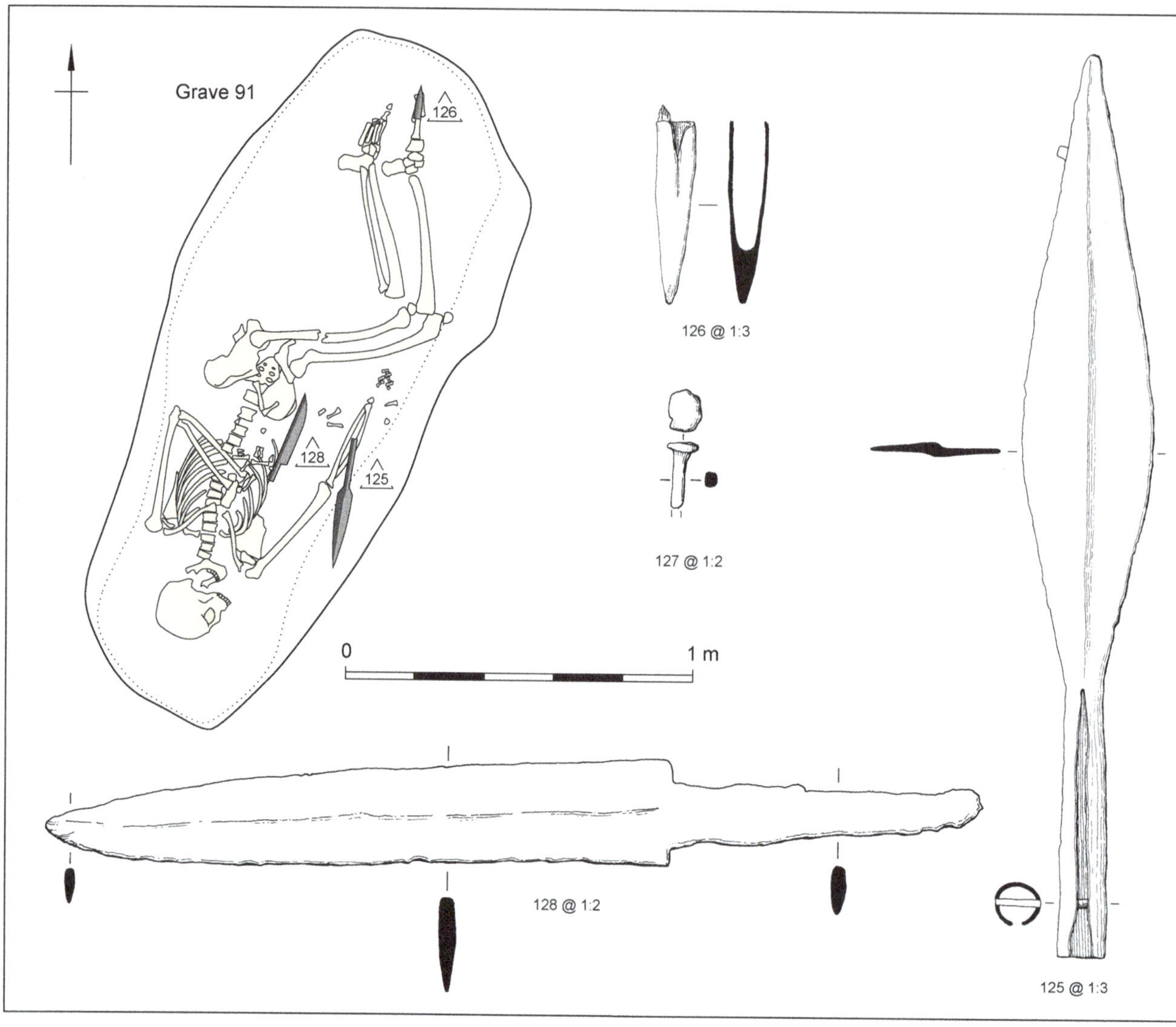

Figure 2.58 Grave 91 and grave goods

ON 126: cleft spear ferrule, overlying right foot. Length 80 mm; diameter 19 mm.
NB ferrule in same alignment as spearhead indicating that the spear had been placed diagonally across the flexed legs.

ON 127: iron nail (location unknown). Length 20 mm; width 6 mm; diameter of head 13 mm.

ON 128: long iron knife, chest to abdomen, handle at left hand, tip towards foot end. Tapering tang central to blade, with sharp angle to back of blade and sharp angle down to cutting edge. Back angled to tip (bowie knife?); blade curves up to tip. Böhner Type C. Length 269 mm; width 30 mm; thickness 5 mm.

ON 129: unidentified (location unknown). Two fragments ?nail. Length 51 mm.

Residual finds: 1 flint; 205 animal bone (amphibian?).

Grave 92: cut 1340 (burial 1300; fill 1299)
(Fig. 2.59; Pl. 2.8)
WSW–ENE, sub-rectangular, rounded ends, steep sides, flat base. 1.90 x 0.70 m, 0.30 m deep (base at 133.44 m OD).
Extended supine, right hand over pelvis, left wrist bent at *c.* 90°, fingers at left hip.
Cremation grave 1297 over left ribs, cut into upper fill of grave 92 (see Fig 1.2).
Human bone: *c.* 95% adult *c.* 20–25 yr. female.
Grave goods:

ON 134: group comprising ONs 135 and 221–223:

ON 135: copper alloy disc brooch (paired with ON 222 (part of Group 134)), left shoulder/neck. Central punched dot surrounded by three concentric inscribed circles. Single hinge and catch with iron pin. Diameter 30 mm.

ON 221 (part of Group 134): copper alloy bell-shaped brooch, lying over right neck/mandible (Pl. 2.9). Obverse is gilded. Chip-carved decoration: human face with pair of prominent eyes and nose, framed by hair; scroll at either end and above a border from which the

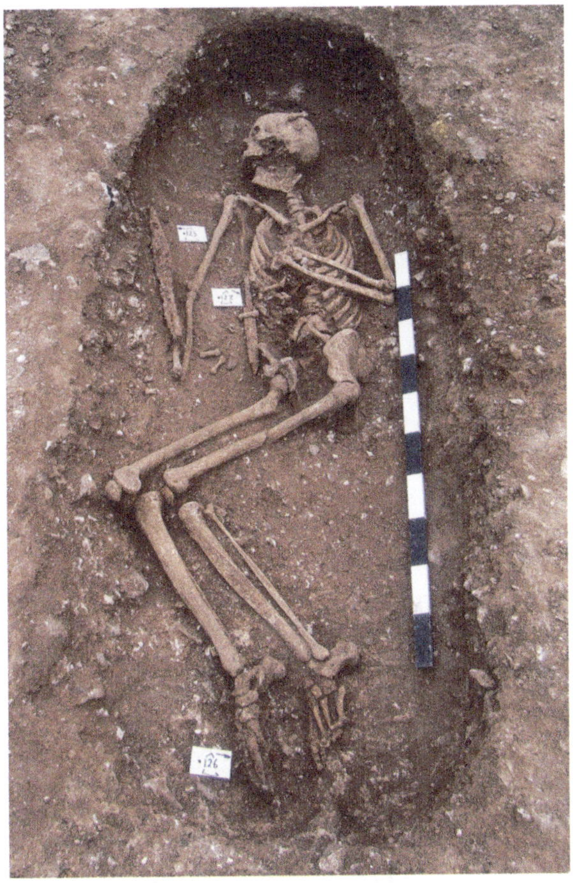

Plate 2.7 *Grave 91 (scale = 1m; from the south-west)*

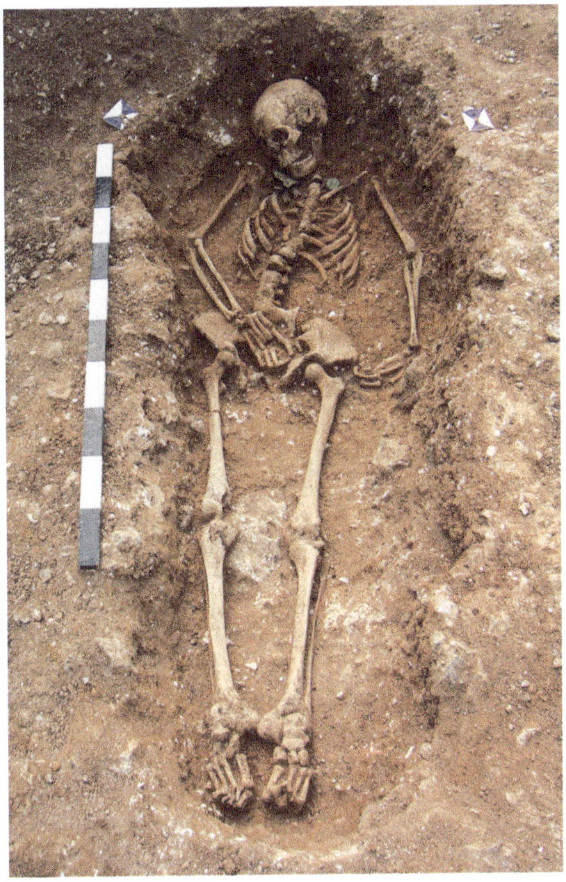

Plate 2.8 *Grave 92 (scale = 1m; from the north-east)*

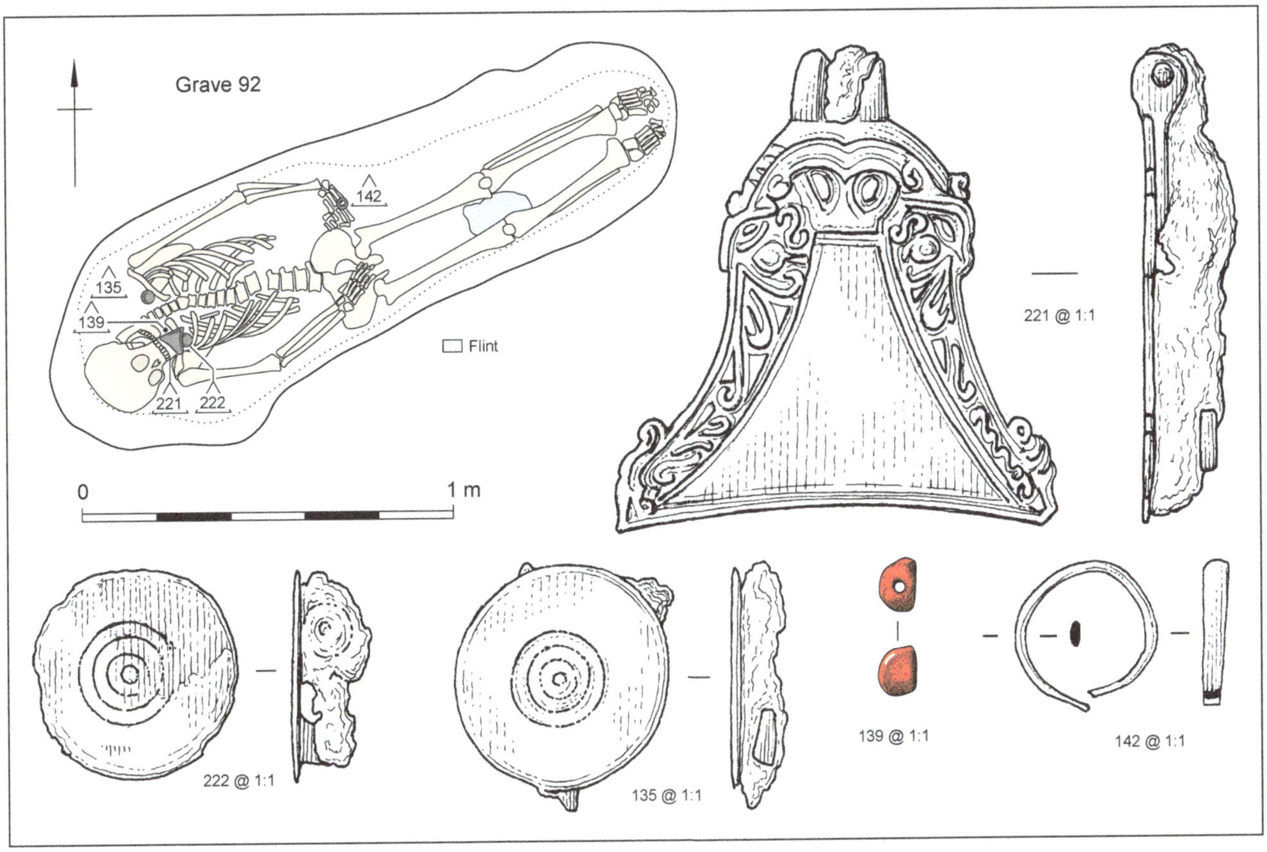

Figure 2.59 Grave 92 and grave goods

Plate 2.9 Detail of grave 93, showing brooch ON 221 at neck (scale = 0.2m; from the north-west)

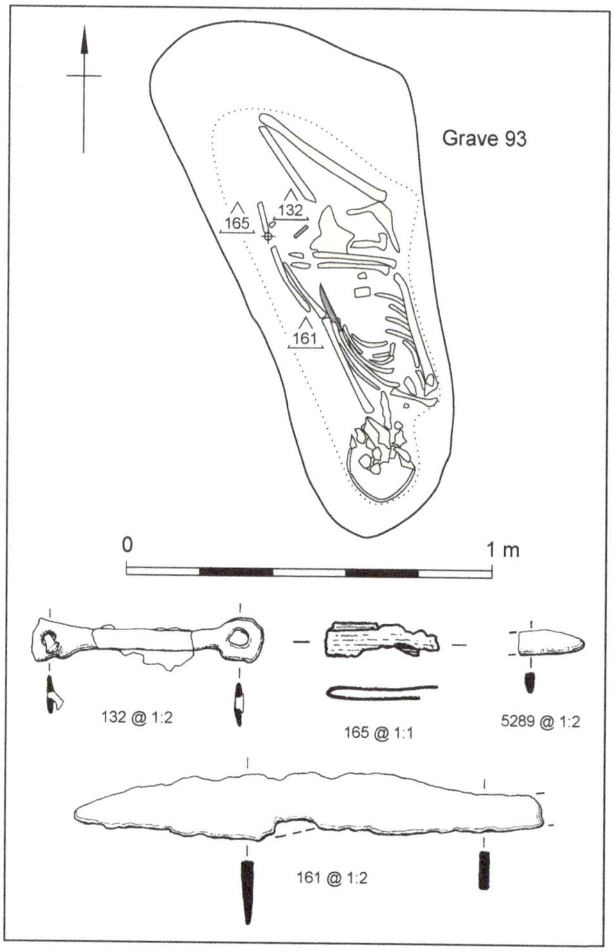

Figure 2.60 Grave 93 and grave goods

hinge extends. The outer border terminates at either end in a simple unmatched motif. A pair of cheek bars delimit the eyes: the example on left is straight, while its counterpart on the right is curved and also thicker. The mouth is formed from a plain triangular centre plate which expands outwards terminating in a concave bottom edge; it is outlined on each side. On the left a scroll separates the face from a Style I animal. The animal consists of an eye, body and three legs. Below the animal is a further scroll motif which terminates at a horizontally-aligned scroll. The animal on the right hand side is also separated from the face by a scroll but in this case it has been forced further down the side of the brooch by the cheek bar. Much of this animal is obscured, but enough is visible to show that it is not an exact parallel of its counterpart. The border around the eye is less angular, while the body is formed from a more prominent but narrower element. The hinge is cast in one with the brooch at the centre top; the catch-plate appears intact but is obscured. The iron pin is *in situ*. Length (centre) 60 mm; width 58 mm.

ON 222 (paired with ON 135 (part of Group 134)): copper alloy disc brooch lying over upper right chest. Wear to the edge. Central punched dot surrounded by three inscribed concentric circles. Single hinge and catch with iron pin. Diameter 29 mm (sub-circular).

ON 223 (part of Group 134): associated with ON 221. Mineral-replaced threads held together with body liquor residue (not illustrated).

ON 139: amber bead. Small, shape A01. Right neck, by ON 221.

ON 142: undecorated copper alloy finger ring on middle finger left hand. Wear to the edges. Formed from a strip of metal. Diameter 20 mm; height 4 mm.

Grave 93: cut 1307 (burial 1308; fill 1309)
(Fig. 2.60)
SSE–NNW, incomplete cut, ?sub-rectangular with rounded head end, shallow sides, flat base. 1.44 x 0.64 m, 0.19 m deep (base at 133.44 m OD). Flexed on left side with hands crossed in front of lap. Truncated below knees. Slight bioturbation. Fill darker than most.
Human bone: *c.* 55% adult >45 yr. female.

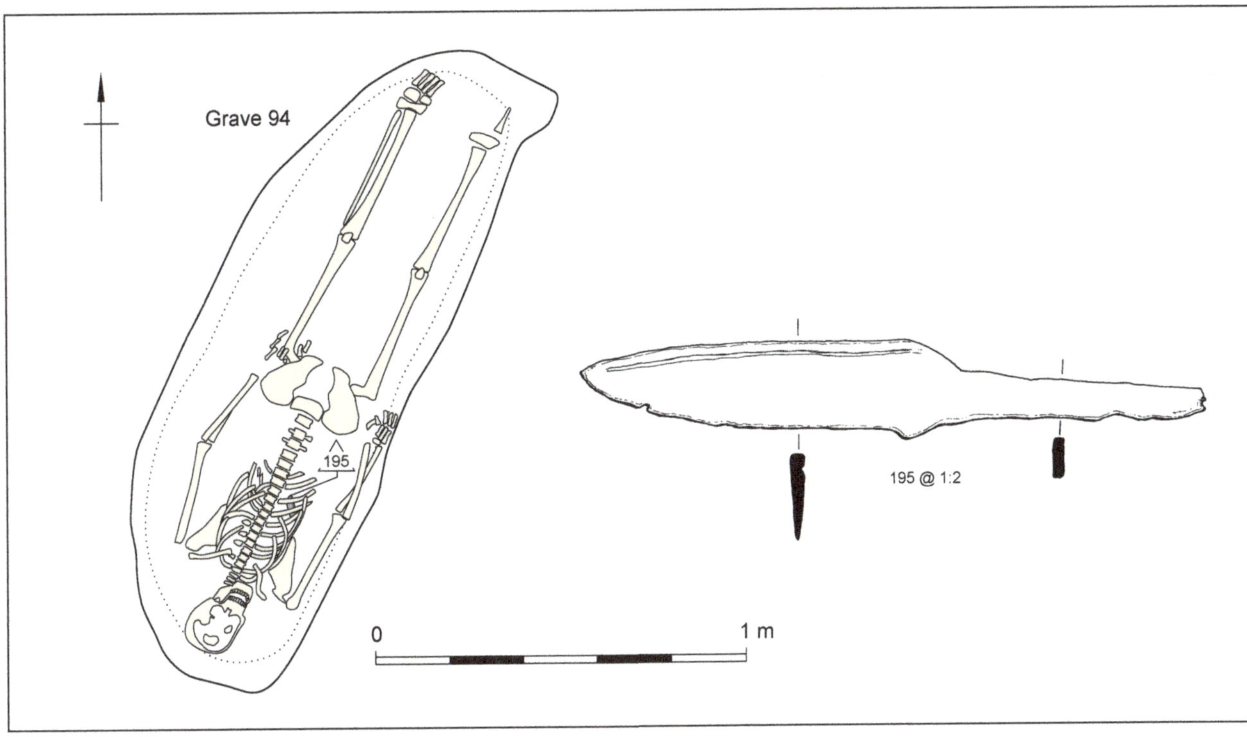

Figure 2.61 Grave 94 and iron knife

Grave goods:

ON 132: iron rod, lap. Perforated either end. Length 64 mm; width 19 mm. Mount probably from same leather object as ON 165.

ON 161: iron knife, left waist, vertical, point to foot end. Tapering tang central to blade, curving to back of blade with pronounced hump, sloping gently to cutting edge; back possibly angled to tip, blade may curve to tip. Böhner Type ?A/C. Length 132 mm; width 20 mm; thickness 6 mm.

ON 165: copper alloy folded strip, a fragment of rim binding, over or on left forearm. Length 16 mm. Mount from leather object (same as ON 132)

Sample 5289: iron fragment by left hand. Length 17 mm; width 6 mm.

3 unidentified (location unknown) including iron ?nail (not illustrated).

Grave 94: cut 1343 (burial 1344; fill 1345)

(Fig. 2.61)

SW–NE, sub-rectangular, rounded ends, steep sides, flat base. 1.80 x 0.80 m, 0.46 m deep (base at 133.40 m OD). Extended supine, arms along sides.

Human bone: *c.* 85% adult *c.* 20–25 yr. male.

Grave goods:

ON 195: short stumpy iron knife, angled behind right mid-back, direction of tip unknown. Tang central to blade, with shoulder angled to back of blade and sloping down to cutting edge; back straight before curving down to tip; blade curves up to tip. Böhner Type A. Length 171 mm; width 25 mm; thickness 6 mm.

Residual finds: 1 sherd pottery (Romano-British).

Grave 95: cut 1381 (burial 1382; fill 1383)

(not illustrated)

SSW–NNE, incomplete ?sub-rectangular, moderate concave sides, flat base. 0.31 x 0.35 m, 0.13 m deep (base at 133.62 m OD). Probably supine.

Human bone: a few frags. s.a.u. neonate.

Grave 96: cut 1468 (burial 1469; fill 1470)

(Figs 2.62–4; Pl. 2.10)

WNW–ESE, rectangular, steep sides, flat base. 2.58 x 1.56 m, 0.40 m deep (base at 136.00 m OD). 'Bed burial'. Extended supine, body slightly slumped to left, left arm along side, right hand over right femur. Cut by cremation-related feature 1480.

Human bone: *c.* 80% adult >45 yr. female.
?placed crd 1470: 8.6 g subadult/adult >13 yr.

Grave goods:

ONs 283–4, 288, 300–53: 55 bed fittings (cleats, pins, eyelets etc). (see Watson, Chapter 4).

ON 349: fragmentary and bent copper alloy disc, about a quarter is missing (location unknown). It may have a burnt patina, which possibly indicates that it was originally associated with the cremation-related deposit 1470, by left forearm. The obverse is decorated with a floriate cross motif (originally four) which is set within a rim. Diameter 16 mm. It may be a mount, or a die for repoussé work, or a model for a similar artefact. There is however, possibly, the very faint trace of a pattern on the reverse.

Residual finds: 1 flint; 14 sherds pottery (1 Late Iron Age; 13 Saxon, organic-tempered).

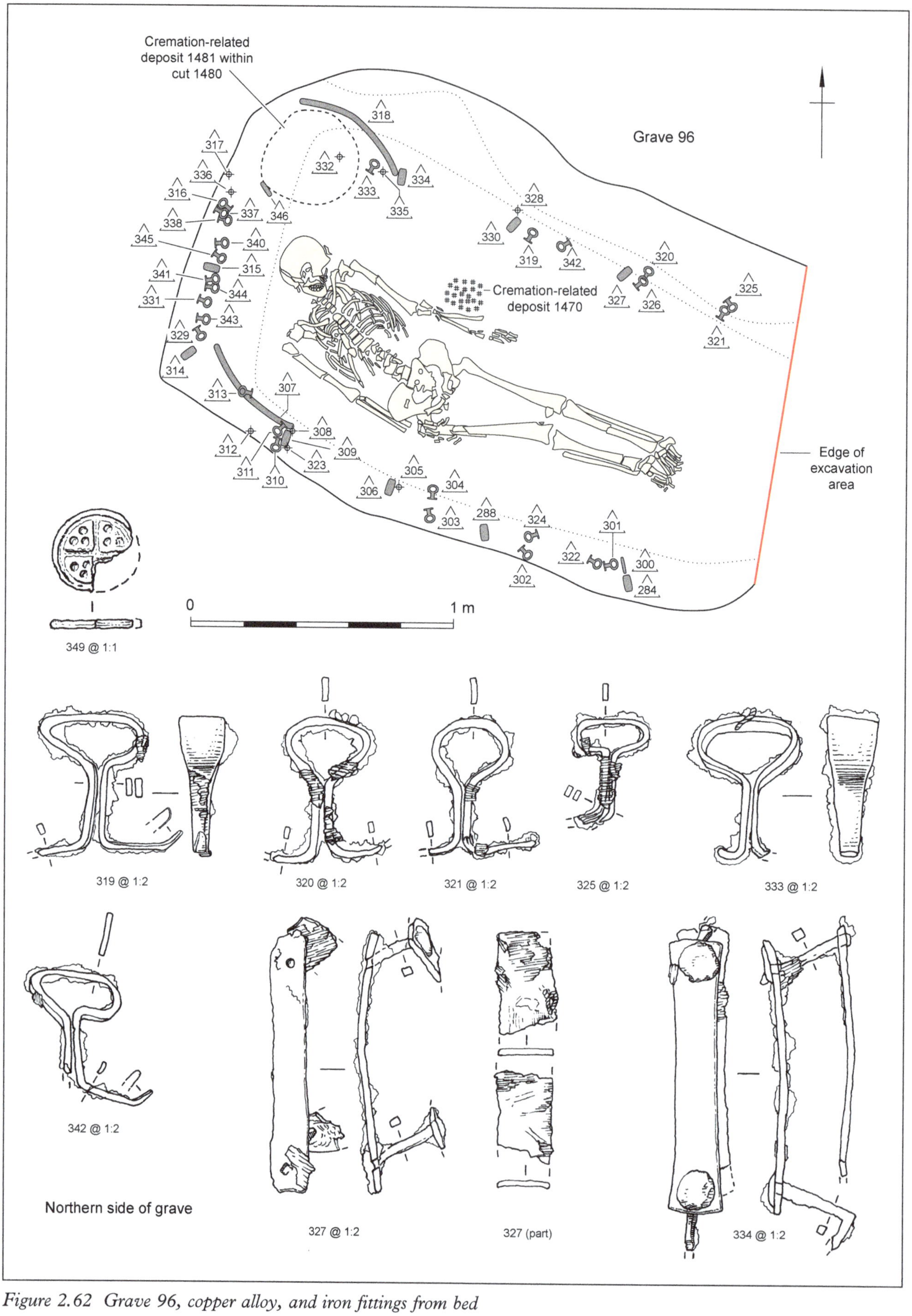

Figure 2.62 Grave 96, copper alloy, and iron fittings from bed

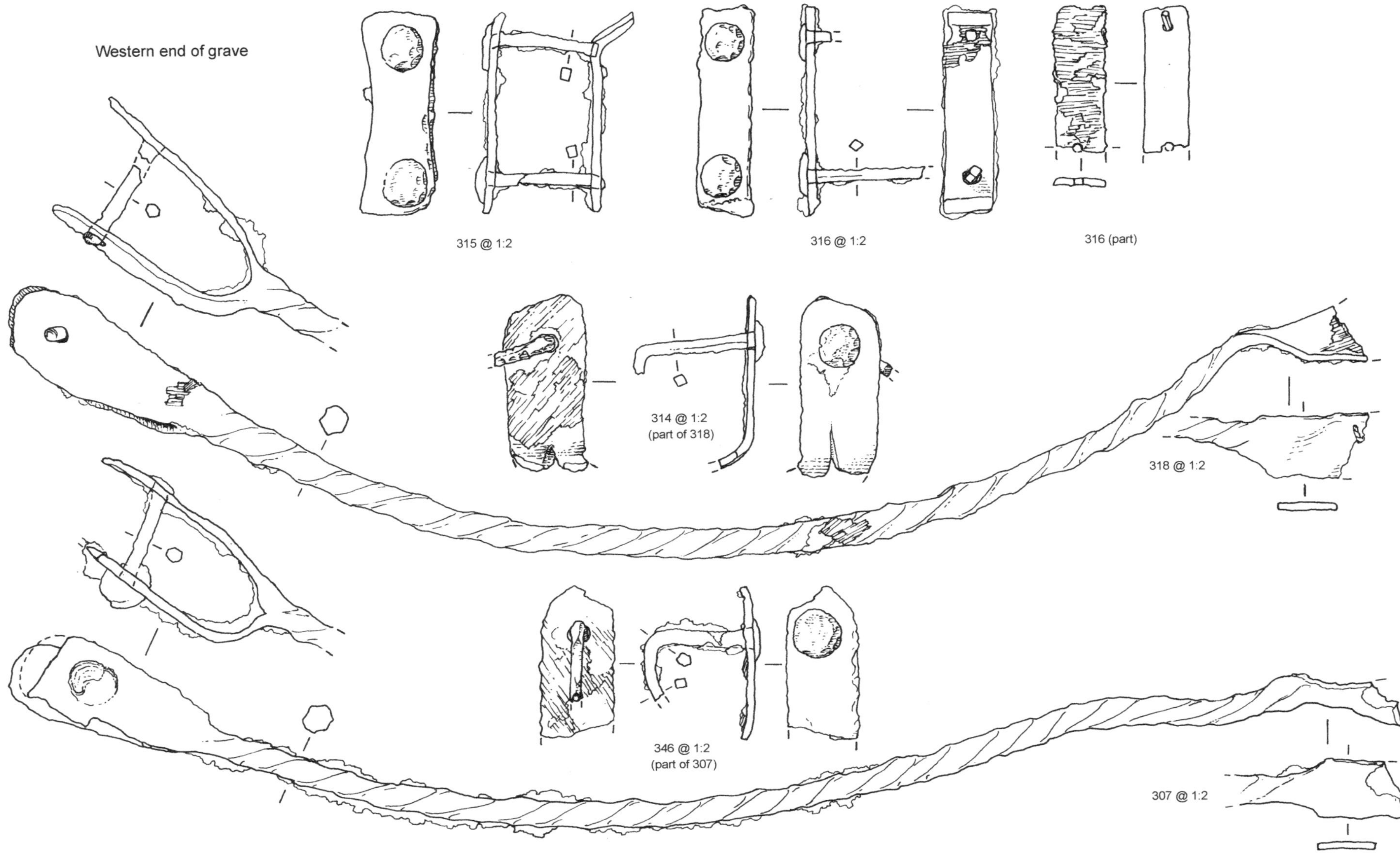

Figure 2.63 Grave 96 iron fittings from bed (continued)

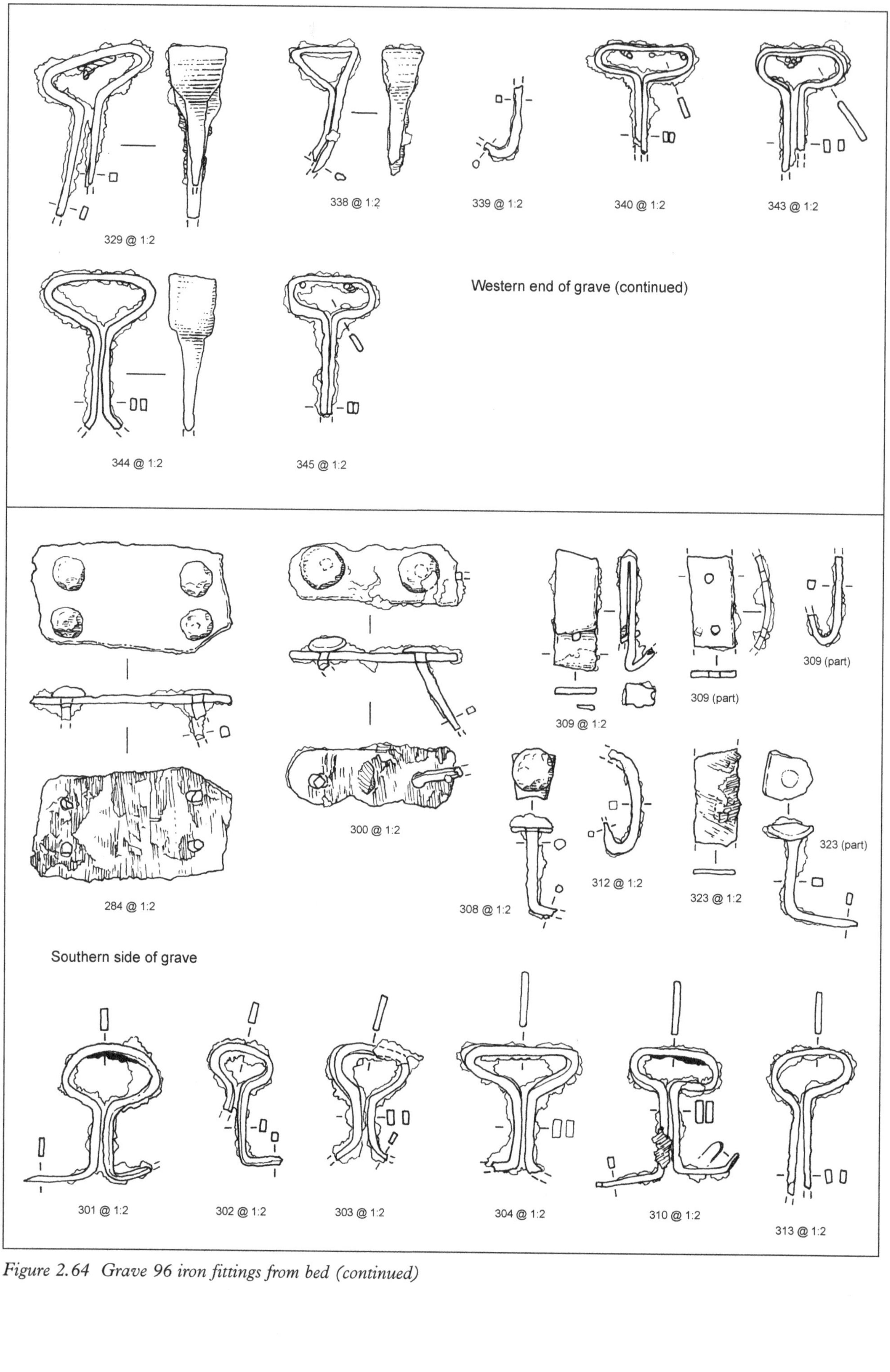

Figure 2.64 Grave 96 iron fittings from bed (continued)

Plate 2.10 Grave 96 'bed burial' under excavation, from the north-west

Grave 97: cut 1477 (burial 1478; fill 1479)
(Fig. 2.65)
SSW–NNE, sub-rectangular, steep sides, flat base. 2.11 x 1.17 m, 0.28 m deep (base at 135.74 m OD). Extended supine, arms along sides.
Human bone: *c.* 65% adult *c.* 25–35 yr. female.
Grave goods:
ON 285: iron knife, over left hip, vertical, tip to foot end? Tip missing; tapering tang central to blade, shoulder curves gently to back of blade and down to cutting edge. Back ?angled down to tip. Böhner Type ?C. Length 171 mm; width 25 mm; thickness 6 mm.

Grave 98: cut 1476 (burial 1475; fill 1474)
(not illustrated)
W–E (unclear), sub-rectangular, rounded ends, shallow sides, sloping base. 1.50 x 0.80 m, 0.10 m deep (base at 135.43 m OD). Posture not discernible. Heavily disturbed (?ploughing).
Human bone: *c.* 20% juvenile *c.* 6–8 yr.

Grave 99: cut 1465 (burial 1466; fill 1467)
(not illustrated)
WSW–ENE, incomplete, sub-rectangular, shallow concave sides, flat base. 1.47 x 0.54 m, 0.06 m deep (base at 135.12 m OD). Extended, supine. Very shallow, truncated and root disturbance.
Human bone: *c.* 10% l. juvenile *c.* 5–13 yr.

Grave 100: cut 1471 (burial 1472; fill 1473)
(Fig. 2.66)
WSW–ENE (burial W–E), sub-rectangular, steep sides,

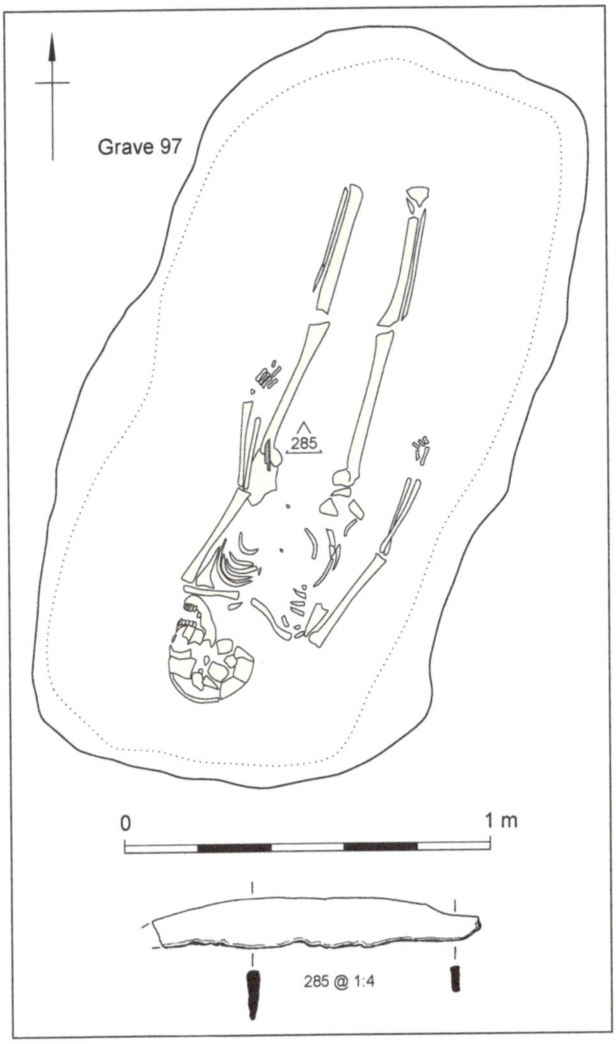

Figure 2.65 Grave 97 and iron knife

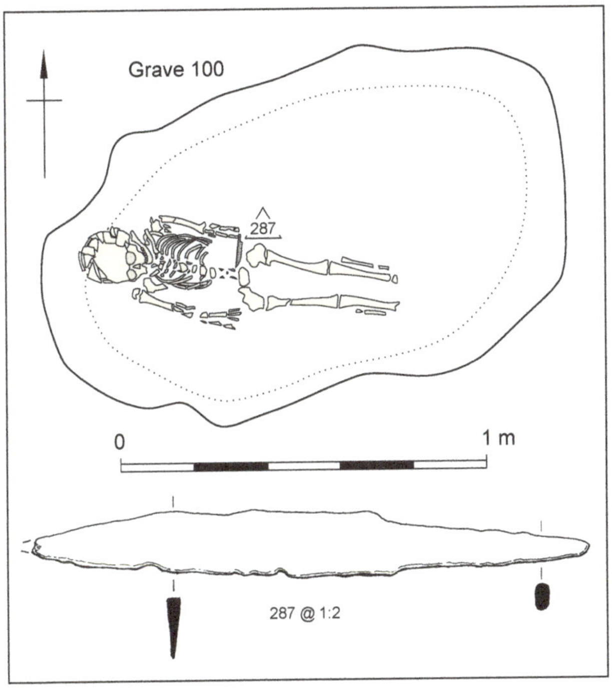

Figure 2.66 Grave 100 and iron knife

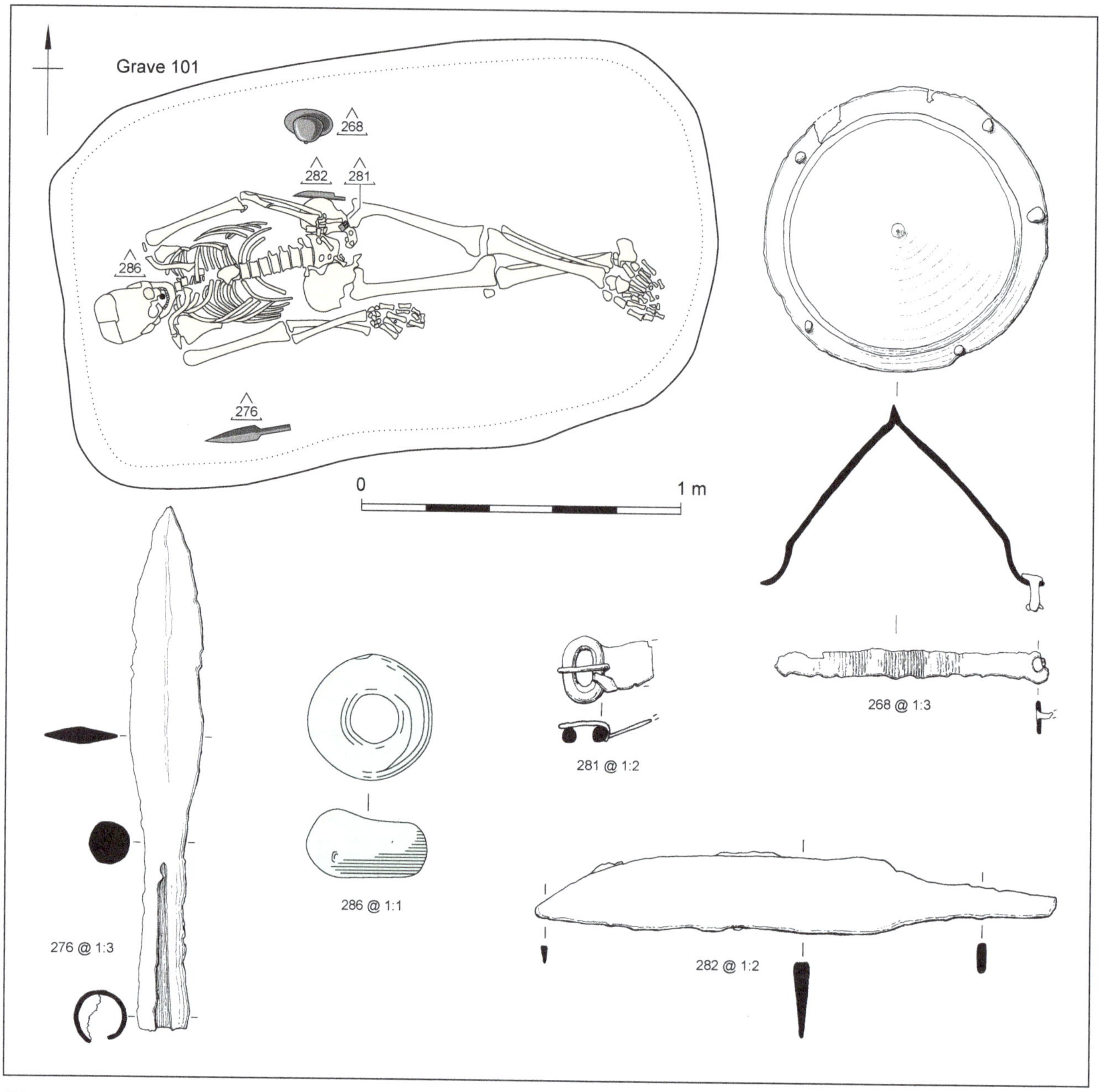

Figure 2.67 Grave 101 and grave goods

flat base. 1.44 x 0.88 m (overcut), 0.33 m deep (base at 134.51 m OD). Extended, supine, arms by sides.
Human bone: c. 50% juvenile *c.* 5–7 yr.
Grave goods:
ON 287: iron knife, at left waist, horizontal, point to right. Tapering tang central to blade, with sharp angle to back of blade and small curve down to cutting edge. Back angled to tip; blade curves to tip. Böhner Type C. Length 151 mm; width 16 mm; thickness 4 mm.

Grave 101: cut 1444 (burial 1445; fill 1446)
(Fig. 2.67)
W–E, rectangular, probable chamber. Vertical sides, flat base. 2.07 x 1.25 m, 0.62 m deep (base at 134.17 m OD). Extended, supine, left leg crossed over right, right arm along side, left hand over left pelvis.
Human bone: *c.* 98% adult *c.* 35–40 yr. male.
redep. cremated bone: 0.4 g human.
Grave goods:
ON 268: iron shield boss, outside left hip, propped against grave side. Straight walls and straight cone terminating in small knob; narrow flange (10 mm width); five rivets remaining. Dickinson and Härke Type 6. Diameter 132 mm; height 85 mm. Fragmentary and thin grip with one rivet *in situ*. Length 129 mm.
ON 276: iron spearhead, along right edge of grave opposite right shoulder, some distance away, vertical, tip to end of grave. Socket cleft. Leaf-shaped blade, lozengiform section. Swanton Group C2. Length 240 mm; width 34 mm.

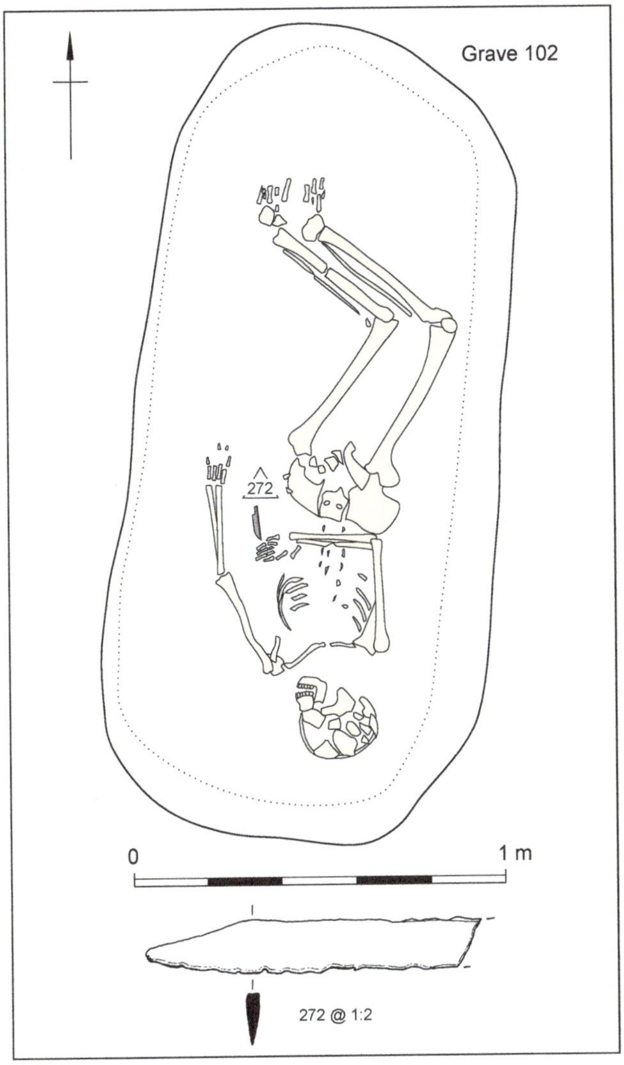

Figure 2.68 Grave 102 and iron knife

ON 281: simple iron buckle over left hip/abdomen. With fragmentary plate broken across rivet hole; oval outline with circular section loop; tongue *in situ* and wrapped around loop. Length of loop 15 mm; width 20 mm. Length of plate *c.* 15 mm; width *c.* 12 mm.

ON 282: iron knife, over left hip, vertical, tip to head end. Tapering fragmentary tang central to blade, curving to back of blade and to cutting edge. Back angled to tip; blade straight to tip. Evison Type 4. Length 164 mm; width 24 mm; thickness 6 mm.

ON 286: glass bead. Wound annular with 3 irregularly spaced 'eyes' (opaque white), 2 missing. Large, colour 6.2a, shape A2. Mouth area.

Grave 102: cut 1450 (burial 1451; fill 1452)

(Fig. 2.68)

S–N, sub-rectangular, concave steep sides, flat base. 2.15 x 1.04 m, 0.25 m deep (base at 134.68 m OD). Supine, legs flexed to the right. Left arm straight, away from body, right hand at left waist.

Human bone: *c.* 85% adult *c.* 35–40 yr. female.

Grave goods:

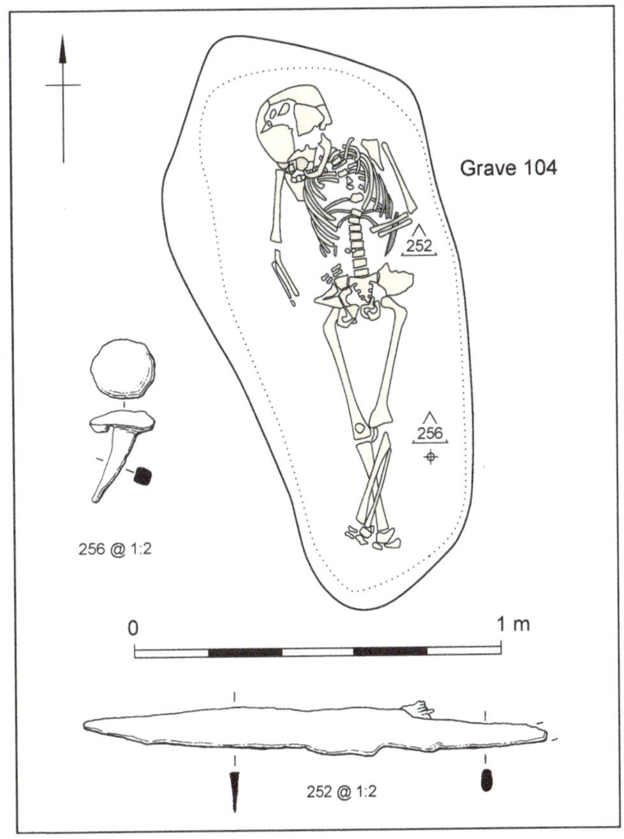

Figure 2.69 Grave 104 and grave goods

ON 272: iron knife, between left waist and left forearm, vertical, tip towards head end, at right hand. Tip missing; long tapering tang central to blade, curves gently to back of blade and ?angled to cutting edge. Back angled to tip; blade straight to tip. Böhner Type ?C. Length 91 mm; width 14 mm; thickness 4 mm.

Grave 103: cut 1453 (burial 1454; fill 1455)

(not illustrated)

WSW–ENE, incomplete sub-rectangular, rounded foot end, irregular sides, base. 1.20 x 0.63 m, 0.07 m deep (base at 135.12 m OD). Extended, supine, left leg crossed over right. Very shallow, truncated and heavy root disturbance.

Human bone: *c.* 15% s.u.l. juvenile *c.* 5–8 yr.
redep. 1 tooth, adult *c.* 18–30 yr.

Grave goods:

ON 277: iron knife, at waist inside lower left arm, vertical, direction of tip unknown. Tip missing; tapering tang central to blade, angled to back of blade and possibly to cutting edge. Back curves down to tip. Evison Type ?4. Length 103 mm; width 14 mm; thickness 4 mm. (not illustrated).

Residual finds: 1 sherd pottery (Romano-British).

Grave 104: cut 1411 (burial 1412; fill 1413)

(Fig. 2.69)

NNW–SSE, sub-rectangular, rounded foot end, pointed head end. Steep irregular sides, concave base. 1.55x 0.75 m, 0.23 m deep (base at 132.91 m OD). Extended, supine with

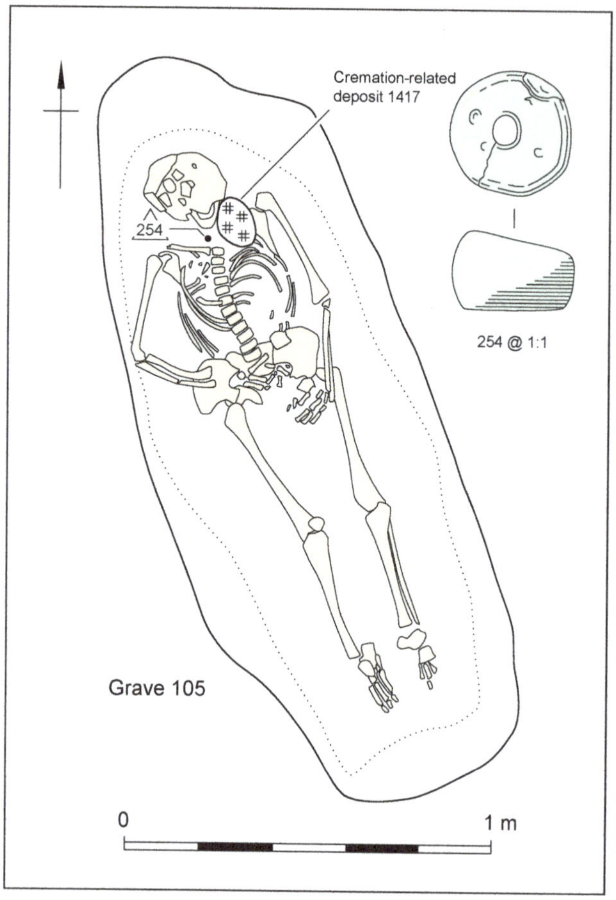

Figure 2.70 Grave 105 and glass bead

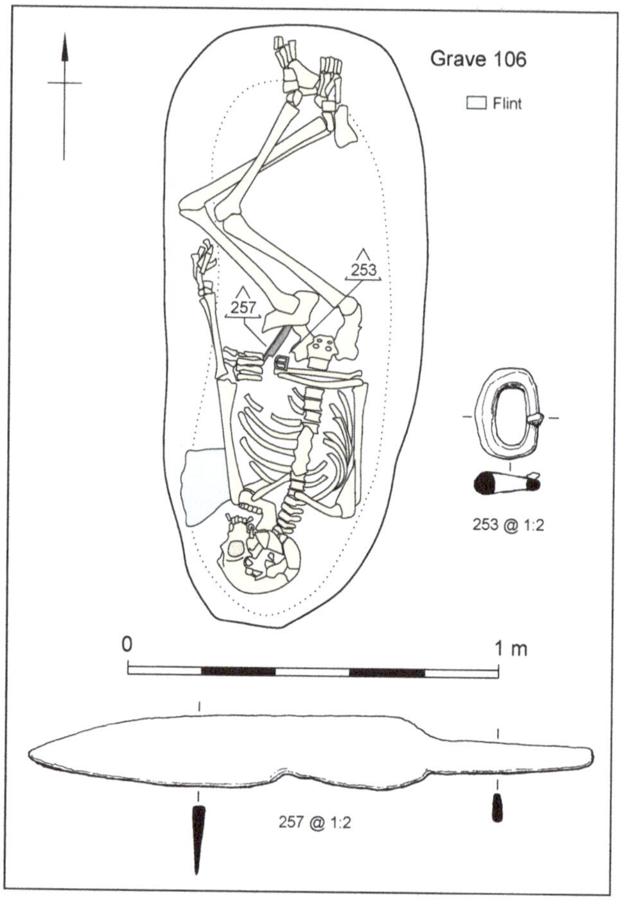

Figure 2.71 Grave 106 and grave goods

left leg crossed over right. Right arm along side, left hand over abdomen. Fill had less chalk than most.

Human bone: *c.* 80% juvenile/subadult *c.* 12–14 yr. ??female.

Grave goods:

ON 252: iron knife, at waist and partly under lower left arm, diagonal, tip towards feet. Tang central to blade, with ?sharp angle to back of blade and ?angled down to cutting edge. Back angled to tip; blade curves gently to tip. Böhner Type C. Length 125 mm; width 18 mm; thickness 4 mm.

ON 256: iron nail, between left shin and grave edge. Length 27 mm; diameter of head 18 mm.

Grave 105: cut 1414 (burial 1415; fill 1416)

(Fig. 2.70)

NW–SE, sub-rectangular, rounded head end, shallow sides, flat base. 2.06 x 0.79 m, 0.14 m deep (base at 133.10 m OD). Extended, supine, left hand over left hip, right hand over centre of pelvis. Below placed cremation deposit 1417.

Human bone: *c.* 85% adult >45 yr. female.

redep. cremated bone (1415): 1 g subadult/adult >13 yr.

?placed crd (1417): 48.4 g adult >18 yr. and 1.6 g ?animal.

Grave goods:

ON 254: glass bead, wound. In neck area. Large, colour 6.2a, shape A1.

Residual finds: 2 sherds pottery (ON 255: Romano-British; ON 259: Saxon, organic-tempered).

Grave 106: cut 1407 (burial 1408; fill 1409)

(Fig. 2.71)

S–N, sub-rectangular, rounded ends, steep sides, flat base. 1.60 x 0.65 m, 0.21 m deep (base at 133.89 m OD). Flexed on left side, slightly slumped back. Left hand towards knees, right hand at left elbow. Single, large flint nodule on SW edge of grave.

Human bone: *c.* 85% adult >45 yr. male.

Grave goods:

ON 253: simple iron buckle and fragmentary plate at waist, under right wrist. D-shaped outline, circular section; tongue missing. Length of loop 20 mm, width 25 mm.

ON 257: iron knife, under left hip, diagonal with tip towards feet. Tang central to blade, angled to back of blade and down to cutting edge; damage to blade possibly from sharpening; back angled to tip; blade possibly curves to tip. Böhner Type C. Length 152 mm; width 18 mm; thickness 4 mm.

Grave 107: cut 1449 (burial 1448; fill 1447)

(Fig. 2.72)

S–N, sub-rectangular, rounded ends, steep sides, concave base. 1.95 x 0.75 m, 0.30 m deep (base at 134.01m OD).

Extended, supine, right arm along side, left hand over sternum. Large flint nodules in backfill (not illustrated). Root disturbance.

Human bone: *c.* 98% adult *c.* 24–29 yr. male.

Grave goods:

ON 270: simple iron buckle, over right waist/elbow. D-shaped outline, circular section; tongue intact and wrapped around loop. Length of loop 19 mm; width 29 mm. X-ray shows presence of possible rivets, and a fragment of ?plate folded around loop.

ON 271: iron knife, at right waist, diagonal, point to left/feet. Tip missing; tapering tang central to blade, curving gently to back of blade and angled down to cutting edge; back angled to tip, blade straight. Böhner Type C. Length 162 mm; width 19 mm; thickness 5 mm (not illustrated).

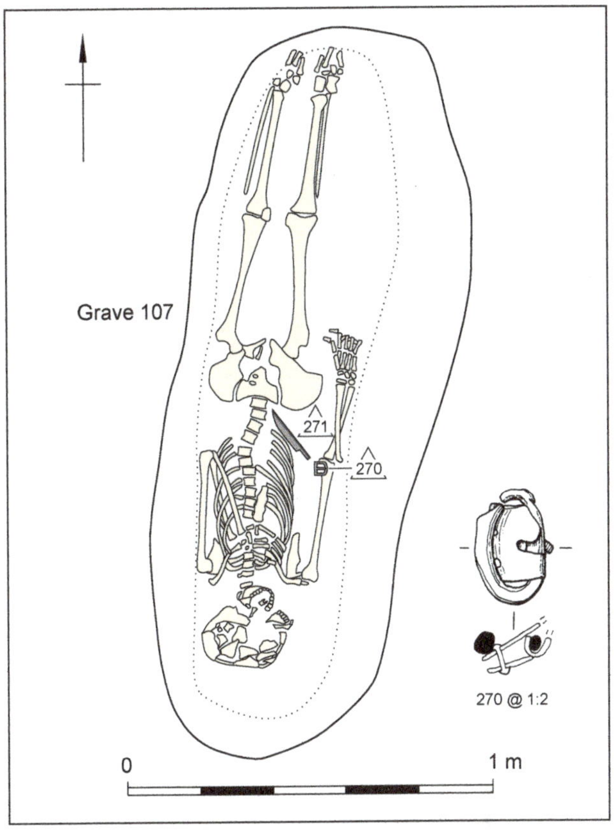

Figure 2.72 Grave 107 and iron buckle

Grave 108: cut 1404 (burial 1405; fill 1406)

(Fig. 2.73)

S–N, sub-rectangular, rounded, wider middle to head end; moderately sloping sides, flat base. 1.86 x 0.97 m, 0.32 m deep (base at 133.73 m OD). Extended, supine, right arm along side, left hand on left hip/abdomen. Skull upright, propped up against grave edge. Large flint nodules around grave sides and over the legs (not illustrated). Heavy root disturbance at foot end.

Human bone: *c.* 80% adult >50 yr. male.

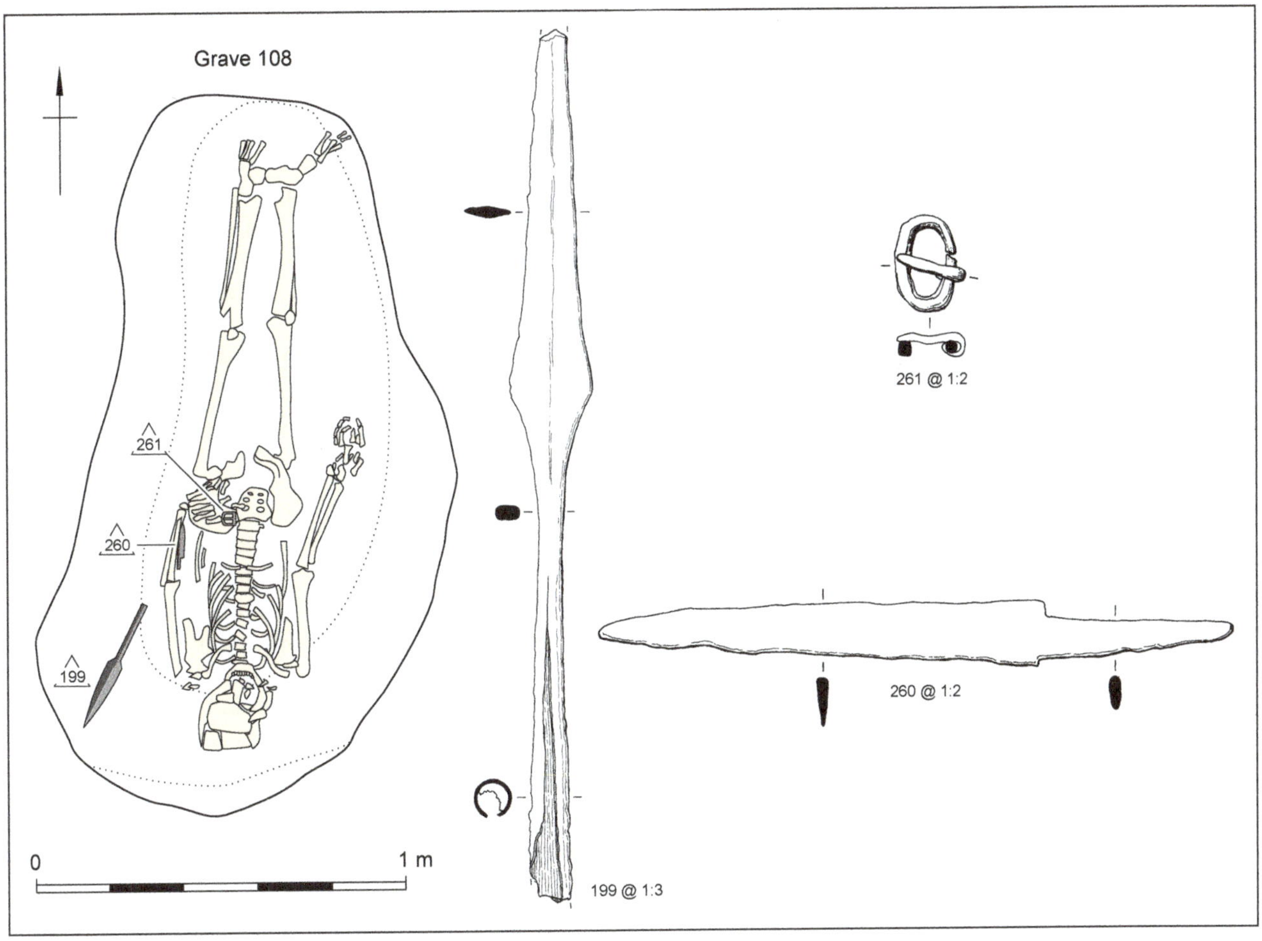

Figure 2.73 Grave 108 and grave goods

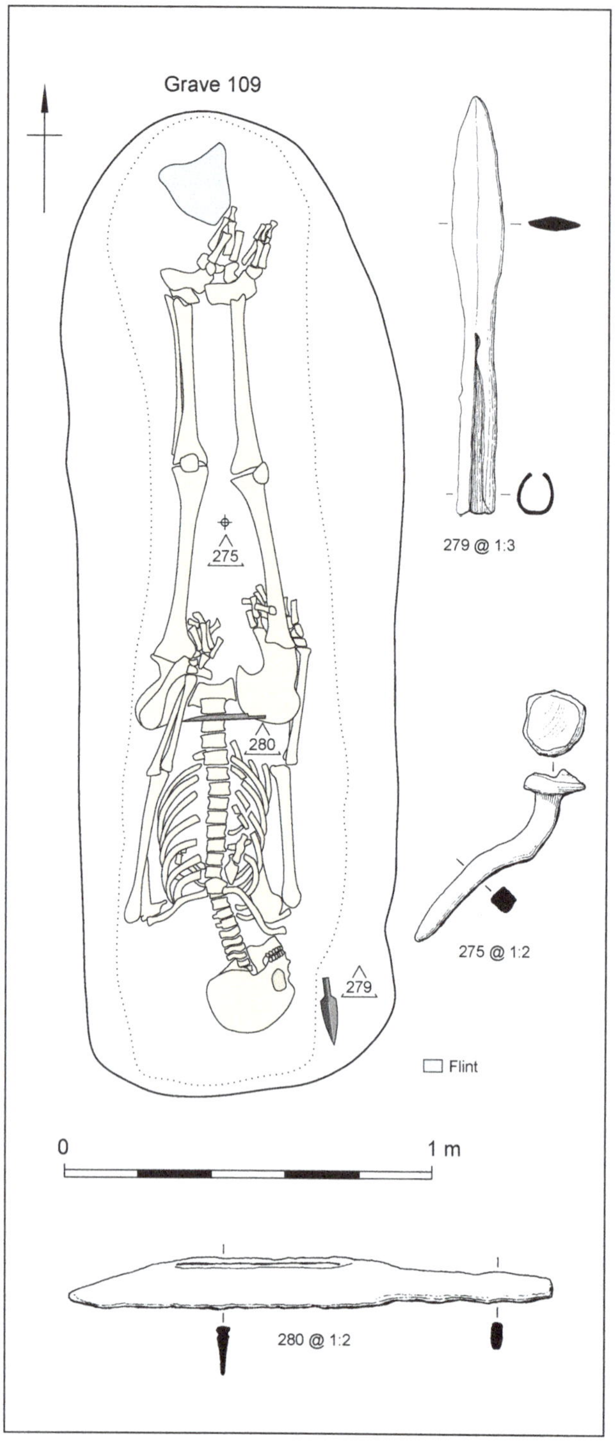

Figure 2.74 Grave 109 and grave goods

Grave goods:

ON 199: iron spearhead, to left of skull/shoulder, diagonal, tip to end of grave. Socket cleft, tip missing. Angular concave-sided blade, lozengiform section. Swanton Group H3. Length 345 mm; width 33 mm.

ON 260: slender iron knife, between waist and left forearm, vertical, direction of tip towards feet. Tapering fragmentary tang central to blade, shoulder angled to back of blade and down to cutting edge. Back straight before curving down to tip; blade apparently curves up to tip. Böhner Type ?A/C. Length 173 mm; width 16 mm; thickness 5 mm.

ON 261: simple iron buckle, centre/left waist. Oval outline and circular section; intact tongue wrapped around loop. Length 18 mm, width 26 mm.

Grave 109: cut 1437 (burial 1438; fill 1439)

(Fig. 2.74)

S–N, sub-rectangular, rounded foot end, steep sides, flat base. 2.55 x 0.90 m, 0.50 m deep (base at 133.82 m OD). Extended, supine, right hand under and left hand over respective hips. ?Shadow of ?wooden box over knees. Large flints in backfill, ? deliberate placement.

Human bone: *c.* 90% adult *c.* 30–40 yr. male.

Grave goods:

ON 275: iron nail, between thighs – ?associated with shadow over knees. Length 58 mm; diameter of head 17 mm.

ON 279: iron spearhead, right of skull, vertical, tip to end of grave. Socket cleft to 65 mm. Leaf-shaped blade; ?lozengiform section. Swanton Group C1. Length 165 mm; width 22 mm.

ON 280: iron knife, across waist, horizontal, tip to left. Tang central to blade, with gentle curve to back of blade and gentle curve down to cutting edge; back angled to tip; blade straight to tip. Böhner Type C. Length 130 mm; width 13 mm; thickness 4 mm.

Residual finds: 1 flint; 10 animal bone; 4 sherds pottery (3 Romano-British; 1 Saxon, organic-tempered).

Grave 110: cut 1434 (burial 1435; fill 1436)

(Fig. 2.75)

NE–SW, sub-rectangular, shallow sides, flat base. 2.92 x 0.87 m, 0.14 m deep (base at 134.27 m OD). Extended supine, arms along sides. Large flint nodules on knees and in other positions (not illustrated). Cut by geotechnical test pit 1456.

Human bone: *c.* 70% adult *c.* 40–50 yr. female.

Grave goods:

ON 266: iron knife, over right thigh and ON 267, vertical, tip to foot end. Tapering tang central to blade, with gentle curve to back of blade and angled down to cutting edge; back angled to tip; blade slightly curves up to tip. Böhner Type C. Length 145 mm; width 15 mm; thickness 3 mm.

ON 267: tiny and fragmentary copper alloy buckle and plate, under knife, on right thigh. Probably associated with a strap belt to which the knife was attached. Only a fragment of the loop survives; it was probably oval in outline and rectangular in section. The sheet metal plate is rectangular in outline and bent symmetrically around the loop creating the back-plate with a slot to accommodate the tongue; a pair of rivets are *in situ*. Tongue now separate but would have been wrapped around the loop. Width of loop 12 mm.

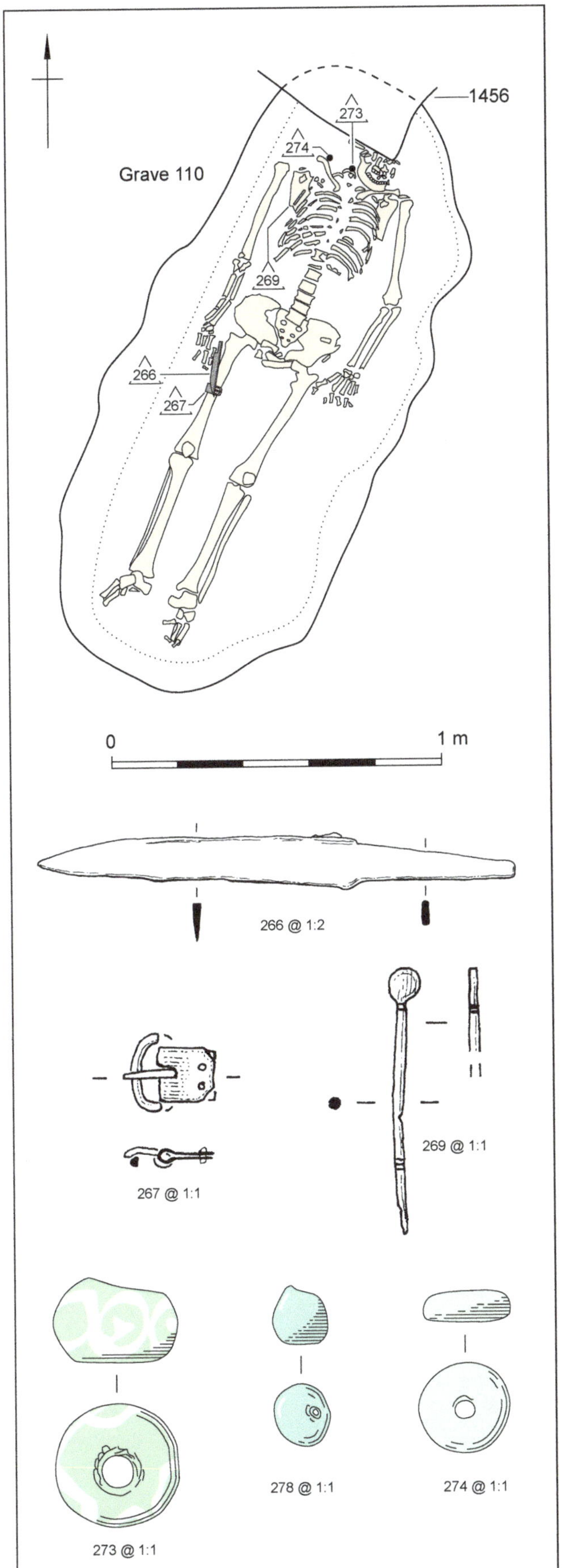

Figure 2.75 Grave 110 and grave goods

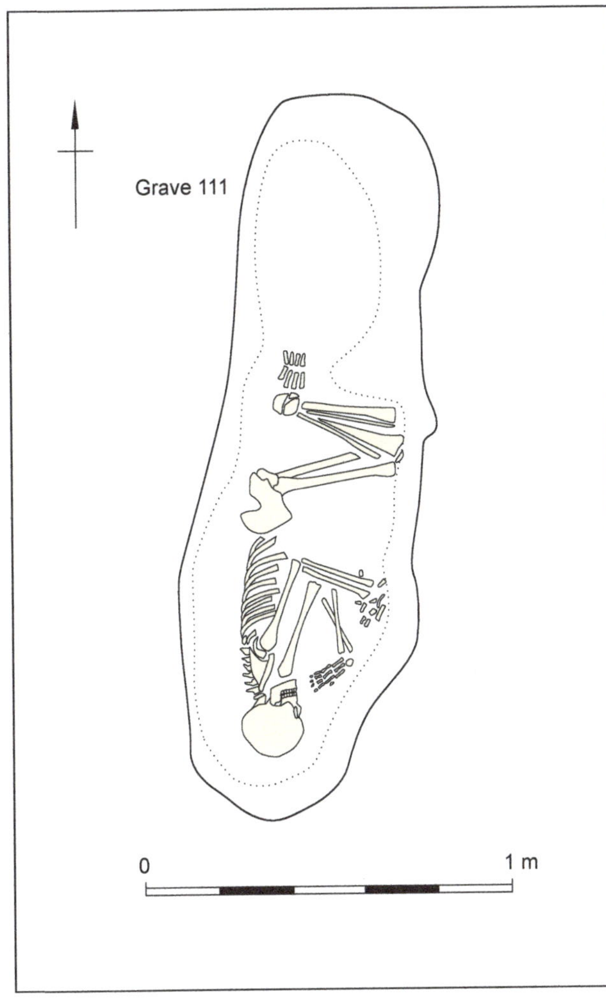

Figure 2.76 Grave 111

Plate length 9 mm; width 8 mm. Length of tongue 8 mm.

ON 269: copper alloy pin, right shoulder. Expanded and flattened circular head; rounded shank tapering to a point. It is decorated below the head by a pair of incised grooves and near the point by three similar grooves. Length 40 mm; diameter of head 4 mm.

ON 273: glass bead. Polychrome (Koch 20?). Large, shape 6.2/8.1, poly P23. Shape B1. Right neck.

ON 274: glass bead. Wound; Brugmann Doughnut. Large, colour 6.2a, shape A1. Right shoulder.

ON 278: glass bead (not located), wound. Medium, colour 7.5, shape C1.

Residual finds: 2 sherds pottery (Saxon, organic-tempered).

Grave 111: cut 1401 (burial 1402; fill 1403)

(Fig. 2.76)

S–N, sub-rectangular, rounded ends, concave moderately sloping sides, concave base. 1.94 x 0.66 m, 0.26 m deep (base at 133.66 m OD). Flexed on right side, right hand to face, left arm bent at 90 degrees to body. 0.70 m space at foot end. Bioturbation and roots.

Human bone: *c.* 90% adult *c.* 24–29 yr. female.

redep. 1 bone s. foetus *c.* 34–38 weeks.

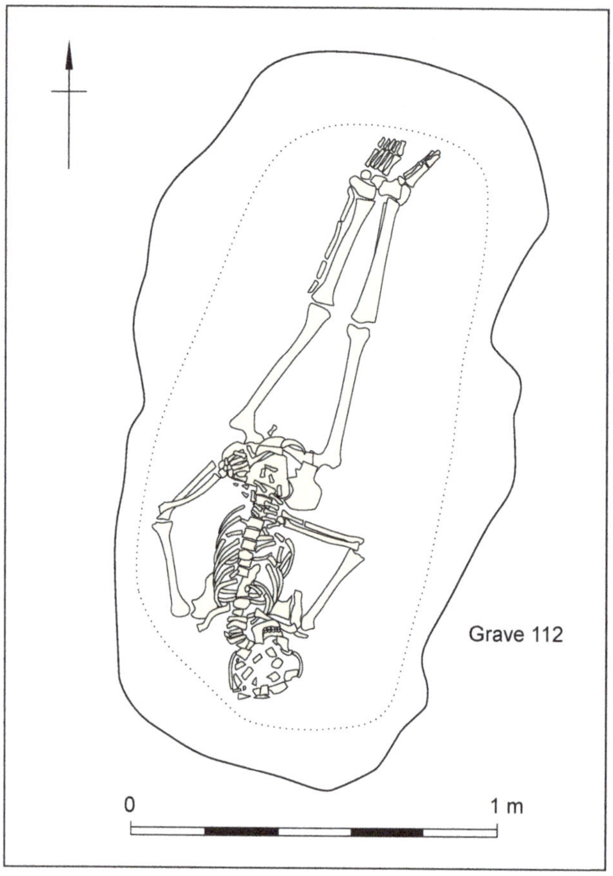

Figure 2.77 Grave 112

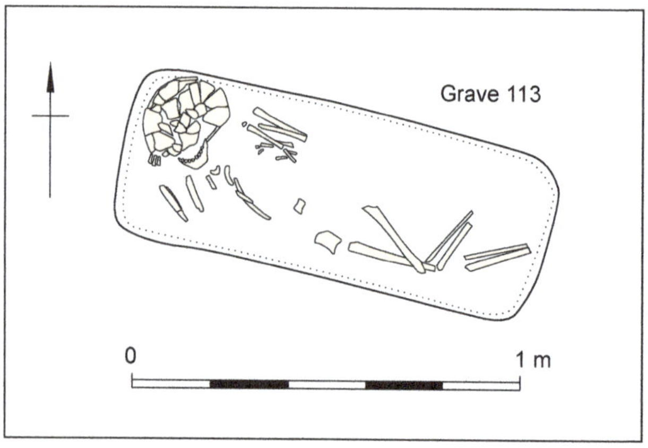

Figure 2.78 Grave 113

Grave 112: cut 1427 (burial 1428; fill 1419)
(Fig. 2.77)
SSW–NNE, sub-rectangular, shallow sides, flat base. 1.84 x 0.97 m, 0.26 m deep (base at 133.60 m OD). Extended supine, hands over pelvis.
Human bone: *c.* 75% adult *c.* 24–29 yr. ?female.

Grave 113; cut 113 (burial 114; fill 115)
(Fig. 2.78)
WNW–ESE, rectangular, steep, concave sides, flat base. 1.11 x 0.43 m, 0.06 m deep (base at 132.72 m OD). Flexed, on right side, torso supine, hands either side of skull. Occasional charcoal flecks in fill. Shallow due to truncation.
Human bone: *c.* 45% juvenile *c.* 6–8 yr.

Grave 114; cut 110 (burial 111; fill 112)
(Fig. 2.79 – ON 1000 only)
SSE–NNW, sub-rectangular, rounded northern end. Steep concave sides, flat base. 1.98 x 1.08 m, 0.17 m deep (base at 132.35 m OD – deepest at N end due to surface slope). Highly disturbed (?revisited in antiquity), but suspect head at S, width suggests flexed. Modern post through S end. Fill has darker patches and contains charcoal flecks.
Human bone: *c.* 15% s.u.l. adult >35 yr. male.
redep. cremated bone: 0.2 g human.
Grave goods:
ON 1000: iron knife blade. Oval-sectioned tang, angled shoulder up to back of blade, slope to cutting edge. Back straight before gently curving down to tip; blade straight. Böhner Type C, Evison Type 4. Length 232 mm, width 18 mm, thickness 4 mm.
Residual/other finds:
ON 1001: iron nails (not illustrated, probably modern.
Pottery: seven sherds (one late prehistoric; two Romano-British; four Saxon, organic-tempered).

Grave 115; cut 119 (burial 120; fill 121)
(Fig. 2.80)
S–N, sub-rectangular, rounded foot end. Steep, straight sides, flat base. 1.64 x 0.87 m, 0.18 m deep (base at 132.34 m OD). supine, legs flexed to left, arms by sides. Shallow due to truncation. Upper part of fill loose indicating disturbance.

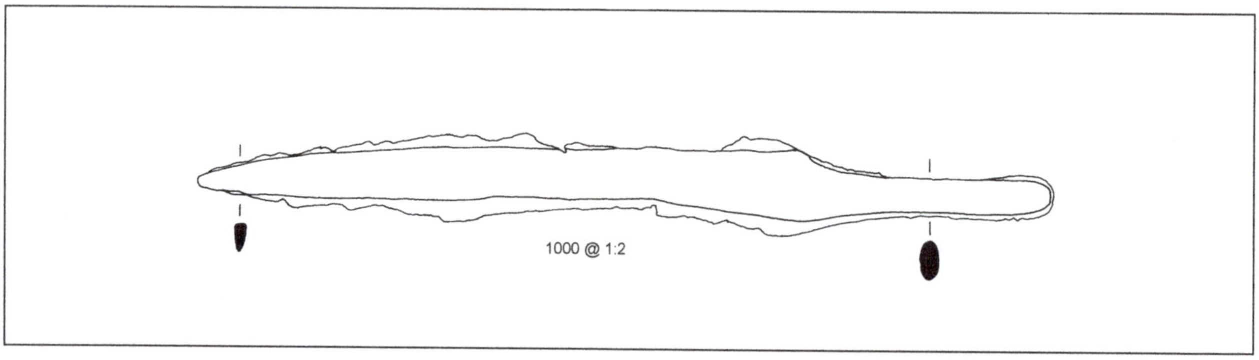

Figure 2.79 iron knife from grave 114

Human bone: *c*. 90% adult >50 yr. female.
Grave goods:
ON 1003: copper alloy object (not located or illustrated). 2 small fragments. Largest 16 x 10 mm, folded over on itself, possibly rim binding. Smallest 10 x 3 mm.
ON 1004: iron knife blade. Left waist, point to left. 3 fragments. Tang and blade. Tang slopes up to back and down to blade. Back appears to slope down to cutting edge, blade may be sloping up to meet back. Possible Böhner Type A. Length 132 mm, width 15 mm, thickness 4 mm.
ON 1005: iron ?pin. By right hand. Fragmentary iron rod in two pieces, with remains of ?textile twisted around it. Probably shank of a pin. Length 36 mm (longest fragment), 10 mm (smallest).

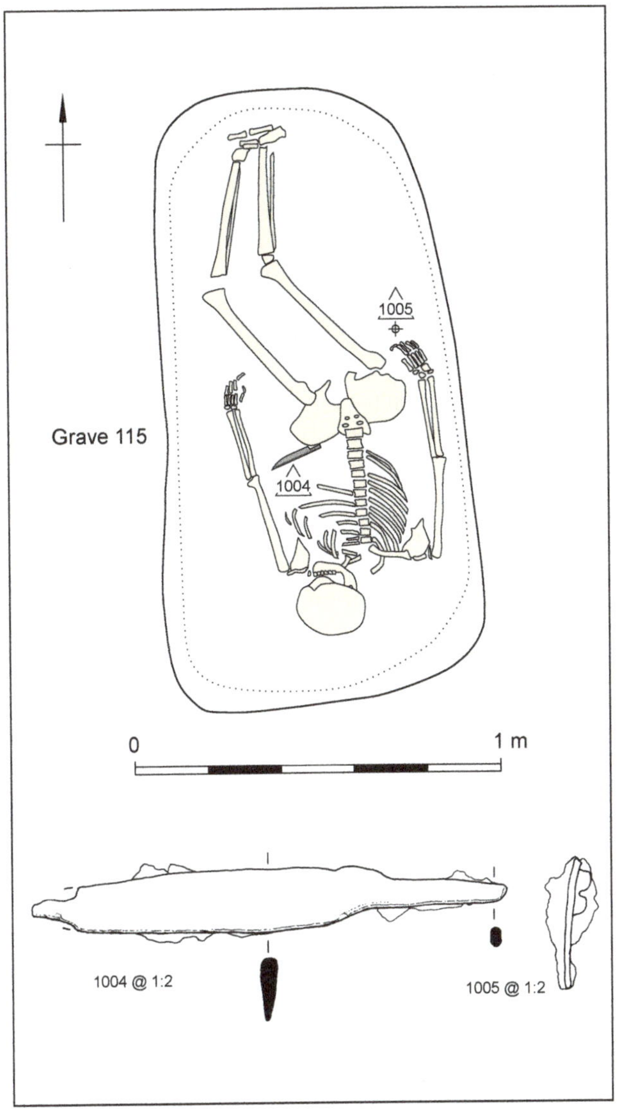

Figure 2.80 Grave 115 and selected grave goods

Grave 116; cut 116 (burial 117; fill 118)
(Fig. 2.81)
W–E, sub-rectangular to oval, steep, straight sides, flat base. 1.85 x 0.90 m, 0.08 m deep (base at 132.25 m OD). Extended, supine with arms by the sides. Shallow due to truncation. Heavy bioturbation (roots).
Human bone: *c*. 90% adult *c*. 35–45 yr. male.
redep. cremated bone 1.4 g subadult/adult.
Grave goods:
ON 1002: ?iron knife blade. Two fragments of blade under right hip, point towards feet. Length 50 mm (longest fragment), width 10 mm, thickness 4 mm. Cannot discern shape of blade or type.
Pottery vessel: 10 sherds organic-tempered pottery, probably from same vessel, form unknown, ?disturbed grave good.
Residual/other finds:
Pottery: two sherds (one Romano-British; one Saxon, organic-tempered).

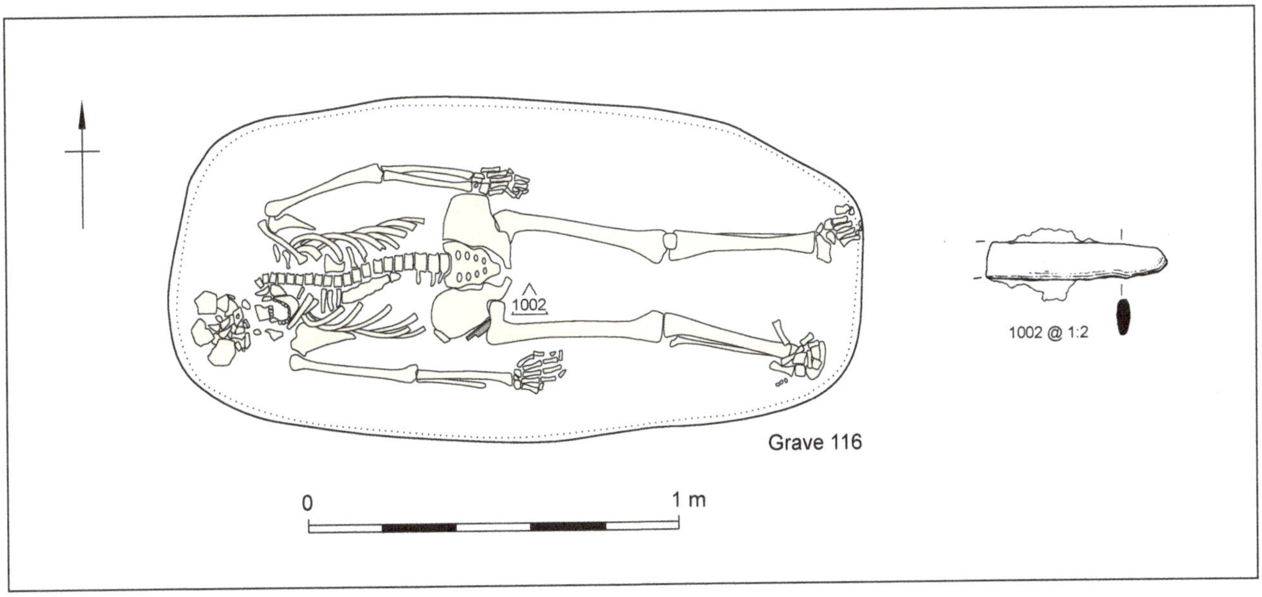

Figure 2.81 Grave 116 and fragmentary knife

Cremation Graves and Cremation-related Features

Key: crd – cremation-related deposit; rpd – redeposited pyre debris; u. – urned; un. – unurned.

NB not including cremated bone from inhumation graves (see above) or structure 1268; (see McKinley, Chapter 3).

Cremation grave 1264 (burial 1501; fill 1265)
(Fig. 2.82)
Sub-circular, moderately sloping sides and flat base. 0.47 x 0.39 m, 0.09 m deep (base at 135.16 m OD), although probably overcut. Shallow and disturbed, potentially *ex situ.*
Cremated human bone: u. burial, 22.3 g, infant *c.* 1–3 yr.
Cinerary urn:
ON 99: Pottery vessel (nine sherds), organic-tempered fabric, very friable. Body sherds only.

Cremation grave 1266 (burial 1502; fill 1267)
(Fig. 2.82)
Incomplete, ?sub-circular, steep sides and flat base. 0.47 x 0.47 m, 0.15 m deep (base at 135.29 m OD), although probably overcut. Very truncated and disturbed, potentially *ex situ*; just the base of the vessel and some of its contents sitting proud of the surface.
Cremated human bone: ?u. burial (+ grave fill), 28.1 g, adult >18 yr.
Cinerary urn:
ON 100: Pottery vessel (23 sherds), sandy fabric, body sherds only.

Cremation grave 1269 (burial 1277; fills 1270, 1278)
(Fig. 2.82)
Circular, moderately sloping concave sides and concave base. 0.59 x 0.59 m, 0.16 m (base at 135.18 m OD). Fairly sterile backfill around, some under urn.
Cremated human bone: u. burial +?rpd, 147.3 g, juvenile *c.* 5–6 yr.
Cinerary urn:
ON 104: Pottery vessel (99 sherds), sandy fabric; rim, body and base sherds; biconical profile with hollow neck and everted rim, and flattened base. Possibly at least partially burnished.

Cremation-related feature 1272 (fills 1503 and 1273)
(Fig. 2.82)
Sub-circular, moderately sloping sides and concave base. 0.35 x 0.34 m, 0.11 m deep (base at 135.37 m OD). Very truncated.
Cremated human bone: ?redep. u. burial, 1.9 g, subadult/adult >13 yr.
Grave goods:
ON 105: Pottery vessel (four sherds), organic-tempered fabric; body sherds.

Cremation grave 1297 (burial and fill 1298)
(not illustrated)
Oval, concave sides and base. 0.28 x 0.23 m, 0.07 m deep (base at 133.46 m OD). Dark greyish brown silty clay loam fill with abundant burnt bone and charcoal inclusions. Cut into grave 92.
Cremated human bone: un. burial + rpd, 296.1 g, adult *c.* 18–25 yr. ?female.

Cremation-related feature 1310 (fill 1311)
(see Fig. 2.1)
Circular, vertical sides and concave base. 0.46 x 0.46 m, 0.49 m deep (base at 134.01 m OD). Single fill dark greyish brown silty clay loam with common chalk and charcoal flecks. Located in centre of mortuary structure 1268. Rpd in fills of structure (1313, 1323, 1325 and 1327).
Cremated human bone: ?redep. u. burial + rpd, 18.8 g, subadult/adult >18 yr.
?Cinerary Urn:
Pottery vessel (six sherds; one may be from second vessel), organic-tempered; rim and body sherds, rounded profile with everted rim.
Residual finds:
ON 1015: perforated stone – bead?

Cremation-related feature 1418 (fills 1415 and 1417)
(not illustrated)
Sub-circular with ?concave sides and base. 0.15 x 0.15 m, 0.06 m deep (base at 133.21 m OD). Dark greyish brown silty clay loam with charcoal and burnt bone. Cut into grave 105 (see Fig. 2.70).
Cremated human bone: ?placed crd, 48.4 g, adult >18 yr.
redep.: 1 g subadult/adult >13 yr.
Other: 1.6 g ?animal bone.

Cremation-related feature 1440 (fill 1441)
(not illustrated)
Sub-circular, steep sides, concave base. 0.42 x 0.42 m, 0.15 m deep (base at 133.23 m OD). Dark grey silty clay loam with charcoal and rare burnt bone.
Cremated human bone: ?redep. 5.9 g, subadult/adult >13 yr.
Other: sheep/pig tooth root.

Cremation-related feature 1442 (fill 1443)
(Fig. 2.82)
Circular, steep concave sides and base. 0.42 x 0.42 m, 0.20 m deep (base at 133.97 m OD). Dark greyish brown silty clay loam with charcoal and burnt bone.
Cremated human bone: ?redep. u. burial + rpd, 56.7 g, adult >25 yr. ??male.
?Cinerary Urn:
Pottery vessel (11 sherds), organic-tempered; body and two small rim sherds; profile not reconstructable.

Cremation-related feature 1462/1464 (fill 1461/1463)
(Fig. 2.82)
Sub-circular, moderately sloping concave sides and base. 0.44 x 0.33 m, 0.16 m deep (base at 134.57 m OD). Dark grey silty clay loam with rare charcoal and burnt bone. Cut into 1464.
Cremated human bone: ?redep./?rpd, 19.5 g, subadult/adult >13 yr.
Other: herring vertebra.

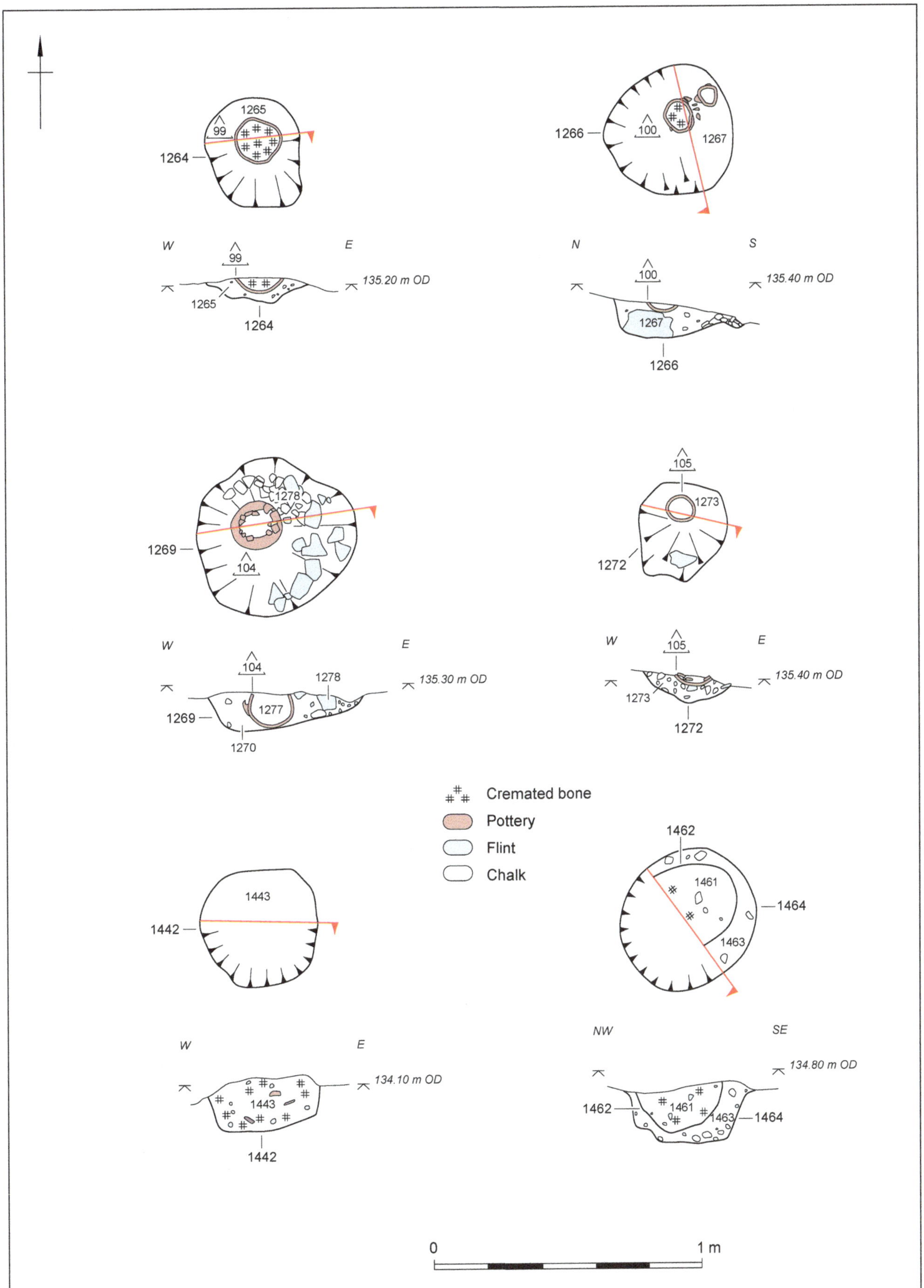

Figure 2.82 Plans and sections of cremation graves and pits containing cremation-related deposits – 1264, 1266, 1269, 1272, 1442, 1462

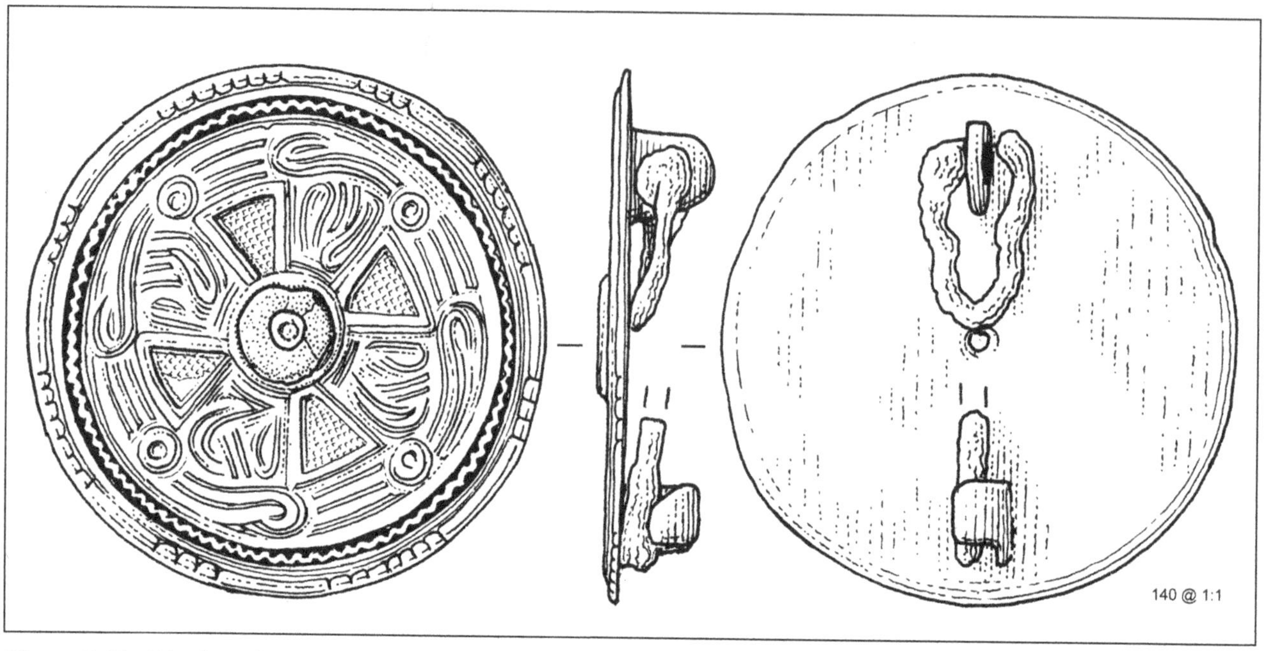

Figure 2.83 Disc brooch

Cremation-related feature 1480 (fill 1481)

(see Fig. 2.62)

Circular, steep sides and concave base. 0.35 x 0.35 m, 0.28 m deep (base at 136.12 m OD). Dark greyish brown silty clay loam with charcoal and burnt bone inclusions. Cut into grave 96 (see grave entry for ?placed crd information).

Cremated human bone: crd incl. rpd, 8.7 g, subadult/adult >13 yr.

Cremation-related feature 1489 (fill 1490)

(not illustrated)

Circular, steep irregular sides and concave base. 0.30 x 0.30 m, 0.08 m deep (base at 137.55 m OD). Very dark grey silty loam.

Cremated human bone: redep. ?inc. rpd, 3.9 g, subadult/adult >13 yr.

?Cremation-related feature 1493 (fill 1494)

(not illustrated)

Sub-circular. 0.85 x 0.55 m, 0.16 m deep (base at 136.85 m OD). Charcoal-rich.

Cremated human bone: ?redep. 5.9 g, subadult/adult >13 yr.

Other: pottery (Saxon, organic-tempered).

Unstratified Metalwork – Probable Grave Goods

ON 3: iron cleat. Length 29 mm; width across top 11 mm (not illustrated).

ON 111: iron spearhead, socket cleft for *c.* 80 mm, rivet *c.* 19 mm from end of socket. Angular, concave-sided blade, lozengiform section. Concavity less marked on one side due to damage to the blade in that area. Swanton Group H1. length 199 mm; width 27 mm (not illustrated).

ON 112: iron spearhead, socket cleft for *c.* 50 mm, rivet *c.* 7 mm from end of socket. Angular, concave-sided blade, lozengiform section. Damage removed one of the 'wings'. Swanton Group H1. length 151 mm; width 25 mm (not illustrated).

ON 140: copper alloy garnet disc brooch (Fig. 2.83). Front displays traces of gilding. The brooch has suffered damage: there are broken and missing garnets and the rim exhibits wear. Central circular boss with a garnet in a setting of shell or bone, and four triangular raised cells contain, or would have contained, triangular garnets. Behind are gold foils stamped with a cross-hatched pattern. Four Style II zoomorphic animals: curving jaws of each grips the hind leg of the one in front. Raised border with a (crude) zig-zag motif and beaded rim with alternating plain and ribbed zones. Closest in style to Avent's Type 7.2.

ON 149: copper alloy rotary key; ring head, hollow shaft (damaged at bottom), flat ward (broken). Length 31 mm; width 4 mm; diameter of ring 12 mm. Comparable examples can be cited from both Roman and later medieval contexts (not illustrated).

Chapter 3
Human Skeletal Material

Unburnt Human Bone

by Kirsten Egging Dinwiddy

Unburnt human bone from 91 contexts was analysed, comprising the remains of 82 *in situ* burials (later 5th–later 7th century), including a 'bed' burial, and redeposited material (16 contexts) from grave fills, subsoil, a lynchet and the coombe (Table 3.1).

Methods

The degree of erosion to the bone was recorded using the standard system of grading (McKinley 2004a, fig. 6.1–7). Age was estimated utilising the stage of tooth and skeletal development (Beek 1983; Scheuer and Black 2000), and the patterns and degree of age-related changes to the bone (Buikstra and Ubelaker 1994). Sex was assessed from the sexually dimorphic traits of the skeleton (Bass 1987; Buikstra and Ubelaker 1994). Where the quantity and quality of sexing criteria was compromised, the indicated sex may be qualified (possible/probable). Measurements were taken (Brothwell and Zakrzewski 2004) and skeletal indices calculated where possible (Trotter and Gleser 1952; 1958; Bass 1987; Schwartz 1995). Non-metric traits were recorded in accordance with Berry and Berry (1967) and Finnegan (1978).

Results

A summary of the results is presented in Table 3.1. Full details are in the archive.

Disturbance and condition

All the graves were cut into the heavily weathered chalk and clay-with-flints geology. Surviving grave depths ranged between 0.03 m and 0.70 m (average: adult 0.28 m, immature 0.17 m). Many had been truncated by erosion and others by landscaping and geotechnical test pits. Root action was the main cause of disturbance in most cases, though it rarely resulted in substantial disruption of the buried remains. Intercutting between features comprised occasional deliberate grave re-use or later insertions (eg, graves 59 and 60, 65 and 66; cremation grave 1297 and cremation-related feature 1480), and minor accidental truncation (graves 76–77). Grave 82 cut through part of structure 1268. Whilst most burials remained undisturbed, the presence of redeposited bone in a number of grave fills implies that this was not always the case. The low level of intercutting and presence of apparent plots (see Stoodley, Chapter 5) suggests that most graves were marked or remembered in some way.

Half of the bone from the *in situ* burial remains and most of the redeposited material is in fair to good condition (grade 3 or better). The poorest preservation was noted amongst the most variably preserved skeletal remains (16% *in situ*). Erosion and root etching were the primary causes of degradation. Fragmentation is common, rarely heavy, and predominantly the result of crushing in antiquity. Though variable, skeletal recovery from *in situ* burial remains was in most cases good to very good – 58% over 60% complete, and 45% over 80% complete (Table 3.1; *Grave Catalogue*). The greater degree of preservation in the redeposited material suggests that the bones had moved prior to, and were consequently relatively protected from the major destructive forces – crushing, root etching and erosive action.

Pale to dark purplish-grey mottling across many bones was probably caused by roots and fungus, while the iron and copper elements of a number of grave goods had stained a number of bones. The remains from graves 70 and 105 have a soapy texture, the reasons for which remain unclear.

Demography

The assemblage comprises a substantial proportion of the original cemetery population. A minimum of 90 individuals (MNI) are represented in the assemblage – 82 from *in situ* remains and eight from the redeposited bone – bringing the excavated total to over 120 (Table 3.2).

The proportion of immature individuals (40%) is comparable to that recorded for Lechlade, Gloucestershire (40%; Harman 1998, 52), Twyford School, Hampshire (39.1%; Egging Dinwiddy 2011), and Andover, Hampshire (36.2%; Cook and Dacre 1985, 67). A higher rate was noted at Blacknall Field, Wiltshire (47.5%; Stuckert 2010, 113), while smaller proportions were recorded at Worthy Park, Hampshire (30.8%; Wells *et al.* 2003, 159, table 3.6) and Aldbourne, Wiltshire (19.2%; Boylston 2012).

Table 3.1 Summary of results from human bone analysis

Grave	*Context*	*Cut*	*Deposit type*	*Quantification*	*Age/sex*	*Pathology*
35	1181	1179	*in situ*	*c.* 10% s.a.l.	infant *c.* 2–3 yr.	–
36	1229	1228	*in situ*	*c.* 55%	juvenile *c.* 5–8 yr. ???male	dental caries; enamel hypoplasia; pd; *cribra orbitalia*; mv – wormian bone
37	1225	1224	*in situ*	*c.* 40%	juvenile *c.* 5–8 yr.	dental caries; enamel hypoplasia; *cribra orbitalia*
38	1203	1202	*in situ*	*c.* 85%	adult *c.* 25–35 yr. female	apical void; calculus; dental caries; enamel hypoplasia; pd; pnb – maxilla; sinusitis – right; destructive lesion – carpals, MtCs, ?right femur, distal phalanges (hands); plastic changes – humeri, radii, ulnae; mv – paramolars, wormian bones
39	1199	1198	*in situ*	*c.* 70%	adult *c.* 35–40 yr. female	calculus; pd; destructive lesions – distal phalanges (hands); Sch – T7, T10–12, L1–2; exo – L2; cortical defect – right clavicle; plastic changes – ulnae; mv – sacralisation (L6)
40	1174a	1173	*in situ*	*c.* 40%	infant *c.* 2–3 yr.	?apical void; *cribra orbitalia*; pnb – orbit (scurvy); cranial hyperporosity & thickening; rickets – limbs (bowing)
	1174b		redep.	frags a.u.	subadult/adult > 16 yr.	–
41	1222a	1221	*in situ*	*c.* 90%	adult >45 yr. female	apical void (infection); amtl; calculus; dental caries; pd; secondary sinusitis; osteoporosis; solitary bone cyst – left carpal; Sch – T10–12, L1–3; oa – C2–5, T1, T8; enth – innominates; ossified cartilage – thyroid, 1st ribs; mv – L6
	1222b		redep	1 tooth	juvenile *c.* 6–8 yr.	–
42	1188	1189	*in situ*	*c.* 30%	infant *c.* 1.5–2.5 yr.	dental enamel hypoplasia
43	1242	1241	*in situ*	*c.* 95%	adult *c.* 24–29 yr. female	calculus; dental caries; enamel hypoplasia; pd; fracture – right distal ulna, right MtC; pnb – right distal ulna; destructive lesion – right distal humerus, proximal right ulna, left carpals; Sch – T9, T11–12, L1–3; cortical defect – left talus; mv – wormian bones
44	1487	1486	*in situ*	10 frags s.u.	adult >35 yr.	calculus; dental caries
45	1250	1251	*in situ*	*c.* 85%	adult *c.* 40–50 yr. male	apical void; calculus; dental caries; pd; *cribra orbitalia*; fracture – left 2nd MtT; pnb – L5; sinusitis (left); ?cysts – left carpals; ddd – C3–5, T5–6, T11, L4–5, S1; oa – T11; op – Ts, Ls; enth – sacroiliac, innominates, left radius, proximal femora; cortical defect – ishium, left proximal radius; ossified cartilage – 1st ribs; MtCs; coalition – left 3rd MtC
46	1234	1233	*in situ*	*c.* 10% a.u.l.	subadult/ adult >14 yr.	–
47	1231	1227	*in situ*	*c.* 60%	adult *c.* 24–29 yr. female	apical void; calculus; dental caries; pd; spondylolysis – L5; secondary sinusitis (left); pnb – left 3rd MtC; Sch – T8, T11; cortical defect – clavicles, right 1st MtT, 1st proximal phalanx (foot), right calcaneum; plastic changes – right 4–5th MtTs; mv – *os acromiale*
48	1238	1236	*in situ*	*c.* 5% s.	neonate/ infant	cranial thickening

49	1248	1246	*in situ*	*c.* 15% s.l.	juvenile *c.* 6–8 yr.	mv – wormian bones
50	1206	1205	*in situ*	*c.* 40%	juvenile *c.* 4–6 yr.	cortical defect – clavicles
51	1167	1166	*in situ*	*c.* 25%	adult >45 yr. ??female	calculus; dental caries; enth – right patella
52	1194	1193	*in situ*	*c.* 30% a.u.l.	adult >45 yr. male	destructive lesion – left distal phalanx; ddd – T, L, S1; Sch – T; oa – T; mv – proximal femora
53	1191	1190	*in situ*	*c.* 60%	juvenile *c.* 4–7 yr.	dental caries; pd; *cribra orbitalia*; ?rickets – right C1, clavicle (deformation) hyperporosity & thinning – exocranial surfaces; mv – additional lamina (C2)
54	1185	1184	*in situ*	2 teeth & frags	adult >45 yr. ??male	calculus
55	1177	1176	*in situ*	*c.* 90%	adult >40 yr. female	apical void; amtl; calculus; dental caries; dental enamel hypoplasia; pd; fracture – left fibula; Rhino-maxillary resorption (leprosy); destructive lesions – distal phalanges (hands & feet); pnb – right femur (?ulcer), right tibia, fibulae; oa – T7; enth – innominates, calcanea; cortical defect – clavicles, right femur
56	1201	1196	*in situ*	*c.* 30%	juvenile *c.* 4–6 yr.	–
57	1216	1215	*in situ*	*c.* 40%	adult >55 yr. female	calculus; pd; cranial thickening & hyperporosity; oa – T; ossified cartilage – thyroid and rib; hydatid cyst; mv – tooth rotation, bipartate Cs
58	1213	1214	*in situ*	*c.* 90%	adult >50 yr. male	amtl; apical void; calculus; dental caries; pd; *cribra orbitalia*; fracture – L4 (body), 3 ribs; fusion – L3–4; ddd – T9–11, L3, L5, S1; Sch – T5–12, L1–2; oa – T2, T11–12; op – L1–2, S1, ribs; enth – ishium, right 1st MtC, 1st proximal phalanx, patellae; exo – left clavicle; ossified cartilage – thyroid; cortical defect – clavicles, 1st distal phalanx (hand); mv – wormian bones, cervical rib
59	1132	1150	*in situ*	*c.* 70%	adult >50 yr. male	calculus; enamel hypoplasia; pd; cranial thickening; sinusitis (right); pnb – endocranial occipital; solitary bone cyst – right carpal; op – right ribs, sacroiliac (bi-) (?ankylosing spondylitis), right glenoid, patellae/distal femora; pitting – right acetabulum; enth – right radius, right ulna, femora, calcanea; cortical defect – right glenoid
60	1104	1103	*in situ*	*c.* 99%	adult *c.* 35–45 yr. male	amtl; apical void; calculus; enamel hypoplasia; hypercementosis; pd; solitary bone cyst – right 1st MtC; destructive lesions – right tibia, fibula, tarsals; ddd – T11–12; Sch – T6–11; oa – T11–12, ribs; op – sterno-claviculars, right proximal humerus, glenoids; pitting – acromio-claviculars; enth – ischia, femora, patellae, right tibia, calcanea; ossified cartilage – thyroid, rib; cortical defect – right glenoid; mv – wormian bones, ribs (articular facets absent)
61	1117	1116	*in situ*	*c.* 75%	adult *c.* 45–55 yr. female	apical void; calculus; dental caries; pd; *cribra orbitalia*; secondary sinusitis (left); pnb – mandible, maxilla, sacrum, tibiae, fibulae, tarsal, left 1st MtT (osteomyelitis?); osteoporosis; ddd – T11–12; oa – T10; op – S1 (bsm, ap), right ribs, fibulae; pitting – left temporo-mandibular, acromio-claviculars, sterno-claviculars; exo – right 1st MtC, left 1st MtT; enth – right femur, tibiae, fibulae; mv – wormian bones
62	1158a	1157	*in situ*	*c.* 70%	adult >55 yr. female	calculus; dental caries; pd; destructive lesion – left humerus, left femur; ddd – 1T, L2–S1; oa – 1T, L1–S1; op – L1–5 ap, left sterno-clavicular; pitting – left sterno-clavicular; enth – right sacroiliac, left humerus, femora, right tibia, calcanea, MtTs; cortical defect – left humerus; ossified rib cartilage; ?kidney stone; hdatid cysts; cortical defect – left tibia; mv – bipartite canine
	1158b		= 1161a	*c.* 5% s.a.	infant *c.* 1.5–3 yr.	–

Table 3.1 Continued

Grave	*Context*	*Cut*	*Deposit type*	*Quantification*	*Age/sex*	*Pathology*
63	1161a	1160	*in situ*	*c.* 20%	infant *c.* 1.5–3 yr.	enamel hypoplasia; pnb – endocranial, ethmoid, left radius, left tibia, right fibula; oa – 1T
	1161b		= 1158a	9 frags a.	adult >55 yr. female	–
64	1101	1100	*in situ* = 1106b, 1109 & 1110	*c.* 95%	adult *c.* 35–45 yr. female	amtl; apical void; calculus; dental caries; enamel hypoplasia; pd; destructive lesion – left 4th MtC; ddd – C4–7, T10, L3–5; Sch – T8, T10, L1–3; op – C1–7 ap, bsm, ribs, left proximal ulna, distal radii, MtPs (hands); pitting – left temporo-mandibular, left proximal humerus; enth – innominates, right glenoid, femora, right fibula; ossified cartilage – rib; mv – wormian bones, incipient *coxa vara*
65	1275	1274	*in situ*	*c.* 65%	infant *c.* 2–4 yr.	*cribra orbitalia*; hyperporosity – left temporal; mv – wormian bones
66	1290	1291	*in situ*	*c.* 85 %	adult *c.* 25–40 yr. female	dental caries; enamel hypoplasia; pd; pnb – 5 left ribs (visceral, ?tuberculosis); *os dissecans* – left femur; Sch – 1T, L3-5; enth – left innominate; cortical defect – left ilium, right clavicle; plastic changes – ulnae; mv – wormian bones, asymmetric C2
67	1336	1335	*in situ*	*c.* 25% s.u.l.	infant *c.* 3–4 yr.	enamel hypoplasia; endocranial 'hair-on-end'
68	1281	1280	*in situ*	*c.* 85%	adult *c.* 30–40 yr. female	amtl; apical void; calculus; dental caries; enamel hypoplasia; pd; hyperporosity – maxilla; plastic change – humeri, ulnae; mv – variant Ps
69	1347	1348	*in situ*	*c.* 60%	adult *c.* 30–45 yr. female	calculus; pd; cranial thickening; ?mastoiditis – right
70	1373	1372	*in situ*	*c.* 65%	juvenile *c.* 12–14 yr.	calculus; enamel hypoplasia; pd; thickening & hyperporosity – maxilla; mv – variant I2s
71	1385	1384	*in situ*	*c.* 5% s.a.u.	infant *c.* 1–2 yr.	mv – wormian bone
72	1388	1387	*in situ*	*c.* 95%	adult *c.* 30–40 yr. male	calculus; dental caries; enamel hypoplasia; trepanation – left parietal; trauma – left proximal femur; Sch – T7, L3; hyperporosity – palate; enth – calcanea; cortical defect – right temporo-mandibular, clavicles, right femur shaft, calcanea, left tarsal; mv – diminutive rib articular surfaces
73	1379	1378	*in situ*	*c.* 45% a.u.l.	adult *c.* 35–45 yr. ?female	Sch – 1T, L3
74	1356a	1355	*in situ*	*c.* 95%	adult *c.* 30–35 yr. female	calculus; enamel hypoplasia; pd; sinusitis (left); pnb – right nasal aperture, left femora; Sch – T6, T8–12, L1–4; cortical defect – right clavicle; right distal humerus; mv – tooth crowding & rotation, wormian bones, double atlas facets, atlas bridging
	1356b		*in utero*	*c.* 45%	foetus *c.* 32–36 weeks	overall poor mineralisation, widespread pnb – ?metabolic deficiency
	1356c		redep.	2 teeth	infant/ juvenile *c.* 2–8 yr.	–
	1356d		redep.	a few frags a	neonate/infant *c.* 0–1 yr.	–

75	1350	1349	*in situ*	*c.* 95%	adult >45 yr. female	calculus; enamel hypoplasia; pd; ?mastoiditis – right temporal; ddd – L5, S1; Sch – L1–4; oa – T1, T4–5, T11; enth – right clavicle, femora, calcanea; cortical defect – left clavicle, distal humeri, 2nd MtCs; mv – asymmetric vertebrae, long femoral necks
76	1391	1390	*in situ*	*c.* 95%	adult >50 yr. male	amtl; apical void; calculus; enamel hypoplasia; pd; *hyperostosis frontalis interna*; fracture – left clavicle; pnb – right fibula; ddd – C3–4, L1–S1; oa – C1–5, T1,1T; op – sacrum, sternum; pitting – left proximal humerus; hyperporosity – palate; enth – innominates, clavicles, left scapula, humeri, proximal ulnae, femora, patellae, calcanea; exo – left 2nd proximal IP (foot); cortical defect – right innominate, left clavicle, left scapula, humeri; left proximal 1st MtT, right 1st proximal phalanx (foot); ossified cartilage – thyroid; coalition – calcanea, left navicular; mv – double atlas facets
77	1370	1369	*in situ*	*c.* 90%	adult *c.* 45–50 yr. male	calculus; dental caries; pd; destructive lesion – right distal humerus; enth – ischia, humeri, patellae, calcanea; mv – dental crowding & rotation, wormian bones, double atlas facet, fused 5th phalanges (feet)
78	1398	1393	*in situ*	*c.* 40%	infant/ juvenile *c.* 4–5 yr. ???female	enamel hypoplasia; pd; *cribra orbitalia*
79	1302	1301	*in situ*	*c.* 85%	juvenile *c.* 10–12 yr.	calculus; enamel hypoplasia; pd; ?impaction; *cribra orbitalia*; cortical defect – clavicles; mv – enamel pearl left M3, supernumery tooth/retained deciduous
80	1353	1352	*in situ*	*c.* 80%	subadult *c.* 12–15 yr.	enamel hypoplasia; pd; *cribra orbitalia*; plastic changes – radii
81	1288	1286	*in situ*	*c.* 99%	adult *c.* 24–29 yr. female	calculus; dental caries; pd; *cribra orbitalia*; destructive lesion – left 4th middle phalanx (foot); hyperporosity – occipital; coalition defect – 3rd MtCs; mv – tooth rotation, shovelled I2s, fused 5th phalanges (feet)
82	1284	1283	*in situ*	*c.* 98%	adult *c.* 24–29 yr. male	calculus; enamel hypoplasia; pd; fracture – sacrum, right 5th MtC, ?right 5th proximal phalanx, right 1st proximal phalanx; destructive lesion – right 1st MtT, left 5th MtT; Sch – T6–7; enth – left femur, patellae, calcanea; cortical defect – tarsal; mv – wormian bones, *os acromiale*
83	1261	1260	*in situ*	*c.* 90%	adult *c.* 24–29 yr. male	calculus; enamel hypoplasia; *cribra orbitalia*; fracture – 4–5th MtC; ddd – C3; Sch – L1–2; enth – innominates; cortical defect – clavicles, right proximal 1st & 5th proximal phalanx (foot); mv – wormian bones; variant ribs
84	1329	1330	*in situ*	*c.* 90%	adult >50 yr. male	amtl; apical void; calculus; dental caries; enamel hypoplasia; pd; *cribra orbitalia*; fracture – right glenoid, right talus; pnb – right tibia, fibulae; ddd – C2–7, T1, T3–12, L2–5; Sch – T11–12, L1–3; oa – C1–4, L3–S1, 2 left ribs, right shoulder, right elbow, distal ulnae, wrists, right proximal 1st MtC, distal femora, proximal tibiae, left 1st distal MtT & sesmoid; op – Ts, Ls, right acetabulum, sacroiliac joints, carpals, right 1–3rd & left 2nd proximal MtCs, distal femora, right distal tibia, left patella, left cuboid; enth – innominates, right proximal humerus, radii, femora, left patella, cuneiforms, calcanea; ivory osteoma; mv – tooth rotation, wormian bones, variant ribs
85	1255a	1254	*in situ*	*c.* 85%	adult <45 yr. female	amtl; apical void; calculus; dental caries; hyper-eruption; pd; secondary sinusitis; pnb – maxilla, T8 (body); destructive lesions – 3 distal phalanges (hands); ddd – C3–4, C6–7, T5–8, S1; Sch – T7–10, T12, L3; oa – T12, L4–5; thickened – skull vault; ivory osteoma – frontal; enth – innominates, patellae, calcanea; cortical defect – right proximal radius, distal femora; mv – wormian bones, non-fusion C1, elongated femoral necks
	1255b		redep.	1 tooth	infant *c.* 1.5–4 yr.	–

Table 3.1 Continued

Grave	*Context*	*Cut*	*Deposit type*	*Quantification*	*Age/sex*	*Pathology*
86	1376a (1371; 1378)	1375	*in situ*	*c.* 90%	adult *c.* 30–35 yr. female	apical void; calculus; dental caries; dental enamel hypoplasia; pd; *hyperostosis frontalis interna*, *cribra orbitalia;* hyperporosity – palate, endocranial; thickening – frontal, parietals; osteomalacia; ?rickets – arms, lower ribs (bowing/deformation); sinusitis; pnb – fibulae; destructive lesions – temporo-mandibulars; Schmorl's node Ts; enth – femora
87	1259	1257	*in situ*	*c.* 40% a.u.l.	subadult *c.* 14–17 yr. male	–
88	1305	1304	*in situ*	*c.* 65%	juvenile *c.* 6–8 yr.	calculus; dental caries; enamel hypoplasia
89	1333	1332	*in situ*	*c.* 55%	juvenile *c.* 5–7 yr.	enamel hypoplasia; 'hair-on-end'– endocranial (?scurvy); hyperporosity – endo- & exocranial; *cribra orbitalia*
90	1396	1397	*in situ*	*c.* 90%	juvenile/subadult *c.* 12–14 yr. ?female	calculus; dental caries; enamel hypoplasia; pd; *cribra orbitalia;* endocranial new bone – occipital; pnb – tibiae
91	1293	1292	*in situ*	*c.* 98%	adult >45 yr. male	amtl; apical void; calculus; dental caries; enamel hypoplasia; hypercemetosis; pd; *cribra orbitalia*; hyperporosity – palate; fracture – T1 (ap); secondary sinusitis; pnb - tibiae; ddd – C3–4, C6, T12, L2, L4–S1; Sch – T10–11; oa – C7, T1, T11–12, T, L2, L5, left 5th metaphalangeal joint; op – T1 ap, L1–4 bsm, feet; enth – supramastoid crest, innominates, femora, patellae, calcanea; cortical defects – proximal 1st proximal phalanges; ossified cartilage – ribs; mv – shovelled I2s, wormian bones
92	1300	1340	*in situ*	*c.* 95%	adult *c.* 20–25 yr. female	calculus; pd; spondylolysis – L5; Sch – T12, L1–2; cortical defect – right humerus; mv – tooth crowding & rotation; wormian bones, cervical ribs
93	1308	1307	*in situ*	*c.* 55%	adult >45 yr. female	amtl; apical void; calculus; caries; pd; osteoporosis; enth – innominates, femora
94	1344	1343	*in situ*	*c.* 85%	adult *c.* 20–25 yr. male	calculus; enamel hypoplasia; pd; ?cyst/tumor – T1 (body); cortical defect – clavicles; mv – C1 – incomplete fusion, left cervical rib – C7
95	1382	1381	*in situ*	a few frags s.a.u.	neonate	cranial thickening
96	1469	1468	'bed' burial	*c.* 80%	adult >45 yr. female	calculus; dental caries; enamel hypoplasia; pd; *hyperostosis frontalis interna*; cranial thickening; osteoporosis; *cribra orbitalia*; sinusitis; ?mastoiditis – left; oa – temporo-mandibulars; ddd – C3–7, L5, 1L; Sch – L; oa – C4–5, 1T, L2–S1; mv – wormian bones
97	1478	1477	*in situ*	*c.* 65%	adult *c.* 25–35 yr. female	apical void; calculus; dental caries; enamel hypoplasia; pd; hypercementosis; ddd – C2–4; mv – cervical ribs
98	1475	1476	*in situ*	*c.* 20%	juvenile *c.* 6–8 yr.	calculus
99	1466	1465	*in situ*	*c.* 10% l.	juvenile *c.* 5–13 yr.	–
100	1472	1471	*in situ*	*c.* 50%	juvenile *c.* 5–7 yr.	calculus; enamel hypoplasia; *cribra orbitalia*; mv – wormian bones
101	1445	1444	*in situ*	*c.* 98%	adult *c.* 35–40 yr. male	calculus; enamel hypoplasia; pd; *cribra orbitalia;* hyperporosity – parietals; trauma – left 5th MtT; pnb – tibiae, fibulae (lamellar); ?solitary bone cyst – right distal ulna, right capitate; ddd – C4–5, T7, L1–4; Sch – T6, T8–12; L1–3; oa – T4–5, T10; enth – parietals, right acetabulum, patellae, calcanea; cortical defect – clavicles, proximal end proximal phalanges (feet) cartilage – manubrium, left 1st rib

102	1451	1450	*in situ*	*c.* 85%	adult *c.* 35–40 yr. female	apical void; dental caries; calculus; enamel hypoplasia; pd; osteoporosis – vertebrae; destructive lesion – temporo-mandibulars; ddd – 1L, S1; enth – radii, right calcaneum
103	1454a	1453	*in situ*	*c.* 15% s.u.l.	juvenile *c.* 5–8 yr.	–
	1454b		redep.	1 tooth	adult *c.* 18–30 yr.	–
104	1412	1411	*in situ*	*c.* 80%	juvenile/subadult *c.* 12–14 yr. ??female	calculus; enamel hypoplasia; pd; hyperporosity – temporals; *cribra orbitalia*; mv – variant teeth, wormian bones, double atlas facets
105	1415	1414	*in situ*	*c.* 85%	adult >45 yr. female	amtl; apical void; calculus; dental caries; pd; *cribra orbitalia*; osteoporosis; tuberculosis:- destructive lesions & pnb – C5–7 body, T1–L1 body, ap, c-v, L2–3 ap, ?sacrum, ribs & kyphosis - T8–L1, ribs; depressed fracture – left parietal; endocranial new bone – spheno-occipital synchondrosis; Sch – T4–7, S1; oa – right temporo-mandibular, T3, T5–7; enth – iliac crests; cortical defect – clavicles, right glenoid; coalition – left calcaneum; ossified cartilage – manubrium, rib; mv – wormian bones
106	1408	1407	*in situ*	*c.* 85%	adult >45 yr. male	amtl; apical void; calculus; dental caries; pd; hyperporosity – left antrum; ankylosing spondylitis – sacro-iliac joints; tumour – C3; fracture – T6, T11–12 (body); right patella; ddd – C-6, L5; Sch – T3; oa – T1–6, T8, T11–12, L5; ribs, right clavicle, glenoids; op – distal humeri, proximal ulnae; enth – proximal ulnae, femora, right tibia, patellae, fibulae, calcanea; cortical defect – right clavicle, right humerus shaft; exo – right distal tibia; plastic changes – bowed ulnae; hydatid cysts; mv – wormian bones, double mastoids, double atlas facets
107	1448	1449	*in situ*	*c.* 98%	adult *c.* 24–29 yr. male	calculus; dental caries; pd; sinusitis; hyperporosity – occipital, parietals; Sch – T7–12, L3–4; enth – clavicles, right acromion, left humerus; cortical defect – left distal tibia; mv – tooth rotation, wormian bones, short 12th ribs
108	1405	1404	*in situ*	*c.* 80%	adult >50 yr. male	apical void; amtl; calculus; dental caries; enamel hypoplasia; pd; hypereruption; fracture – left parietal, left distal radius, left 2nd distal phalanx (hand), right distal tibia and fibula shaft, ?left fibula; destructive lesion – temporo-mandibulars, L5; ddd – C3–6, T12, L3-5; Sch – L1; oa – C1–2, C4–5, C7, T1–3, T11–12distal ulnae, carpals; op – Ts, L2–5; enth – innominates, right clavicle, right fibula, calcanea; mv – tooth impaction & rotation; cervical ribs, bony nodule – right 1st MtC
109	1438	1437	*in situ*	*c.* 90%	adult *c.* 30–40 yr. male	calculus; enamel hypoplasia; pd; hyperporosity – endocranial; *cribra orbitalia*; mastoiditis; pnb – left orbit; destructive lesion – left frontal; fracture – left tibia & fibula; ddd – C4–6, T6–8, L5; enth – innominates, right humerus shaft; mv – wormian bones
110	1435	1434	*in situ*	*c.* 70%	adult *c.* 40–50 yr. female	apical void; amtl; calculus; pd; ?destructive lesion/?cyst – carpals, left 1st MtP, proximal phalanx (hand); Sch – T11, T, L; cortical defect – clavicles; exo – 2/3rd MtC shaft
111	1402a	1401	*in situ*	*c.* 90%	adult *c.* 24–29 yr. female	calculus; dental caries; enamel hypoplasia; pd; spondylolysis – L5; cortical defect – clavicles; mv – wormian bones; *os acromiale*; incipient *coxa vara*
	1402b		redep.	1 bone s.	foetus *c.* 34–38 weeks	–
112	1428	1427	*in situ*	*c.* 75%	adult *c.* 24–29 yr. ?female	calculus; dental caries; enamel hypoplasia; pd; *cribra orbitalia*; fracture – left 2nd middle phalanx (hand); Sch – T11–12; pitting – left glenoid; enth – clavicles (deltoid), right proximal humerus; exo – left distal humerus; cortical defect – C (ap), navicular; plastic changes – arms;

Table 3.1 Continued

Grave	*Context*	*Cut*	*Deposit type*	*Quantification*	*Age/sex*	*Pathology*
113	114	113	*in situ*	*c.* 45%	juvenile *c.* 6–8 yr.	calculus; dental caries; enamel hypoplasia; endocranial new bone; mv – shovelled Is
114	111	110	disturbed	*c.* 15% s.u.l.	adult >35 yr. ?male	calculus
115	120	119	*in situ*	*c.* 90%	adult >50 yr. female	calculus; dental caries; pd; ?cyst – T1; spondylolysis – L5; fracture – T1 ap; ddd – C3-7, T1; Sch – T7–12; oa – C1–2, T1, 5 right, 4 left ribs, right proximal humerus, left distal humerus, right 1st carpo-metacarpal, knees; op – Cs, 1st rays (hands), distal IPs (hands); pitting – 1st rays (hands); enth – ischium, left distal humerus, calcanea; cortical defect – left 1st proximal phalanx (foot); mv – distomolar; tooth rotation
116	117	116	*in situ*	*c.* 90%	adult *c.* 35–45 yr. male	calculus; dental caries; enamel hypoplasia; pd; oa – 1st ribs; op – left costo-clavicular, left distal ulna, distal radii, carpals, 1st MtPs (hands); enth – clavicles, right MtCs, right proximal phalanges, left patella;; mv – mandibular torus, coalition – calcanea
-	1106a	1106	redep.	1 bone u.	juvenile < 13yr.	–
-	1106b	1106	redep. = 1101	*c.* 30 long bone frags	subadult/adult >14 yr.	–
-	1109	1109	redep. = 1101	1 frag. s.	subadult/adult >14 yr.	–
-	1110	1101	redep = 1101	*c.* 10% l.	subadult/adult >14 yr.	–
-	1245	1244	redep.	1 frag human?	unid.	–
-	1410	coombe	redep.	*c.* 50 frags l. +?	adult >18 yr.	–
-	Unstrat A	?	redep.	6 frags left	adult >18 yr.	–
-	Unstrat B	?	redep.	a few frags a.	subadult/ adult >14 yr.	–
-	Unstrat C	?	? = 1213	*c.* 15 frags and some teeth	adult *c.* 35–45 yr. ?male	calculus; pd
-	Unlabelled B	?	redep.	8 frags l.	adult >18 yr.	–

s. a. u. l. – skull, axial, upper limb, lower limb (when not all elements are represented); amtl – *ante mortem* tooth loss; pd – periodontal disease;
pnb – periosteal new bone; C, T, L, S cervical, thoracic, lumbar, sacral vertebrae; ap – articular process; c-v – costo-vertebral; tp – transverse process; sch. – Schmorl's node;
ddd – degenerative disc disease; r. – right; l. – left; oa – osteoarthritis; op – osteophytes; enth – enthesophytes; exo – exostoses; IP – interphalangeal joint; MtC/T – metacarpal/metatarsal;
MtP – metaphalangeal; cort. def. – cortical defect; MV – morphological variation

Table 3.2 Minimum number of individuals (MNI) 2007/9 excavation

Age	*2007/9*	*after Fielden 1978*	*Total*
Immature			
Foetus *c.*32–38 wk.	2	–	2
Neonate *c.* 0–6 mth.	1	1	2
Neonate/infant 0–5yr.	2	–	2
Infant *c.* 6 mth.–5 yr.	8	3	11
Infant/juvenile 6 mth.–12 yr.	5	–	5
Juvenile *c.* 5–12 yr.	12	2	14
Juvenile/subadult 5–12 yr.	1	–	1
Subadult *c.* 13–18 yr.	5 (1??F, 1?F, 1M)	4	9
Subtotal	36 (2F, 1M)	10 (3M)	46 (2F, 4M)
Subadult/adult	2		2
Adult			
c. 18–25 yr.	–	6 (1?F, 1F, 3M)	6 (1?F, 1F, 3M)
c. 20–30 yr.	11 (1?F, 5F, 4M)	–	11 (1?F, 5F, 4M)
c. 25–35 yr.	3 (F)	–	3 (F)
c. 30–40 yr.	6 (4F, 2M)	–	6 (4F, 2M)
c. 35–45 yr.	8 (1?F, 3F, 1?M, 3M)	–	8 (1?F, 3F, 1?M, 3M)
c. 40–50 yr.	3 (2F, 1M)	–	3 (2F, 1M)
>18 yr.	–	3 (1??F)	3 (1??F)
c. 26–45 yr.	–	11 (1??F, 4F, 1?M, 4M)	11 (1??F, 4F, 1?M, 4M)
>45 yr.	13 (1??F, 7F, 1??M, 4M)	1 (M)	14 (1??F, 7F, 1??M, 5M)
>50 yr.	8 (3F, 5M)	–	8 (3F, 5M)
Subtotal	52 (30F, 21M)	21 (8F, 9M)	73 (38F, 30M)
Total MNI	90	31	121

F – female, M – male

Individuals below *c.* 6 months (including foetus and neonate/infant) accounted for 13.9% of the immature assemblage, a high rate – far greater than the 2.1% from Blacknall Field (Stuckert 2010, 113), where a more distinct peak in subadult deaths was attributed to increased responsibilities and stress associated with reaching the age of majority (around 15 years). The lowest proportions of adult deaths occurred between the ages of around 20 and 35 years (30% female; 19% male), and a third of each sex died between the ages of *c.* 35 and 50 years. The greatest proportion of adult deaths occurred after 45 years (36.6% females; 42% males). In contrast Stuckert (2010, 114–5) remarks on a peak in the 20–29 year range in the male assemblage and the more typical 30–39 year peak for females from Blacknall Field.

It was possible to establish the sex of most adults (90.4%; Table 3.2). Of the 52 adults, 57.7% were assessed as female and 40.4% male. Combined with the data from 1974, this slight preponderance of females is maintained (52.1% female/40.1% male; after Fielden 1978). A similar pattern was recorded in the assemblage from Blacknall Field, (52.8% /43.4%; Stuckert 2010). A greater proportion of females was also noted at Droxford, Hampshire (63.6%/36.4%; Cook and Dacre 1985, 67), whereas more males were recorded in the assemblage from Alton, Hampshire (53.1% males/46.9% females; Evison 1988, 59–62), and fairly equal proportions were seen at Twyford School (Egging Dinwiddy 2011, 95–100).

The demographic proportions of the Collingbourne Ducis assemblage are generally consistent with a normal domestic population; the slight preponderance of females may be due to migration of a small percentage of the males (particularly in the younger adult group) for social and/or economic reasons, or their burial elsewhere.

Skeletal indices

Skeletal indices allow the comparison of various aspects of the skeleton both within an assemblage and between assemblages (Mays 1998, 96–100). Inferences may then be made regarding the degree of homogeneity, health and nutritional status, biomechanical stresses (ie, activities, environment) and/or parent populations.

Stature was estimated for 46 adults (88.5%; Table 3.3). The average male stature was slightly greater than that calculated by Roberts and Cox for the period (1.72 m; 2003, 220), and for the males from Twyford School, Worthy Park and Blacknall Field (1.73 m; Egging Dinwiddy 2011; Wells *et al.* 2003, 159; Stuckert 2010, 115). The female stature was comparable to those from most of these assemblages, and to the average for the period (1.61 m; Roberts and Cox 2003, 220). Those from Twyford School, however, were generally a little taller (1.64 m; Egging Dinwiddy 2011). A comparatively large stature range, as seen at Collingbourne Ducis, implies a greater variability in either access to

Table 3.3 Main skeletal indices

Sex	*Number*	*Range*	*Mean*
		Estimated stature	
Male	19	1.58 m – 1.83 m (*c.* 5' 2¼"– 6' 0")	1.74 m (*c.* 5' 8½") (SD 0.0730)
Female	27	1.54 m – 1.76 m (*c.* 5'0½" – 5'9¼")	1.61 m (*c.* 5'3½") (SD 0.0684)
		Cranial index	
Male	11	67.02–79.89 (dolicho-mesocranic)	73.81 (SD 3.79) (dolichocranic)
Female	13	67.72–78.02 (dolicho-mesocranic)	73.70 (SD 2.76) (dolichocranic)
		Platymeric index	
Male	19	74.01–97.69 (platymeric – eurymeric)	83.87 (SD 6.91) (platymeric)
Female	25	67.68–95.50 (platymeric – eurymeric)	80.13 (SD 6.10) (platymeric)
		Platycnemic index	
Male	18	64.13–79.69 (mesocnemic – eurycnemic)	71.85 (SD 3.91) (eurycnemic)
Female	23	62.50–90.66 (platycnemic – eurycnemic)	73.30 (SD 7.12) (eurycnemic)
		Robusticity index	
Male	15	108.92–136.60	120.46 (SD 7.53)
Female	13	114.81–138.33	125.43 (SD 6.84)

nutrition, or in the genetic make-up of the group (ie, more diverse parent populations). The achievement of average or greater stature suggests that most of the Collingbourne population had access to good food resources during growth, or were able to use what they had more effectively. Alternatively, especially considering other factors (cranial indices, non-metric traits and general health – discussed below), it may be that some of the community had a genetic predisposition to grow taller.

It was possible to calculate the cranial index of 24 (46.2%) of the adults (Table 3.3). Both male and female skulls ranged between dolichocranic and mesocranic (long/narrow and medium), the average for both falling within the dolichocranic range, and following the general trend toward long-headedness in the Anglo-Saxon period (McKinley 2004c, 36). The skulls from Blacknall Field were also dolichocranic (Stuckert 2010, 117). Other cranial indices range widely, indicating a degree of heterogeneity within the cemetery population, probably related to a varied genetic input.

The platymeric index reflects the anterior/ posterior flattening of the proximal femur. The average score for both sexes fall within the platymeric (laterally flattened) range, the females being on average slightly more flattened. In both sexes, however, femora vary from platymeric to eurymeric (broad). Where both sides are measurable (36 cases, 69.2% adults) there is a strong tendency for the females to have a higher scoring (broader) right femur (89.5%), whilst in male femora there is no preference. A platymeric average score was also calculated for the femora of both sexes at Blacknall Field, Twyford School and Aldbourne (Stuckert 2010, 117; Egging Dinwiddy 2011; Boylston 2012). The platycnemic index (Table 3.3) reflects the meso-lateral flattening of the tibiae. Male and female average scores are eurycnemic (broad/normal) range, though the female tibiae are more variable. Where both sides were measurable (33 cases, 63.5% of adults), the right is broader in most female tibia pairs, whilst no such preference is evident in the male remains. The female scores are comparable to those from Blacknall Field, though there the male tibiae were broader – falling into the mesocnemic range (Stuckert 2010, 117–118). The purported link between platycnemia and squatting facets (Brothwell 1972, 91) was not upheld – none of those with squatting facets (more than 75% of the observable tibiae) were platycnemic. The robusticity index reflects the robusticity of the femoral shaft. Little difference was noted between the sides, whilst there was only a small tendency for males to have more robust femora. The shortest male had the most robust femora, whilst those of the tallest females were the least robust.

Various factors are reflected in these indices, such as genetic predisposition, lifestyle and environmental conditions, however, the data indicate clearly that the lower limbs of males and females were differentially subject to forces determining bone shape. Physical activity seems the most likely cause due to the strength and nature of the patterning.

Non-metric variation

Variations in skeletal morphology can indicate genetic relationships within a population, and others can be the result of activities involving repeated stresses, though heritability and aetiology of many remain unclear, and interpretations regarding particular traits, especially from a small sample, can be problematic and potentially misleading (McKinley 2009a, 18).

Examples are listed in Table 3.1, and the more noteworthy are discussed below. Within the assemblage there was some variation, and some repetition, of traits.

Some common dental variations include shovelled incisors and double-rooted canines. More unusual examples include supernumerary teeth: peg-like paramolars between the left first and second molars (grave 38), and a small distomolar found distal of a left maxillary third molar (grave 115). Wormian bones (extra ossicles within the cranial sutures) were observed in 29 adults (55.8%), most commonly in the lambdoid suture – a common site generally. One individual had a metopic suture (grave 93; 2.6% of observable).

Palatine tori (a clinically common condition consisting of bony masses along the midline of the palate) can be genetic, or reflect localised trauma, such as persistent consumption of hard foods (Neville *et al.* 2002, 20). Two individuals (graves 86 and 115) had slight palatine tori. Mandibular tori (bony masses on the lingual surface of the mandible, usually bilateral, near the premolars) are less common, and relate to localised pressure such as bruxism (teeth-grinding) (*ibid.*, 21). Two mandibles had distinct tori (4.5% of mandibles – grave 110 and 116). Slight tori were observed in the mandibles of a further five individuals (graves 76 and 77, 102, 105 and 106). The tori were bilateral in four cases, and on the right side in three.

Spinal variations include a sixth lumbar vertebra (present in two spines – graves 39 and 41). Cervical ribs were identified in five individuals (graves 58, 97, 108, and adjacent graves 92 and 94). Accessory sacral facets (pseudo joints between the ilium and second sacral vertebra (Berry and Berry 1967; Ehara *et al.* 1988, 857)) may be congenital, or a result of weight-bearing which often increases with age (Ehara *et al.* 1988, 857–9). The six examples were observed in both males and females, most over *c.* 40 years old – implying most were due to age and activity.

Os acromiale is the non-fusion of the acromion epiphysis, indicative of strenuous activity involving the shoulders, initiating prior to the expected age of fusion (Stirland 2005, 121; Scheuer and Black 2000, 268; Roberts and Cox 2003, 152). There is also a degree of genetic predisposition (Hunt and Bullen 2007, 309). The anomaly was observed in two females both *c.* 24–29 years of age (graves 47 and 111).

Spondylolysis (non-union of part of the posterior portion of a vertebra, most often the fifth lumbar) is understood to be a morphological variation though it can develop with repeated hyperextension of the vertebral column, particularly in those with some predisposition (Aufderheide and Rodríguez-Martín 1998, 63–4; Ward *et al.* 2010). Examples were observed in the fifth lumbar vertebra of three females, all of whom died in their twenties.

Squatting facets – anterior extensions of the tibial distal articular facets (most commonly laterally positioned) – are created by repeated hyper-dorsiflexion of the ankle joint, as occurs with the habitual adoption of a squatting position (Boulle 2001). Of the observable tibiae, 75% had lateral squatting facets, and 3.3% had medial facets. There was no preference between the sides, or sexes, and there was no correlation with platycnemia (see above). A similar rate was seen at Twyford School (80%; Egging Dinwiddy 2011, 100–1), but of the 26 individuals at Aldbourne only eight had lateral and three had medial facets (Boylston 2012).

Coalition abnormalities include fusion between two bones, either by fibrous, cartilaginous or bony tissue. An ossicle may form which can adhere to any surrounding bones, or may remain as a separate, accessory bone. Calcaneonavicular variations (Bergman 1998) were evident in the feet of three individuals, and a calcaneocuboid variation in a fourth (graves 72, 76, 105 and 117); metacarpostyloid variations were observed in the left third metacarpal of the individual in grave 45, and both of another (grave 81). The same anomaly was observed in the remains of an older female from Twyford School, where a portion of the third metacarpal styloid process had become part of the capitate (Egging Dinwiddy 2011, 97, table 2).

A number of inferences may be made on the basis of the evidence reviewed above. There is some evidence for familial relationships, whilst a reasonable degree of variation (including some less common traits) indicates a degree of diversity in parent populations. Other traits, particularly when considered with other skeletal evidence, are likely to be activity-related.

Pathological lesions

Pathological lesions were observed in the remains of 76 individuals (84.4%). A summary of the observed lesions is presented in Table 3.1. Details are held in the archive. All rates are True Prevalence Rates (TPRs) unless otherwise stated.

Dental disease

All or parts of 64 erupted permanent dentitions were recovered from 20 males, 30 females and 14 unsexed individuals (Table 3.4). Dental lesions were observed in all.

Dental calculus (calcified plaque/tartar) has been linked to a diet dominated by soft, carbohydrate rich foods such as porridge or gruel (Hillson 1986, 278). The condition was observed in 1–32 teeth (average 18.5) in 57 permanent dentitions (89.1%) (Table 3.5). Most deposits were mild, evident as tide-marks at the

Table 3.4 Summary of erupted permanent dentitions (excluding supernumerary)

	Max. teeth	*Man. teeth*	*Total no. teeth*	*Max. tooth positions*	*Man. tooth positions*	*Total no. tooth positions*
Female (secure sexing)	333	382	715	351	407	758
Female (all levels)	381	429	810	395	453	848
Male (secure sexing)	239	264	503	259	281	540
Male (all levels)	245	265	510	262	281	543
Unsexed	55	72	127	31	69	100
Total	681	766	1447	688	757	1491

gumline, and occasionally stained pale green. Build-up was most frequently observed on the mandibular canines, and least so on maxillary incisors, though overall the distribution was fairly even. The rate was marginally greater in females, with examples of heavier deposits on the mandibular teeth, and the most severe examples (affecting adults over *c.* 35 years of age) associated with general poor oral health. Two juveniles had moderate deposits on deciduous teeth; one (grave 100) had clearly suffered periods of either nutritional or health stresses in infancy (see below), and may have had a softer diet as a result. The calculus rate at Collingbourne Ducis is considerably higher than the average (39.2%) calculated for the period by Roberts and Cox (2003, 193–4), though similarly high rates, severity and distribution were recorded at Twyford School (70.1%; Egging Dinwiddy 2011, 101, table 4). At Aldbourne all dentitions were affected (Boylston 2012), whilst at Worthy Park nearly half the dentitions had deposits (Wells *et al.* 2003, 160–2). The nature of calculus, however, predisposes it to post-depositional damage and loss, making interpretations potentially misleading.

Periodontal disease (gingivitis) can lead to bone resorption, root exposure and eventual tooth loss (Ogden 2005; 2007). The condition has been linked to dental calculus deposits and both are purported to increase in severity with age (Wells *et al.* 2003, 162–3). The disease was recorded in up to 21 alveoli of 50 permanent dentitions (78.1%), and three deciduous dentitions. The condition is most frequently evident in the molar and premolar sockets, where the examples are also most severe. There is little difference in extent and severity between the mandible and maxilla, and most cases coincide with calculus deposits. Females were affected to a greater degree than males (60% compared with 32%), however, extent and severity were comparable. In general, severity was mild (score 2) though in a few examples flaring and sclerosis of the alveolus was marked (graves 38, 104, 106, and 115). Whilst these severe cases include older individuals, one was a subadult, and one was *c.* 25 to 35 years old. In the three youngest cases (graves 40, 53 and 78) there is an apparent link to metabolic disorders, for example scurvy and/or iron deficiency anaemia (see Table 3.1, and below). Extreme attrition was noted in some of the most severe examples of the condition (eg, grave 106). The rate (78.1%) is notably higher than from other sites in the region, eg, 56.3% from Twyford School (Egging Dinwiddy 2011, 101, table 4), though rates from other contemporaneous assemblages vary substantially (Roberts and Cox 2003, 194, table 4.18).

Dental caries (destruction of the tooth by acids, produced by oral bacteria present in dental plaque) were recorded in 1–12 teeth, in 40 permanent dentitions (13 male, 26 female and one unsexed). Lesions are present in similar proportions of mandibular and maxillary teeth (Table 3.5). The most commonly affected teeth are the first and second molars, though most parts of the dentition were involved. Where evident, the origin of the lesion was three times more likely to be interdental and at the cemeto-enamel junction, than on any other surface. Following the typical pattern, more female than male dentitions had carious lesions (86.6%/65%). There is an age-related link in frequency, with 70% of those with more than five lesions aged over *c.* 40 years.

Table 3.5 Summary of dental lesions with TPRs (erupted permanent dentition)

	Teeth	*Socket positions*	*Calculus*	Ante mortem *tooth loss*	*Caries*	*Abscesses*	*Hypoplasia*
Female	810	848	652 *(80%)*	32 *(3.8%)*	97 *(12.0%)*	27 *(3.2%)*	165 *(20.7%)*
Male	510	543	372 *(72.9%)*	30 *(5.5%)*	49 *(9.6%)*	15 *(2.8%)*	79 *(15.5%)*
Unsexed	127	100	28 *(22.0%)*	–	1 *(0.8%)*	–	30 *(23.6%)*
Total	1447	1491	1052 *(72.7%)*	62 *(4.2%)*	147 *(10.2%)*	42 *(2.8%)*	274 *(18.9%)*

Exceptions include a *c.* 30–40 year old female with 12 lesions and a *c.* 24–29 year old male with seven. Several lesions were associated with extreme wear, and approximately 19% probably contributed to the formation of granuloma and abscesses. Five deciduous dentitions have caries in 1–3 teeth (4.5% of deciduous teeth). The maxillary teeth are most commonly affected (8.3% maxillary/1.9% mandibular). Four of these individuals also have evidence for severe nutritional or health stresses. As discussed above, it may be that a different diet was provided either as a result of, or perhaps aggravating their conditions. Rates of 4% and 3.3% were recorded at Blacknall Field and Worthy Park (Stuckert 2010, 120, table 41; Wells *et al.* 2003, 161; table 3.10), and a similarly low rate was given by Roberts and Cox for their sample (2003, 190–1, table 4.14) – though some sites had rates similar to Collingbourne Ducis.

Most apical voids are related to chronic inflammation and death of the tooth pulp where it has been exposed to micro-organisms (eg, via caries, fracturing or wear). The resultant formation of granulation material leads to permanent bone loss in the form of a smooth-walled cavity up to 3 mm in diameter, which increases should the granuloma become cystic; other cysts, however, can produce similar lesions (Soames and Southam 2005, 65–84). Subsequent infection can lead to a dental abscess, which in turn can lead to secondary infection of the surrounding tissues (Katzenberg and Saunders 2008, 322–3; Ogden 2007, 283–308; Soames and Southam 2005, 45–63; Dias and Tayles 1997, 548). Granuloma probably caused the apical voids in first molars and second premolar in six individuals over *c.* 35 years – four female (13.3%), two male (10%); all would have been cystic at between 4 and 7 mm diameter. All but one (grave 64) also had dental abscesses, and two have extreme tooth wear. Dental abscess lesions were recorded in 42 sockets, with 1–4 lesions in 19 dentitions (12 (40%) female; 7 (35%) male), most over *c.* 45 years. The right first molar positions are more frequently affected, and canines least so. The main causes of infection were carious lesions and extreme wear. Secondary sinusitis is evident in five cases, whilst long-standing, occasionally healed infection of surrounding tissues is manifest in three maxilla and four mandibles. The rate corresponds with the average calculated by Roberts and Cox for the period (2003, 191–2, table 4.15), a higher rate being recorded at Blacknall Field (4%; Stuckert 2010, 122, table 44), whilst the rate from Worthy Park is somewhat lower at 1.7% (Wells *et al.* 2003).

Ante mortem tooth loss was noted in 1–11 tooth positions in 15 dentitions (seven male, eight female). Slightly greater prevalence was observed in males, and the most commonly lost teeth were first molars. An age-related link to tooth loss was also found – nearly two thirds of those affected were over 45 years of age. In four cases tooth loss was associated with a dental abscess; the loss of maxillary incisors in one individual (grave 55) was associated with leprosy (see below). Roberts and Cox (2003, 191, table 4.16) calculated a much higher rate of 8% for the period. Rates from some other sites in the region include 6.2% at Worthy Park (Wells *et al.* 2003, 161), and 4% at Blacknall Field (Stuckert 2010, 122, table 44).

Dental enamel hypoplasia (reflecting the disruption of enamel production due to nutritional or health stresses) is evident as linear or pitted defects in the tooth surface. The position of the defect may be used to estimate the general age at which the stresses occurred (Hillson 1986, 37), though the extent to which the defects can be interpreted has been the subject of some contention (Lewis and Roberts 1997, 581–2). Lesions were evident in between one and 22 teeth in 43 dentitions (67.2%; 13 male (65.0%); 16 female (53.3%) and all 14 immature). Defects were most commonly identified in the canines, followed by the maxillary incisors. In most cases, multiple episodes of stress are indicated. Most affected individuals had lesions that formed around the 'traditional' age of weaning (2–4 years), though periods of stress throughout childhood are indicated. The evidence suggests that those affected in their youngest years were prone to further episodes, possibly due to an already weakened system, and/or perhaps they lived in a community which suffered repeated economic stress. Much higher rates were observed in the dentitions from Twyford School (30.4%; Egging Dinwiddy 2011, 102), whilst Roberts and Cox (2003, 188, table 4.12) record a substantially lower rate for their sample (7.4%).

Dentitions from 24 adults had particularly marked attrition eg, faceted polishing, grooves and notches, extreme and irregular attrition, and damage. Anterior teeth were most frequently involved in all but the latter. Similar patterns have been noted at Twyford School and Blacknall Field, as well as sites further afield eg, Saltwood and Mill Hill, Kent (McKinley 2006a, 22; Anderson and Andrews 1997, 236–7). Most changes were probably related to diet and abnormal mastication, whether due to dental lesions or malocclusion. Non-masticatory use of the teeth, eg, during craft or similar tasks, may also have been a factor, though this is difficult to prove.

Dental hygiene was generally poorer than seen in several contemporaneous assemblages, with dental calculus build-up a major cause of both periodontal disease and carious lesions due to trapped decaying food and plaque. Conditions may have been exacerbated by general poor health, for which there is evidence in both the adult and immature population (see below).

Plate 3.1 Trepanation – location on skull; posterior view. Skeleton 1388 (grave 72)

Plate 3.2 Trepanation – detail showing bevelling and extent of remodelling; superior left view. Skeleton 1388 (grave 72)

Trauma

Signs of trauma were manifest in the remains of 18 individuals, including fractures, a dislocation and trepanation (Table 3.1).

Between one and six fracture sites were identified in 17 adult skeletons (total 35 sites). The axial skeleton is more commonly involved (40%), followed by the upper limb (28.6%), lower limb (25.7%) and the cranium (5.7%). Males had twice as many fractures, affecting more injury sites than the females.

Well-healed depressed fractures of the left parietals are evident in two older adults: a female from grave 105 and a male from grave 108. In the female the oval lesion (30 x 18 x max. 2 mm) is located across the coronal suture adjacent to the bregma. In the male the lesion is linear (*c.* 40 x 18 x 0.75 mm) and located adjacent to and parallel with the coronal suture. Due to advanced healing and remodelling it was not possible to determine the methods of injury with confidence, though their locations suggest infliction by a right-handed assailant.

Trepanation is the removal of a piece of skull to create a communication between the cranial cavity and the environment (Roberts and McKinley 2003, 55). A slightly curved, triangular lesion is present in the left parietal of the adult male found in grave 72 (Pl. 3.1). The external dimensions of the excised portion would have been around 44 x 36 mm, bevelling to approximately 28 x 24 mm (endocranial; Pl. 3.2). There is no sign of any head injury, nor are there any other pathological changes that indicate a reason for such an operation. The individual clearly survived long after the treatment, without any noticeable complications. Though no associated head injury was evident in this example, trepanation is more usually associated with the reduction of a depressed fracture. Anglo-Saxon trepanations account for just over a third of recorded British examples. Nearly all come from cemetery sites, and were derived from relatively normal and undistinguished burials (Roberts and McKinley 2003).

Uncomplicated wedge compression of vertebral bodies, as seen in the spines of two males, are most often caused by hyperflexion or combined flexion and rotation, occurring when vertical force is applied eg, falling debris or a fall onto the head, feet or buttocks (Adams 1987, 100–1). In the T1 of two older individuals the superior articular processes are cracked and 'folded' anteriorly, and the inferior processes posteriorly (*perimortem*). Such fractures are usually associated with fracture-dislocation – when one vertebra is violently forced forwards upon the one below, often whilst flexing and rotating – though the Collingbourne Ducis examples lack overt damage to the vertebral body. Falls are a common cause of spinal injuries, though such a location high in the spine are akin to injuries sustained in car accidents ie, violent force (Adams 1987, 101, 105).

Well-healed fractures were identified in three left ribs of an older adult male. Such injuries are consistent with a direct impact or a fall against a hard object. Most heal well without intervention (Adams 1987, 107).

Partial detachment of a small portion of the sacral lateral mass – at the usual attachment site of the *iliacus*, which connects the sacrum, innominate and femur – was observed in the remains of the robust young adult male from grave 82. The healed possible stress fracture (noted clinically in long-distance runners) is likely to have been associated with activity involving strenuous use of the legs (Major and Helms 2000, 727–29).

Most of the upper limbs injuries were probably caused by falls, either onto the shoulder or arm (often outstretched), or by direct blows (Adams 1987, 119, 128–9, 158). Healed fractures were identified in the left distal clavicle of the male from grave 76, and in the right distal ulna of the young adult female from grave 43 (greenstick). In addition to a number of other injuries sustained during his life (Table 3.1; see below), the male from grave 108 had fractured his left wrist, where the scaphoid and/or lunate had been forced into the distal radius around the time of his demise. Changes to the right shoulder of one adult female (grave 64) are indicative of humeral head dislocation.

Lower limb injuries were observed in five males, comprising healed fractures of the patella, two tibiae, three fibulae, a talus and metatarsal (Table 3.1). The knee injury (grave 106) was probably the result of a blow to the patella (Adams 1987, 235), causing a small depression on the lateral, inferior edge of the articular surface, and a fracture along the medial edge. The tibiae and fibulae injuries were probably the consequence of rotational force, resulting in a spiral break (Adams 1987, 254). A more anatomically correct alignment was achieved in the left leg of the man buried in grave 106, compared to the right leg of that from grave 108.

A fracture of the left talus (inferior articular surface; grave 83) is fairly unusual as the calcaneus normally takes the force of any falls onto the feet (Adams 1987, 280). Breaks to the metatarsal shafts (eg, the left second metatarsal, grave 45) are more common and are often the result of a heavy object dropping onto the foot.

Most of the traumatic injuries appear to be the result of falls and accidents, some of which would have been serious. In general, the pattern is consistent with those found in many other contemporaneous cemetery assemblages (Roberts and Cox 2003, 202–9).

Enthesopathies and exostoses

Pathological changes to the bone at the insertion sites of tendons, ligaments and joint capsules include bony growths (enthesophytes) and lesions or gaps in the cortical bone (cortical defects). The main causative factors include traumatic or repeated stress (often activity related), various diseases and advancing age. It is not always possible to determine the aetiology of particular lesions (Rogers and Waldron 1995, 24–5; Havelkova and Villotte 2007, 51). Exotoses (bony protrusions) can result from stress or injury to the bone. Multiple exotoses are known to occur with some diseases and conditions. Lesions are listed in Table 3.1.

Metabolic

Deficiencies in iron and vitamins C and D often affect individuals concurrently (Ortner and Putschar 1985, 273) making it difficult, or impossible, to determine which is responsible for particular lesions, especially in immature individuals (Lewis and Roberts 1997, 584; Lewis 2007).

Cribra orbitalia (pitting of the orbital roof) has traditionally been linked to iron deficiency anaemia, though more recently reconsiderations suggest some lesions may result from megaloblastic anaemia due to vitamin B12 deficiency and gastrointestinal infections (Lewis 2010, 408; Walker *et al.* 2009). The aetiology is more complicated than a merely poor diet; factors such as blood loss, parasitic infestation and chronic disease are also potential factors (Molleson 1993; Roberts and Manchester 1997, 163–9). Twenty-two individuals had lesions in one or both orbits (40.2% orbits; 23.9% female, 38.7% male; Table 3.1). The immature rate was notably high at 80%, corresponding with the high rates of enamel hypoplasia, another stress indicator (see above). Of all those with *cribra orbitalia*, 72.7% had dental enamel hypoplasia defects, and in 36.4% disease or chronic infection was evident. Manifestations of other deficiencies were also noted (Table 3.1). The overall TPR is substantially higher than those recorded for other contemporaneous sites in the region – Blacknall Field: 27%; Twyford School: 25%; and Worthy Park: 27.9% (Stuckert 2010, 132; Egging Dinwiddy 2011, 104–5; Wells *et al.* 2003, 164).

Vitamin C deficiency (scurvy) disrupts the production of bone and collagen, leading to bleeding into the skin and beneath the periosteum, and periodontal disease. The resultant haemorrhages can manifest as new bone formation anywhere on the skeleton, but particularly the jaws and orbit (Roberts and Manchester 1997, 171). Extended deficiency can lead to osteoporosis; however, administration of vitamin C rapidly rectifies all aspects of the condition (Salter 1999, 190). Potential scorbutic characteristics were identified in the remains of two infants

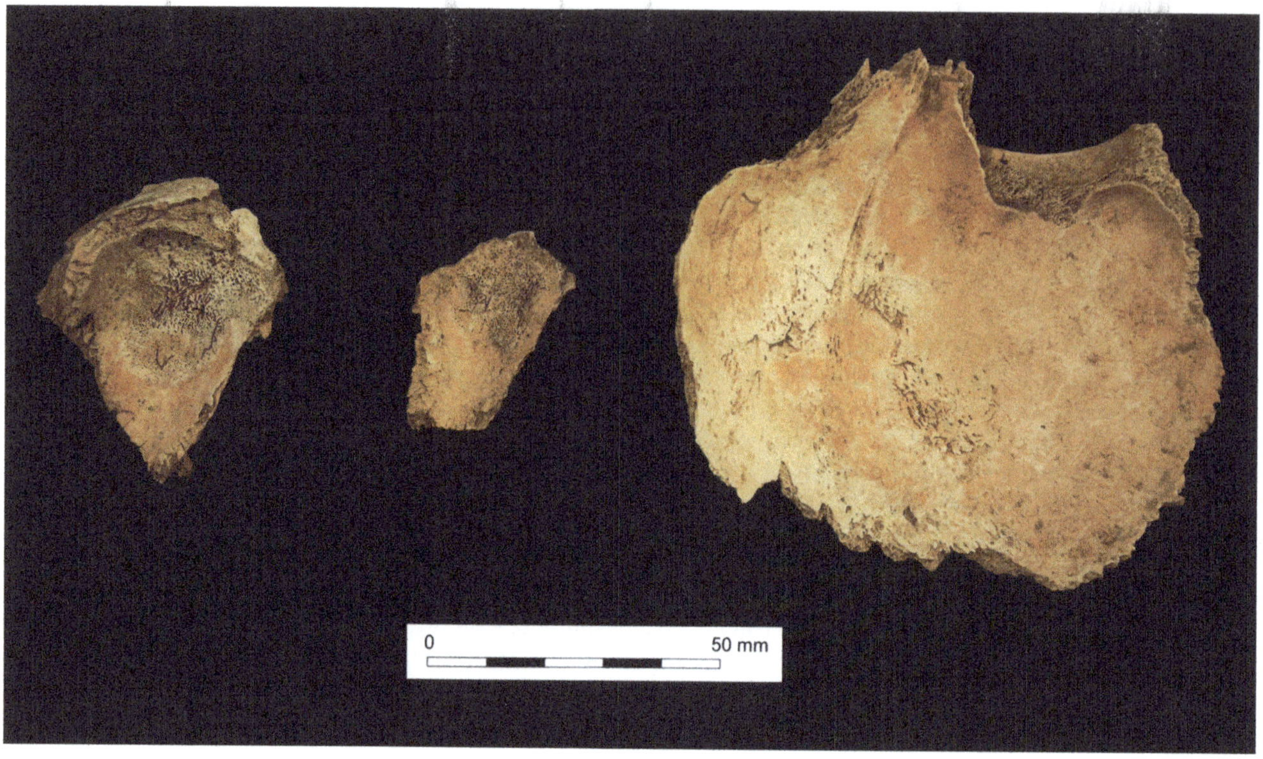

Plate 3.3 Probable vitamin C deficiency – left: cribra orbitalia*; right: endocranial lesions (skull – orbits and frontal; inferior view). Skeleton 1174 (grave 40)*

Plate 3.4 A: Congenital deformity of atlas; posterior view. Skeleton 1191 (grave 53). B: Probable vitamin D deficiency – thinned exocranial surface (right parietal); superior right view. Skeleton 1191 (grave 53)

c. 2–3 years of age (graves 40 and 63). The most striking changes evident in one infant (grave 40) include extensive new bone deposits in both orbits, and patches of endocranial lamellar new bone featuring abundant vessel impressions (Pl. 3.3) – probably a result of haemorrhage, though pronounced such patterning also occurs with vitamin D deficiency (Roberts and Manchester 1997, 173). Less extensive endocranial lesions were observed in the infant from grave 63, though extensive lamellar new bone was observed on the ethmoid, and woven new bone on several limb bones. Lesions consistent with other metabolic deficiencies (some severe) were recorded in both infants (Table 3.1). Roberts and Cox (2003, 189) report low rates of scurvy in ancient populations, but highlight problems in the recording of the deficiency in past analyses.

Vitamin D, produced by the exposure of the skin to sunlight, and present in small quantities in mother's milk, fish oil and animal fat, is essential for the mineralisation of bone. During the growing stage, under-mineralised bone is subject to plastic change caused by weight-bearing and muscle contracture. This can cause chronic skeletal abnormalities, with characteristic changes including bowing of the limbs, dental development problems and general poor health. In infants the skull tables may become thinned due to pressure from resting on one side. In adults the condition is termed osteomalacia, where bone density is affected, often resulting in vertebral collapse. Causes in adults include poor diet, kidney or intestinal disease, closely spaced pregnancies and lactation (Ortner and Putschar 1985, 274–6; Salter 1999, 184). Changes potentially indicative of childhood vitamin D deficiency were observed in three individuals (Table 3.1), an adult female, an infant and an infant/juvenile. More widespread long bone bowing (Rickets) was noted in the infant remains from grave 40, whilst thinning of the exocranial parietal surface with exposure of the diploe was seen in the infant/juvenile from grave 53 (Pl. 3.4B). Changes to the remains of the woman from grave 86 suggest osteomalacia. Many also had lesions consistent with other metabolic problems. Conditions associated with a lack of vitamin D are normally associated with urbanisation, and are generally rare in archaeological contexts.

Osteoporosis – evident in the skeletons of six females, five over *c.* 45 years – is the reduction in trabecular bone mass and structure, weakening the bones and making them more prone to fracture. The condition can affect either sex, and is strongly associated with advancing age. However, factors such as disease, diet and lifestyle, and genetics play a role (Roberts and Manchester 1997, 177–180). Roberts and Cox (2003, 189) report low rates of osteoporosis in the period, but suggest that the actual occurrence must have been higher.

Infection

Infection can result from invasion of the body tissues by bacteria, viruses, parasites or fungus (Roberts and Manchester 2005, 124–5). The most common cause of infection observable on bone is bacteria. Bacterial infections are either non-specific, where the cause is unidentifiable, or specific, where changes form a pattern typical of a specific disease, for example tuberculosis or leprosy. Irritation of the periosteum (the membrane covering bone) can stimulate growth, whilst abscesses and direct infection of the bone may cause destructive lesions.

Tuberculosis (TB)

Tuberculosis is a complex condition resulting from bacterial infection (*Mycobacterium bovis* and *M. tuberculosis*; Aufderheide and Rodríguez-Martin 1998, 118–41) thought to be linked to close and long-term contact with animals (Roberts and Cox 2003, 40–2). Two forms of bacteria cause tuberculosis in humans – these can spread via water droplets in the air and enter the lungs, causing the pulmonary form of the disease. Alternatively, ingestion of infected milk or meat, and possibly even contact with infected hides, can result in manifestation within the bowel and lymph nodes (Roberts and Cox 2003; Salter 1999, 226-8). Infection of the soft tissues has the potential to spread to bone, for example pulmonary infection can lead to the deposition of new bone on the visceral surfaces of the ribs. Both forms can cause erosive, sclerotic bone lesions created by the bacteria-filled cysts or tubercles in the vertebrae and joints. Large abscesses within the bone (osteomyelitis) often cause the total destruction of joints and severe curvature of the spine (Pott's disease) (Salter 1999, 226–8; Roberts and Manchester 1997, 135–42; Aufderheide and Rodríguez-Martin 1998, 118–41). Tuberculosis of the spine is characterised by the progressive destruction of the vertebral body, usually in the lower thoracic and upper lumbar regions. Without intervention the infection is ultimately fatal.

Tuberculosis is the most likely cause of the pathological changes in the spine and ribs of the older adult female from grave 105 (Pl. 3.5). Most dramatic is the massive destruction of the bodies of T8–L1, with associated fusion and anterior/posterior kyphosis of the neural arches and remaining body portions; greater destruction occurred between T11–L1, the twelfth vertebra body having been completely destroyed. Less severe lesions were observed in T5–7 and C5–7 bodies. Associated deformation was recorded in the eighth to twelfth ribs, with plastic changes, pseudo facets, erosion and woven new bone on the articular surfaces. Lamellar bone on the tenth rib heads could indicate pulmonary infection. Other changes that may or may not be related to the infection include erosive lesions in some toe joints and endocranial new bone deposits. The disease may

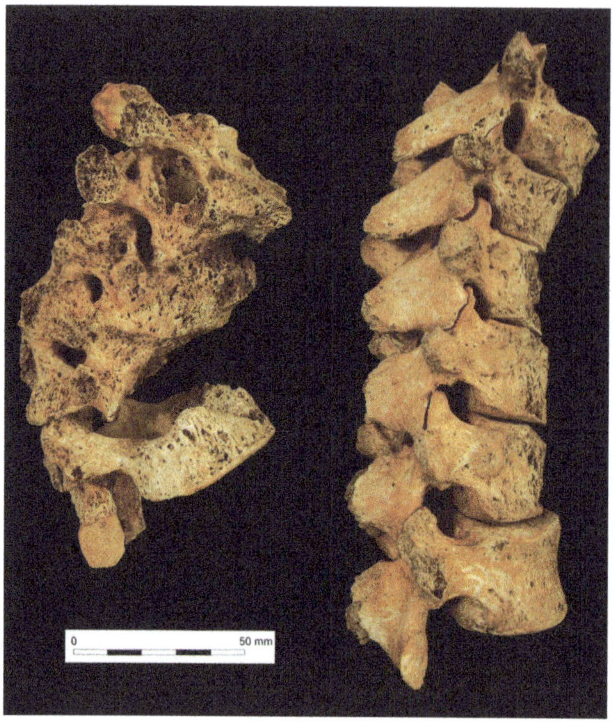

Plate 3.5 Tuberculosis – left: tuberculosis of the spine (T8 to L1) in skeleton 1415 (grave 105); right: 'normal' spine (T8 to L1). (Both showing right side)

also have caused, or exacerbated the osteoporosis evident in this individual. A layer of lamellar new bone was noted on the internal (visceral) surfaces of at least five left ribs of an adult female (grave 66). It appears that this individual had suffered chronic inflammation of the left viscera. Possible factors include chronic infection (eg, pulmonary TB, pleurisy and pneumonia), or exposure and sensitivity to irritants such as smoke and dust.

Tuberculosis has been proven to be present in humans in Britain during the Middle Iron Age (Mays and Taylor 2003; Taylor *et al.* 2005), though a recent discovery at Cherry Lodge Farm, Shrewton, Wiltshire suggests that the condition was affecting humans as early as the Middle/Late Bronze Age (McKinley 2010). It appears that the frequency increases during the Anglo-Saxon period; 18 contemporaneous examples from across England are listed by Roberts and Cox (2003, 184, table 4.10, 390).

Leprosy

Leprosy, a chronic infection caused by *M. leprae*, spreads between humans through skin-to-skin contact, and mucous droplets. It takes a number of years to incubate and manifest itself with the infection affecting the peripheral nerves, skin, mucous

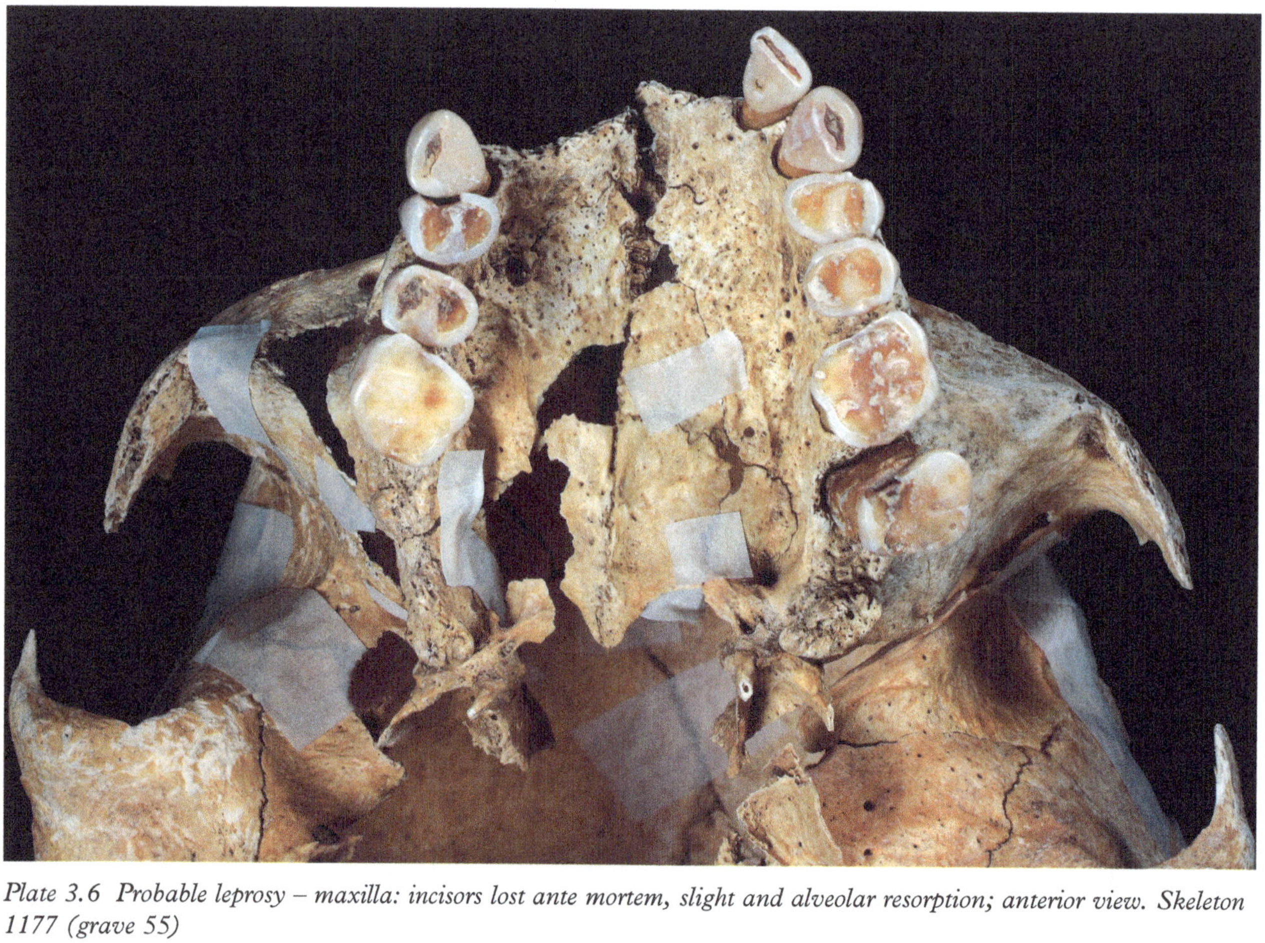

Plate 3.6 Probable leprosy – maxilla: incisors lost ante mortem, slight and alveolar resorption; anterior view. Skeleton 1177 (grave 55)

membranes and soft tissues (Roberts and Manchester 1997, 142; Aufderheide and Rodríguez-Martín 1998, 141–54). It can produce distinctive pathological skeletal changes such as destruction/resorption of maxillary bones, periosteal new bone on the tibiae and fibulae, atrophy of the hand and foot bones, osteomyelitis and septic arthritis (Ortner and Putschar 1985, 176–180).

The skeletons of three adult females (graves 61, 55 and 85) had potentially leprous bony changes (Table 3.1; Pls 3.6–3.8). The nasal spine and nasal margins of the individual from grave 55 are resorbed, as are the maxillary incisor sockets. The resultant bony structure is disorganised, and there is porotic new bone on the palatal aspect of the incisive positions. Large patches of partially healed periosteal new bone are manifest on the right tibia and both fibulae shafts, whilst lesions on the right femur shaft indicate a chronic ulcer. Tapering atrophy was evident in five hand distal phalanges, and in the feet an intermediate and distal phalanges were similarly affected. Distinctive depressions on the palmar side of three hand proximal phalanges are indicative of prolonged finger contracture. The poorly preserved skull of the individual from grave 85 revealed the *ante mortem* loss of a maxillary incisor, and secondary sinusitis, whilst three distal hand phalanges are atrophied, and signs of finger contracture are evident on the palmar surface of a proximal phalanx. Given the evidence discussed above, the pattern of extensive new bone formation on the anterior maxilla and sinuses, tibiae, fibulae and metatarsals, along with osteomyelitis of the left third metatarsal, suggest that the individual from grave 61 was also infected with *M. leprae*.

Possible cases of leprosy have been observed in Middle Bronze Age (Horton, Berkshire, McKinley pers. comm.) and several Roman-British skeletal assemblages (eg, Poundbury, Dorset, Cirencester, Gloucestershire and West Thurrock, Essex; Roberts and Cox 2003, 120; Roberts and Manchester 1997, 147; McKinley 2009b). The disease is still not commonly recorded in Anglo-Saxon material – Roberts and Cox (2003, 218) list 18 Anglo-Saxon examples from across the country.

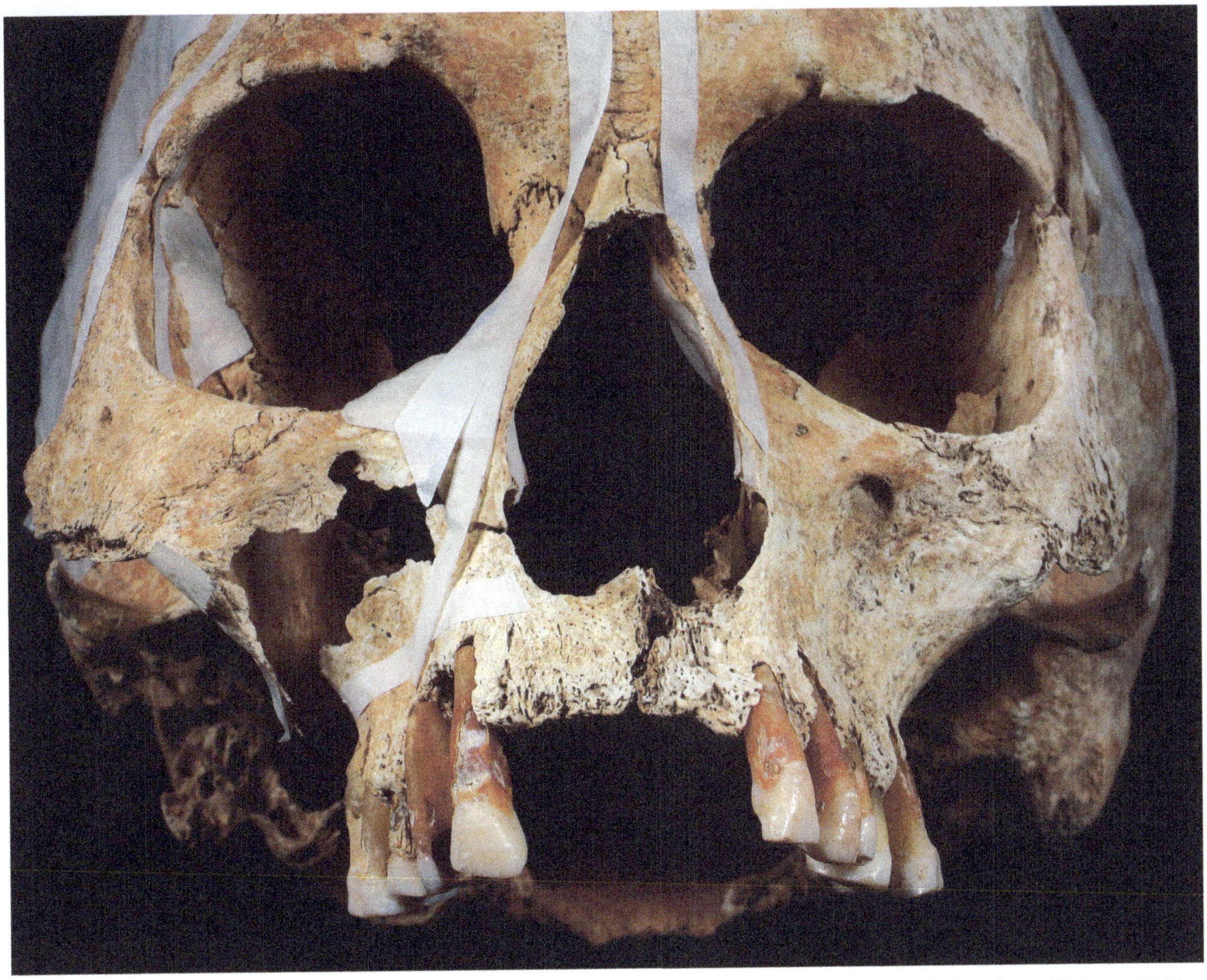

Plate 3.7 Probable leprosy – maxilla: substantial resorption and remodelling of anterior; inferior view. Skeleton 1177 (grave 55)

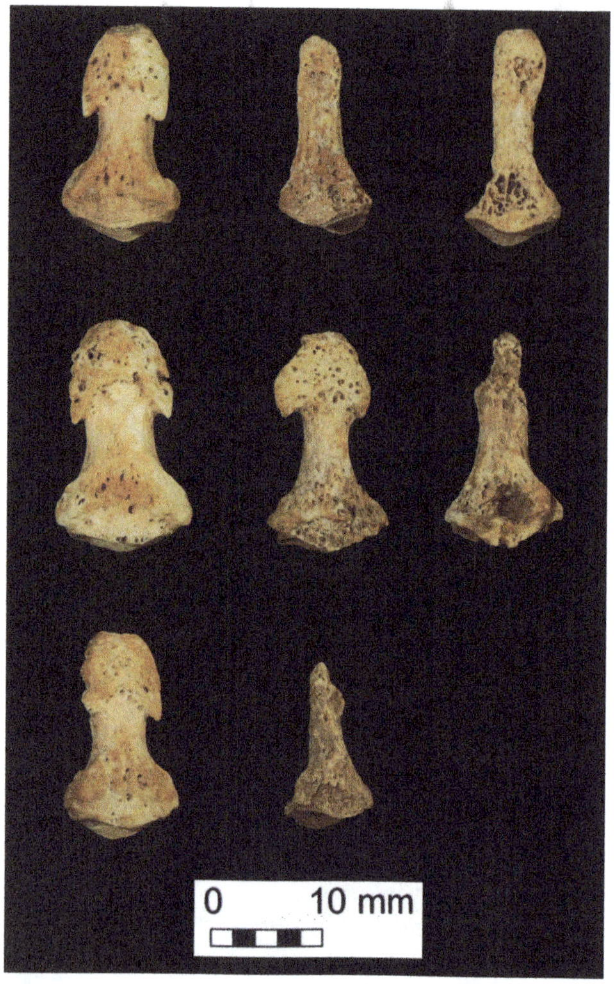

Plate 3.8 Probable leprosy – tapered distal phalanges (finger tips, palmar view); left: 'normal'; top: right hand, skeleton 1177 (grave 55); middle: right hand, skeleton 1255 (grave 85); bottom: left hand, skeleton 1255 (grave 85).

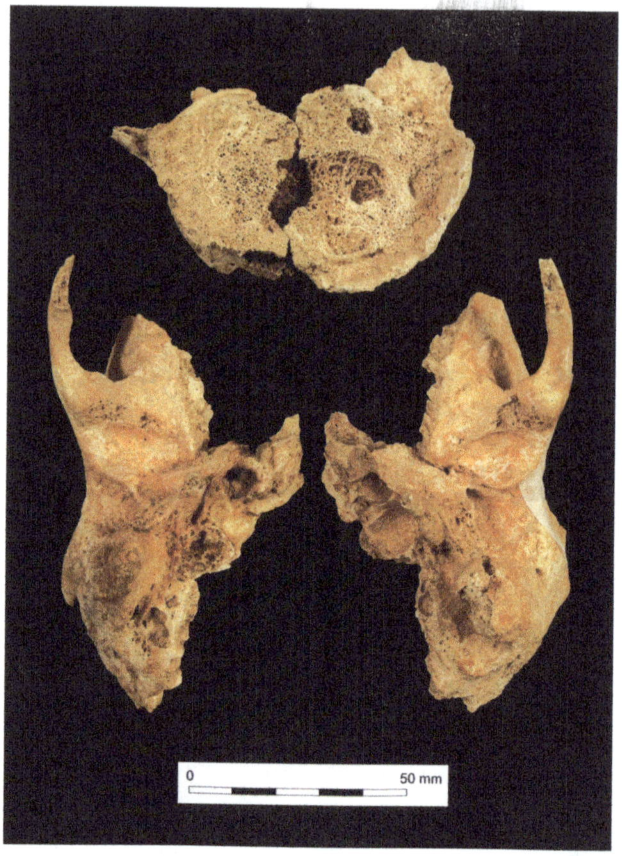

Plate 3.9 Destructive lesions – top: L5 with lesion in the anterior body; superior view; bottom: temporo-mandibular joints with lesions; inferior view. Skeleton 1405 (grave 108)

Non-specific infection

Lamellar bone on the endocranial occipital surface of an adult male (grave 59) suggests that the individual had sustained endocranial inflammation, potentially as a result of disease/infection or injury.

Destructive lesions were observed in the right lower leg and foot of a young adult male (grave 60), and in the arm and wrist of a young adult female (grave 43). The sclerotic lesions were typically concave and fairly ragged, with darkly discoloured margins. Lytic lesions can occur with various infections such as tuberculosis, leprosy and syphilis (though the latter is generally bilateral), as well as multi-focal neoplastic diseases.

The older adult male in grave 108 had a destructive lesion affecting the left temporo-mandibular joint (?psoriatic arthritis (Farronato *et al.* 2010)) and a larger, lobate destructive lesion (33 x 22 x 5.5 mm) on the superior surface of the fifth lumbar vertebral body (Pl. 3.9).

Osteomyelitis, possibly caused by a penetrating wound or fracture was identified in the left hand of another female (grave 64), where the distal, dorsal aspect of the fourth metacarpal had been substantially destroyed, with a small cloaca on the lateral surface.

The relatively high rate of what are ususally considered conditions associated with overcrowding and urbanisation is intriguing in the rural setting of Collingbourne Ducis, and may imply strong links with larger settlements.

Parasites

Tapeworm *Echinococcus granulosus*, which when eggs are ingested, can lead to Echinococcosis or hydatid disease, the most common being cystic echinococcosis. Larvae hatch and migrate through the blood, attaching primarily within the liver. Hydatid cysts then form slowly, and whilst symptoms depend on location, the liver can become enlarged and painful (Aufderheide and Rodríguez-Martín 1998, 240–4). Rupture of a cyst can cause potentially fatal anaphylactic shock. Fragments of hydatid cyst were recovered from the burial remains of three older adults, one male, and two female (graves 57, 62 and 106).

Table 3.6 Summary of spinal lesions by sex (including unnumbered vertebrae)

	Total no. vertebrae	*Schmorl's nodes*	*Degenerative disc disease*	*Osteoarthritis*	*Lone osteophytes*	*Lone pitting*
Female	453	68 *(15.0%)*	49 *(10.8%)*	43 *(9.5%)*	129 *(28.5%)*	21 *(4.6%)*
Male	402	54 *(13.4%)*	85 *(21.1%)*	52 *(12.9%)*	160 *(39.8%)*	58 *(14.4%)*
Unsexed	2	–	–	–	–	–
Total	*857*	122 *(14.2%)*	134 *(15.6%)*	95 *(11.1%)*	289 *(33.7%)*	79 *(9.2%)*

Joint disease

Joint diseases represent the most commonly recorded conditions in archaeological bone assemblages. Osteophytes and other forms of new bone development, and pitting, may occur as lone lesions. These may reflect age-related 'wear-and-tear', or may form in response to various disease processes. Many conditions increase in frequency and severity with age, though other factors are often involved. The aetiology of some conditions is not fully understood.

All or parts of 49 adult spines (19 males, 29 females and one unsexed) were available for analysis (Tables 3.6–7). A total of 4765 adult extra-spinal joints (2151 male, 2592 female and 22 unsexed) were recorded.

Schmorl's nodes (represented by pressure defects in the surface of vertebral bodies) result from intervertebral disc rupture, which commonly affect young adults, and frequently persist into later life (Rogers and Waldron 1995, 27; Roberts and Manchester 1997, 107). Lesions were observed in 30 adult spines (61.2%), affecting 1–10 vertebrae in 13 male spines and 1–11 vertebrae in 17 female spines. The predominantly slight lesions were of mixed appearance (crescent, linear and circular); more severe examples include those involving prolapse of the extrusion into the spinal cord cavity. The TPR is a little less than the average calculated by Roberts and Cox (16.6%; 2003, 197–8, table 4.2) from their sample, and that for Twyford School (14.5%; Egging Dinwiddy 2011). Only 2.2% of vertebrae from Worthy Park were affected (Wells *et al.* 2003, 165, table 3.15).

Degenerative disc disease (represented by pitting and marginal osteophytes of the vertebral body surfaces) results from the breakdown of the intervertebral disc, most often reflecting age-related wear-and-tear (Rogers and Waldron 1995, 27). Clinical studies also suggest a biochemical factor in the disease, which may explain the presence of the condition in younger individuals (see below; Buckwalter 1995; Sobajima *et al.* 2004, 390). Lesions were evident in 22 adult spines (44.9%; Table 3.7); 1–21 vertebrae in 13 male spines, and 2–14 vertebrae in nine female spines (averaging 7 and 6.9 vertebrae respectively). Patterns of distribution are broadly similar between the sexes, whilst there is a strong age-related link to severity and extent – most of those affected being over *c.* 40 years old. Exceptions include the individuals from graves 83 and 97 – both under *c.* 35 years of age at death (see above). Most lesions were slight to moderate. Similar TPRs were seen in the small assemblage from Twyford School (14.5%; 10.1% female; 26.5% male; Egging Dinwiddy 2011).

Lesions indicative of osteoarthritis (Rogers and Waldron 1995, 43–44) were recorded in 20 spines (40.8%; 11 male and nine female) and 144 extra-spinal joints from 21 individuals (10 male, and

Table 3.7 Summary of spinal lesions by spinal region and sex (including unnumbered vertebrae)

Area	*Total no. vertebrae*	*Schmorl's nodes*	*Degenerative disc disease*	*Osteoarthritis*
Cervical	261	0	49 *(18.8%)*	24 *(9.2%)*
	F: 144	F: 0	F: 21 *(14.6%)*	F: 9 *(6.25%)*
	M: 117	M: 0	M: 28 *(23.9%)*	M: 15 *(12.8%)*
Thoracic	373	80 *(21.4%)*	39 *(10.5%)*	51 *(13.7%)*
	F: 186	F: 40 *(21.5%)*	F: 12 *(6.5%)*	F: 21 *(11.3%)*
	M: 185	M: 40 *(21.6%)*	M: 27 *(14.6%)*	M: 30 *(16.2%)*
	U: 2	U: 0	U: 0	U: 0
Lumbar	178	41 *(23.0%)*	37 *(20.8%)*	17 *(9.6%)*
	F: 96	F: 27 *(28.1%)*	F: 12 *(12.5%)*	F: 11 *(11.5%)*
	M: 82	M: 14 *(17.1%)*	M: 25 *(30.5%)*	M: 6 *(7.3%)*
First sacral	45	1 *(2.2%)*	9 *(20%)*	3 *(6.7%)*
	F: 27	F: 1 *(3.7%)*	F: 4 *(14.8%)*	F: 2 *(7.4%)*
	M: 18	M: 0	M: 5 *(27.8%)*	M: 1 *(5.6%)*

Table 3.8 Summary of extra-spinal joint disease

	Joint count	*Osteoarthritis*	*Eburnation*	*Osteophytes*	*Pitting*
Temporo-mandibular	85	12 *(14.1%)*	1 *(1.2%)*	–	11*(12.9%)*
Costo-vertebral (ribs)	737	94 *(12.8%)*	–	246 *(33.4%)*	79 *(10.7%)*
Sterno-clavicular	57	5 *(8.8%)*	–	4 *(7%)*	18 *(31.6%)*
Acromio-clavicular	41	–	–	–	17 *(41.6%)*
Shoulder – glenoid	79	3 *(3.8%)*	1 *(1.3%)*	19 *(24.1%)*	3 *(3.8%)*
Shoulder – humerus	69	2 *(2.9%)*	–	7 *(10.1%)*	4 *(5.8%)*
Elbow – humerus	71	2 *(2.9%)*	1 *(1.4%)*	8 *(11.3%)*	2 *(2.9%)*
Elbow – radius	65	1 *(1.5%)*	1 *(1.5%)*	3 *(4.6%)*	2 *(3.1%)*
Elbow – ulna	82	–	–	21 *(25.6%)*	–
Wrist – radius	65	–	–	12 *(18.5%)*	–
Wrist – ulna	54	2 *(3.7%)*	2 *(3.7%)*	5 *(9.3%)*	–
Hand – carpals	434	5 *(1.2%)*	5 *(1.2%)*	40 *(9.2%)*	–
Hand – carpo-meta	270	3 *(1.1%)*	2 *(0.7%)*	19 *(7%)*	–
Hand – meta-phalangeal	296	–	–	39 *(13.2%)*	–
Hand – proximal IP	312	1 *(0.3%)*	–	29 *(9.3%)*	7 *(2.2%)*
Hand – distal IP	279	–	–	35 *(12.5%)*	–
Sacro-iliac	90	–	–	17 *(18.9%)*	–
Hip – pelvis	92	4 *(4.3%)*	–	18 *(19.6%)*	5 *(5.4%)*
Hip – femur	91	–	–	6 *(6.6%)*	2 *(2.2%)*
Knee – femur/patella	81	4 *(4.9%)*	4 *(4.9%)*	15 *(18.5%)*	2 *(2.5%)*
Knee – lateral	68	2 *(2.9%)*	1 *(1.5%)*	5 *(7.4%)*	2 *(2.9%)*
Knee – medial	73	2 *(2.7%)*	1 *(1.4%)*	3 *(4.1%)*	–
Ankle	82	–	–	2 *(2.4%)*	2 *(2.4%)*
Foot – tarsals	473	–	–	34 *(7.2%)*	–
Foot – tarso-meta	291	–	–	10 *(3.4%)*	–
Foot – meta-phalangeal	191	2 *(1.0%)*	1 *(0.5%)*	3 *(1.6%)*	13 *(6.8%)*
Foot – proximal IP	145	–	–	13 *(8.9%)*	1 *(0.7%)*
Foot – distal IP	279	–	–	1 *(0.4%)*	–
Total	4952	144 *(2.9%)*	20 *(0.4%)*	614 *(12.4%)*	170 *(3.4%)*

Table 3.9 Rates of osteoarthritis in the extra-spinal joints, by sex

Joint	*Joint count (incl. unsexed)*	*Male (all)*		*Female (all)*	
		Total	*Osteoarthritis*	*Total*	*Osteoarthritis*
Temporo-mandibular	85	34	8 *(23.5%)*	51	4 *(7.8%)*
Costo-vertebral (ribs)	737	321	19 *(5.9%)*	416	75 *(18.0%)*
Sterno-clavicular	41	27	2 *(7.4%)*	30	3 *(10.0%)*
Shoulder – Glenoid	79	31	3 *(9.7%)*	48	–
Shoulder – humerus	69	31	1 *(3.2%)*	38	1 *(2.6%)*
Elbow – humerus	71	36	1 *(2.8%)*	35	1 *(2.9%)*
Elbow – radius	65	29	–	36	1 *(2.8%)*
Wrist – ulna	54	28	2 *(7.1%)*	26	–
Hand – carpals	434	195	5 *(2.6%)*	239	–
Hand – carpo-meta	270	133	1 *(0.8%)*	137	2 *(1.5%)*
Hand – proximal IP	312	141	1 *(0.7%)*	170	–
Hip – pelvis	92	38	2 *(5.3%)*	54	2 *(3.7%)*
Knee – femur/patella	81	35	2 *(5.7%)*	46	2 *(4.3%)*
Knee – lateral	68	34	2 *(5.9%)*	34	–
Knee – medial	73	36	2 *(5.6%)*	37	–
Foot – meta-phalangeal	191	93	2 *(2.2%)*	94	–

NB – No lesions were observed in the possible/probable sex categories

11 female) (Tables 3.6–9). Lesions were observed on 1–19 vertebrae in the female spines, and 1–13 vertebrae in the male spines. Overall, the thoracic region is most commonly affected with changes seen in all joint types, though most examples were mild to moderate. The condition is most prevalent in the temporo-mandibular and rib joints, the former being more prevalent in males, whilst the reverse is true in regard to rib lesions (Tables 3.8–9). Factors in temporo-mandibular lesions can include mis-alignment, injury, infection, ageing and overuse (including bruxism). Osteoarthritis in other extra-spinal joints appears to have been fairly evenly distributed within the body, a pattern recognised by Roberts and Cox (2003, 195). The majority of lesions can be described as slight, or slight–moderate; the most severe were predominantly manifest in the remains of individuals *c.* 45 years or older. Comparative TPRs are limited, and where they exist, caution regarding preservation has been suggested (McKinley 2006a; Egging Dinwiddy 2011).

Lone osteophytes were observed on all types of vertebral articulations, the most commonly involved being the articular facets of the first and second cervical vertebrae closely followed by the joints of L3–5. The transverse process joints and rib facets had a greater frequency of lesions in the mid-range and lower two thoracic positions respectively. Osteophytes were manifest on the body surface margins in 31 adult spines (65.3%), on 1–22 vertebrae in 16 male spines, and 1–20 in 17 female spines. The L5/S1 region was most commonly affected, whilst the upper cervical and upper thoracic regions were least so. Most lesions were mild to moderate, with occasional more prolific examples in the cervical and lower lumbar/sacral regions. As expected, the individuals with the most advanced osteophyte growth were older adults, over *c.* 45 years. Lesions were seen in 614 extra-spinal joints, with peaks in the ribs, shoulders, elbows and wrists, hips and knees respectively. At Twyford a similar rate of spinal osteophytes was recorded (39.5% vertebrae), whilst the wide range of affected extra-spinal joints included a slightly elevated prevalence in those of the shoulders (Egging Dinwiddy 2011, 108).

Lone pitting was observed in the vertebral articular process joints and rib facets in 29 adult spines (14 male and 15 female), with peaks in the fifth and tenth thoracic vertebral positions. The extent of pitting was slight in all but a few cases, and the rate was higher in males. Of the 1701 affected extra-spinal joints, those of the clavicle were most commonly involved, followed at some distance by the temporo-mandibular and rib joints (Table 3.8). At Twyford lower rates were seen in the vertebrae (5.3%) and extra-spinal joints (1.5%).

Changes consistent with rotator cuff damage, generally a result of the degeneration and rupture of the tendinous cuff of the shoulder (Adams 1987, 129), were identified in the right shoulder of an older adult female (grave 115). A few individuals (five females, one male) had noticeably bowed upper limb bones, possibly a result of vigorous, repeated arm movements – as may be seen in certain crafts or processing tasks.

As with other contemporaneous groups in the region, those buried at Collingbourne were participating in fairly rigorous activities, such as those associated with agriculture, though there is little evidence to suggest that these were excessively strenuous. The evidence also suggests a general, slightly greater/heavier use of the upper limbs.

Cysts

Most of the lesions described as cysts (Table 3.1; six individuals) represent 'pseudo-erosions' or solitary bone cysts, considered to be the result of vascular disturbance and/or fibroplastic proliferation, and predominantly asymptomatic (Rogers and Waldron 1995, 61-3; Eiken and Jonsson (1980, 285).

Ankylosing spondylitis

Large bony projections extend superiorly and medially from the superior margin of both sacroiliac joints of an older male (grave 59) (Pl. 3.10). Pronounced calcification of the *ligamentum flavum*

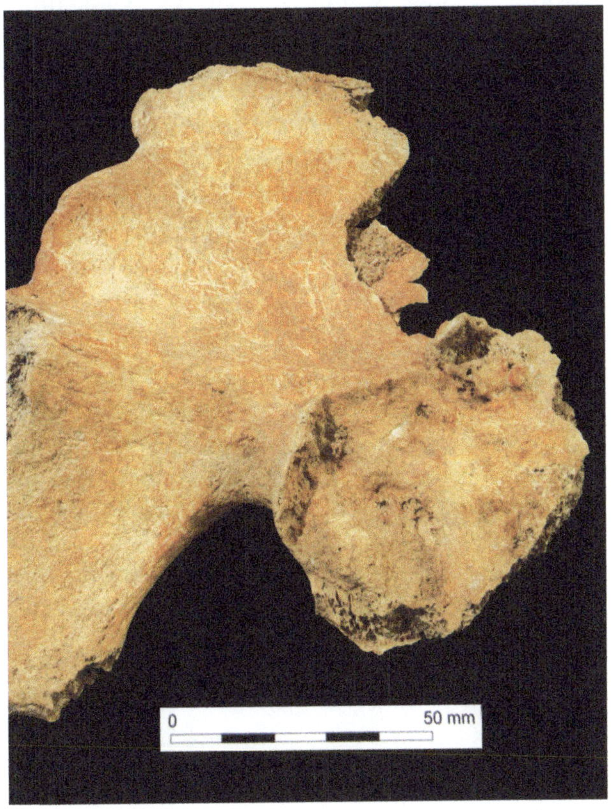

Plate 3.10 DISH or ankylosing spondylitis – extensive osteophytes around the right sacroiliac joint margin; medio-anterior view. Skeleton 1132 (grave 59)

was also noted on the thoracic and lumbar vertebrae. A more advanced example was seen in the sacroiliac joints of another elderly male (over 45 years, grave 106). Although damaged, it is clear that both joints are substantially fused with large, smooth proliferations.

The most likely diagnosis is ankylosing spondylitis, a rare inflammatory, possibly genetically-linked disorder that causes entheses and synovial fluid to calcify in the spinal, sacroiliac and some other joints. The condition, which predominantly affects males, commences in early adulthood at the sacroiliac joints and gradually progresses up the spine, with extreme cases resulting in complete fusion of all or part of the spine ('bamboo spine' or 'poker back') (Salter 1999, 242–5; Roberts and Cox 2003, 32). Whilst similar lesions can occur in Diffuse Idiopathic Skeletal Hyperostosis (DISH; Rogers and Waldron 1995, 54), further diagnostic changes were not present elsewhere on the skeleton.

Archaeological examples of ankylosing spondylitis are rare; Roberts and Cox (2003, 195) list two cases from contemporaneous sites in Kent and Suffolk. A probable example was identified in the Twyford School assemblage (Egging Dinwiddy 2011, 109).

Congenital disease

Incipient *coxa vara* was identified in the femora in grave 64. The condition can be congenital, developmental, related to trauma or to metabolic deficiencies (Aufderheide and Rodríguez-Martín 1998, 74). Incomplete fusion of the neural arch, ie, spina bifida (*ibid.*, 61–2) in the atlas was observed in the individuals from graves 85 and 94, whilst the axis of one individual was asymmetric (grave 66), and a further individual had a double lamina on the left side – possibly an example of incomplete segmentation (grave 53; Pl. 3.4A; *ibid.*, 62–3).

Miscellaneous

Other conditions are listed in Table 3.1 and summarised below.

Hyperostosis frontalis interna, seen in three adult females, is an often age-related accumulation of smooth bone on the endocranial surface of the frontal bone, predominantly affecting females.

Ossified rib and thyroid was present in the remains of several, predominantly older, adults – as is usually the case. The calcification of cartilaginous tissue may also be triggered by a variety of processes, including diseases, or a predisposition to hyperostosis.

Concluding Remarks

The cemetery was probably used for several generations by most members of the local community, some of whom may have originated from outside the locale, as implied by the degree of heterogeneity within the assemblage, and the variety of grave goods and burial rites.

Diet and inferior oral hygiene may have been responsible for the comparatively poorer dental health of the group, whilst childhood stress, malnutrition, infection, disease and parasitic infestation indicate generally poorer overall health compared to contemporaneous communities in the region. Socially and/or culturally related preferences may also have been factorial, eg, swaddling, whereby the access to sunlight and therefore production of vitamin D is restricted.

Though the relative level of traumatic injuries is slightly higher than expected for the period, the patterns are comparable, with most representing falls and accidents, and a few potential cases of interpersonal violence.

There remains considerable potential for further research. Radiocarbon dating would, for example, establish a better understanding of the temporal and spatial development of the cemetery (Hines and Bayliss 2013). Investigation of the origins of the population can be undertaken through stable isotope analysis, whilst analysis of aDNA may reveal familial links and potentially identify strains of disease pathogens.

Cremated Human Bone and Aspects of the Cremation Rite

by Jacqueline I. McKinley

Cremated human bone was recovered from 30 contexts including the remains of a minimum of four burials, three urned and one unurned (Table 3.10). The nature of the remaining deposits is uncertain. Some appear to represent the remains of formal deposits of bone and/or pyre debris (inclusive of cremated bone) either within inhumation graves or in specifically cut features. Other finds of cremated bone probably represent the remains of incidentally redeposited material within the backfills of various feature types including postholes, inhumation graves and a ditch.

The majority of the features from which the deposits derived lay in the southern third of the site to the east and west of the coombe (Fig. 2.2). Although little direct dating evidence was associated with any of the deposits of cremated bone, the more closely dated remains of inhumation burials from this part of the site have been assigned late 5th–early 6th century or late 6th–7th century dates. The allocation of a tighter date range to the cremation-related deposits themselves is difficult. The vessels functioning as

Table 3.10 Summary of the results from the analysis of the cremated bone

Context	*Cut*	*Deposit type*	*Bone weight (g)*	*Age/sex*	*Pathology*	*Comment*
111	114	R	0.2	human	–	–
117	116	R	1.4	subadult/adult >13 yr.	–	–
1277 inc. 1270	1269	u. burial * +?rpd	147.3	juvenile *c.* 5–6 yr.	–	Only 0.6 g in grave fill
1298	1297	un. burial + rpd	296.1	adult *c.* 18–25 yr. ?female	–	–
1311	1310	?R u. burial + rpd	18.8	subadult/adult >13 yr.	–	Central feature in Group 1268
Gp 1268		R	4.4	subadult/adult >13 yr.	–	From 4 of 8 components
1338	1337	R ?rpd	14.9	subadult/adult >13 yr.	–	–
1364	1360	R	0.1	human	–	–
1415	1418	R inh. grave 105	1.0	subadult/adult >13 yr.	–	–
1417	1418	?placed crd	48.4	adult >18yr.	–	1.6 g ?animal
1441	1440	?R	5.9	subadult/adult >13 yr.	–	Sheep/pig tooth root
1443	1442	?R u. burial + rpd	56.7	adult >25 yr. ??male	Pitting – thoracic articular process; periosteal new bone – femur shaft	–
1446	1444	R inh. grave 101	0.4	human	–	–
1459	1458	R	0.1	human		–
1461/3	1462/4	?R/?rpd	19.5	subadult/adult >13 yr.	–	Herring vertebra
1470	1468	?placed crd in grave 96	8.6	subadult/adult >13 yr.	–	–
1481	1480	crd inc. rpd in grave 96	8.7	subadult/adult >13 yr.	–	–
1482	1483	R	0.6	?infant	–	–
1490	1489	R ?inc. rpd	3.9	subadult/adult >13 yr.	–	–
1494	1493	R ?inc. rpd	0.5	subadult/adult >13 yr.	–	–
1501	1264	u. burial	22.3	infant *c.* 1–3 yr.	–	–
1502 inc. 1267	1266	?u. burial (+ grave fill)	28.1	adult >18 yr.	–	–
1503 inc. 1273	1272	?R u. burial	1.9	subadult/adult >13 yr.	–	–

* undisturbed; u. burial – urned burial; un. burial – unurned burial; rpd – redeposited pyre debris; crd – cremation-related deposit; R – redeposited

urns are not chronologically distinctive (Mepham, Chapter 4) and no other artefactual remains were recovered from the deposits. There is stratigraphic evidence to suggest that some cremation-related deposits were disturbed by inhumation graves and conversely that some postdated inhumation burials, though the latter may be complicated by the possible curation of cremated remains, with final deposition occurring some time after the primary mortuary rite of cremation itself. Although cremation is generally viewed as a 5th–6th century rite (Lucy 2000, 119–200), suggesting those from Collingbourne Ducis are likely to relate to the earlier half of the cemetery's use, 7th century examples have occasionally been recovered from a few cemeteries in southern England including Apple Down, Sussex (Down and Welch 1990, 108) and St Mary's Stadium, Southampton (Allen 2005).

Methods

Osteological analysis followed the writer's standard procedure for cremated remains (McKinley 1994, 5–21; 2004b). The remains of urned burial 1277 had been excavated in five 20 mm deep spits to enable details of the burial formation processes to be analysed. These divisions were maintained throughout analysis, though only the data for the overall context is presented in Table 3.10. Cremated bone was recovered from five of the samples recovered from the fill of inhumation grave 96 (the 'bed burial'); this was also recorded and analysed separately, but the data has been amalgamated in Table 3.10.

Age was assessed from the stage of tooth and skeletal development (Beek 1983; Scheuer and Black 2000), and the patterns and degree of age-related changes to the bone (Buikstra and Ubelaker 1994). Sex was ascertained from the sexually dimorphic traits of the skeleton (Gejvall 1981; Bass 1987; Buikstra and Ubelaker 1994). The variable integrity of the attributed sex has been denoted as confident, probable ('?' in Table 3.10) and most likely ('??').

Results and Discussion

A summary of the results is presented in Table 3.10; full details are held in the archive.

Disturbance and condition

The depth of features from which cremated bone was recovered (excluding inhumation grave 101 and penannular ditch 1360, both of which contained only very small quantities of incidentally redeposited material) ranged from 0.07 m to 0.49 m; the majority (*c.* 58%) were 0.10–0.20 m deep and a substantial proportion were over 0.20 m (*c.* 26%). Although possible 'placed' deposits of cremated bone were recovered from the fills of two inhumation graves (96 and 105; see below), most of the features containing cremated bone were discrete cuts and not subject to disturbance by later features (Fig. 2.82).

Many of the cremation-related deposits were recognised by their dark, charcoal-rich fills visible at surface level, and this, together with the relatively shallow surviving depth of some features (ie, *c.* 26% at less than 0.15 m), suggests some level of truncation may have occurred and that bone may have been lost as a result. Set against this possibility, however, is the fact that the maximum weight of bone recovered from any of the deposits was from the shallowest feature; cremation grave 1297 cut into the upper fill of inhumation grave 92 and containing the remains of an unurned burial. The charcoal-rich fill of the grave was evident at surface level, and it is possible that additional bone may have been removed as a result of truncation, but intact unurned burials recovered elsewhere have shown depths of only 0.07–0.10 m (eg, Dinwiddy and Schuster 2009, figs 36–38); hence, even in this case there was probably little, if any, bone loss.

Graves may often have been truncated but the burial remains (unurned or urned) within them, generally made at the base of the cuts, were frequently unaffected or only slightly so. For example, the intact remains of an urned burial were recovered from an obviously truncated grave (1269) of 0.16 m depth (see *Formation Processes*, below for further discussion). The remains of the two other probable urned burials, from graves 1264 and 1266, had both been substantially truncated, possibly in antiquity. Both vessels appear to have been dragged out of position leaving only a few body sherds within the grave fills, despite the graves themselves surviving to 0.09 m and 0.15 m depth respectively. Alternatively, the deposits could have been deliberately disturbed in antiquity and what survived could represent wholly redeposited remains. In both cases some bone, potentially substantial amounts in the case of grave 1266 (only a 30 mm 'depth' of the vessel remained in the fill), is likely to have been lost.

The bone from the majority of contexts is slightly worn and chalky in appearance, and trabecular bone (generally the first to be lost in acidic soil conditions; McKinley 1997, 245; Nielsen-Marsh *et al.* 2000) is absent from all except four deposits. The small quantities of bone from the two deposits associated with inhumation grave 96 (1470 and 1481) are the most severely affected. The bone from two of the burials – the undisturbed urned burial in grave 1269 and the unurned burial in grave 1297 – is in good condition, as is that from the deposit of uncertain type (see below) in cut 1442. Trabecular bone is relatively well represented in only three deposits; those from graves 1269 and 1297, and the 'placed' deposit 1417 from inhumation grave 105. A small amount was also included amongst the bone from pit 1310 set central to the rectilinear features defining mortuary structure 1268.

The silty clay texture of the local soils and free-drainage on the valley slope will have combined to create a slightly acidic burial environment. Minor variations in the burial environment may benefit or adversely effect bone preservation. The urned burial 1277 will have been afforded protection from the environment by the vessel while disturbance in antiquity would have removed this protection from the other proposed deposits of this type. The location of cremation grave 1292 in the upper levels of the fill of inhumation grave 92, together with the neutralising effects of the charcoal-rich environment, may explain the better preservation of the bone in this case. The bone from grave 105 and cremation-related feature 1310 was also in charcoal-rich environments. Both the cremated and the unburnt bone from inhumation grave 105 is in good condition, perhaps affected by grave location and the inclusion of organic materials in the grave. The poorly preserved cremated bone from inhumation grave 96, where the unburnt bone was in fairly good condition, suggests the former may originally have derived from a more aggressive burial environment.

Demographic data and deposit types

Minimum number of individuals (MNI)

A minimum of four individuals are represented, one from each of the confidently identified burials (graves 1264, 1266, 1269 and 1297). All four graves were situated in the western half of the site, those containing the remains of the three urned burials forming a *c.* 10 m arc just to the north of the mortuary structure 1268, while that containing the unurned burial (1297) was cut through the upper levels of the early 6th century inhumation grave 92 on the southern margins of the site (Fig. 1.2). The identified individuals comprise one infant, one juvenile and two adults – one a young female and the other an unsexed individual (Table 3.10).

Four individuals is undoubtedly a minimum number in this instance and it is likely that a greater number, probably at least nine, are represented (see below). The additional numbers are likely to include three subadult/adult individuals (1311, 1470 and 1503) and two adults including one possible male (1417 and 1443; Table 3.10). The difficulty surrounding the confident identification of a higher MNI stems from uncertainty regarding the types of deposit from which the rest of the assemblage derived and the form of the assemblage itself.

Deposit types

Irrespective of the probable loss of small quantities of trabecular bone from most deposits (see above), the quantities of bone recovered from most non-grave features are very small (0.1–56.7 g) with an average weight of 12.9 g; ie, less than 1% of the expected weight of bone from an adult cremation (McKinley 1993a). Few of the deposits contained identifiable fragments of those skeletal elements useful for minimum number counts (mostly skull; McKinley 2000a, figs 2 and 3), most comprising undistinguished fragments of long bone shaft. Consequently, there is very little duplication of skeletal elements between the deposits, including the confidently identified remains of burials (a fragment of volmer – one of the facial bones – was the only duplicate fragment in the assemblage, one recovered from a deposit in inhumation grave 105 and one from cut 1442).

The features from which these very small quantities of bone were recovered were generally of a relatively substantial depth (see above). The method of excavation employed in most cases involved the fill being recovered as a single sample, rather than in accordance with the advised procedure for cremation burials of using a sample series with divisions by quadrants and, where necessary, spits (eg, McKinley forthcoming). Consequently, there is no mechanism by which the distribution of the bone within the individual features can be ascertained. For example, the 18.8 g (equivalent to a tablespoon full) of cremated bone from the 0.46 m diameter and 0.49 m deep pit 1310 (central within mortuary structure 1268) could have comprised a concentration within one part of the pit or have been dispersed throughout. The forms of deposit indicated by these two possibilities are vastly different but neither would be indicative of a formal *in situ* 'burial' as represented by the deposits in graves 1269 and 1297 for example – the quantities of bone are simply too small and unrepresentative. In view of the potential variety of deposit types which may be represented within the assemblage – including redeposited pyre debris, 'placed token' deposits or *memento mori*, and incidentally redeposited bone – and in the absence of clear duplication of skeletal elements or variations in indicated age/sex, the remains from one cremation may have been deposited in several features and it cannot be assumed that the contents of different features derived from different pyres.

Careful consideration has been given to each individual deposit with a view to their most probable interpretation, drawing on all the available evidence: stratigraphic information, archaeological components and where possible their distribution, and the data from the cremated bone itself.

Two deposits made within inhumation graves appear to represent deliberate placements, probably within textile or skin bags, made contemporaneously with the inhumation burial. In grave 105, the bone was recovered as a 0.15 m diameter, 0.06 m deep concentration (context 1417, containing some flecks of fuel ash) set over the left shoulder of the unburnt skeletal remains (Fig. 2.70). In this case, the cremated bone appears to have been deposited in direct contact with the inhumed individual. The majority of the cremated bone (77%) from inhumation grave 96 (the 'bed burial') was recovered from a 0.16 m diameter (no thickness recorded, possibly similar to diameter) concentration of fuel ash (1470) situated in the area above and to the left of the left forearm of the inhumed remains (Fig. 2.62). In this instance there was no direct physical contact between the skeletal remains and the cremation-related deposit, the latter being recovered at the same level as the bed-fittings which generally lay *c.* 0.10 m above the level of the skeleton (the latter presumably having dropped slightly as the organic components of the bed disintegrated; see below). The evidence suggests that a placed deposit of pyre debris (by definition inclusive of cremated bone) was made during backfilling of the grave. A further, similarly sized deposit of cremated bone within pyre debris (1481) was made in a pit (1480) dug through the upper levels of the fill in inhumation grave 96, situated to the left of the skull (but not disturbing it). The absence of bed fittings from this small area of the grave fill (Fig. 2.62) suggests the insertion of this deposit postdated the inhumation burial by several years. Whilst the evidence is not conclusive, it seems likely that the cremated bone from both these inhumation graves (96 and 105), apparently deliberately placed and inserted as 'token' *memento mori* deposits, represents the 'curated' remains of individuals known to the occupants and not represented elsewhere within the cemetery assemblage. Both have tentatively been included in the possible extended minimum number counts.

Two sherds from the body of a pot and a very small quantity of cremated bone were recovered from the upper levels of pit 1272 (0.11 m deep). The remains were clearly not *in situ* but may represent the redeposited remains of an urned burial, a possibility strengthened by the location of the feature in close proximity to other deposits of this type (Fig. 2.2). A second such example but inclusive of redeposited pyre debris is represented by the material from cut 1442 (0.20 m deep) in the eastern half of the site, which contained several body sherds and a small quantity of bone in a charcoal-rich matrix. There is no obvious cause for disturbance in either case, which suggests both may have been deliberately disturbed ('robbed') in antiquity. Again both have tentatively been included in the possible extended minimum number counts.

Mortuary group 1268 and its interpretation is discussed in detail below. It is, however, believed unlikely that the individual represented by the small quantity of bone recovered from this feature has otherwise been included within the MNI.

On the strength of the available evidence, the small quantities of bone from the remaining features all appear likely to be redeposited, representing either scattered material from pyres not collected for inclusion in the burial and incidentally incorporated into the fills of non-grave features, or in a few cases, possibly formal deposits of pyre debris (Table 3.10). As such, all could have derived from one of the cremations already represented within the minimum number counts discussed above.

Pathology

Unsurprisingly, given the form and condition of the assemblage and the paucity of trabecular bone, lesions were recorded in the remains of only one individual (Table 3.10). The pitting observed in the thoracic spine was probably related to early stage osteoarthritis. The lamellar new bone evident on a fragment of femur shaft is indicative of a healed infection of the periosteal membrane covering the bone; in the absence of supporting evidence it is not possible to suggest the aetiology of the condition in this case.

Pyre technology and cremation ritual

Oxidation

The majority of the cremated bone is white in colour, indicative of full oxidation of the bone (Holden *et al.* 1995a and b). A few bone fragments from six deposits, including two urned burials, exhibit colour variations indicative of incomplete oxidation. The variations are very minor involving slight blue or grey colouration of one or occasionally two or three fragments from any one skeletal element. Skull elements are most commonly involved (four cases including the two urned burials); fragments of individual lower limb elements are affected in three cases, and upper limb and axial skeleton in one case each. The most extensive variations were observed in the juvenile remains from grave 1269 where individual elements from across the skeleton were affected.

Factors affecting the efficiency of oxidation have been discussed elsewhere by the writer (McKinley 1994, 76–78; 2004a, 293–295; 2008a). The common involvement of the skull may reflect the peripheral position of the head on the pyre, particularly if the body was not positioned centrally. Alternatively, it could reflect the muffling effect resulting from the head being covered by some form of hat/hood or resting on a 'pillow'. The variability in oxidation (degree and extent) appears less than that noted in the broadly contemporaneous cremation cemeteries at St Mary's Stadium, Southampton (McKinley 2005, 19–21) and the London Transport Museum (AOC Archaeology Group 2009). Some colour variation was also noted at Portway, Andover, Hampshire (Henderson 1985), and at Alton, Hampshire the bone was almost uniformly a pale grey (Powers 1988). This suggests that sufficient fuel and time was generally employed to facilitate full oxidation of the bone.

Bone weight

There has already been some discussion related to the weight of bone recovered from individual contexts and its probable significance in reflecting the type of deposits represented. Few of the deposits from the site appear to represent the remains of burials and only two of the latter are sufficiently well preserved to enable their comparison with material recovered from other sites.

The weight of bone from the undisturbed urned burial 1277 (grave 1269) is slightly above the mean of 126.7 g calculated for the undisturbed urned burials of juveniles (with no animal bone; 27 burials) at Spong Hill, Norfolk, though a broad range of 17.2–580 g was recorded (McKinley 1994, table 2). Only one deposit of adult bone, that from the unurned burial 1298 (grave 1297), is likely to be representative of a relatively undisturbed burial deposit. The 296.1 g of bone recovered, representing *c.* 18.5% of the expected weight of bone from an average adult cremation (McKinley 1993a), falls within the lower range of weights recovered from contemporaneous cemeteries of similar date. For example, the average for the undisturbed adult burials at Sancton, Yorkshire, is *c.* 882.2 g (McKinley 1993b) and 806.3 g from Ringlemere, Kent (McKinley 2009c). Cemeteries in southern England generally appear to have lower weight ranges and averages than those in central and northern England, with few deposits of more than 500 g (AOC Archaeology Group 2009; Bayley 2003; Cameron 1988; Henderson 1985; McKinley 2005; Powers 1988; 2008, fig. 16). Although limited conclusions can be drawn from the meagre evidence from Collingbourne Ducis, in this respect the site appears to be in keeping with others from the region (though the potential levels of disturbance observed at some comparative sites is not always clearly stated).

Fragmentation

Meaningful consideration of the levels of bone fragmentation is hampered by the lack of undisturbed burial deposits and the uncertain or redeposited nature of the bone from most features. Cremated bone is very brittle and repeated manipulation and disturbance of deposits inevitably increases fragmentation, breakage occurring along the dehydration fissures formed in cremation. This is clearly reflected in the small maximum fragment size recorded from most deposits (65% below the average of 20 mm); the majority of the bone in 71% of deposits was recovered from the 5 mm or 2 mm sieve fraction. The maximum fragment size of 60 mm was recovered from the unurned burial 1298, where the majority of the bone (*c.* 73%) was in the 10 mm sieve fraction. The figures from the undisturbed urned burial 1277 were smaller, maximum 38 mm with only 44% of the bone in the 10 mm fraction, but this in part reflects the young age of the individual.

The figures from both burials are within the ranges commonly recorded from contemporaneous burials, with average maximum fragment sizes of 42 mm from Spong Hill, 35.5 mm from Sancton, 35 mm from Portway and 52 mm from St Mary's Stadium (Henderson 1985; McKinley 1993b; 1994, 84; 2005). There is no evidence to suggest deliberate fragmentation of bone prior to burial.

Skeletal elements

Most cremation burials of any period (unless substantially disturbed) will include fragments of elements from all four skeletal areas (skull, axial skeleton, upper and lower limb). The identifiable proportions from each are often skewed from what may be referred to as a 'normal' distribution due to the ease with which skull fragments may be recognised, even as very small fragments, and the difficulties in distinguishing individual long bones (McKinley 1994, 6). The potential taphonomic loss of trabecular bone may also reduce the proportion of the axial skeleton (mostly trabecular) identified (see above). The proportion (by weight) of the bone identifiable to individual skeletal elements within the two burials 1277 and 1298 was relatively high at 55% and 62% respectively. The proportions within the other deposits varied widely dependent on the quantity of bone recovered, fragment size and bone condition.

The undisturbed urned burial of the juvenile (1272) shows the common bias towards skull elements (*c.* 50%), but the other three areas are represented in relatively normal proportions to each other. In the unurned burial (1298), skull, is unusually, fairly poorly represented (*c.* 13%) at the expense of the axial skeleton (24%) and lower limb (48%). Given the ease of recognition of skull elements this limited representation is noteworthy. It is possible, given the shallow depth of the deposit (0.07 m), that some bone was lost from the grave due to truncation and that skull fragments could have been concentrated in these potentially lost upper levels. Alternatively, there may have been deliberate de-selection of skull fragments for inclusion within the burial. An absence or paucity of skull elements was also observed in several of the deposits from Rayleigh, Essex (Powers 2008). The mortuary rite of cremation did not require burial of all the bone that remained at the end of cremation and while there is evidence to indicate some other forms of deposition for what remained, eg, inclusion in deposits of pyre debris, the fate of at least some of this material is a point of conjecture (McKinley 2006a). In the case of skull fragments, potentially still identifiable and viewed as representative of the individual even after cremation, they may have been selected for some other form of deposition such as curation or distribution as *memento mori* (*ibid*; Hiatt 1969). Other deposit types did not demonstrate any obvious pattern in terms of skeletal elements represented. Where more than a few grammes of bone were present there was no apparent bias towards specific skeletal areas or elements, and where very little bone was recovered it did not consistently represent only one part of the skeleton.

Tooth roots and the small bones of the hands and feet are commonly recovered from the remains of cremation burials of all periods, and the writer believes their frequency of occurrence may provide some indication of the mode of recovery of bone from the pyre site for burial (McKinley 2000a; 2004b, 299–301). Between one and 12 elements were recovered from six deposits (1277, 1298, 1338, 1441, 1443 and 1463) at Collingbourne Ducis. The greatest number of elements were recovered from the intact urned burial (1277) and the redeposited urned burial (1443), with 11 and 12 elements respectively, the former showing a bias towards hand/foot bones. Of the remaining deposits, three elements were included in the unurned burial (1298) and one or two elements in the redeposited material. The data suggest that different modes of recovery of remains from the pyre may have been employed for different cremations, with a possible link to the mode of burial. For those deposits with fairly high numbers of small elements the bone may have been recovered from the pyre site by raking-off and winnowing, thereby increasing the recovery of the smaller skeletal elements as well as the larger ones. In the case of the unurned burial (1298), where only a few such elements were found, collection of bone for burial may have been effected via the hand recovery of individual bones/fragments, creating a bias towards the more easily recoverable large bones. At Ringlemere it was observed that burials apparently falling in the latter category contained bone weights in the lower part of the range for the site, but currently there is limited data from other Anglo-Saxon sites to support or contradict this observation (McKinley 2009c).

Pyre goods

Very small quantities of cremated animal bone occurred in three deposits comprising one possibly placed deposit and two redeposited contexts (Table 3.10). The species could be confidently identified in two cases (identifications by Jessica Grimm) and included the rare recovery of a fish bone. The inclusion of cremated animal bone (ie, pyre goods) in burials is a common characteristic of the rite across the temporal range which appears to have reached its zenith – both in terms of quantity and variability of species – in the earliest Anglo-Saxon phases as represented in the large cremation cemeteries in the central-eastern areas of England (McKinley 2000a; 2006b; 2014; Hills and Lucy 2013). The quantities recovered from these sites are frequently large, with between one and five species per burial, the most frequently occurring species being horse (Bond 1993; 1994; Bond and Worley 2006; McKinley and Bond 1993; McKinley 1994). In contrast, no animal bone has been noted in burials from many of the contemporaneous cemeteries in southern England including Worthy Park (Bayley 2003), Portway (Cook and Dacre 1985) and Alton (Evison 1988). Where it is found, as here, the quantities are small and the species restricted; eg, St Mary's Stadium and Ringlemere (McKinley 2005; 2009c). Recent re-analysis of data from Spong Hill, Norfolk, suggests this variation in the mortuary rite is probably temporal rather than regional (Hills and Lucy 2013), and in these later cases the bone is likely to represent the remains of food offerings.

Redeposited pyre debris

Ten deposits contained varying quantities of redeposited pyre debris including the remains of urned and unurned burials, and discrete formal and incidental deposits of pyre debris alone (see *Deposit Types*, above). With the exception of Anglo-Saxon cemeteries in central and north-eastern England, the inclusion of pyre debris in grave fills is a common characteristic of the rite throughout its use, and it is generally believed to reflect the proximity of the pyre site to the place of burial (McKinley 2000b; 2000c; 2009c). Such may have been the case at Collingbourne Ducis where, given the distribution of the features from which bone was recovered, the most likely location for the pyres would be in the southern area of the cemetery. The presence of pyre debris in what appear to represent curated 'placed' deposits within two of the inhumation graves may indicate one use to which remains not collected for inclusion in a formal burial was put, in this case retention not necessarily just of the bone but of pyre debris as *memento mori*.

Formation processes

The majority (96%) of the bone from the intact urned burial 1277 was recovered from the lower 40 mm of the 100 mm urn fill. This demonstrates, as has previously been observed, that vessels were often not used to full capacity (though other organic material may occasionally have been incorporated in such burials) and that burial remains may sometimes suffer considerable levels of truncation without the loss of any of the bone (McKinley 1993b, 299; 1994, 85–7; 2009c). There was an even distribution of elements from the different skeletal areas within the vessel, but where they could be sided those from the right occurred higher-up in the fill (spits 3 and 4) than those from the left (spits 4 and 5), the overlap in spit 4 being restricted to skull elements. This may be indicative of an ordered collection/deposition of remains from the pyre, commencing on the left side and progressing down the right from the head-end.

Mortuary structure 1268

The square mortuary structure 1268 comprised four shallow slots (1.08–1.20 m long; 0.26–0.38 m wide, 0.12–0.19 m deep) with postholes (0.42–0.56 m diameter, 0.16–0.29 m deep) at each corner. There was no intercutting between the individual components of the structure which enclosed an area 1.25 m square. Pit 1310 (0.46 m diameter, 0.49 m deep) was situated slightly off-centre to the south-east within the enclosed area. The postholes generally had steep sides with concave bases, whilst the profiles of the slots were slightly more variable, either V-shaped or convex and occasionally with one side steeper than the other. The uniform fills of mid-greyish brown silty clay with sparse flint nodules and chalk pieces contained few finds; very small quantities of cremated bone came from three slots (north, south and west) and one posthole (north-west; Table 3.10), and a few sherds of Saxon pottery from two slots (south and east) and two postholes (south-east and north-west). Several sherds, all from one vessel, were also recovered from the charcoal-rich fill of pit 1310. Despite it not being possible to ascertain the location of the various archaeological components within the pit fill (see above), this evidence, together with the recovery of a small quantity of cremated bone, suggests the fill may have incorporated the partial redeposited remains of an urned burial with redeposited pyre debris.

The mortuary structure is of a form observed in several Anglo-Saxon cremation cemeteries both in southern England and continental Europe, including Apple Down in West Sussex, Alton in Hampshire, Croydon in Surrey and Leibenau in north Germany (Evison 1988, 35–6; Cosack 1983; Down and Welch 1990, 25–33; McKinley 2003, 15–18; Lucy 2000, 118–19). At Apple Down, 32 square mortuary structures were excavated; only one appears to have had slots running between the postholes, the slots being cut by the postholes, and only 11 had a (surviving) central posthole/pit (Down and Welch 1990, fig. 2.13, plate 5). Small quantities of cremated bone (maximum 40 g), sometimes with associated vessels or sherds and redeposited pyre debris, were recovered from various components of some of the structures at Apple Down. It is debatable if all nine of the deposits interpreted as 'burials' did actually represent the remains of *in situ* burial deposits; there is insufficient data regarding potential levels of truncation (no depths) and some bone weights are missing, but on the available evidence many of these deposits appear to represent redeposited material, possibly from burials though not necessarily ones made in the same features as those in which they were found.

The various deposits associated with feature 1268 at Collingbourne Ducis appear remarkably similar to those described at Apple Down, but there is no question of an *in situ* burial deposit here. The inclusion of the bone, pot and fuel ash in pit 1310 does, however, seem rather more than fortuitous and may be related to the interpretation given to these structures by Down and Welch (1990, 29 and plate 53). It has been suggested that the cut features supported a structure which functioned as an above-ground 'mortuary house'. Such features may have contained the remains of one or more burials but being fashioned of organic materials would presumably not have survived for an extensive period of time. The cremation-related deposits, which appear to represent the remains of redeposited burials rather than *in situ* ones, may have been made if the structure fell into disrepair and needed to be replaced or removed.

There are close similarities in form and possibly function between these Anglo-Saxon mortuary features and those recorded from numerous Romano-British cremation cemeteries. The latter, four-post structures describing areas of 0.76–2 m square, often with linking slots as in the Collingbourne Ducis example, have most frequently been recorded at urban and military sites in southern England and Wales (Black 1986; Struck 2000; McKinley 2008b, 107, 188–9). They have been variously interpreted as the bases of wooden 'shrines', cheaper or native versions of stone mausolea, or cenotaphs. It is likely that the Anglo-Saxon features represent a continuation of this Roman tradition, both practising populations possibly being linked to a common continental European origin, the former via foreign military personnel and the latter as recent migrants.

Concluding Remarks

Irrespective of the most representative MNI, whether four or nine, cremation was clearly the minority rite within the cemetery, there currently being 116 excavated inhumation graves (inclusive of the previously excavated features; see above). The cemetery is likely to continue downslope to the south and, the cremation-related deposits being concentrated in the southern portion of the site, further deposits associated with this mortuary rite may still remain unexcavated in this area (redeposited cremated bone was recovered from the southern-most inhumation graves). In keeping with the majority of early Saxon cemeteries from southern England, however, the proportion of cremation graves is likely to remain relatively low. Inclusion of individuals across the age range and members of both sexes indicates that neither age nor sex was a factor in the choice of mortuary rite. It appears that some cremations were undertaken at least in the early part of the 6th century (eg, grave 1297) but the potential curation of remains renders evidence associated with the later 6th century inhumation grave (where cremated bone was deposited in a cut through the grave fill) open to debate. Consequently it cannot be stated with confidence that cremation was preferentially undertaken at any one stage of the cemetery's use. The apparent clustering of a group of cremation graves in the south-western area of the cemetery may suggest the use of the rite by a specific family group. This leaves open to question the nature of the deposits in the eastern half of the cemetery which appear to represent either placed 'token'/*memento mori* deposits of possibly curated material, or redeposited material of some form. If the latter interpretation is correct and the material includes, as it appears to, redeposited pyre debris, the possibility also exists that corpses were being cremated in the vicinity of the cemetery but that the majority of the bone was being removed for burial elsewhere, perhaps entirely outside the region.

The curation and/or transportation of cremated bone is known to have been practiced in the Roman period, particularly for military personnel serving away from home (Table X, Law IX of the Roman Laws of the Twelve Tables; McKinley 2004a). Oestigaard (1999) has argued that such activity formed a common part of the mortuary rite across a wide temporal range in parts of Scandinavia. The duality (some may argue multiplicity) of the cremation rite certainly lends itself to a potentially wide range of individual practices. At Collingbourne Ducis, with its unusual variety of deposit types, not all of which have the characteristics of formal burials, it may be that we have the remains both of material transferred to the site from elsewhere – in the form of curated token/*memento mori* deposits intended for eventual deposition with a loved-one – and debris derived from cremations undertaken within/adjacent to the cemetery from which the bone collected for burial was transported back to the individual's place of origin rather than their being buried where they died. The site lies close to the 6th century western margins of Saxon expansion, and these western-most cemeteries tend to have few, if any cremation graves (Eagles 1994; Davies 1985; Musty and Stratton 1964). What the evidence from Collingbourne Ducis may represent is an adaptation within the mortuary rite, developed in order to maintain a link with their place of origin, by migrants living on the edge of their range of expansion.

Chapter 4
Finds

Bed Burial (Grave 96)

by Jacqui Watson

Little organic material has been preserved on the many iron fittings (Figs 2.62–4), and an initial assessment of the assemblage indicated that the metalwork associated with the bed itself could be separated into the following groups:

- Headboard stays
- Double cleats
- Eyelets or split spiked loops

Detailed examination of the organic traces has made it possible to put forward a possible reconstruction of the original bed, but this can only be an approximation of how it originally looked in the absence of any evidence for decoration and covers that were almost certainly present. The bed appears to have been made from boards of ash, *Fraxinus* sp., the same wood used for all the Anglo-Saxon beds from cemeteries in England (eg, Speake 1989; Malim and Hines 1998; Watson 2006; for further discussion of bed burials and grave 96 see Stoodley below, and Table 4.1).

Many of the iron fittings appear to have been broken prior to burial, which suggests that the bed was dismantled before placing the pieces against the sides of the grave. The woman was then placed in the grave and the position of the skeleton indicates that the body was extended and supine, slumped slightly to the left, with the left hand alongside and the right hand over the right femur. Its position low in the grave is in keeping with lying on a bed – see the distribution of skeleton and metalwork in the grave section (Fig. 4.1; see also Fig. 2.62).

In addition to the metalwork incorporated in the bed structure are two iron brackets that have been fixed over a join between two planks of oak, *Quercus* sp., and may belong with a grave cover.

Headboard Stays

The headboard stays found on Anglo-Saxon beds are an important starting point in establishing the basic structure of the main wooden components of the bed, and these elements may provide an indication of grain orientation so that the other pieces can be positioned accordingly. The stays on the Collingbourne Ducis bed are broken and twisted out of shape (see Fig. 2.63), but they indicate that the headboard was made from wood *c.* 35 mm thick. The sides were 30–36 mm thick, probably with a curved top. The broken

Table 4.1 Dimensions of the recorded Anglo-Saxon and Viking beds with fixed headboards

Site	*Length (m)*	*Width (m)*	*Comment*
Collingbourne Ducis Grave 96	approx. 1.50	0.60	Bed dismantled to place in grave. Oak cover over grave
Barrington, Cambridgeshire Grave 18B (Malim and Hines 1998)	1.60–1.80	0.80	Bed appears to fit closely within the grave, and personal items, including a sword beater, are placed on the body
Barrington, Cambridgeshire Grave 60 (Malim and Hines 1998)	1.50–1.60	approx. 0.70	Large grave with bed and accompanying items
Cherry Hinton, Cambridgeshire (Geake 1997, 147)	1.56	0.72	–
Coddenham, Suffolk (Watson 2006)	1.90	>0.60	Bed dismantled and sections laid out in grave
Shudy Camps, Cambridgeshire (Geake 1997, 147)	1.80	0.80	–
Swallowcliffe Down, Wiltshire (Speake 1989)	approx. 1.83	approx. 0.84	Accompanied with many high status objects
Oseberg Ship burial, Vestfold, Norway (Sjovold 1969)	1.80	1.80	Made from oak with no metal fittings

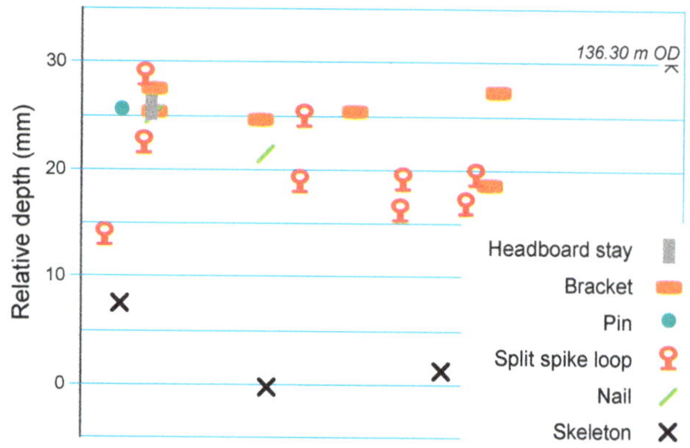

Figure 4.1 Bed burial 96 – section illustrating distribution of skeleton and metalwork within the grave

ends of the headboard stays (ONs 314 and 346) have wood preserved on them that suggests that they were mounted pointing inwards on boards with the grain running horizontally (Fig. 4.2). The headboard appears to have been made from two or three boards which, on the evidence from the wood grain, were probably arranged horizontally and held together with the double cleats.

The headboard stays, although damaged, indicate that the headboard was fixed at an angle of between 96°–99° from the horizontal (Fig. 4.2), in keeping with the angle of 100° noted on the other beds found in England, and the decorated bed from the Oseberg ship (Sjovold 1969).

Double Cleats

It is presumed that the double cleats were used to join two planks or boards together, but no evidence remains in the wood preserved on the broken cleats and the sets are positioned at different heights along the length of the sides and width of the headboard. On both the north and south sides of the grave the cleats are located about 300 mm apart (see Fig. 2.62), and the wood thickness is only 23–28 mm, so maybe they were later additions to the bed, possibly used to add another section to facilitate its carriage.

Eyelets or Split Spiked Loops

There are at least 25 eyelets amongst the metalwork distributed around the perimeter of the grave; nine on the headboard and a further nine on the south side of the bed, with just seven on the north side (see Fig. 2.62). All seem to be located within a 100 mm band across the middle of the headboard and the upper part of the sides, although some were found close together. Where wood is present, the grain suggests that the heads are in a horizontal position. Some eyelets have traces of possible leather strapping passing through the loop, but the ones associated with the headboard appear to have housed thin cords (not included in McCormick, below).

The eyelets have different types of loops, with some made from flat strips and others that have a circular cross-section, and come in three different widths of *c.* 18 mm, 24 mm and 32 mm (see Fig. 2.62). This variation could be an indication of different function or different episodes of repair or modification.

Grave Cover

The only evidence for a grave cover comes from two flat sheets of metalwork (ONs 284 and 300) that were mounted over the joint between two pieces of oak; there is no obvious position for them within the bed structure itself. Both brackets were fixed to the narrow edge of planks of 38.5 mm thickness and appear to be holding a separate piece of oak in position between them (Fig. 4.2) – possibly some crude form of handle to put this wooden structure in place over the burial, unless the brackets are residual fittings from reused pieces of timber.

Discussion

The original structure was probably a plain box bed with the sides held together with tusk tenon joints, which could be dismantled when it was moved (Fig. 4.2). This plain bed could have been adapted to have an upright reclining headboard held in position with twisted metal stays; this would have been fixed and might have been important for the comfort of someone with long term health problems. However, fixing the headboard in this one position would mean it could no longer be easily dismantled and force had to be used to separate the pieces to put it into the grave, which would account for the damage to the metalwork. The placing of bed sections within a grave rather than the intact bed has been recorded at Coddenham, Suffolk (Watson 2006; Penn 2011).

The bed appears to have been approximately 1.5 m long, and 0.6 m wide, which makes it slightly smaller than some of the other beds (Table 4.1), but not significantly so. The dimensions of these beds indicate that they are in the main short and narrow, so only suitable for single occupancy unlike the carved bed found in the Oseberg ship burial (Sjovold 1969).

When it came to the burial, the bed could have been used as a bier or carrier for the body, similar to those identified and illustrated in the Anglo-Saxon cemeteries at Mucking, Essex (Hirst and Clarke 2009), but the fixed headboard might have been too

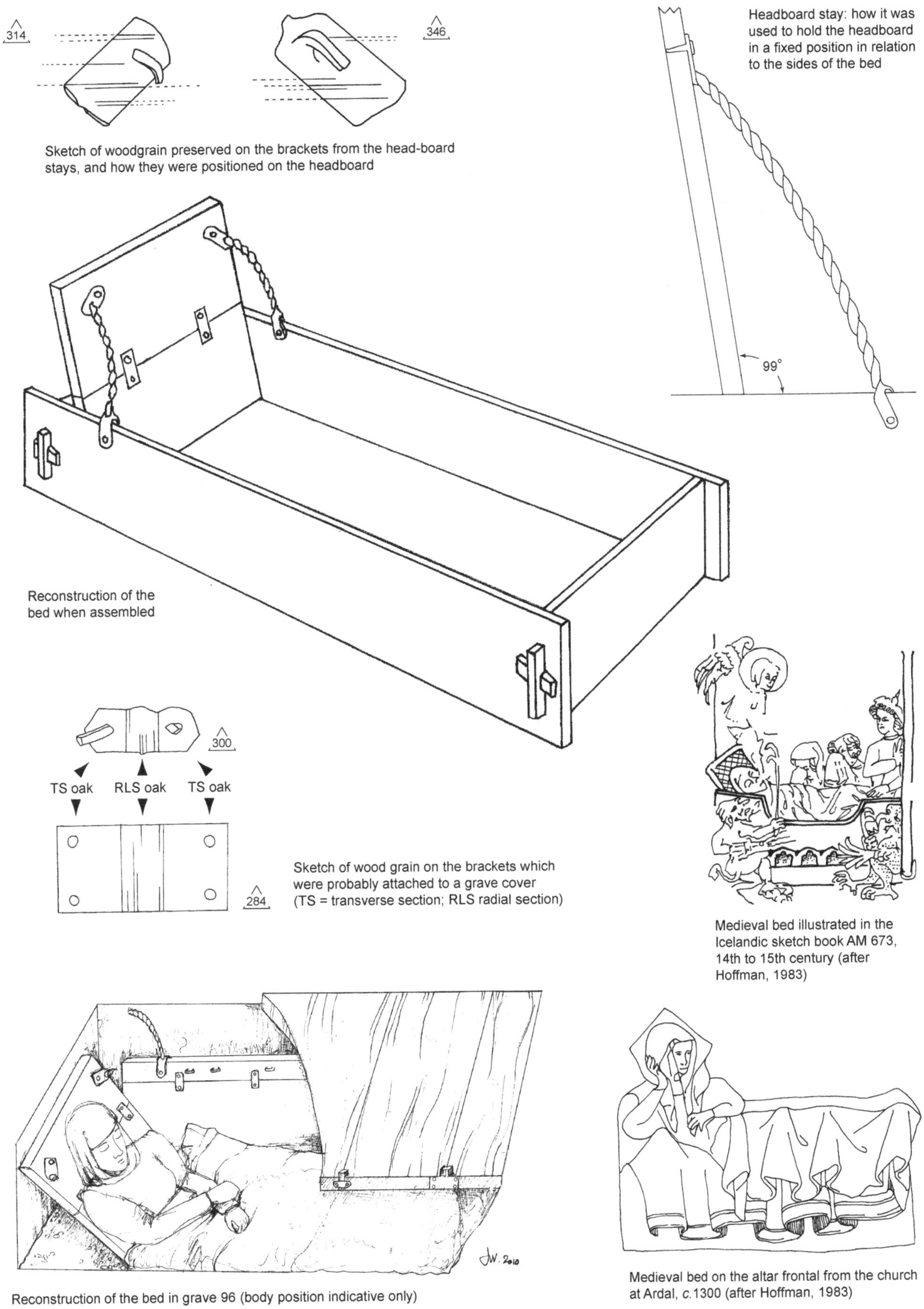

Figure 4.2 Bed burial 96 – details of bed construction, reconstruction of the bed, and illustrations of medieval beds

high for the grave and would have required breaking from the sides in order to be accommodated (Fig. 4.2) (but see Stoodley, below).

Unfortunately no evidence for any textile has been preserved on these bed fittings, although it is difficult to imagine that this burial did not include covers or pillows as has been recorded in other examples (Fig. 4.2). However, the presence of cords through the loops associated with the headboard could point to the presence of upholstery or covering that was held in position, as seen in the 14th–15th-century bed illustrated in the Icelandic sketch book (Fig. 4.2).

Metalwork

by Nick Stoodley

In total, 232 metal objects (excluding the bed fittings in grave 96) were recovered, comprising 63 copper alloy objects and 169 of iron. The majority (205) came from inhumation graves (see *Grave Catalogue*, Chapter 2), while many of the remaining 27 were unstratified. The artefacts have been placed into one of four main assemblages (weapons, jewellery, personal equipment and vessels). Each one is split into object type and then, using the main classificatory schemes, further divided by subtype allowing the date of deposition and cultural association of each piece to be considered. The text integrates the metalwork from the 1974 excavations (Gingell 1978) to provide an overall assessment of the use of metal grave goods within this community.

Weapons

Weapons were recovered from 11 male graves (Fig. 4.3), to which can be added two unstratified spearheads that came from layer 1110 (ONs 111 and 112). The majority of weapon burials contained a single spearhead or one combined with a shield boss (Table 4.2). The four weapon burials from the 1974 excavation mainly consisted of single spears. In total, the spear is the most common weapon type (13/15: 80%) and this concurs with both the national (85%) and regional picture (86%). Overall the proportion of burials with just a spear (53%) is very similar to Market Lavington, Wiltshire (50%; Williams and Newman 2006), but higher than other Wiltshire cemeteries at Petersfinger (43%; Leeds and Shortt 1953) and Blacknall Field, Pewsey (25%; Annable and Eagles 2010). The figure from the latter is explained by the greater number of spear and shield combinations (35%); for comparison the proportion at Collingbourne is 27%. With the exception of Kent and Surrey, swords were rarely placed in the grave, but in Wiltshire, Petersfinger and Blacknall Field produced three and four examples respectively, with most of these accompanied by a shield and spear. The simplicity of the two Collingbourne sword burials is notable.

Table 4.2 Weapon combinations (1974 and 2007)

Weapon combination	*Grave*
Spear	3A, 15, 34, 45, 58, 91, 108, 109
Spear and shield	77, 82, 83, 101
Shield	52
Sword	59
Sword and shield	2

All the weapons had been buried with males (that from grave 3 is unidentified) which is not surprising, and has parallels in other Wiltshire burial grounds (Stoodley 2010). Weapon burials account for 13% of the total, which is lower than that recorded in contemporary cemeteries in the county: for example, Blacknall Field (19%), Petersfinger (20%) and Market Lavington (24%). Under half of the males within the assemblage were interred with weapons (42%), which is broadly in agreement with Härke's (1989a, 49) national study (47% of males) but in the context of Wiltshire is lower than that at Blacknall Field (53%) and Petersfinger (55%) and considerably less than Market Lavington (71%), although the incomplete nature of the investigation at the latter may be partly responsible for the high figure.

The weapon burials were distributed fairly evenly throughout the cemetery with examples in the groups to the east and west of the coombe. In several places they were found close together, such as graves 82 and 83 that both had a shield and a similar type of spearhead, and graves 108 and 109 that were adjacent and also shared the same orientation.

Swords

Two swords were recovered from the cemetery, one in 1974 (grave 2), and another in 2007 (grave 59). Grave 2 contained a double-edged parallel-sided sword that had not been pattern-welded. The metal fittings to the sword and scabbard identify it as a Menghin Type 5 (Menghin 1983). The weapon was interred in the early or mid-6th century and examples can be cited from both Blacknall Field (G22) and Petersfinger (G20). The example from grave 59 (ON 15) is also a double-edged weapon with an overall length of 910 mm. It has a hilt made from horn, and wood from the scabbard's plates has been identified as willow/poplar (see McCormick, below). In both cases the weapon had been placed on the left side of the body probably indicating that the individuals had been right-handed.

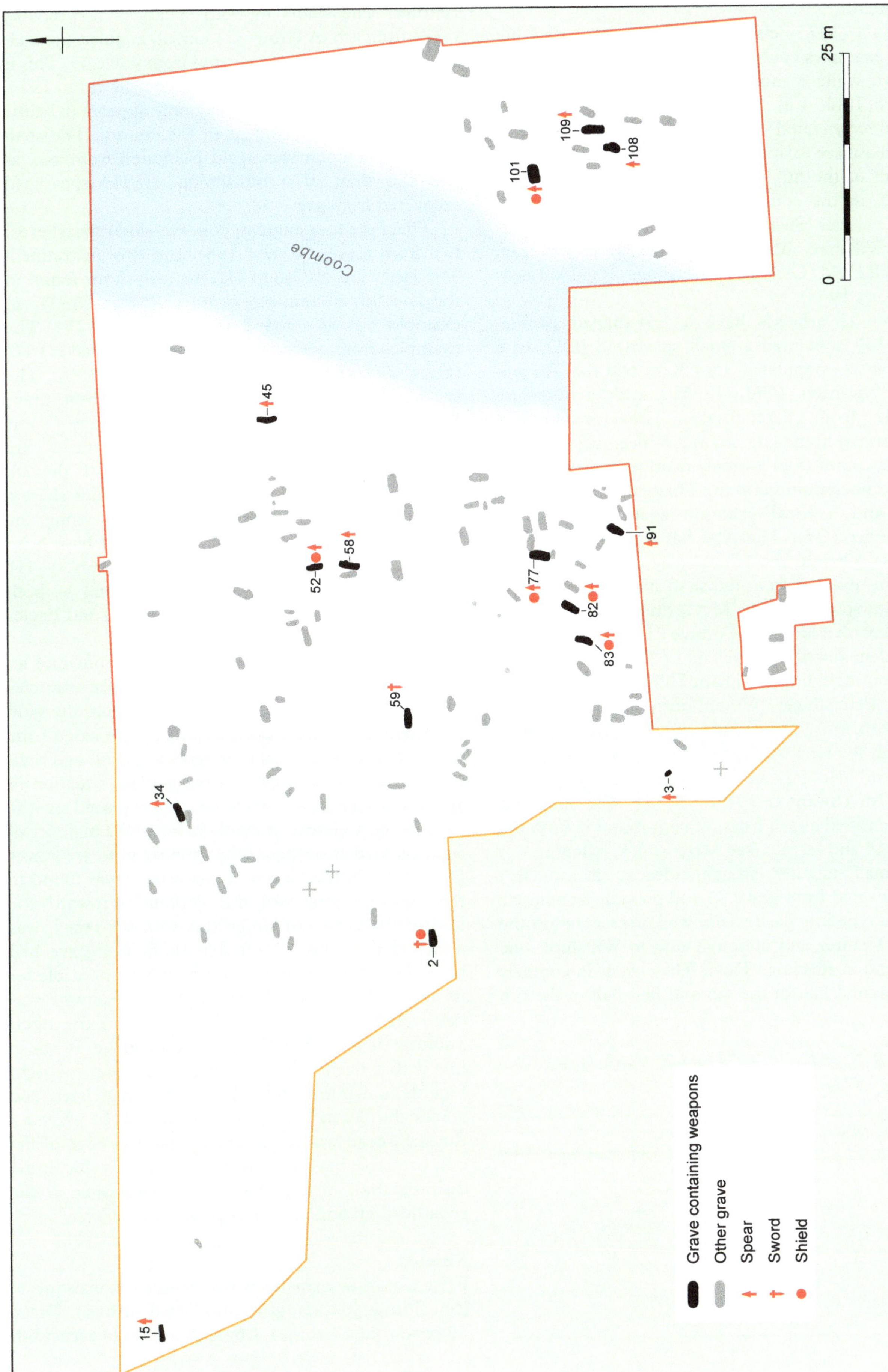

Figure 4.3 Cemetery plan: distribution of weapons

Spearheads

Swanton's (1973) classification has been used but several examples could only be tentatively ascribed to a group, while a number also exhibit intermediary features (Table 4.3).

Two corrugated K1 spearheads were found in 1974: these are early forms dating to the late 5th and first half of the 6th century and come mainly from contexts in the south of England, particularly the Upper Thames (Swanton 1973, 128–31). The type is rare in Wiltshire, although examples are known from Blacknall Field (G94) and Petersfinger (G55A; Leeds and Shortt 1953).

Three spearheads have a leaf-shaped profile. Grave 109 contained a small spearhead (C1), of a type that was popular in East Kent and the Thames Valley (Swanton 1973, 49–51), with a Wiltshire example from Petersfinger. They are mainly concentrated in the late 5th and 6th century. The C2 example comes from a widely distributed group, with notable concentrations in the Thames Valley and East Kent, and a local example again comes from Petersfinger (G7). The type has a wide date range from the 5th into the 7th century (*ibid.*, 51–53). A fragment of wood from the shaft has been identified as willow/poplar (see McCormick, below). An example with a long blade (grave 91) is one of a small but widely distributed group of C3 spearheads in Wiltshire, including Harnham Hill (Akerman 1855 a and b), Petersfinger, Winterbourne Gunner (Musty and Stratton 1964) and Ford (Musty 1969). Although the type was deposited in graves as early as the second half of the 6th century, it was more prolific in the 7th (Swanton 1973, 55–57). The shaft has been identified as ash from remains found in both the spearhead and ferrule (see McCormick, below).

A small, angular, straight-sided spearhead (E1) was recovered from grave 83 and possibly from grave 82. As a type it is particularly well represented in the Upper Thames and although rare in Wiltshire, one was found at Blacknall Field. They occur in contexts of the second half of the 5th and first half of the 6th century. The shafts of both spears were probably made from ash. A Group G1 (small, angular, parallel-sided) spearhead was recovered from grave 45. This is a widely distributed 6th-century type (Swanton 1973, 99), but the Collingbourne example appears to be the first from a sealed context in the county. The shaft from this weapon was again fashioned from ash, as was the shaft of a transitional E2/H2 spearhead recovered from grave 58.

Table 4.3 Spearheads (1974 and 2007) (following Swanton 1973)

Spearhead (Swanton Group)	*Grave*
C1	109
C2	?101
C3	91
E1	?82, 83
E2/H2	58
G1	45
H1	15
H1/H2	77, 108
K1	3A, 34

There are four angular, concave-sided spearheads: two from graves (77 and 108), and two unstratified. The latter are of Group H1, an early form found in the late 5th to mid-6th century (*ibid.*, 103–7); an example was also found in 1974 (grave 15). The examples from graves consist of a transitional H1/H2 (grave 77) example and a H2 (grave 108). The species of wood used for the spear shaft from grave 108 is unknown, but the example from grave 77 was made from hazel/alder. Type H2 spearheads are found in contexts from the 5th through to the 7th century (*ibid.*, 107–11). All these spearheads share a similar distribution with concentrations along the Thames Valley and in the Midlands, and have been retrieved from most Wiltshire cemeteries; H1 spearheads are especially well represented at both Blacknall Field and Petersfinger (Annable and Eagles 2010; Leeds and Shortt 1953).

The locations of the spearheads demonstrate an unusually high degree of variability. In six examples the artefact was in a typical location close to the skull indicating that it had been laid along the side of the grave. There were equal numbers on the left and right hand sides, which differs to the general situation in Wessex where most spears had been placed on the right of the skeleton, probably indicating a majority of right-handed spearmen. Of particular note are graves 58 and 91. In the former the spearhead was found to the left of the torso with the tip pointing towards the foot of the grave. Although this suggests that it was attached to a short or broken shaft, the grave had been disturbed and this was probably responsible for its unusual position. In grave 91 the example was discovered in a similar position, only to the right, pointing diagonally to the head of the grave. It was in line with a ferrule that was discovered over the right foot demonstrating that the weapon had been laid across the flexed legs of this individual. In grave 82 the spearhead was found against the top edge of the cut, probably having been laid on top of a shield, the disintegration of the shield board resulting in the spearhead ending up in this position.

Shields

Evidence of five shields was recovered, consisting of iron fittings (bosses, grips and board fittings). Grave 82 produced a Group 1.1 boss (later 5th to earlier 6th century), a form that is concentrated in the Upper Thames Valley and Wessex (Dickinson and Härke 1992, 12–3) and is by far the most common boss in Wiltshire, occurring in 74% (n=20/27) of interments. It was found with a Type 1a 1 grip. The wood for the board has been identified as lime, and there is also evidence that it had a leather cover (McCormick, below). Two pairs of circular iron board studs were associated with the boss. These are the most frequent type of fitting (Dickinson and Härke 1992, 27) and provided a simple form of decoration. A Group 1.1 boss was also recovered in grave 2 along with a short grip (Type 1a 1).

The other types of boss are more frequently encountered outside Wessex. This is particularly so for Group 3 bosses (mainly 6th century; graves 52(?) and 77), which were popular in East Kent and Essex (Dickinson and Härke 1992, 15–16), although a pair was recovered from Petersfinger (graves 7 and 60). At Collingbourne, the shield board in grave 77 was made of lime, and it had a leather covering on both sides. A pair of circular board studs was also associated with this boss. A Type 1a 1 grip was present and revealed evidence of a leather carrying strap (see McCormick, below). The example from grave 52 was badly damaged and its identification is not certain. The (possible) Group 2 (grave 83) boss is a form more readily encountered in Anglian districts, especially East Anglia (*ibid.*, 13–14), but another example is also known from Wiltshire (Charlton Plantation G59, Davies 1985). This board also had a leather cover, while its Type 1b grip was bound by straps of leather. A low curved boss (Group 6) was retrieved from grave 101. This type is found mainly in eastern areas (Geake 1997, map 35), in contexts dated to the late 6th to mid-7th century. The board was fashioned out of willow/poplar and covered with leather (see McCormick, below). It was associated with a thin, narrow grip with terminals that appear to be expanding (Type 1a 2) and the central part of it was wrapped with plied thread.

The size of this weapon restricted where it could be placed and the majority of shields have been found horizontally along the centre axis of the grave (Dickinson and Härke 1992, 65). The boss in grave 2 (Gingell 1978) was found over the pelvis, while the example in grave 83 was to one side of it, but it is worth mentioning that at this point the grave widens, possibly to accommodate the weapon. In grave 52 it covered the abdominal area to mid-chest and in grave 77 the weapon had been placed over the upper body, while in grave 82 it was discovered overlying the skull. In grave 101 a different situation was found: it was on its edge against the north wall of the grave. The position may be linked to the use of a coffin: the width of the shield prevented it from being deposited inside the container, but the gap between the coffin and grave wall would have allowed it to be secured in a vertical position. In a similar fashion, the spearhead in grave 101 lay close to the south wall of the grave, and approximately 0.4 m from the skull, further away than in the other examples, suggesting that this too had been placed outside the container. Although there was no structural evidence, the shape of grave 101 suggests that it had once accommodated a coffin, and at 0.62 m deep it was the deepest grave investigated.

The position of the circular fittings allows the minimum diameter of the board in grave 82 to be estimated. Each pair of board studs was close to the edge of the grave, indicating that the board could not have been much wider and a minimum diameter is estimated at between 350–400 mm. In grave 77 the two pairs of studs were 320 mm apart, possibly suggesting a slightly smaller board.

Three of the burials were made in close proximity in the southern part of the cemetery to the west of the coombe: graves 82 and 83 were adjacent, while grave 77 was only a few metres to the north-east. This is the only grouping of weapon burials and suggests that a possible relationship existed between these individuals. A similar situation involving the shield burials was also noted at Market Lavington (Williams and Newman 2006, 76).

Personal Equipment

Knives

Fifty-three knives were recovered from 49 graves in 2007 (and 14 from 14 graves in 1974), making them the most common type of grave good (Fig. 4.4; see also Blakelock, below). Böhner's (1958) and Evison's (1987) classifications have been used here; although in the case of fragmentary knives it was often impossible to identify type. Both schemes are based on the shape of the blade and its point in relation to its centre. All the major blade types are present: A (12, ?3), B (9, ?1), C (6, ?2), plus rarer types D (1) and Evison Type 4 (2, ?1). There are 13 blades that cannot be classified; plus several where the identification is uncertain (one A/B and two A/C). Types A and B are found from the 5th to the 7th century, while Type C, although occurring earlier, is predominantly a 7th-century form. The same can be said of Type D and Evison Type 4. As is normal, most of the burials included a single knife (Stoodley 1999a, 30–3). Two adult females were found with multiple knives, and although this is rare, it is a practice associated with females (*ibid.*, 30–3).

Type A blades are the most common form and this is also the case at Market Lavington and Blacknall

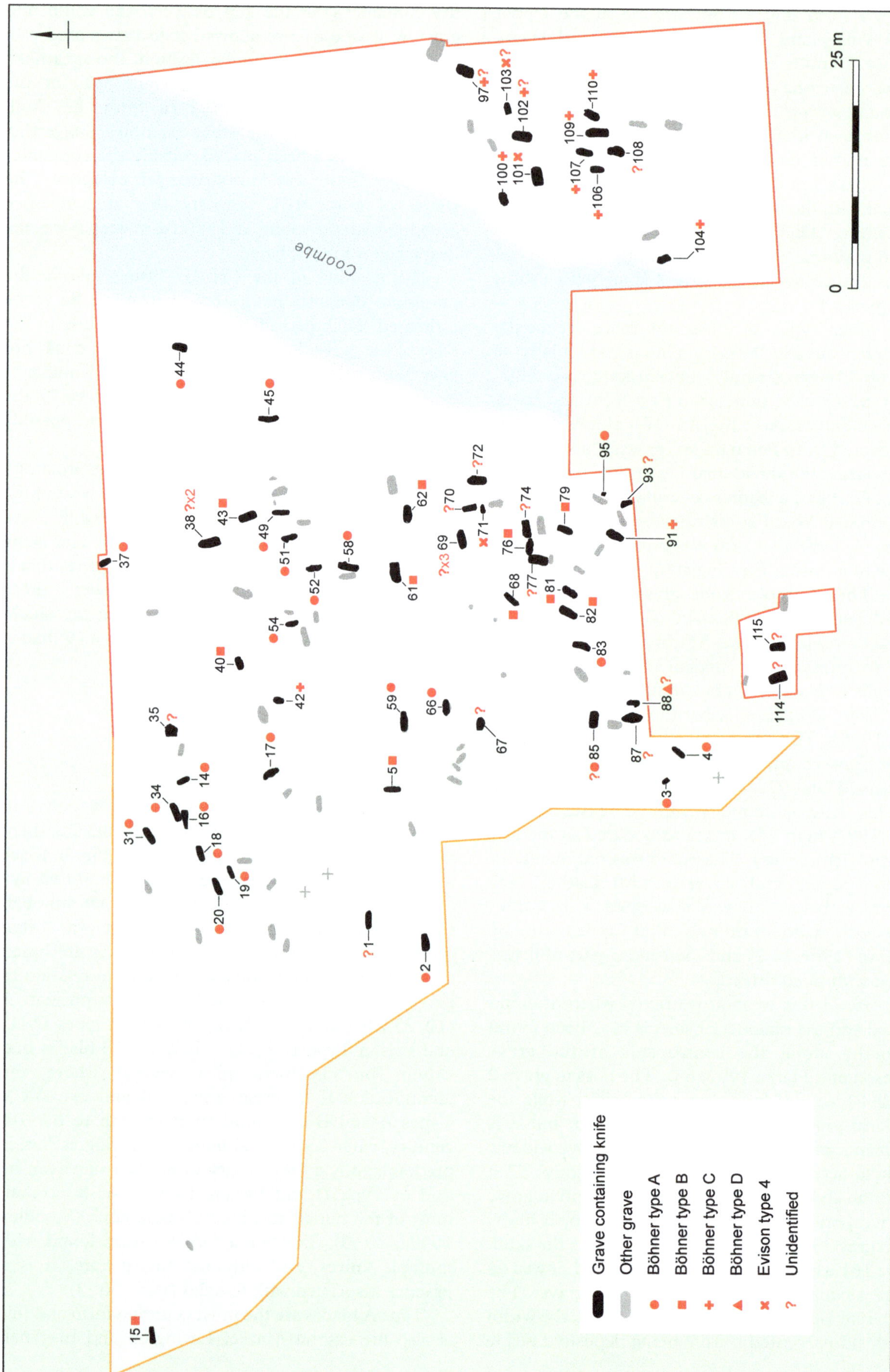

Figure 4.4 Cemetery plan: distribution of knives

Table 4.4 Knife types from selected Wiltshire cemeteries (following Böhner 1958)

Cemetery	*Type A*	*Type B*	*Type C*	*Type D*	*Others*	*Type ?*
Collingbourne Ducis (all years)	25 (37)	12 (18)	8 (12)	1 (1)	6 (9)	15 (22)
Charlton Plantation	1 (6)	7 (44)	4 (25)	1 (6)	0	3 (19)
Market Lavington	11 (52)	6 (29)	0	0	0	4 (19)
Petersfinger	7 (27)	11 (42)	1 (4)	0	0	7 (27)
Blacknall Field	15 (35)	9 (21)	3 (7)	0	0	16 (37)

Number in brackets = %. Others = Evison Types and transitional types. Type ? = unclassified

Field, while at Petersfinger and Charlton Plantation Type B's have a numerical advantage (Table 4.4).

Knives were recovered with individuals of all ages and sexes, and broadly similar numbers of males and females were accompanied by one. This is not unusual and a similar situation is found in the other Wiltshire cemeteries. For example, at Market Lavington knives were found with equal numbers of males and females and the statistics from Blacknall Field are similar (Williams and Newman 2006, 76; Annable and Eagles 2010). The youngest individual discovered with a knife was an infant of 1–2 years (grave 71), who had a short one of unusual form (Evison Type 4). The possible Type 4 was accompanying a juvenile of 5–8 years (grave 103), while the rare Böhner Type D was found with a juvenile of 6–8 years (grave 88). Härke (1989b) discovered that blade length was related to age; perhaps blade shape is also determined by this variable.

The most common location for a knife was to the left of the waist/pelvis (23/53%), while 33% (n=14) were found on the opposite side, and it seems likely that it had been attached to a belt or slipped behind it. Where a buckle was absent it is possible that the knife had been secured by a rope belt.

Over two-thirds of the knives had remains on the tang, and in the vast majority of cases it was identified as horn (see McCormick, below). In several examples the handle extended onto the blade shoulder, for example on ON 133 (grave 88) horn was found up to 11 mm on the surface of the blade. This is believed to have been a technique to help secure the handle. In a similar way, a rivet near the junction of the tang and blade shoulder (eg, ON 87, grave 49) would have helped to fasten the handle to the tang. Very little evidence for a scabbard was identified, although the blades of ON 18 (grave 59) and ON 133 (grave 88) produced traces of leather, while a pelt, identified as pig, was found on ON 29 (grave 59). Finally, the examination of ON 195 (grave 94) revealed a <1 mm recessed line near the back of the blade, which may have originally contained an inlay.

The knives are evenly distributed throughout the cemetery, although, as expected, the later types were mainly found in the part of the cemetery to the east of the coombe.

Toilet implements

Toilet implements were recovered from five graves. A pair of stout copper alloy tweezers was discovered in the waist area of the older adult male in grave 59. In Wiltshire tweezers have a strong association with males (n=13: 9/69%) and six of these were also accompanied by weapons. Grave 59 contained a sword and it seems that tweezers have an association with the weapon burial rite; perhaps this particular group of males was concerned with personal grooming or the tweezers were involved in preparing the deceased for burial and were deposited in the grave following this rite.

The other four graves contained toilet sets, plus a handle from a cosmetic brush. Graves 39 and 69 each held a copper alloy toilet set consisting of an ear scoop and pair of pickers. The implements had been threaded onto wire slip-knot rings and were found in the chest region. Picks were probably used to clean nails, although they may also have been used to remove food from between teeth (MacGregor and Bolick 1993, 216). Very similar toilet sets were recovered from Blacknall Field (graves 31, 35 and 55). The handle of a cosmetic brush (Pl. 4.1) was found to the left of the skull in grave 39, but it may originally have been part of the toilet set found at chest level and the disturbance to the grave resulted in its movement. The examination of the object revealed the remains of bristles which have been identified as being either horse or hog (see McCormick, below). In the 1974 excavation a brush handle was found with the adult female in grave 31 (Gingell 1978), while further examples can be cited from Blacknall Field G50 and Charlton Plantation G24. Grave 38 is more complicated because it was found to contain several complexes that can probably be identified as toilet items. A copper alloy scraper (ON 64) was threaded onto a wire slip-knot ring and was associated with the chatelaine complex found between the legs, while another scraper was associated with two copper alloy strips and slip-knot rings in the area of the upper chest/left shoulder. The Collingbourne burials with

Plate 4.1 Copper alloy cosmetic brush (grave 39/ON 48)

toilet sets are all those of females and overall these are objects that record strong feminine associations (Stoodley 1999a, 33), although at Petersfinger, G21 (a male weapon burial; Leeds and Shortt 1953) produced an ear scoop in association with a pair of tweezers.

Iron toilet sets are rarer than their copper alloy counterparts (Dickinson 1976, 224), although because of poor preservation many cases have probably been overlooked. An example may have been found in grave 38 (ON 215, ON Group 76): a collection of rods was excavated from the thigh area along with the remains of a chatelaine and the copper alloy toilet set. The object's position and general form, however, support its interpretation as a set of latchlifters. A fragmentary iron toilet set from grave 47 was recovered from the left chest area. Parallels from Wiltshire are rare, although a small iron scoop with perforated end can be cited from Market Lavington G15 (Williams and Newman 2006, 81).

Pursemount

An incomplete iron pursemount (ON 54), comprising a pair of crescentic arms and a centrally placed attachment buckle, was found in the abdominal area of the infant in grave 40. The buckle would have attached it to a belt. The Collingbourne example is of a typical 6th-century type, and similar examples are known from weapon burials at Winterbourne Gunner (G1) and Petersfinger (G20) (Musty and Stratton 1964; Leeds and Shortt 1953). These are relatively rare finds (less than 2% of the Wiltshire sample), especially so from the burials of younger individuals. A fragment of a probable pursemount was found in grave 54, but its location in the grave is unknown due to disturbance.

Accessory rings

Grave 85 contained a large iron ring. It has the appearance and dimensions of a bag ring, but its location to the outside of the upper right arm is unusual: such receptacles are usually discovered at the waist. For example, a similar ring was found at the left side of the individual's waist in Petersfinger G29. A small copper alloy suspension ring was found at the waist of the young infant in grave 42. The different sizes and locations of the rings may indicate that they served a variety of functions, particularly as one was with an adult and the other with a baby.

Purses

Grave 39 produced a group of objects that included an iron ring (ON 204), perhaps a purse ring, plus several iron objects that include a possible fitting and a rod. The objects were discovered over the chest/right shoulder area. A ring, and associated objects, was found to the outside of the right arm of the adult female in grave 85 (see above), and this assemblage also included a ?fitting. It is possible that in these cases, rather than suspending the purse from the waist in the usual manner, it had been placed over, or next to, the upper body/shoulder.

Chatelaines and girdle groups

This group comprises either single objects or complexes that would have originally been suspended from the waist of adult females. A chatelaine complex consisting of both copper alloy and iron objects was discovered with the adult female in grave 38. The main elements are an iron L-shaped fragment and rods, and some possible latchlifters, but there is also a group of disparate objects, such as toilet implements, a disc brooch, a ring, copper alloy bands, a buckle and a knife. It is possible that the latter group were part of the chatelaine, although it is not clear how these items would have attached. Alternatively they may have been in a pouch suspended alongside the chatelaine and some, or all, of the objects were 'scrap' or had been deliberately concealed.

A heavy iron latchlifter with a hooked bottom terminal and fragmentary attachment ring was found at the left waist of the infant in grave 42. These are fairly common objects, although they are more usually associated with adult females (Stoodley 2000, 466). Grave 16, excavated in 1974, contained a key and attachment ring, also at the left waist (Gingell 1978), while in Petersfinger G8 an iron ring and several keys were in a similar position (Leeds and Shortt 1953). An iron rod with perforated terminals was found by the left pelvis of the older adult female (grave 93), and was possibly associated with the girdle.

Vessels

A wooden stave-built bucket bound by copper alloy strips and decorated with triangular appliqués was discovered to the right of the adult woman's skull in grave 69. Here, as is usual elsewhere, the bucket is only represented by its metal fittings. These vessels record an association with adult males, both nationally (Stoodley 1999a, 33) and regionally: the 11 Wiltshire examples are, however, divided between five males and three females (plus one unsexed adult and two children). Buckets are also linked with greater quantities of burial wealth, for example in Wiltshire all the male burials had weapons; especially noteworthy are Blacknall Field graves 22 and 47, each of which had a sword, shield and spear (Annable and Eagles 2010). It is not, therefore, surprising that the Collingbourne example was recovered from one of the better furnished female graves. It may be that these vessels symbolised an aspect of the deceased's lifestyle; possibly they had more leisure time at their disposal, perhaps spending it on activities such as feasting.

The wider fragments of copper alloy strip would have formed the upper hoop of the vessel (Fig. 2.36). Measurements taken during the excavation indicate that the top edge had a diameter of about 200 mm, which makes for a relatively large vessel. The average width of eight buckets from Wiltshire is 127 mm, the largest having an upper rim diameter of 177 mm (Harnham Hill G63; Akerman 1855a and b). Moreover, a national survey found that the vast majority record diameters of between 75–210 mm (Cook 2004, 40). Most of the Wiltshire buckets have three or even four hoops, but the remaining copper alloy strips from the Collingbourne example derived from just one other hoop, probably positioned at the base of the vessel. There is no evidence of a handle but this is not that unusual; the example in Blacknall Field G21 also had no obvious method of carrying, and perhaps organic handles were used (*ibid.*, 33). In addition, while most buckets had vertical uprights (*ibid.*, 32–3), that from grave 69 lacked these elements. This might explain why there was no handle: buckets were usually suspended from hoops attached via perforations at the top of (extended) uprights (*ibid.*, 37). There are eight appliqués that would have decorated the upper hoop of the vessel. They were secured under the bottom edge of the hoop and fastened to the vessel by rivets at the top and bottom of the appliqué. Despite its large diameter, it is rather simple and the closest parallel comes from Charlton Plantation G13, which although being much smaller (diameter of 80 mm) had just two hoops, no uprights and no handle.

A fragment of copper alloy rim clip/reinforcing strip was found in the vicinity of the adult female's left forearm in grave 93. It would probably have been riveted over the rim of a wooden vessel to reinforce a damaged area (MacGregor and Bolick 1993, 263).

Jewellery and Dress Accessories

This category includes brooches, pins, finger-rings and necklaces. Twenty-five graves (30%) were found with these objects (with possibly two more where the identification of an artefact is uncertain (graves 54 and 93) (Fig. 4.5). When the data from the 1974 excavations (n=10; Gingell 1978) is combined, a total of 35, or 30%, is returned. Jewellery was mainly discovered with adult females and the proportion is exactly the same as the national average (60%; Stoodley 1999a, 75) (NB 1974 data not included because of the low number of sexed individuals). The figure is lower than Blacknall Field, where an uncharacteristically high proportion of adult female graves contained jewellery (82%; Annable and Eagles 2010).

Jewellery was recovered from the graves of two infants and a juvenile (graves 35, 42 and 89), but they did not have brooches and thus differed significantly to the way adult women were treated. One male (grave 84) was discovered with a single disc brooch. The possible male in grave 54 was found with a circular iron object which may be a brooch, although the presence of a single lug on its reverse indicates that it is more likely to be a mount. Grave 11 – from the 1974 excavations (Gingell 1978) – contained a Roman disc brooch, found at the individual's shoulder. Nationally, a small number of men were buried with a single brooch (Stoodley 1999a, 34) indicating a fashion amongst sections of the male population to have worn a cloak clasped at the shoulder (Walton Rogers 2007, 206–7). In grave 84, the brooch was by the left shin, perhaps attached to a cloak laid over the legs, while in grave 54 the remains were too disturbed to tell.

There are 64 certain items of jewellery (a collection of beads is counted as one necklace/group/bracelet). When the assemblage is broken down by individual type (Table 4.5), it is seen that brooches are the most common artefact, followed by collections of beads. Pins are next, while other types

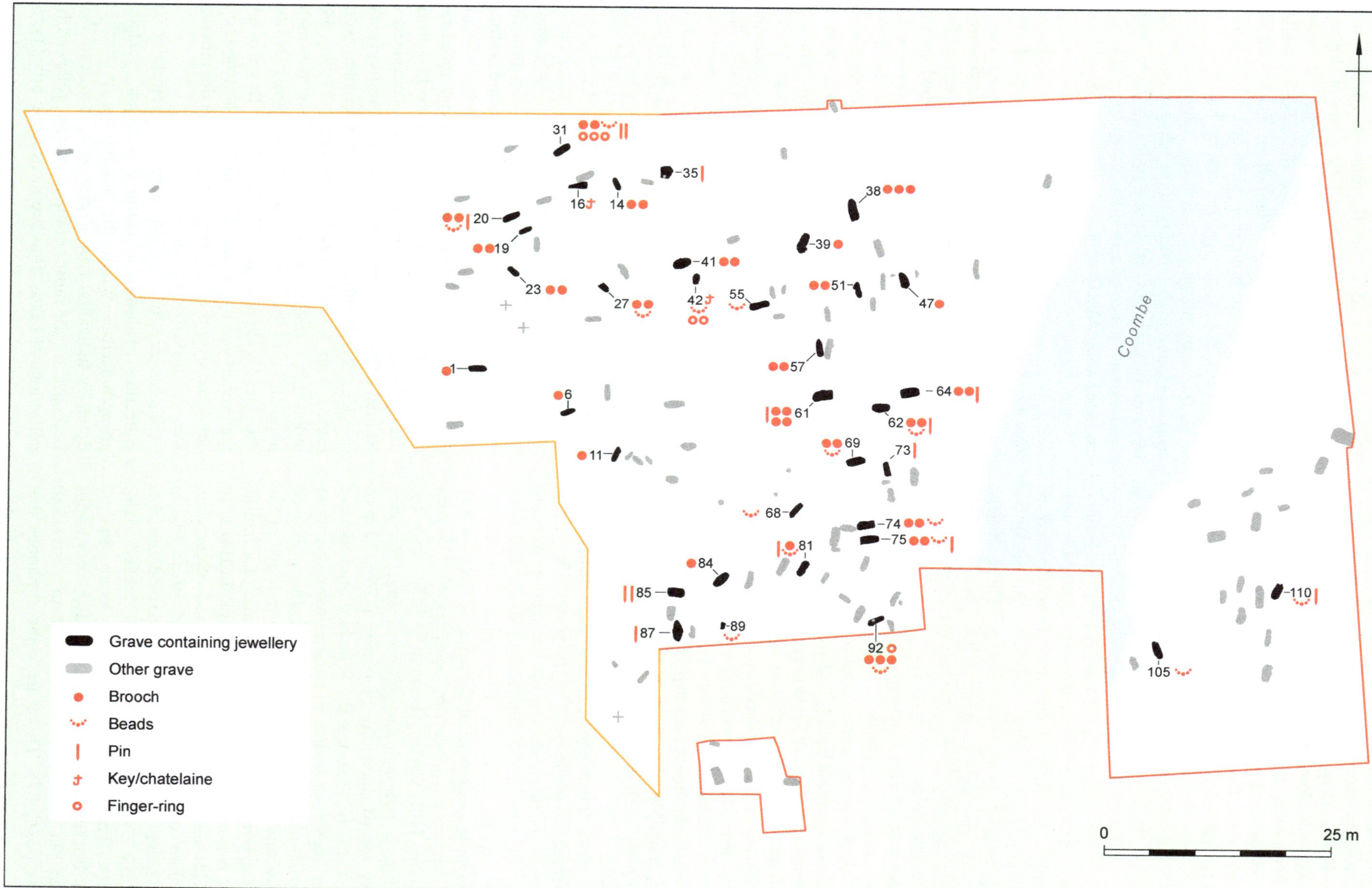

Figure 4.5 Cemetery plan: distribution of jewellery

are much rarer. It is interesting that the data from the 1974 excavations give a slightly different picture, with pins being relatively common, reflecting a greater preference for this fastener in the western part of the cemetery.

A broadly comparable situation is found elsewhere in Wiltshire (Table 4.6). Brooches were the main type of costume accessory at Market Lavington and Blacknall Field (Williams and Newman 2006; Annable and Eagles 2010), though at Petersfinger beads were slightly more popular (Leeds and Shortt 1953). Overall, the statistics reveal that the key elements of a costume were the brooches to fasten the cloth and beads to embellish it. Pins were also an important costume element being more popular than beads at Market Lavington. The topic is examined in more detail when an attempt is made to reconstruct the style of costume (see below).

Table 4.5 Jewellery by type

Dress accessory		*1974*
Brooch	30 (47)	14 (56)
Finger-ring	3 (5)	3 (12)
Necklace	21 (33)	3 (12)
Pin	10 (16)	5 (20)

Number in brackets = %

Brooches

Thirty brooches were recovered from graves in 2007 (Fig. 4.6), and a garnet inlaid disc brooch was found in subsoil/colluvium. Most brooches were found accompanying adult females; the most notable exception is the adult male from grave 84 (see above). Eight burials had a pair of brooches. Two burials had three brooches: grave 92 contained a pair of disc brooches plus the rare bell-shaped brooch and grave 38 a pair of small-long brooches and a disc brooch – the latter associated with a pouch or chatelaine. Grave 61 had the largest number of brooches: a pair of penannular brooches plus a pair of disc brooches. Most brooches were only paired with the same type, the exceptions being disc brooches, penannular/annular brooches (?single example with grave 47) and the bell-shaped brooch (grave 92). In grave 39 the disc brooch was over the upper right chest/shoulder of the adult female, and immediately below this was an annular brooch. A similar range of brooch types were found in the 1974 investigations, although it is notable that Anglo-Saxon disc brooches were absent. Two small button brooches were discovered in grave 31 and are the only examples of this type from the site.

Most pairs of brooches were found in the shoulder area; a possible exception is grave 51 where a small-long brooch was found at the left shoulder but the location of the other is unknown (the grave was truncated). Grave 61 is unusual in that a penannular brooch was found on either side of the neck, possibly having been used as ear-rings or veil rings (see below); in addition, there were also two disc brooches: one was at the neck (possibly associated with the veil), while the other was lower down the body. A number of individuals had single brooches. The penannular brooch in grave 47 was on the left shoulder of the adult female. In grave 81 the disc brooch was over the upper chest of the adult female.

When the data from the entire assemblage (including 1974) are combined it is clear that there are three predominant brooch types: applied, disc and small-long brooches (Table 4.7). The first two are typical Saxon types and, along with the saucer brooch, are found throughout the region. The small-long brooch is the most numerous type of brooch and this is also the case at Blacknall Field (Annable and Eagles 2010). Small-long brooches are prevalent in Anglian regions, although there are certain types that are more commonly found in the south of the country (Leeds 1913, 77–8; 1945). Compared to other Wiltshire cemeteries, both Collingbourne and Blacknall Field have a relatively wide range of brooch types, and this might reflect a greater range of cultural influences in this part of the county (Table 4.8).

Annular and penannular brooches

The pair of copper alloy penannular brooches discovered on either side of the skull in grave 61 may have been used as ear-rings. Frankish women wore such jewellery, but there is no evidence that the fashion was adopted in England (Walton Rogers 2007, 133–4). Given the width of the terminals it is difficult to see how they would have fitted through a pierced ear, although early medieval body piercing is little understood. Perhaps the brooch pin was used to

Table 4.6 Jewellery types from selected Wiltshire cemeteries

Cemetery	*Brooch*	*Bracelet*	*Finger-ring*	*Girdle item*	*Necklace*	*Pin*
Market Lavington	9 (41)	0	0	1 (5)	4 (18)	8 (36)
Petersfinger	13 (33)	2 (5)	2 (5)	6 (15)	14 (35)	3 (8)
Blacknall Field	52 (49)	5 (5)	1 (1)	4 (4)	31 (29)	13 (14)

Number in brackets = %

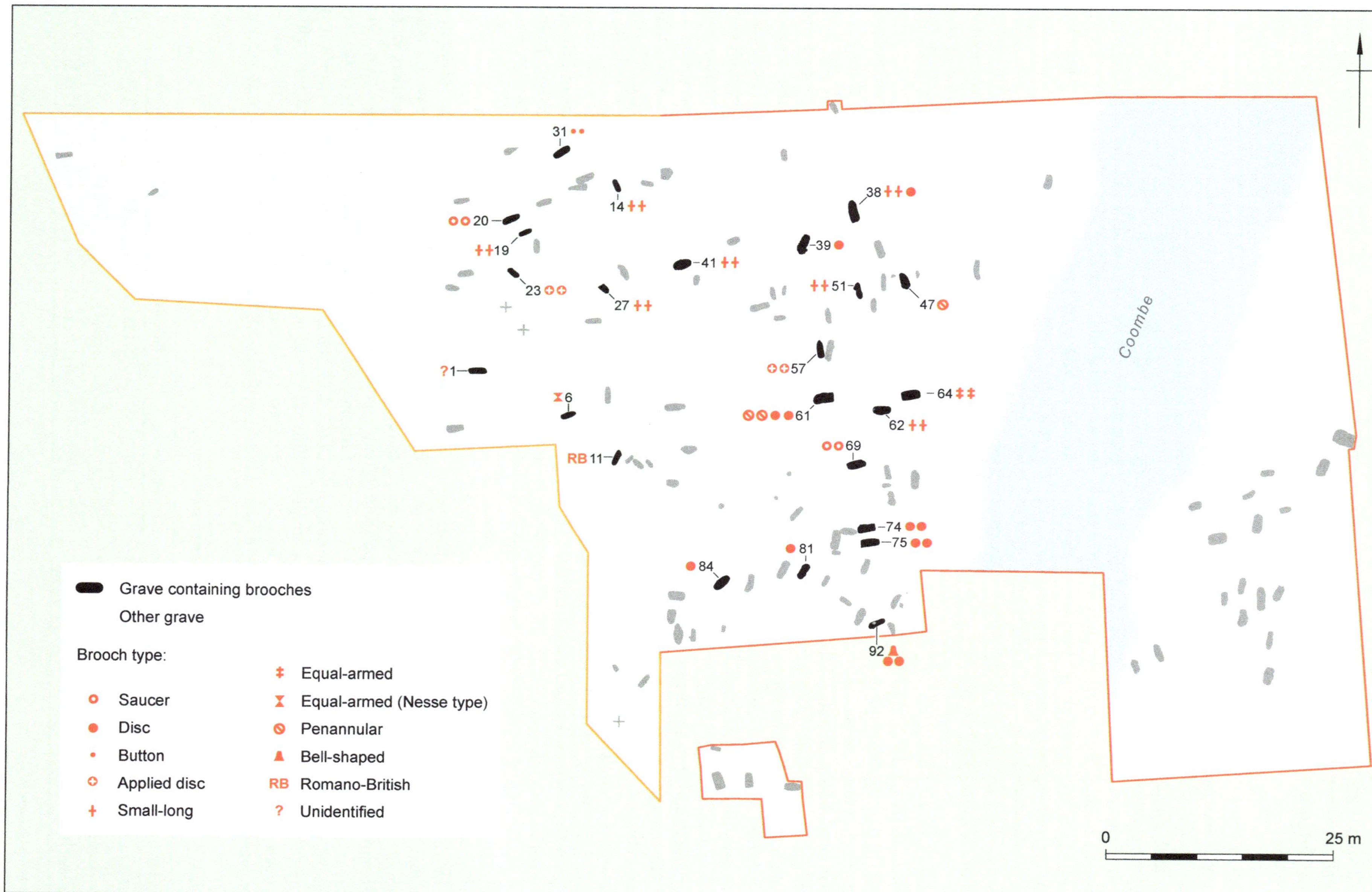

Figure 4.6 Cemetery plan: distribution of brooches

secure it through a piercing. Alternatively the brooches may have functioned as veil rings. Pairs of wire rings and clips/staples that have been found by the ears of women are interpreted as securing tie-bands on the veil, or on a coif or cap which the veil was draped over (*ibid.*, 159). Walton Rogers can only cite one example that is comparable to Collingbourne: Finglesham grave 57, where a pair of small annular brooches was found on either side of the woman's skull in a 7th-century grave (*ibid.*, 159), and although a pair of clips was found at Holywell Row, Suffolk, in a grave that may be as early as the mid-6th century, this is a practice that is mainly found in the 7th century (*ibid.*, 159). It is possible that the Collingbourne burial represents an early instance of the practice or, as suggested above, it is a very rare example of a pair of ear-rings. The brooches are classified on the shape and decoration of the terminals and each of the Collingbourne specimens are different. One is a Fowler Type E, the other a Fowler Type D4. A Type D was found at Blacknall Field G102 paired with a Type F in a grave dated to the late 5th century. The disc brooches from grave 61 imply a date of deposition in the later 5th or earlier 6th century.

A single iron penannular brooch lay on the left shoulder of the young woman in grave 47, and in grave 39 a fragmentary iron annular brooch was found on the woman's right upper chest (close to a disc brooch). Annular brooches are uncommon finds in southern England, although a pair were found with an adult male (G9) at Portway East (Cook and Dacre 1985).

Applied brooches

Two pairs of applied brooches were recovered but, unfortunately, close parallels cannot be identified because of the very fragmentary state of their faces. It is known that the pair from grave 57 both had a central glass stud (Pl. 4.2), which is a feature they share with several other examples from Wiltshire. Harnham Hill G42 produced a pair decorated with a star motif, each having a central blue glass bead, while two pairs from Winterbourne Gunner (graves 8 and 9) that are decorated with Style I decoration also have central blue glass beads (Akerman 1855a and b; Musty and Stratton 1964). The brooches from grave 57 may possibly have had scrolls which, if correct, would place their manufacture in the 5th century. The brooches from grave 75 (Pl. 4.3) have Style I decoration and were manufactured at some point in the late 5th or 6th century. Grave 23 (Gingell 1978) contained a pair of applied brooches of Mahndorf Type.

Bell-shaped brooch

A rare type of bell-shaped brooch was found in grave 92. It is gilded and decorated with a human mask with bulbous eyes that was surrounded by Style I animals (Pl. 4.4). These animals extend down either side framing a central flat triangular 'mouth'/plate. At the apex is a pair of hinges through which the pin was secured. No parallel can be cited, but a pair of bell-shaped gilt brooches was found in G136 at Lechlade, Gloucestershire (Boyle *et al.* 1998, 162–3). Each brooch consists of a human mask surrounded by a pair of Style I animals, below which is a rectangular baseplate. The pins were secured using a

Table 4.7 Brooches (from graves) by type

Brooch type	*No. (2007)*	*No. (combined including 1974)*
Annular	1 (3)	1 (3)
Applied	4 (14)	6 (14)
Bell-shaped	1 (3)	1 (2)
Button	0	2 (5)
Disc	10 (33)	11 (25) (1 RB type)
Equal-armed	2 (7)	3 (7)
Penannular	2 (7)	2 (5)
Saucer	2 (7)	4 (9)
Small-long	8 (27)	14 (32)

Number in brackets = %

Table 4.8 Brooch types from selected Wiltshire cemeteries

Brooch type	*Market Lavington*	*Petersfinger*	*Blacknall Field*
Annular	0	0	0
Applied	0	4 (31)	9 (17)
Button	0	3 (23)	5 (9)
Disc	3 (33)	2 (15)	5 (9)
Equal-armed	0	0	0
Penannular	0	0	5 (9)
Saucer	6 (66)	2 (15)	8 (15)
Small-long	0	0	13 (25)
Square-headed	0	0	4 (8)
Other	0	2 (15)	4 (8)

Number in brackets = %

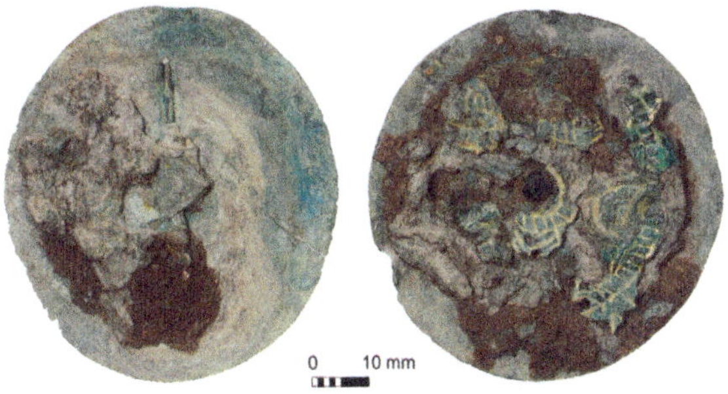

Plate 4.2 Pair of copper alloy applied brooches (grave 57/ONs 73 and 74)

Plate 4.3 Pair of copper alloy applied brooches (grave 75/ONs 166 and 167)

conventional catchplate and hinge and thus differ to the mechanism of the Collingbourne example.

On the basis of the hinges and triangular 'mouth' the Collingbourne brooch has more in common with a series of bell-shaped pendants. For example, a gilt copper alloy openwork pendant of 6th-century date from Weymouth, Dorset (PAS find SOMDOR-A8DD87). The upper section of this specimen is decorated with two symmetrical downward-looking Style I animals with open curling jaws. The lower section is in the form of a triangle that would have been covered by a sheet of silver foil. The original means of suspension is unknown, but it was replaced by a cylindrical loop; it may originally have had a pair of apex hinges like the gilt copper alloy pendant from 'Suffolk' (MacGregor and Bolick 1993, 162–3). The upper part of each side of the 'Suffolk' pendant is covered with Style I animals, each extending into downward-looking animal heads with gaping jaws. Between each head is a triangular terminal flaring outwards, below which is a rectangular band. Chessel Down G85, Isle of Wight (Arnold 1982, 68 and fig. 18), contained a bell-shaped pendant with apex loop and Style 1 animals with open curling jaws. Other similar examples are known from Barrington, Cambridgeshire, Brighthampton, Oxfordshire (MacGregor and Bolick 1993, 163) and Kingsworthy G77, Hampshire (Hawkes and Grainger 2003, 76). Although the Collingbourne brooch is clearly related to the series of bell-shaped pendants, it does not have an openwork panel and it is larger. If the pin is an original feature then it must have functioned as a dress fastener, while if it is a later modification then it would appear to have started life as a pendant.

Plate 4.4 Copper alloy bell-shaped brooch (grave 92/ON 221)

Disc brooches

These are the most common brooch type in the Upper Thames Valley (Dickinson 1979, 39) and they figure prominently throughout the south. At Collingbourne six disc brooches were paired, two were on their own, and the final two were combined with other brooches. None of the paired brooches are identical, although the examples in grave 61 are very similar, as are those in grave 92. The majority were decorated with simple motifs and a repeating theme is a central perforation surrounded by inscribed circles (graves 39, 61, 74 and 92). Exceptions are from grave 81 which displays a double row of punched dashes around the periphery, and grave 84, with a central perforation and notching around the edge.

Given the very random nature of the decoration (Dickinson 1979, 40–1), it is not surprising that it has been impossible to find exact parallels in Wiltshire. In fact a wider search has also been largely unsuccessful. One brooch from Brighthampton, Oxfordshire (G29) is very similar to the simply decorated example in grave 84, while at Fairford, Gloucestershire, and Haslingfield, Cambridgeshire, there are brooches with a punched double ring-and-dot motif in the centre and a row of small circles around the periphery (MacGregor and Bolick 1993, 58), which are not too dissimilar to the brooch from grave 74 (ON 173). The other brooch from grave 74 (ON 170) is roughly comparable to one from Charlton Plantation (burial 17; Davies 1985), although the central perforation is enclosed by three rather than two circles.

Equal-armed brooches

A pair of unusual equal-armed brooches was recovered from grave 64 (Pl. 4.5). They are very different to the series of brooches that developed during the 5th century in the continental homelands of the Saxons (Evison 1977) and occur in southern England, such as the Nesse Type brooch from grave 6 (Gingell 1978). Although no exact parallel can be cited, similar types have been found in Kent and on the Isle of Wight. A copper alloy equal-armed brooch with a symmetrical triangular head and foot-plates on either side of a bow comes from Lyminge, Kent (PAS find KENT-346441). Both head and foot-plate terminate in a round knop, and both are flat and plain. More similar still is a fragmentary brooch from Shalfleet, Isle of Wight (PAS find IOW-A71E22). Both arms probably ended in circular terminals and on each side at the top there is a projecting lobe decorated with a ring-and-dot motif. Another brooch comes from Halling, Kent (PAS find KENT-8A0D63), and although this example has triangular terminals, the lobes on either side of the foot are decorated with ring-and-dot decoration. The Collingbourne pieces can be described as belonging to a rare and little understood corpus of brooches that are restricted to the Jutish regions of Kent and the Isle of Wight and thus provide important evidence of links between Wiltshire and these coastal areas.

The arms of these brooches are reminiscent of the feet of certain types of small-long brooches, both in form and the employment of ring-and-dot decoration. Magnus (1999, 164–6) has argued that one particular type of 6th-century Scandinavian equal-arm brooch was formed by joining the foot-plates of small square-headed brooches together with a bow. It seems probable that the design of these English brooches was also inspired by an existing type of brooch.

It is unfortunate that the Collingbourne brooches were not associated with closely datable objects and that most of the comparisons are metal detector finds. A similar equal-armed brooch was found in a grave at Ringlemere, Kent, where most interments date from the mid-5th to very early 6th century (Martin Welch, pers. comm.). The simple form of these brooches, and the ring-and-dot decoration that they share with disc brooches, may suggest a date in the later 5th and earlier 6th century.

Keystone garnet disc brooch
Kentish influence is also evidenced by a silver keystone garnet disc brooch found in the subsoil (Fig. 2.82 and Pl. 4.6). It is unfortunate that it was not recovered from a sealed context because this may have helped to explain its presence in a Saxon region. The piece has suffered damage: there are broken and missing garnets/coloured glass and the rim exhibits wear. The brooch consists of a central circular boss and four triangular raised cells that each contain, or would have contained, garnets/coloured glass. There are four Style II zoomorphic animals, the curving jaws of each beast grips the hind leg of the one in front. On the basis of these features the brooch can be ascribed to Avent's Type 7.2 (early 7th century), which consists of a single brooch from Faversham, Kent (Avent 1975, 38). The Collingbourne brooch does display some differences, however. The boss has a central garnet/coloured glass setting and although the raised border with a (crude) zig-zag motif is similar to that of the Faversham brooch, it differs by having an additional beaded rim with alternating plain and ribbed zones. Class 7 consists of a small number of brooches that are linked together on the basis of their ornament (*ibid.*, 37), the other parts, as demonstrated by the Collingbourne piece, exhibiting variation. Consequently it is difficult to say whether the brooch was an export or a local copy of a Kentish model.

Plate 4.5 Pair of copper alloy equal-armed brooches (grave 64/ONs 5 and 6)

Saucer brooches
In 1974 a pair of 6th-century gilt saucer brooches was excavated from grave 20, each displaying a pair of long-and-short bar motifs (Dickinson Group 15). Grave 69 produced a pair of matching saucer

Plate 4.6 Copper alloy keystone garnet disc brooch (unstratified/ON 140)

Plate 4.7 Pair of copper alloy saucer brooches (grave 69/ONs 163 and 164)

brooches with a seven running scroll design (Pl. 4.7) (Dickinson's Group 1.3) (Dickinson 1976, 123). Examples have been found throughout south-east England in contexts of the early to mid-6th century, but this is the first piece from Wiltshire. The closest known example is a fragmentary brooch from Portway, Andover (C78; Cook and Dacre 1985, 50), while a metal detector user recovered one from Soberton in the Meon Valley (Stedman and Stoodley 2000, 137–8). Dickinson's (1993, 17) detailed analysis of the type has produced a number of sub-types and the Collingbourne brooches are closest to her Group 4 (outer field of pellets) that has a distribution in the west, especially the Upper Thames Valley. On the Collingbourne pair, a beaded circle has been substituted for the field of pellets, which may be evidence of a localised production centre.

Small-long brooches

A relatively large number of small-long brooches (n=14) has been recovered from Collingbourne, including six from the 1974 excavations (Gingell 1978). Leeds (1945) classified the brooches into types based mainly on the form of the headplate. Since then there has been no overall study of the type and a reassessment is urgently required. Two graves (62 and 51) contained pairs of Type IV brooches (square-headed). The examples from grave 62 have triangular feet and parallels can be cited from the earlier excavations at Collingbourne (graves 14 and 19), Blacknall Field (graves 19, 74, and 85), Harnham Hill (G26), and Winterbourne Gunner (G7) (Gingell 1978; Annable and Eagles 2010; Akerman 1855a and b; Musty and Stratton 1964). These types occur in the later 5th century, but continued to be deposited into the earlier 6th (Dickinson 1976, 175). At Collingbourne an early date is confirmed by the kidney-shaped buckle in the grave (62). The pieces from grave 51 have crescentic feet and can be paralleled at Blacknall Field G9. They are mainly a 6th-century type (Leeds 1945, 26; Dickinson 1976, 176). A pair of Type V brooches (square headed with lozenge foot and round terminals) was recovered from grave 38 and is paralleled in the Upper Thames Valley, at Blacknall Field (graves 15 and 27) and again from the earlier work at Collingbourne (grave 27, but with angled footplate). It is a relatively early type with parallels dated to the late 5th and earlier 6th century, and a similar date is suggested for the deposition of the Collingbourne brooches by the associated disc brooch. All these types are more common in Saxon regions; in contrast is the pair of Type III brooches from grave 41 (cross patee with square-topped headplate and basal notches), which are generally found in Anglian areas.

Pins

Iron pins are relatively common, being recovered from both settlement and funerary contexts (Geake 1997, 66). A fairly large number (n=10) were found, all except one with an adult female (grave 35 infant). Six burials included iron objects that on the basis of form, and in some cases location, can be identified as dress pins (graves 35 (location within grave unknown), 64, 73, 75, 81 and 85 (two pins) and, in addition, possibly 115). The fragmentary pin from grave 73 was recovered from the pelvic region where it may have secured a garment around the waist. Although this appears to be in an odd position, Geake's (1997, 66) study revealed that a greater number of iron than bronze pins were found at the waist. The grave had suffered considerable truncation and this may explain its location.

The style of head is used to classify the pin, although it is often hard to identify the type because of poor preservation. The examples from graves 35 and 64 had the end of the shaft looped over to create a hooked end – a typical style with examples from Market Lavington and Blacknall Field, dated by Ross (1991, 198–201) to the early 6th century. An additional number of artefacts may also be pins, but their fragmentary state precludes a firm identification (graves 51, 57, 62, 77 and 82). However, apart from grave 51, their location suggests that this is the case.

Copper alloy pins were recovered from graves 61 and 110. The former contained a slender pin with a flattened and perforated head through which it was attached to a copper alloy slip-knot ring. It was discovered in an unusual position to the right of the skull (Walton Rogers 2007, 159–61) and may have fastened a garment around the head or alternatively functioned as a hair pin. Ross (1991) places this type in the late 5th to early 6th century, a date which is consistent with the disc brooches in this grave. The small pin with an expanded, flattened and circular head from grave 110 was found near the right shoulder of the woman. It belongs to Ross's Kingston disc-head type (Ross 1991, 224–31) and mainly occurs in 7th-century graves. Examples can be cited from Edix Hill (Barrington A), Cambridgeshire, graves 60 and 66 (MacGregor and Bolick 1993).

Finger-rings

Copper alloy finger-rings were recorded from two graves in 2007. The infant in grave 42 had a pair: the location of one is unknown (ON 224), but a fragmentary example (ON 38), formed from a thin piece of folded metal, was found to the right of the waist. It is unusual for such a young individual to have been buried with this item of jewellery (Stoodley 2000, 462–63), though it is not certain that either were actually worn. The only other broadly comparable example from Wiltshire is from Petersfinger (G57) and is described as a 'girl's skeleton' (Leeds and Shortt 1953). The ring worn by the adult female in grave 92 was formed from a plain strip of metal (and most of the Wiltshire rings are plain), but ON 224 in grave 42, also formed from a plain strip, was decorated with a border line that encloses a field of ring-and-dot motifs and one of hatching. Grave 31, excavated in 1974, contained three rings, one decorated with punched dots; a similar example was also found in Charlton Plantation G24 (Davies 1985).

Buckles

The buckle is the second most common artefact, having been recovered from 24 (31%) inhumation graves. When the data from the 1974 excavation are added the proportion falls to 26%, which brings it into line with most of the other Wiltshire cemeteries (Table 4.9).

Buckles do not record an association with a particular gender; they were almost equally distributed between males and females, and the addition of the 1974 information does not really alter the observation. A similar picture is found elsewhere, for example at Market Lavington (Williams and Newman 2006, 82) and Blacknall Field (Annable and Eagles 2010), where 10 male and nine female graves contained buckles. Buckles were not restricted by age, though none was found with individuals of less than 2–3 years (grave 40), which is similar to Blacknall Field, for example, where the 3 year old in G100 was the youngest.

Most buckles are simple iron fasteners, the majority oval in outline, while just over a third are D-shaped (5/14). There is also one example of a kidney-shaped loop. This concurs with Marzinzik's (2003, 33) national study that found oval buckles are the most popular type. Half of the buckles (n=12) had a circular-shaped section, followed by five that are D-shaped. Both these forms occurred in contexts ranging from the 5th to the 7th century (Marzinzik 2003, 30–33).

Table 4.9 Frequency of buckles in Wiltshire cemeteries

Cemetery	*No.*
Charlton Plantation	10 (22)
Harnham Hill	6 (8)
Market Lavington	8 (19)
Blacknall Field	27 (25)
Petersfinger	16 (23)

Number in brackets = %

Just under half (10) have plates. They were folded over the loop with a central perforation to accommodate the tongue. Most are unremarkable rectangular examples, although one tapering plate (grave 88) was found, which also had an unusual loop of rectangular section. Triangular plates are rare in England, being more common on the Continent in Frankish and Saxon territories (Marzinzik 2003, 49). The Collingbourne piece does not, however, have protrusions like the continental examples, and is similar to the buckle from Barrington G63. Grave 12, excavated in 1974, contained a buckle with tapering plate, while a similar example came from Charlton Plantation G82 (Davies 1985). In these and grave 88 the plate is much less obviously triangular when compared to the other examples. A rare kidney-shaped buckle with rectangular cellwork plate (Marzinzik Type II.10) was recovered from grave 62, and two out of the other three known examples also come from Wiltshire (Petersfinger G21 and Blacknall Field G49), perhaps indicating an origin in the county for this type. The other Wiltshire buckles have circular loops and it is possible that the Collingbourne specimen is unique. It could have been produced in the 5th century, but examples are found in graves spanning the 5th and early 6th century.

There are only two copper alloy buckles. Grave 59 contained a kidney-shaped loop, which has faint traces of ribbing. It belongs to a slightly larger and more widely distributed group than the iron buckles of this shape (Marzinzik 2003, 27). The hinge bar is particularly thin, linking it to two examples from Mucking II, Essex (graves 493 and 648; Hirst and Clark 2009). It was probably manufactured in the 5th century, but may not have been interred until the earlier 6th. Grave 110 held a tiny fragmentary buckle with a plate that was secured by a pair of rivets. Its location suggests that it was serving as a fastener for a strap to which a knife's sheath was attached. These delicate buckles appear to be more common in the 7th century than either the 5th or 6th (Geake 1997, 79; Marzinzik 2003, 52), and in Hampshire parallels can be cited from the late cemeteries at Portway West G8 (Stoodley 2006a, 71; fig. 7) and Snell's Corner graves 19 and 22 (Knocker 1956, 135–36; figs 11 and 14).

Discussion

The range of artefacts recovered from these graves is typical of an assemblage from an early Anglo-Saxon cemetery from southern England. Brooches provide the clearest evidence for cultural associations and the examples are generally in keeping with what one would expect from an area of Saxon settlement. The disc and saucer brooches provide the best indication of connections with other southern English sites, for example, the pair of cast saucer brooches with seven running spiral designs in grave 69 has parallels in the Upper Thames Valley and Hampshire (Dickinson 1993, fig. 19). Other cultural influences are represented by the pair of unusual equal-armed brooches and certain small-long brooches which between them demonstrate links with both Kentish and Anglian regions.

Costume reconstruction

The actual cloth and linen hardly ever survives, yet the position of the fasteners in relation to the skeleton has the potential to provide information about the type of costume that the deceased was laid to rest in (Fig. 4.7). The predominant style of costume found throughout most of south-east England in the 5th and 6th centuries was the *peplos* dress – a tubular type of costume that was fastened over the shoulders (Walton Rogers 2007, 144–8; Welch 1992, 62–4 and fig. 42). The following discussion considers the data from the entire excavated cemetery (including 1974) and focuses on those individuals that had their costume secured by brooches. In total, 25 burials included metal dress fasteners. By breaking this group down further, it is found that 14 have pairs of brooches in a position consistent with that expected for the *peplos* dress (Table 4.10). Grave 81 had a single disc brooch and a pin, but the positions are again suggestive of the *peplos* and it is similar to Market Lavington G8 (Williams and Newman 2006) which contained a saucer brooch and a pin at the left and right shoulder respectively. Only one individual had a triumvirate of brooches: grave 92 with a pair of disc brooches at the shoulders and a bell-shaped brooch. The latter is lying over a disc brooch and suggests that it was fastening an outer cloak (Walton Rogers 2007, 167–70). In fact, one of the disc brooches (ON 222) has textile on its front, which will have come from the garment it clasped (see McCormick, below). Brooches that secured outer cloaks could be large and showy, for example at Blacknall Field the woman in G21 had, amongst other jewellery, a fine great square-headed brooch. It is likely that the bell-shaped brooch was chosen because of its size and sophistication. Moreover, textile has survived on the right-hand side of the brooch and is interpreted as the border of a garment or linen veil. In a similar way, mineral-preserved textile from a pair of equal-arm brooches has contributed to an understanding of the costume in grave 64: ON 6 included textile that related to an undergarment, while the textile identified on ON 5 was from a garment which was worn over the top of this (see McCormick, below).

Table 4.10 Location of brooches

Position of brooches	*Frequency*	*Brooch type*
Pair at shoulders	14	Various
Single on right shoulder	1	Disc
Single on left shoulder	1	Annular
Three over upper chest	1	Disc & bell-shaped
2 x pairs: chest & head	1	Disc & penannular

Table 4.11 Brooch pairs used for the peplos

Types of brooches combined (all pairs)	*No. of pairs*
Applied	1
Button	1
Disc	3
Equal-armed	1
Saucer	2
Small-long	6

Only brooches of the same type were used to secure the *peplos*, the most popular variety being the small-long brooch (Table 4.11). This regularity is typical of Saxon areas, for example at Market Lavington and Petersfinger only paired types were used (burials with two brooches) and at Blacknall Field, of the 15 individuals wearing a *peplos*, only two had non-matching brooches (Stoodley 2010, 91).

Studies of early Anglo-Saxon costume have revealed the presence of other dress styles (Brush 1993; Walton Rogers 2007, 196–8) and grave 61 provides the clearest evidence for an alternative costume. In addition to the possible ear-rings/veil rings, there are two disc brooches: one was on the upper chest, while the other was lower down the torso which is consistent with a form of Kentish costume (Walton Rogers 2007, 197). Given the close links between Kent and Frankia, this could support the interpretation of the penannular brooches as ear-rings. The burial is broadly contemporary to those of the other women with disc brooches and it is likely that this style existed alongside the *peplos* dress – perhaps a woman who was expressing a different cultural identity. In addition, there are several individuals that were found with single brooches. In grave 6 (from 1974) a single brooch was found over the right shoulder and in grave 47 a penannular brooch was positioned on the left shoulder. At Market Lavington, graves 24 and 33 both had single brooches on the right shoulder and at Blacknall Field, G23, an

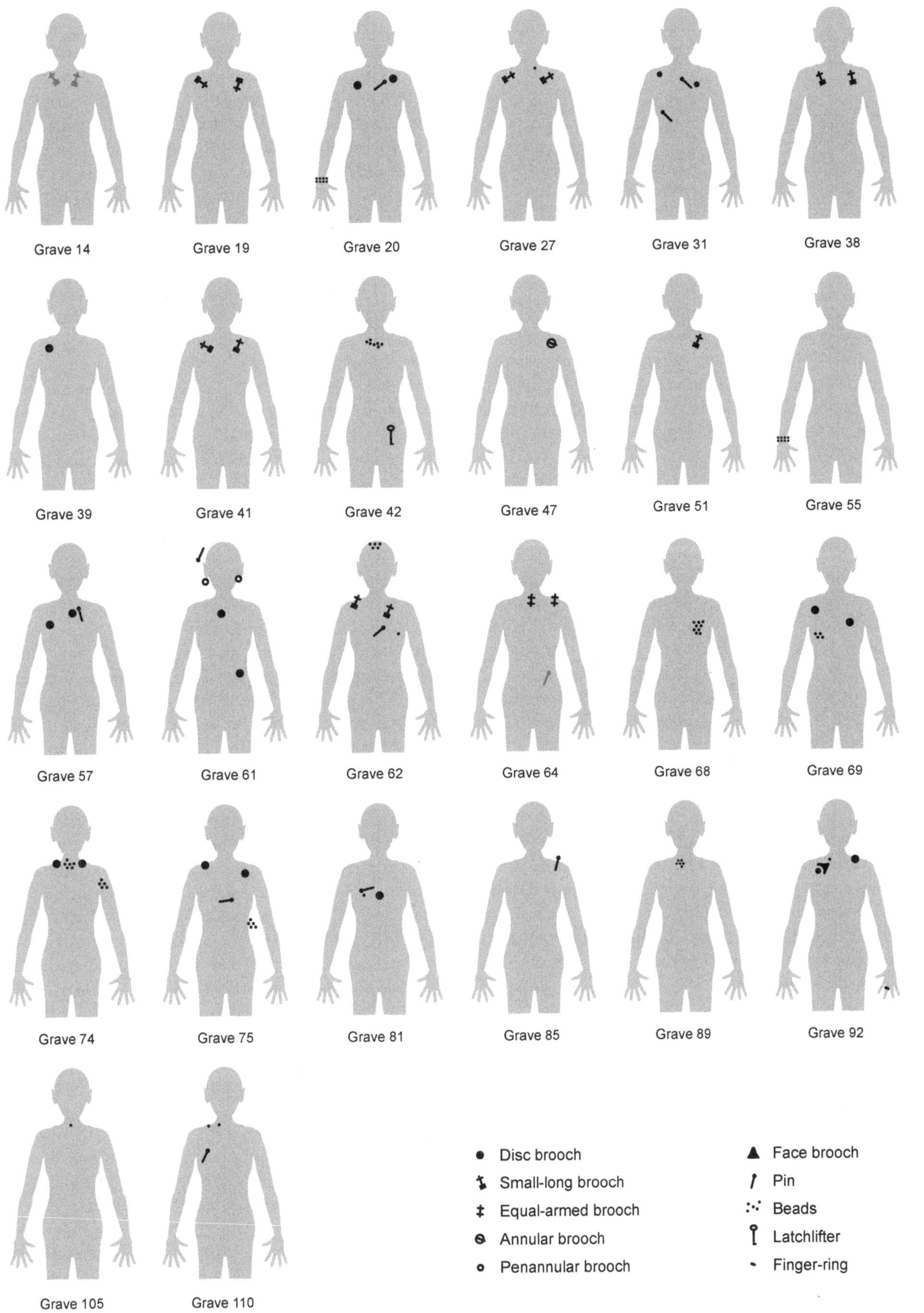

Figure 4.7 Position of jewellery/fasteners on body

Table 4.12 Cemetery phasing

Phase	*Date range*	*Grave*
I	Late C5	6, 23, ?11,
II	Late C5–early C6	3A, 15, 19, 27, 34, 38, 39, ?57, 59, ?61, 62, 74, ?76, ?81, 82, 84
III	C6	2, 14, 20, 31, ?35, 40, ?41, 42, 45, 51, 52, 60, ?63, 64, 69, ?73, 75, 77, ?83, 89, 92
IV	Late C6–C7	12, 44, 71, 88, 91
V	C7	96, 97, 100, 101, ?102, ?103, 104, ?105, 106, 107, ?108, 109, 110

8–9 year old was found with an applied disc brooch in the same position. The evidence may suggest that an organic type of fastener was used to secure the dress over the other shoulder, or that a different style of dress altogether was being worn. Despite these variations, the majority of adult women in this community wore, for the funeral at least, traditional Saxon folk costume.

Chronology

The site consists of two separate groups of graves, which can be interpreted as representing spatially distinct burial areas within a single cemetery. To the west of the coombe the graves have a date range extending from the later 5th, through the 6th and possibly into the early 7th century. The smaller group of graves on the eastern side of the coombe are mainly of 7th-century date.

Western part of the cemetery

A sequence of burials is mainly derived from chronologically diagnostic grave goods (see Table 4.12; *Grave Catalogue*). The earliest burials were probably made in the late 5th century (Phase I) and comprise several of those from the 1974 excavation. Grave 23 produced a pair of 5th-century applied brooches of Mahndorf Type. In the absence of similarly early material in Wiltshire, it is safest to place its interment in the late 5th century. An equal-armed brooch of Nesse Type was discovered in grave 6. These are dated to the second half of the 5th century (Evison 1977), but this specimen was damaged and a date in the early years of the 6th century cannot be ruled out. Grave 11 is tentatively placed in this phase on the basis of the Roman disc brooch that was being worn by its occupant; it is possible that the burial took place at a time when this was a current fashion. Grave 57 with a pair of applied brooches with possible scrolls may be as early as Phase I, but it may be safer to place it in Phase II.

Phase II contains burial remains that included artefacts indicating that they were made sometime within the later 5th and earlier 6th century (AD 450–550). Out of necessity it overlaps with Phases I and III. It is in this phase that the earliest weapon burials are found. For example, grave 59, with its sword and kidney-shaped buckle loop, and grave 82 with Type 1.1 boss and ?E1 spearhead. Most of the burials with disc brooches can be attributed to this phase, while several of the small-long brooches should be contemporary, such as grave 62 with its Type IV brooches found in association with an iron kidney-shaped buckle of later 5th- to early 6th-century date.

Phase III covers the first three-quarters of the 6th century. Grave 92, with its Style I decorated bell-shaped brooch and pair of disc brooches, was dug and used in the first half of the century. The applied brooches with zoomorphic decoration from grave 75 were found with amber beads and a date in the 6th century can be ascribed. The pair of rare equal-armed brooches (grave 64) may, according to similar examples from Kent, date to the 5th century, yet the quartz bead lifts the date of deposition to sometime in the (?earlier) 6th century. Graves 73, and possibly grave 35, contained a loop-headed pin, which Ross (1991) places in the early 6th century. A male equivalent is probably grave 83 with Type E1 spearhead and Type 2 shield boss. A number of female burials can be ascribed a more general date in this phase, for example grave 69 with a pair of seven-spiral saucer brooches and grave 51 with a pair of square-headed small-long brooches with crescentic feet. The majority of the remaining weapon graves can be satisfactorily accommodated in the 6th century, such as grave 45 with a Type G1 spearhead.

Phase IV is a small group comprising burial remains inclusive of grave goods that occur in both the later 6th and 7th centuries. Because these were made in the western part of the cemetery, it is argued that their deposition occurred before the eastern part of the cemetery was established and they should, therefore, date no later than the end of the 6th or early 7th century. Grave 12 contained an iron buckle with triangular plate of a form usually found in the late 6th–7th century and grave 91 a spearhead of a type more commonly encountered in the later 6th and 7th century (Swanton Group C3). The other burials all included knives of a type more commonly encountered in the 7th century, but which could occur in the 6th.

There are a small number of stratigraphic relationships that supplement the artefactual information. Grave 82 (Phase II) cut the south-east corner of structure 1268. It is possible that an unurned cremation burial (cremation grave 1310) had been made in the centre of this structure (see McKinley, Chapter 3); if this is correct then it would pre-date grave 82, making it one of the earliest burials. Grave 60 (no grave goods) cut grave 59 (Phase II), which should place it safely within the 6th century. In a similar way grave 63 cut a Phase II grave (62) (the beads, assigned a mid-5th–mid-6th-century date, possibly deriving from grave 62 rather than grave 63), and the end of grave 76 had been clipped by grave 77 (Phase III). Grave 65 was found to be overlying grave 66; neither unfortunately have closely datable grave goods and only a relative sequence can be inferred. Grave 92 (first half of the 6th century) was cut by cremation grave 1297 (unurned burial), demonstrating that cremation was still taking place in the latter part of the century. Without chronologically diagnostic grave goods it is impossible to predict where the remainder of the burials belong and out of necessity they are allocated a broad date range covering the period that the western part of the cemetery was used.

Eastern part of the cemetery

The evidence from the grave goods indicates that these interments postdate their counterparts in the western part of the cemetery and represent the relocation of burial at some point in the early 7th century. Grave 101 is dated to the first half of the 7th century by its Type 6 shield boss, while grave 110 is placed in the middle decades of the century by its monochrome 'doughnut' type bead. The latter was also accompanied by a small copper alloy buckle and pin (Ross' Kingston disc head Type) that are typical of late burial. Grave 96 contained the remains of a bed (see Watson, above), which is a practice considered to have taken place in the second half of the 7th century (Speake 1989, 226). The other graves contained various forms of late knives, but these are not closely datable and a general date covering the period that the eastern part of the cemetery was in use must apply. Deposits of cremated bone were found in the fills of both graves 96 and 105 which may demonstrate that cremation-related practices were still an important element of mortuary practice in the 7th century (see McKinley, Chapter 3). Several burials were devoid of artefacts, but their spatial relationships to those with artefacts suggest that they are contemporary and not isolated 5th- or 6th-century graves. It is difficult to know when the last burials were made, but if the absence of later 7th- and earlier 8th-century artefacts is anything to go by, the cemetery did not outlast the 7th century.

Mineral-Preserved Organics and Compositional Analysis of Metalwork

by Elizabeth McCormick

Condition of the Metalwork

The soil environment at Collingbourne Ducis is predominantly alkaline and the metals have survived in relatively good condition. Consequently little organic material has survived, as organics are best preserved where corrosion is prevalent because ferrous corrosion products mineralise the organic material and copper corrosion products are toxic to micro-organisms (Cronyn 1990, 244). The majority of organic material that has survived is either partly or wholly mineralised. A few fibres, all identified as plant, have also survived in a more natural, non-mineralised form suggesting the burial environment favoured plant preservation over that of animal material. This is confirmed by little leather surviving.

Investigative Conservation

The metalwork underwent investigative conservation in 2009–2010 to identify materials and aid understanding of manufacture, use, and function of the objects. Prior to examination the metalwork was mechanically cleaned of accretions and corrosion products (by Wiltshire Council Conservation Service (WCCS) and Wessex Archaeology's in-house conservator) to reveal surface detail.

Examination and analysis were undertaken at the English Heritage Archaeological Conservation and Technology Team (ACATT) laboratories and included:

- Optical microscopy to increase understanding of the manufacture and function of the metalwork, and to identify and classify organic material, identify wood species, and record weave patterns and thread counts of textiles;
- Scanning Electron Microscopy (SEM) to identify textile fibres, as well as wood species unable to be identified using low-powered optical microscopy, and to examine animal pelt;
- Fourier Transform Infrared spectroscopy (FTIR) to identify fibres;
- X-ray fluorescence (XRF) analysis to identify the composition of copper alloys, and any surface coatings such as gilding and tinning;
- X-radiography to identify features relating to manufacture and function. X-radiography of all of the finds prior to cleaning was carried out largely by Wessex Archaeology, with a number by WCCS, and a few objects were X-rayed again by ACATT staff after cleaning to answer specific questions raised during examination.

The metalwork excavated in 2007 comprised 290 objects, the vast majority of which have been examined, including weapons (one sword, five shields, 12 spearheads), personal items (50 knives, 31 brooches, 2 brooches/veil rings, 25 buckles, 8 cosmetic sets/implements or possible implements), a bucket binding, and fittings from a bed burial. For a

Table 4.13 Summary of sword ON 15 details

	Measurement	*Comment*
Sword	length 910 mm	–
Hilt	length 123 mm	3 pieces of horn
Upper guard	length 21 mm	–
Grip	length 89 mm	–
Lower guard	length 13 mm; extends 6 mm over blade	–
Blade	width 48 mm	–
Scabbard	unknown (not enough surviving MPO evidence)	Wood, identified as willow/poplar using SEM. No other organics remain

catalogue of all objects examined see Appendix 1; for XRF results see Appendix 2 (see also McCormick and Watson 2010).

It should be noted that the exact orientation of objects within the graves was not recorded which has affected the interpretation of the organic remains found on the surface of some of the metalwork. Exemplary are objects found on top of skeletal remains; as it is not known which face of the object was uppermost any preserved textile could be either evidence of costume or a grave covering. In such cases the most probable interpretations are given.

Sword

One sword (ON 15) was found, in grave 59; it has a broad two-edged blade and measurements that are characteristic of the 5th–7th century (see Table 4.13; *Grave Catalogue*), although the grip is somewhat shorter than average and the upper guard longer (*cf.* Underwood 1999, 47; Watson 2009, 566).

Mineral-preserved horn has survived on the tang, in differing orientations corresponding to the lower guard, grip and upper guard, signifying that the hilt was manufactured from three different sections of horn; such manufacture is typical of swords from the 5th–7th century (Cameron 2000, 34; Watson 2009, 565). Raised lines in the corrosion also indicate the location of joins between the different hilt sections, and the arching grain pattern of the horn on the upper guard suggests that it was made from the tip of a horn.

The only remaining evidence of the scabbard is areas of mineral-preserved wood on the blade which has been identified using SEM as willow/poplar, the standard scabbard wood used in the Anglo-Saxon period (Cameron 2000, 34; Watson 2009, 565). There are two longitudinal ridges visible on the surface of the wood, on one side of the blade near to the tip, that appear to be converging slightly towards the blade tip; these may be remnants of the scabbard's decoration (*cf.* Cameron 2000, 35–6). None of the scabbard fleece lining has survived. Similarly, there are no remains of the leather covering. However, the dark layer of corrosion products on top of the mineral-preserved wood is indirect evidence of the cover and that an adhesive was used to help attach it to the wood; the adhesive would have formed an impermeable layer that the corrosion products solidified against.

The sword was positioned on the left side of the body, lying across the left arm, from shoulder to hip (Fig. 2.25), with the lower part resting beside the left thigh; this is a common positioning of Anglo-Saxon swords within graves (Watson 2009, 566). The grave contained no other weapons. No textile remains were found on the sword, but possible evidence of the male's costume has been preserved on the knife by his right hip (ON 18; see below).

Shields

The five shield bosses and grips were examined for organic evidence relating to the shield boards and grip binding. Wood relating to the shield board was found on three of the shields and identified using SEM; two as lime (ONs 106, 178; graves 82, 77), one as willow/poplar (ON 268; grave 101). Studs were found with two of the shields (ONs 106; 178), and their positioning in the graves in relation to the centre of the associated boss was used to give minimum diameters of the boards: 0.36 metres and 0.34 metres respectively. These correspond to the lower end of the 0.35–0.45 metres range for minimum diameters given by Härke (1992, 45).

All of the wooden boards were probably covered in leather, the thickness of which could be accurately measured for ONs 106 and 178 due to the survival of mineral-preserved organic material on the associated shield studs; in both cases it was found to be especially thick leather (4 mm). The latter of these has thinner leather on the front (1 mm), presumably to allow decoration, whereas the former has thick leather (3–4 mm) on either side of the 3–5 mm wooden board. This illustrates that the leather covering was probably much more important to the strength and, therefore, functionality of the shields than the wood, which provided the rigidity (Jacqui Watson pers. comm.). It should be noted that the wood on the front of boss ON 102 (grave 83) relates to a possible grave covering and is probably oak, evidence of which was also found on buckle ON 103 from the same grave.

Grips which are inserted into the board have a grain orientation perpendicular to it to add strength and three inserted grips have been identified on the Collingbourne shields (ONs 102, 106, 178; graves 83, 82, 77). Leather was commonly used to bind grips, and evidence of this survives on the grip of ON 102 which is bound in strips of leather 5–7 mm wide. Unusually, the central section of the grip of ON 268 (grave 101) has been bound with plied thread.

Evidence of a carry strap survives on the grip of ON 178 which is wound in two places with leather strips 16 mm wide, 3 mm thick.

Two-thirds of Anglo-Saxon shields are found buried in the middle of graves, between the head and feet, with most on top of the body (Härke 1992, 65). The Collingbourne Ducis shields follow this trend; two bosses were found on the torso (ONs 1, 178; graves 52, 77), two to the side of the torso – one of which was against the side of the grave (ONs 102, 268; graves 83, 101), and one on the face (ON 106; grave 82). Consequently textile remains were found on two of the shields (ONs 1, 178), potentially evidence of male costume. The textile on the boss fragments and grip of ON 1 is tabby weave with ZZ spin and a thread count of 20 x 12 over 10 mm². SEM identified the textile fibres to be plant. The textile on the outer side of the grip of ON 178 is 2/1 twill with ZZ spin and a thread count of 12 x 8 over 10 mm². SEM identified the fibres to be animal, probably sheep wool.

Spears

Mineral-preserved wood relating to shafts remains in all 12 spearheads and one spear ferrule. The shaft remains were identified using a combination of optical microscopy and SEM as: five ash (ONs 69, 77, 107, 111, 125 and corresponding ferrule ON 126; graves 58, 45, 82, subsoil, 91), two possible ash (ONs 101, 405; graves 83, 52), one willow/poplar (ON 276; grave 101), one possible willow/poplar (ON 112, subsoil), one hazel (ON 179; grave 77), one willow/poplar/hazel/alder (ON 199; grave 108) and one unidentified (ON 279; grave 109). The ash shafts were mature timber, evidenced by the characteristic bands of vessels relating to annual cycles of growth. The hazel shaft was conversely identified as sapling wood due to the rays being arranged towards the centre in cross-section. The predominance of ash with occasional examples of other woods is typical of Anglo-Saxon spear shafts (Underwood 1999, 39; Watson 2009, 570). The classifications willow/poplar and hazel/alder have been given as the pairings have such similar features it is currently not possible to distinguish between the former, and only occasionally possible to distinguish between the latter.

The spearhead in grave 91 (ON 125) was found alongside the right arm of the adult male, and the ferrule (ON 126) was found on the right foot. Evidence for an ash shaft was observed in both, suggesting they are from the same object. The distance from spear tip to ferrule end as found in the grave was 1.34 m.

Knives

The majority of the 50 knives examined have mineral-preserved organic remains relating to handles on the tangs, most of which could be positively identified as horn using optical microscopy. In a number of cases there is evidence that the handle extended onto the blade shoulder, a manufacturing technique to secure their position. This is indicated by mineral-preserved horn remains on the blade (ONs 34, 68, 97, 133, 190, 195; graves 54, 37, 87, 88, 77, 94) and/or a raised line on the blade where corrosion products once seeped into the gap between the handle and the sheath, later solidifying (ONs 53, 96, 118, 271; graves 40, 43, 83, 107).

However, there is little remaining organic evidence of the sheaths, with just a few examples of mineral-preserved leather surviving on blades (ONs 18, 29, 53, and possibly ONs 97, 133; graves 59, 51, 40, 87, 88), and where it does survive it is little more than a fine layer of compacted powder so the species is unidentifiable. The one exception is the knife from grave 51 (ON 29) which has mineral-preserved leather on the now detached blade pieces, an area of which can be described as pelt with hair impressions left in the surface, evidence that the sheath's leather was not de-haired before manufacture. The pelt has been identified as pig from the grain pattern, best visible using SEM.

The positioning of knives in the grave, both in relation to the body and other objects, is evidence that they were suspended from or tucked into belts, (ONs 18, 29, 34, 53; graves 59, 51, 54, 40), although little evidence of the belts or sheaths themselves has survived.

Textile has survived on a few of the knives (ONs 12, 18, 43, 68, 189, and possibly 175; graves 61, 59, 55, 37, 69, 74), and due to their placement on the body it is possible evidence of costume. However, the textile is highly mineralised and deteriorated meaning that the features are not discernible. The exception is the knife from grave 59 (ON 18) which has a strip of mineralised textile along the blade edge that is 2/2 twill with ZZ spin and a thread count 14 x 14 over 10 mm². This is potential evidence of male warrior costume as the knife was found at the waist of the man buried with the sword. The mineralised textile on knife blade ON 189 (grave 69) is visibly twill but too deteriorated to identify features further. It was placed on the lower torso below one of the saucer brooches (ON 163); fibres from the brooch's pair (ON 164) were identified as animal, possibly sheep wool, and are likely related to the twill textile on the knife.

Brooches

Textile has survived on most of the 31 brooches, predominantly in a mineral-replaced state around the iron pins. All of the textile remains on the back of the brooches have survived around the pin and/or catch so it is safe to presume they are all evidence of costume and that the brooches lay with their fronts uppermost. This is also confirmed in a number of

Table 4.14 Summary of textile material on the brooches

Grave/ ON	*Location of fibres*	*Weave*	*Spin*	*Thread count over 10 mm²*	*Analysis*	*Interpretation*
41 ON 72	Pin fulcrum	2/2 twill	–	–	–	Garment
51 ON 2	Pin fulcrum	tabby	–	–	–	Garment
61 ON 10	Front	2/1 twill	ZZ	10 x 10	–	Veil or Outer garment
64 ON 5	Back	–	–	–	SEM; animal, possibly sheep	Garment
	Between woollen garment and body	threads appear twisted	–	–	SEM; plant	Braid edge, probably of undergarment (found on ON 6)
64 ON 6	Back	tabby	–	–	SEM; plant	Undergarment
69 ON 164	Catch	–	–	–	SEM; animal, possibly sheep	Garment. *cf.* twill found on knife ON 189
	Associated piece	threads appear twisted	ZZ	14 x 6	–	Garment border (tablet weave) or bead cord (braided cord)
74 ON 173	Catch	–	–	–	SEM; plant	Bead cord
75 ON 167	Catch	–	–	–	SEM; sheep	Garment
92 ON 221	Front	–	–	–	SEM, FTIR; plant	Garment border or veil. Extant fibres
	Back	2/2 twill	ZZ	14 x 14	SEM; animal	Cloak
92 ON 223	Associated textile pieces to ON 221	–	–	–	SEM; sheep	Cloak
92 ON 135	Between textile and brooch back	2-ply thread	–	–	SEM, FTIR; plant	Bead cord. Extant fibres. Other end of cord on ON 222

cases by the placement of human body residue/bone on top of the textile, indicating that the textile lay between the body and brooch back (ONs 72, 115, 135 and 222, 163; graves 41, 81, 92, 69). However, in the majority of cases the textile is too deteriorated or abraded to discern features. Table 4.14 gives the exceptions where certain textile features are visible and/or fibres were able to be sampled.

The 2/1 twill textile on the front of ON 10 – a brooch found on the sternum of the burial in grave 61 – could relate to a veil, for which ONs 8 and 14 (found at the sides of the skull) could be veil rings. However, most veils were a lightweight linen tabby rather than a twill (Walton Rogers 2007, 157) and ONs 8 and 14 could equally be penannular brooches minus their pins, or (less likely) ear-rings. No organics were found on ONs 8 and 14 to directly aid their identification. Alternatively, the textile on ON 10 may relate to a grave covering, or an outer garment that could have been fastened by brooch ON 11, found on the lower left ribcage.

Anglo-Saxon cloaks were typically wool twills (Walton Rogers 2007, 170). Brooch ON 221 from grave 92 has been identified as a cloak brooch due to the 2/2 twill textile found around the pin, and the associated textile fibres (ON 223) being identified as sheep by SEM. The cloak brooch is significant: it is unusual in style, with central cloak brooches rarely found in the Saxon region of the country, and textile remains on such brooches from the region being especially sparse (Walton Rogers 2007, 170). The plant textile on the front of the brooch may be from a garment border, evidence of a linen veil, or a grave covering.

Evidence of bead cords has been found on ONs 135, 164, 173 and 222, further confirmed by beads being found between the brooch pairs (ONs 135–222, ONs 163–164, ONs 170–173; graves 92, 69, 74), although that found on ON 164 could be a tablet weave from the border of a garment instead, given its larger size. Bead strings were often worn strung between brooches, presumably fastened around the catches, and the cords were generally made from plied or braided linen (Walton Rogers 2007, 193). This fits in with the identification of the fibres found on ONs 135 and 173 as plant using SEM, the fibres on ONs 135 and 222 being plied, the fibres on ON 164 being braided, and the positioning of the plied fibres on ONs 135 and 222 between mineral-replaced textile (garment) and the brooch backs.

Human body residue was found on the back of a number of brooches (ONs 72, 115, 135 and 222, 163, S5115; graves 41, 81, 92, 69, 57), as well as human bone (ONs 72, 222) and a skin surface cast (ON 163). ON 223 (grave 92), found associated with brooch ON 221, consists largely of mineral-replaced threads with some extant threads, all held together by the residue of body liquor.

X-Ray fluorescence (XRF) analysis (Appendix 2) revealed that all of the brooches that have been gilded (ONs 140, 163 and 164, 221, S5115 and S5128; unstratified, graves 69, 92, 57) were done so by amalgam gilding, indicated by the presence of mercury. The analysis also confirmed surface tinning (ONs 2, 5 and 6; graves 51, 64 and probably ONs 10 and 11; grave 61), tin solder on catches (ONs 24, 170 and 173, S5115; graves 62, 74, 57) and tin/lead solder on catches (ONs 19 and 20; grave 62). It is likely that the tin solder found on the central stubs of the disc brooches ONs 10 and 11 is evidence that there was originally a central attachment on each. A comparison of the alloy compositions of brooches found in pairs but which look stylistically different was utilised to verify when such brooches were not originally a pair (ONs 2 and 26; ONs 8 and 14, ONs 170 and 173; graves 51, 61, 74). Brooch ON 140 (unstratified; Fig. 2.82) is a keystone garnet disc brooch and XRF analysis identified the base metal as a copper alloy high in silver, that gilding originally covered the entire front of the brooch, and that the stones are almandine garnets. The white setting into which the central garnet has been directly embedded was examined visually and analysed using XRF and is either bone or shell.

Buckles

Most of the 25 buckles are simple loops, with the exceptions of two kidney-shaped buckles (ONs 16, 22; graves 59, 62). ON 22 has an iron buckle and back plate, with copper alloy front plate and inlays on the buckle both identified using XRF as leaded gunmetal with a significant amount of zinc.

The majority of the buckles, 17 of 25, were found at the waist, and are almost certainly from belts. In grave 51 the position of knife ON 29 strongly suggests it was tucked into the belt represented by buckle ON 55. The pair of tweezers (ON 17) alongside a knife (ON 18) were probably both suspended from the belt (evidenced by buckle ON 16) worn by the male buried in grave 59. Similarly, the position of knife ON 53 suggests it was suspended from the belt represented by buckle ON 46 (grave 40). In addition, buckle ON 270 (grave 107) may represent a disturbed belt as its positioning on the inner right elbow is peculiar.

The remainder of the buckles include one (ON 216) associated with a possible purse group (ON Group 76) placed between the thighs of the individual in grave 38, and three probable carry strap buckles (ONs 70, 188, 267) for the knives (ONs 71, 187, 266) in graves 58, 70 and 110 – the buckles found in the chest region of the former two (one left, one right), and on top of the right thigh of the latter, underneath the knife tip. The buckle ON 181 found on the right shoulder of the female in grave 75 may have been related to an outer garment such as an animal cape (*cf.* Walton Rogers 2007, 173). The purpose of buckles ONs 103 and 91, which were both found positioned outside the left lower leg (graves 83 and 85), is unknown.

Buckles were examined for evidence of the belts and straps they originally fastened, as well as textile from adjacent clothing or grave coverings. Mineral-preserved leather was found between buckle plates, definite on three examples (ONs 55, 70, 253; graves 51, 58, 106) with another three possibly leather but too abraded to ascertain (ONs 22, 130, 270; graves 62, 88, 107). The grain pattern on both ONs 55 and 70, visible using optical microscopy, was identified as pig. Belt buckle ON 184 from grave 80 has no pin so it may have had a textile rather than a leather strap; unfortunately not enough mineral-preserved organic has survived to verify this (only a small area of abraded mineral-replaced textile survives).

Mineral-replaced textile was found on a number of the buckles and buckle plates, however, the weave pattern has only been identified in two cases – ONs 70 and 253 (graves 58, 106) – as most of the textile is too deteriorated and fragmentary. Buckle ON 70 has mineral-replaced textile remains on the buckle and outer surfaces of the plates. On the back plate, which would have been adjacent to the male's costume, is a tabby tablet weave at the edge of a 2/1 twill, ZZ spin, thread count 13 x 13 over 10 mm^2. The position of the buckle and, therefore, the tablet weave (which occur at the edge of garments) on the left chest suggests that the costume was similar to that of a 7th-century man's warrior dress (*cf.* Walton Rogers 2007, 206). The orientation of the tablet weave indicates that the buckle sat perpendicular to the edge of the garment. It may, for example, have been part of a carry strap that passed from the left chest over the right shoulder. The mineral-replaced textile on ON 253, an iron buckle and back plate with a copper alloy front plate, is visible as tabby, ZZ spin, but there is not enough to do a thread count.

Cosmetic implements

Cosmetic implements were found in five female graves (ONs 13, 48 and 78, 50, 80, 168; graves 61, 39, 38, 47, 69) and one male grave (ON 17; grave 59); the latter – containing tweezers (ON 17) – being that of the warrior accompanied by a sword. Little organic evidence remains on the cosmetic implements, and where it does it is mineral-replaced textile that is too deteriorated to identify the features (ONs 50, 80). The exception to this is the cosmetic brush (ON 48), found next to the skull of the female buried in grave 39.

There are few examples of cosmetic brushes in which the organic material has survived (Hirst and Clark 2009, 544), which makes ON 48 extremely significant. It consists of an iron core, visible on the broken edge and the X-ray, surrounded by a bundle of coarse mineral-replaced fibres tied together with a plied thread made from finer fibres (still extant). The coarser fibres that would have formed the brush bristles have been identified as either horse or hog hair using SEM; it has not been possible to narrow this identification further as both horse and hog have similar features. The finer, extant fibres have been identified as plant using SEM and Fourier Transform Infrared spectroscopy (FTIR). The brush would have been held within the copper alloy cover, a tapering tube the narrow end of which is attached to a suspension ring; the decorative spangle would have also been attached to this ring. The tip of the cover's narrow end was tinned, confirmed using XRF (Appendix 2), and the wider end is decorated with incised transverse lines.

Wooden grave cover

Evidence of a wooden grave cover was found on the shield boss and buckle (ONs 102, 103) from grave 83; although wood was a component of Anglo-Saxon shields the positioning of the wood on the front of the shield boss does not correlate with any wooden features of a shield. The wood was examined with optical microscopy and is most probably oak.

Bucket binding

The copper alloy binding (ON 169) was found next to the skull of an adult female in grave 69. There is mineral-preserved organic around some of the rim rivets, which would be expected to be wood but there is too little material to ascertain this. The length of a rim rivet measures 4 mm, the length of a base rivet 15 mm, which is likely to be due to the base rivets passing through the sides and base of the vessel rather than an indication that the vessel walls were thicker at the base. XRF analysis showed evidence of tinning on the fittings, base and rivets (Appendix 2).

Grouped objects

Objects found closely associated with each other were examined for features and organic evidence that might confirm whether they were from the same object or part of a defined group, such as a purse or bag. For example, the mineral-replaced textile on ON 237, from grave 38, strongly suggests that it is the iron pin from brooch ON 49 which it was found associated with. The similar features of the associated objects ONs 132 and 165 (grave 93) were used to identify them both as mounts, probably from the same leather object; the maximum width for rivets through ON 132 and the width of the open end of ON 165 are both 2 mm, which is so small it indicates they were both mounted on leather.

The group (ON 92) found in the female grave 85 has been identified as a purse and its contents. This consists of a purse ring with six separate items likely to be the contents as similar-looking mineral-replaced textile survives on all the objects; unfortunately the textile is too abraded to see details such as the weave and thread count that would further support this. The ring is too small for a hand to pass inside it, so it probably passed over the top of the pouch to hold the textile around the contents. ON 235, found associated with the purse ring, is likely to be a purse fitting as the small width of the gap between its front and back indicates it was mounted on leather, such as a purse strap. However, no mineral-preserved organics survive to verify this.

The identification of ON Group 85 from the female grave 39 as a purse ring (ON 204) and contents (ON 205 copper fragment and ON 206 iron mount and two implements) is somewhat more tenuous; the group was found in the upper chest area and so the mineral-replaced textile on the iron ring and iron objects could be from the costume rather than remains of a purse. The features of the textile are too obscured by corrosion to help determine this. However, it is most likely to be a purse because of the close association of the objects and, furthermore, as there seems little other use for ON 204, which is too small to be a bangle.

Most of the grouped objects had none or not enough substantial mineral-preserved organic material remaining to draw any conclusions about the association of the objects (ON Group 4, grave 64; ON Group 40, grave 42; ON Group 62, grave 38; ON Group 76, grave 38; ON Group 141, grave 89; and a possible group from the subsoil).

Metallographic Examination of Knives

by Eleanor Blakelock

Introduction

A combination of metallographic and X-radiographic analysis of knives can reveal far more about iron technology in the Anglo-Saxon period than measuring and typology alone. Metallographic analysis is used to determine the iron alloys available and used, methods of manufacture and heat treatments. Analysis may even provide hints as to how knives were used and repaired. It is impossible to metallographically examine all iron artefacts from a site, therefore X-radiographs can be used to reveal the quality of preservation, the overall distributions of shapes, wear and manufacturing types of the entire assemblage (Blakelock and McDonnell 2007; Fell and Starley 1999; McDonnell 1992; McDonnell *et al.* 1991; Starley 1996).

The Saxon smith made good use of the different iron alloys available by creating composite knives, for example using a hard steel cutting edge welded on to a soft and more flexible ferritic or phosphoric iron back. Tylecote and Gilmour's pioneering study of edged tools in 1986 produced a typology of six different methods of manufacturing knives (Fig. 4.8), though this typology has since been simplified (Blakelock and McDonnell 2007; Tylecote and Gilmour 1986). To get the most out of the steel cutting edge heat treatments such as quenching (the artefact is plunged into a liquid to cool it rapidly) and tempering (heating again to *c.* 500°C to remove some of the stress) would be carried out to create a much harder cutting edge (Pleiner 2006, 65–70; Samuels 1999, 5–37).

A total of 53 knives were recovered from graves during the 2007 excavations at Collingbourne Ducis. The X-radiograph analysis and survey has shown that the most common were curved-backed. The survey also revealed that the preferred type of tang to blade interface was distinct on both sides, followed by knives with a distinct tang interface on the knife back.

Methods

Samples were chosen for metallurgical analysis based on the state of preservation and features seen in the X-radiographs. Sections from the knives were taken across the cutting edge of the blade and back, and where possible staggered to preserve the overall knife shape. The samples were mounted in resin and prepared by grinding on successively finer paper before being polished to a 1-micron finish.

Metallographic examination was undertaken using a Nikon Optiphot Reflected Light microscope with various objective lenses ranging from x2.5 to x40. The samples were then etched for approximately 5 seconds in a weak solution of acid (Nital, 4% nitric acid in alcohol) to reveal the microstructure of the metal. The Vickers micro-hardness test was used to determine the hardness of different microstructures present in each sample. The Scanning Electron Microscope with Energy Dispersive X-Ray Analysis (SEM-EDX) was used to determine the elemental composition of the metal.

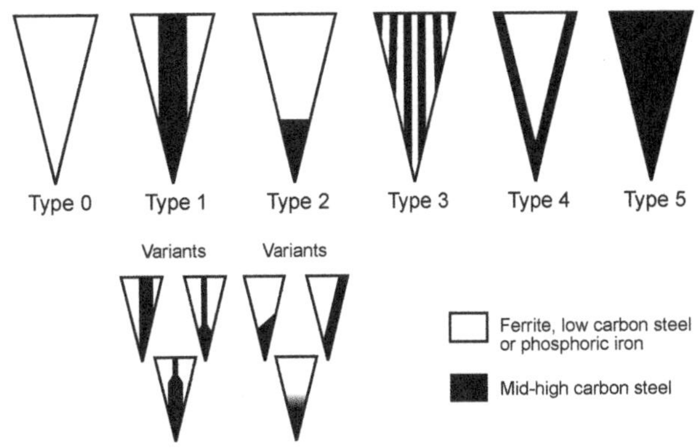

Figure 4.8 Knife manufacturing typology based on blade cross sections (adapted from Tylecote and Gilmour 1986). 0 = all ferrite (or phosphoric iron) with no steel cutting edge; 1 = steel core flanked by ferritic or phosphoric iron; 2 = steel cutting edge butt-welded to the iron back; 3 = piled or banded structure throughout the section; 4 = steel forms a jacket around an iron core, 5 = all steel blade

Results

Twenty-five knives were examined, 15 from 6th- to 7th-century graves and 10 from later, 7th-century graves (Fig. 4.9).

The 6th–7th-century knives were constructed using a range of different manufacturing techniques. The highest proportions were plain iron type 0 knives or all steel type 5 knives, and eight were heat-treated. One (ON 123; grave 66) was very unusual in construction as it appeared to be a reverse type 1 knife with a phosphoric iron core sandwiched between two pieces of heat-treated steel.

The 7th-century knives on the other hand were mostly type 2 knives, with a steel cutting edge and an iron back. The rest of the group consisted of one type 0, one type 1 and one type 3; six of the 10 had been heat-treated.

Discussion

A recent review showed that the vast majority of knives from early medieval settlements are those manufactured by butt-welding a cutting edge, often of high quality steel, on to a ferritic or phosphoric iron back. This is dramatically different from the knife assemblages from cemeteries where a range of different manufacturing techniques are present (Blakelock and McDonnell 2007).

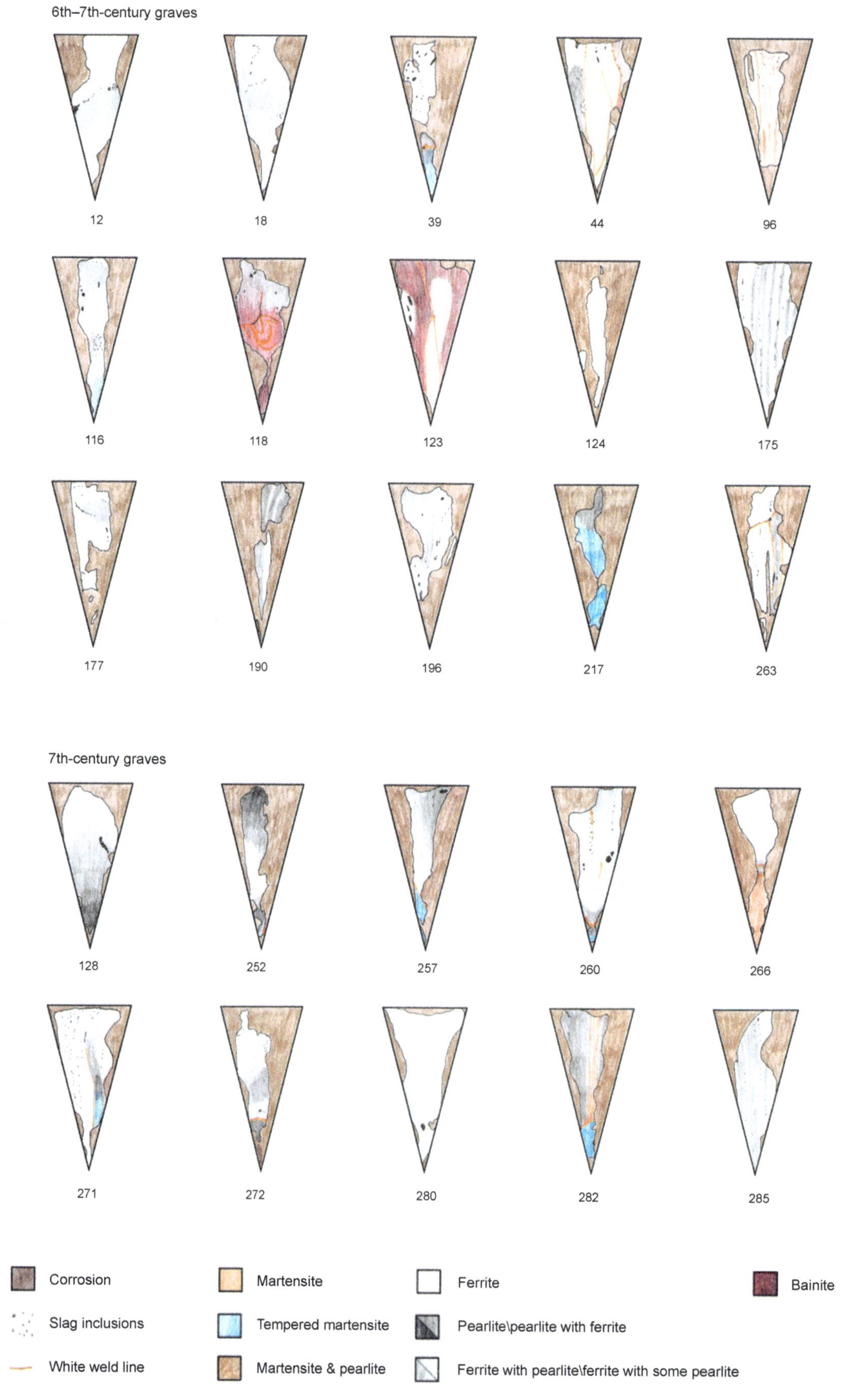

Figure 4.9 Diagram of the knives from 6th–7th-century graves (top) and 7th-century graves (bottom) at Collingbourne Ducis

At Collingbourne, where there appears to be a spatial separation of the later, 7th-century graves from the earlier 6th–7th-century ones, there is a distinct split in manufacturing techniques. The earlier knives were made using a range of different techniques, similar to other cemeteries and early Anglo-Saxon settlements, whilst those of 7th-century date appear to be more standardised, similar to those seen in later Anglo-Saxon settlements.

Therefore, it is possible to argue that there is a shift in iron technology in the 7th century, not only in the variety of manufacturing techniques but also in the quality of the knives, the heat-treatments carried out and alloys used. The knives from Collingbourne were slightly better quality than those from earlier cemeteries, possibly relating to the higher number of standardised type 2 knives seen.

Conclusion

This analysis has clearly shown that the differences in knife manufacturing technology during the Anglo-Saxon period reflect changes through time. It is very rare to associate changes of this magnitude with a specific date or even period, especially when many sites span multiple centuries and have poorly-stratified contexts. An exception to this pattern are early Saxon graves, which can be dated to specific centuries based on the grave goods present or other dating techniques (Lucy 2000, 16–64; Lucy and Reynolds 2002). To determine a specific time frame for these manufacturing changes in knives, those from graves that have been securely dated to the 7th century were separated from the other early Saxon cemetery knives.

There is a distinct change to a standardised manufacture in the 7th century. This occurred at the same time that kingdoms developed, Christianity was introduced and urban settlements re-emerged. It is unknown exactly which of these three developments resulted in this change, or if it was a combination. However, the sudden standardisation of knives could have been influenced by the specialised blacksmiths present in urban and high status settlements, particularly as urban settlements were markets and ports which would have facilitated new ideas, innovations and technologies to diffuse into the country.

This programme of metallographic examination was carried out in conjunction with a larger research project, and a more comprehensive overview of changes in iron technology in the early medieval period is available in Blakelock 2011 (electronic copies can be requested from the author).

Coins

by Nicholas Cooke

Three coins were found in two graves; all are *nummi* – small copper alloy Roman coins of the 4th century AD. All are in reasonable condition, although they bear evidence of heavy wear.

Two (ONs 201 and 202) were found together as part of ON Group 4 in grave 64, the former struck by Gratian between AD 367 and 375, and the latter a commemorative 'Constantinopolis' issue of the House of Constantine minted between AD 330 and 335. ON Group 4 comprises a collection of objects which Mepham (below) suggests may represent an amulet group, perhaps originally contained in a pouch and placed by the right hand in the mid-chest area (see *Grave Catalogue*; Fig. 2.30). Both coins were pierced for suspension, although in neither case was the piercing intended to display the engraving on either the obverse or the reverse of the coin.

ON 239, from grave 89, is too worn to be identified closely, but is clearly one of the numerous 4th-century issues bearing a votive wreath on the reverse. Although not pierced, it appears to have been incorporated within a necklace – along with a small number of beads (ON 141), it formed part of a necklace apparently worn by the 5–7 year old juvenile at the time of burial. It is not clear how the coin was attached to the necklace.

Catalogue

ON 201 Context 1101. Cu Alloy AE3
Obv. Bust r -GRA-
Rev. Emperor l with standard and shield. GLORIAN (O VISAECVLI). Mint Mark: OFIII / CON (3rd *officia* in Arles)
18 mm diam. 1.40 g. Very worn. Die Axis 360°. Pierced for suspension. Issue date: AD 367–375. LRBC II, 517

ON 202 Context 1101. Cu Alloy AE3
Obv. Bust l, helmeted, spear. (CONSTAN)T INOPLIS
Rev. Winged victory on prow. Mint Mark: Illegible
16 mm diam. 1.70 g. Very worn. Die Axis 360°. Pierced for suspension. Issue date: AD 330–335. As LRBC I, 52

ON 239 Context 1333. Cu Alloy AE3
Obv. Bust r. CON-
Rev. Wreath containing text -T /- /-X
15 mm diam. 0.90 g. Very worn. Votive C4 *nummus*. Issue date: 4th century AD

Beads

by Lorraine Mepham

A total of 190 beads (86 glass, 99 amber, five other), plus fragments, was recovered from one cremation and 20 inhumation graves. Table 4.15 gives the breakdown of bead types by grave; numbers per grave ranged from one to 112, although the latter is exceptional – the other 20 graves contained 11 beads or less.

The beads have been classified following the scheme recommended by Hirst (2000), with correlations where appropriate to Brugmann's classification (2004). Reference has also been made to the Dover Buckland assemblage (Evison 1987).

Glass Beads

Monochrome

The majority of the beads (74) are monochrome types; these are summarised in Table 4.16. Disc, annular, globular, drawn globular, biconical, cylindrical and ribbed types are all present, although the drawn globular (32 examples), annular (22 examples) and disc (10 examples) types are by far the most common. One unusual type is also present: a large, globular or biconical bead, flattened on four sides to give a 'horned' shape.

All of the drawn globular beads (Brugmann ConSeg) came from grave 38. The number of segments in each ranged from one to four, although a few beads show signs of breakage at the ends (particularly those comprising single segments), suggesting that some at least were originally longer. There is no sign that these beads are of 'gold-in-glass' type; they appear simply colourless.

Seventeen of the annular beads are blue (Brugmann Blue); these were found in four graves (55, 62, 69, 74), in numbers ranging from one to six. Other annular beads are opaque yellow (four examples from grave 89) and very pale green (one example from grave 101).

Disc beads occurred in blue, opaque white, opaque red, colourless, and very pale green.

One fragment of Romano-British vessel glass may have been reused as a bead (grave 81); this came from a tubular rim or footring in pale blue glass, and was found by the right shoulder. No other beads came from this grave.

Polychrome

Polychrome beads were found in five graves; their types are summarised in Table 4.17. Just over half came from a single grave (grave 44), and these comprise Koch 34 (double crossing wave) and Koch 20 types (double crossing wave and spots). Another Koch 34 (Yellow) came from grave 89, and another Koch 20 from grave 110.

There is one possible example of Brugmann's Traffic Light type from grave 38, with opaque yellow and green trails on an opaque red ground, but the bead is very abraded. The single polychrome bead from grave 41 is also very degraded, so much so that the design cannot be discerned.

Table 4.15 Bead types by grave

Grave	*Glass Mono*	*Glass Poly*	*Re-used vessel*	*Amber*	*Rock crystal*	*Carnelian*	*Stone*	*Total*
38	39	2	–	69	1	1	–	112
39	–	–	–	–	1	–	–	1
41	–	1	–	–	–	–	–	1
42	–	–	–	7	–	–	–	7
44	3	6	–	–	–	–	–	9
51	2	–	–	frags	–	–	–	2+
55	5	–	–	–	–	–	–	5
61	1	–	–	–	–	–	–	1
62	6	–	–	–	–	–	–	6
64	–	–	–	–	1	–	–	1
68	–	–	–	10	–	–	–	10
69	2	–	–	2	–	–	–	4
74	8	–	–	3	–	–	–	11
75	–	–	–	6+frags	–	–	–	6+
81	–	–	1	–	–	–	–	1
89	4	1	–	1	–	–	–	6
92	–	–	–	1	–	–	–	1
101	1	–	–	–	–	–	–	1
105	1	–	–	–	–	–	–	1
110	2	1	–	–	–	–	–	3
1310 C	–	–	–	–	v	–	1	1
	74	11	1	99+	3	1	1	190+

C = Cremation burial

The final bead, a ribbed form from grave 38 with horizontal marvered trails, does not fall into a common type.

Amber Beads

The 99 amber beads derive from eight graves, in numbers ranging from one to 69, although seven graves produced 10 or fewer. In addition, fragments, probably from a single bead, were recovered from grave 1166. The bead forms have been classified according to the scheme used for the Dover Buckland cemetery (Evison 1987), and these are summarised by grave in Table 4.18. Two forms account for the majority of the amber beads – A01 (73 examples) and A04 (23 examples) – with only two other forms represented: A09 and possibly A02. One of the two examples of the latter form had been broken in antiquity (hence the difficulty in ascertaining form)

Table 4.16 Monochrome bead types by grave

Grave	*No.*	*Colour*	*Form*	*Comment*	*Dating*
Grave 38	3	Blue	Thick-walled cylinder	Buckland B51	–
Grave 38	2	Colourless	Disc	–	–
Grave 38	1	Blue	Thin-walled cylinder	Brugmann ConCyl	*c.* AD 480–580
Grave 38	3	Colourless	Drawn globular, segmented (4 segments)	Brugmann ConSeg	mainly *c.* AD 480–580
Grave 38	7	Colourless	Drawn globular, segmented (3 segments)	Brugmann ConSeg	mainly *c.* AD 480–580
Grave 38	12	Colourless	Drawn globular, segmented (2 segments)	Brugmann ConSeg	mainly *c.* AD 480–580
Grave 38	10	Colourless	Drawn globular	Brugmann ConSeg	mainly *c.* AD 480–580
Grave 38	1	Blue	Disc	Buckland B45	–
Grave 44	1	Opaque pale blue	Thick-walled cylinder	Brugmann CylRound	*c.* AD 555–650
Grave 44	1	Blue	Thick-walled cylinder	Brugmann CylRound	*c.* AD 555–650
Grave 44	1	Uncertain	Globular	–	–
Grave 51	2	Opaque white	Disc	Buckland B57	–
Grave 55	5	Blue	Annular	Brugmann Blue	mainly *c.* AD 450–530
Grave 61	1	Uncertain	Disc	–	–
Grave 62	5	Blue	Annular	Brugmann Blue	mainly *c.* AD 450–530
Grave 62	1	Pale olive green	Biconical/'horned'	–	–
Grave 69	1	Blue	Annular	Brugmann Blue	mainly *c.* AD 450–530
Grave 69	1	Opaque red	Disc	Buckland B01	phases 3–6
Grave 74	1	Very pale green	Disc	Buckland B23	–
Grave 74	6	Blue	Annular	Brugmann Blue	mainly *c.* AD 450–530
Grave 74	1	Pale blue	Ribbed	Brugmann Melon	*c.* AD 530–580
Grave 89	4	Opaque yellow	Annular	–	–
Grave 101	1	Very pale green	Annular	–	–
Grave 105	1	Very pale green	Disc	Buckland B23	–
Grave 110	1	Very pale green	Disc	Brugmann Dghnt	*c.* AD 650+
Grave 110	1	Pale blue	Biconical	–	–

Table 4.17 Polychrome bead types by grave

Grave	*No.*	*Colours*	*Type and pattern*	*Comments*	*Dating*
Grave 38	1	Opaque red body with opaque yellow and ?green trails	Globular	Brugmann Traffic Light?	–
Grave 38	1	Opaque red body with opaque yellow trails	Ribbed; three horizontal trails	–	–
Grave 41	1	Uncertain	Thick-walled cylinder; pattern undiscernible but possibly crossing waves and spots	–	–
Grave 44	1	Opaque red with opaque yellow trail	Barrel; double crossing wave and spots	Buckland D46; Koch 20 Yellow	AD 555–650
Grave 44	1	Opaque white with pale blue trail	Disc; double crossing wave	Buckland D24; Koch 34 Blue	AD 580–650
Grave 44	1	Opaque red with opaque white trail	Disc; double crossing wave and spots	Buckland D42; Koch 20 White	AD 555–650
Grave 44	1	Opaque red with opaque white trail	Annular; double crossing wave	Koch 34 White	AD 580–650
Grave 44	1	Opaque red with trail missing	Barrel; double crossing wave and spots	Koch 20	AD 555–650
Grave 44	1	Opaque white with pale blue trail	Globular; irregular double crossing wave	Koch 34 Blue?	AD 580–650
Grave 89	1	Opaque yellow with opaque red trails	Annular; double crossing wave	Koch 34 Yellow	AD 580–650
Grave 110	1	Pale green with opaque white trail	Globular; double crossing waves and spots	Koch 20	AD 555–650

and re-perforated through the side. One example of an A04 form has a double perforation.

Other Beads

The five beads in other materials comprised three crystal, one carnelian, and one stone (?perforated flint/quartz pebble), the latter (rather dubious example) from cremation-related feature 1310. One of the crystal beads is faceted (grave 38); the other two are globular.

Distribution of Beads

One inhumation grave (grave 38) stands out from the assemblage – this yielded over half of the total (112 beads), comprising 41 glass, 69 amber, one crystal and one carnelian bead. With this exception, the highest total from a single grave was 11 beads from grave 74. Apart from grave 38, only four graves contained both glass and amber beads (graves 51, 69, 74, 89); amber beads alone occurred in graves 42, 68, 75 and 92.

The majority of the beads accompanied adult females (see Table 4.19) – 15 individuals. Two of the graves contained the remains of adult males; there were also one infant and one juvenile. One heavily disturbed grave (grave 44) probably contained an adult but the sex is unknown.

Beads were found in varying positions within the graves (Table 4.19). In several cases they were found at the neck, either singly or in groups, where it is assumed they were worn as pendants or necklaces. This certainly seemed to be the case for the infant and the juvenile, and also for the individuals in graves 74, 92, 105 and 110, and possibly also for those in graves 41, 60, 68, 69, 81 and 101. In a few cases beads were found by the wrist or elbow – in grave 38 the four blue cylindrical beads were recorded as lying around the right wrist, while the female in grave 75 had six amber beads (plus fragments) in a tight group by her left elbow, where they may have formed an armlet. The large crystal bead in grave 64 was found by the right wrist, together with an iron pin and two pierced Roman coins; these objects may have formed an 'amulet group', perhaps contained in a small pouch. Other bead groups possibly held in pouches came from graves 38 (a tight group of 108 beads by the right hip) and 55 (a loose group of five beads in a similar position).

Table 4.18 Amber bead types by grave

Grave	*No.*	*Type*	*Comments*
Grave 38	56	A01	–
Grave 38	13	A04	1 with two perforations
Grave 42	7	A01	–
Grave 51		uncertain	Fragments only
Grave 68	2	A04	–
Grave 68	8	A01	–
Grave 69	1	?A02	Broken and re-perforated through side
Grave 69	1	A04	–
Grave 74	1	A01	–
Grave 74	1	A04	–
Grave 74	1	A09	–
Grave 75	6	A04	–
Grave 89	1	A02	–
Grave 92	1	A01	–

Table 4.19 Position of beads in graves

Grave	*Age/Sex*	*No. beads*	*Position in grave and associations*
38	Adult female	112	Two groups: four blue cylindrical beads around right wrist; remaining beads by right pelvis
39	Adult female	1	By left elbow
41	Adult female	1	By right shoulder
42	Infant	7	At neck
44	?Adult	9	Heavily disturbed and dispersed
51	Adult ??female	2+	Glass beads retrieved from soil sample; position of amber bead not recorded
55	Adult female	5	In right pelvic area
61	Adult female	1	Retrieved from soil sample
62	Adult male	6	Five monochrome beads (annular blue) in head area; one monochrome bead (pale green 'horned') in torso area
64	Adult female	1	By right wrist, with iron pin and two Roman coins
68	Adult female	10	In upper torso/neck area
69	Adult female	4	In torso area
74	Adult female	11	Two groups: three amber and six glass from neck; two glass by left shoulder
75	Adult female	6+	By left elbow
81	Adult female	1	By right shoulder
89	Juvenile	6	At neck
92	Adult female	1	At neck
101	Adult male	1	By left shoulder
105	Adult female	1	At neck
110	Adult female	3	At neck

Discussion

The majority of the beads, including the large group from grave 38, appear to be of early date – types present (wound blue, constricted segmented, constricted cylindrical, possible 'Traffic Light') fall within Brugmann's Group A1 and A2 beads, dated *c.* AD 450–580 (2004, 28, 70). Amber beads, too, are considered to fall within this date range (Evison 1987, 60).

It may be noted that beads recovered from the previously excavated part of the cemetery at Collingbourne Ducis were also considered to be early, perhaps all pre-dating the 6th century (Guido 1978). Of interest here are the close similarities between graves 31 and 38, the former from the earlier excavation (Gingell 1978, 90). Both produced high quantities of beads (292 and 112 beads respectively), and in both cases a high proportion comprised drawn globular segmented beads, and amber beads. Both also contained faceted crystal beads.

There are also, however, some beads which fall later within Brugmann's chronological framework, dated *c.* 555–650 (Koch 20 and Koch 34 polychrome types); these are concentrated in the group from grave 44, but also occurred in graves 89 and 110. One 'doughnut' monochrome form is amongst the latest types found in this country, dating after *c.* AD 650 (grave 110).

General parallels can be observed with other Wiltshire cemeteries (Brugmann 2004, table 10). Blacknall Field, Pewsey and Petersfinger, Salisbury, both contained bead types dated to the later 5th or 6th centuries, including high proportions of amber beads. Annular blue and drawn globular beads were particularly common at Black Patch. 'Traffic Light' beads occurred at both these cemeteries, and also at Harnham, Salisbury. Late beads, however, are largely absent from other Wiltshire sites, restricted to Mildenhall and Swallowcliffe.

Pottery

by Lorraine Mepham

The small pottery assemblage includes sherds of prehistoric (two sherds), Late Iron Age/Romano-British (37 sherds), Anglo-Saxon (244 sherds) and medieval date (six sherds), amounting to a total of 289 sherds. Only the Saxon pottery is discussed here; much of the remainder occurred as residual finds in Saxon graves (see *Grave Catalogue* for details).

The Saxon sherds are in relatively poor condition. This reflects the fact that those recovered from inhumation graves appear to be entirely residual in these contexts, while the cremation graves had been heavily disturbed and truncated, and any vessels contained therein were in a very fragmentary condition. Mean sherd weight for the Saxon assemblage is 7.0 g.

The Saxon assemblage can be divided into two broad ware types: organic-tempered (120 sherds) and sandy (124 sherds). No more detailed fabric analysis has been undertaken; the assemblage is likely to represent a spectrum of variation rather than discrete types, as demonstrated by the fact that most of the organic-tempered sherds also include at least some sand, while the sandy wares also generally include some organic inclusions.

Cremation Graves

Most of the sandy wares are accounted for by a single vessel, found as a grave good (container) in cremation grave 1269 (99 sherds). This vessel had been broken in antiquity, and sherd edges are abraded, but the form can be reconstructed as biconical and hollow-necked, with a flattened base (Fig. 4.10, 1).

Five other certain or possible cremation graves (1264, 1266, 1272, 1310, 1442) produced pottery sherds which could represent further grave goods, either containing or accompanying the burials. Two of these were recorded as urned or probably urned burials (1264, 1266) and three as possibly redeposited urned burials (1272, 1310, 1442). All the vessels represented were very fragmentary (quantities ranged from two to 23 sherds per grave), and clearly only represented very partial vessels; the possibility

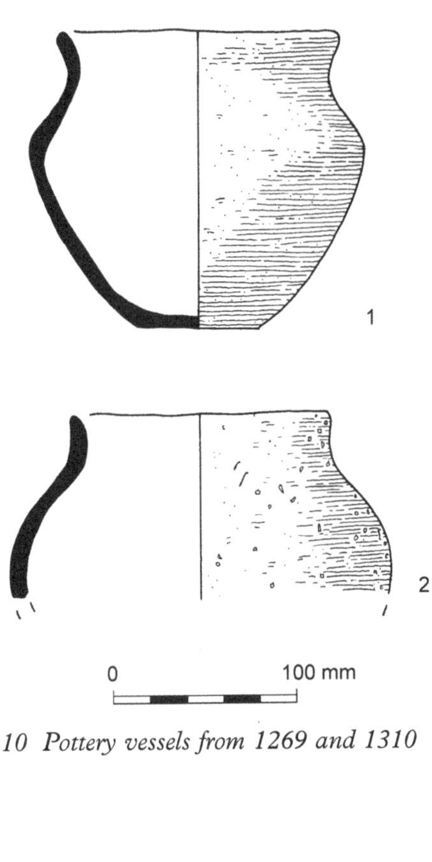

Figure 4.10 Pottery vessels from 1269 and 1310

that at least some sherds were residual cannot be ruled out. Only one grave (1310) contained diagnostic sherds – rim/shoulder sherds from a rounded vessel (Fig. 4.10, 2).

None of these vessels are decorated in any way, and dating is therefore difficult. All that can be offered is the fact that biconical vessels are generally considered to fall relatively early within the Saxon sequence, in the 5th century, although their use may have continued into the 6th century (Myres 1977, 3). No other grave goods, datable or otherwise, were recovered from the cremation graves.

Inhumation Graves

A further 31 sherds came from inhumation graves, where they all appear to be redeposited, perhaps from earlier, disturbed burials, or from settlement activity in the vicinity. Both sandy and organic-tempered fabrics are represented in this group, which included no diagnostic sherds.

Other Features

In addition, 48 sherds were recovered from subsoil and unstratified contexts, and from several cut features; again, some of these sherds could be redeposited in these contexts. Both sandy and organic-tempered fabrics are represented, and there are no diagnostic sherds.

List of illustrated vessels
(Fig. 4.10)

1. Vessel profile: hollow-necked biconical form with flattened base. ON 104, context 1278, cremation grave 1269.
2. Partial vessel profile: rounded with upright rim. Context 1311, cremation-related feature 1310.

Charcoal

by Catherine Barnett

Six contexts of Anglo-Saxon date were selected for wood charcoal analysis during assessment of environmental samples (Wessex Archaeology 2008). All were related to inhumation or cremations burials and the wood charcoal was found to be abundant and in relatively good condition.

Methods

Up to 200 randomly selected fragments of charcoal were taken from each sample, a number felt to be representative of the sample. The fragments were

Table 4.20 Wood charcoal identifications

Grave	Mortuary structure 1268	77	77	77	–	–
Feature	1310	1369	1369	1369	1442	1480
Context	1311	1422	1422	1422	1443	1481
Feature type	?R. urned cremation burial + rpd	Large timber in inhumation grave	Large timber in inhumation grave	Large timber in inhumation grave	?R. urned cremation burial + rpd	Cremation-related deposit inc. rpd
Comments	Medium size sample good cond.	V large sample, good cond. but many pieces vitrified	Highly fragmentary medium sample	Highly fragmentary medium sample, occasionally vitrified	Small sample good cond. But several vitrified	Medium size sample good cond.
Alnus glutinosa	–	–	–	–	1	–
Corylus avellana	1	1	–	–	1	–
Fraxinus excelsior	2	–	–	–	–	–
Quercus sp.	194	199	99	100	24	105
Quercus roundwood	3	–	–	–	–	20
Pomoideae	–	–	–	–	17	–
Prunus sp.	–	–	–	–	4	–
Salix/Populus sp.	–	–	–	–	1	–
Unidentified	–	–	1	–	2	–
Total no. fragments	200	200	100	100	50	125
% of assemblage >2 mm used for ID	*c.* 25%	*c.* 10%	*c.* 25%	*c.* 25%	*c.* 80%	*c.* 20%

rpd – redeposited pyre debris ; R. – redeposited

prepared for identification according to the standard methodology of Leney and Casteel (1975, see also Gale and Cutler 2000). Identification was undertaken according to the anatomical characteristics described by Schweingruber (1990) and Butterfield and Meylan (1980). Identification was to the highest taxonomic level possible, usually that of genus, and nomenclature is according to Stace (1997). The results are given in Table 4.20.

Results

The samples from inhumation grave 77 were overwhelmingly dominated by pieces of oak (*Quercus* sp.). Of the 400 fragments identified, only a single piece of another type was found (hazel, *Corylus avellana*), which may well be intrusive. The field interpretation of a single large split timber (of mature oak), 1.75 m in length, is therefore supported. The exact nature of the relationship to the inhumation it lies next to is unclear, but the timber was apparently deliberately burnt and included in the grave at the time of the burial (Fig. 2.44).

The cremation-related deposits were also dominated by oak, and in the case of feature 1480, which cut into the corner of the bed burial (grave 96), only oak was present, 16% or more of which was of young roundwood. The charcoal assemblage from pit 1310, in the centre of the four-post mortuary structure (1268), was again heavily dominated by mature oak, or pieces too small to gauge their maturity, but there were small quantities of oak roundwood, ash (*Fraxinus excelsior*) and hazel. Given their low presence, it cannot be said whether these woods formed part of a pyre construction or whether they relate to pyre goods or offerings.

The probable cremation grave 1442 yielded a smaller quantity of charcoal, but this was much richer in terms of species presence, perhaps surprisingly so. Oak was still dominant at approximately 50%, but pomaceous fruit wood (Pomoideae, a group of anatomically similar wood types that include hawthorn, whitebeam and apple) formed over 30% of the assemblage, and there were small numbers of alder (*Alnus glutinosa*), hazel, cherry-type (*Prunus* sp.) and willow/poplar (*Salix/Populus* sp.). While this variety of species might have formed kindling, none of the pieces was conspicuously narrow or juvenile. This sample demonstrates that a variety of common deciduous tree and shrub types were available to the users of the site and the presence of alder and willow/poplar indicate that wetter areas were also exploited for wood.

The heavy reliance on oak for pyre construction demonstrated here is commonly found for all archaeological periods, for oak is a readily available dense wood of high calorific value (Edlin 1949; Gale and Cutler 2000), capable of providing the high, even temperatures required to cremate a body. It was noted that a number of oak pieces in this analysis were glassy and vitrified, some experimental work suggests this indicates high temperatures (> 800° C, Prior and Alvin 1983). More recent work (McParland *et al.* 2010) refutes this but the high reflectance of several pieces does on balance suggest a fierce heat. Pyre debris from few Saxon cremation burials has been subject to wood charcoal analysis so comparable material is rare, though Murphy (1994) and Williams (2004) suggest Saxon pyres were generally of oak covered with small hazel branches. Of particular interest, given the large oak timber in inhumation grave 77, is a cremation burial made on a five foot long oak 'tray' or board at Sutton Hoo (Carver 1986, 149), which some have since suggested might be the remains of a dug-out boat. Whether such an interpretation can be sustained for the timber in grave 77 is unlikely, but, if not part of a coffin, then it may have been some form of grave good, or possibly a charred timber from a pyre.

Chapter 5
Discussion of Burial Practices

by Nick Stoodley

Cemetery Layout and Organisation

With 115 inhumation graves (including those excavated in 1974) and a minimum of four cremation burials (maximum nine), Collingbourne Ducis is currently the largest sample of burials from early Anglo-Saxon Wiltshire. Moreover, it is the only example of a double cemetery complex (ie, with two spatially separate areas of burial) from Wiltshire; the closest comparable cemetery lies across the county boundary in Hampshire at Portway Industrial Estate (Cook and Dacre 1985; Stoodley 2006a; 2007) (Fig. 5.1). The limits of the western part of the cemetery have probably been reached in the north, west and east, but graves are known to continue to the south of the excavated area, as confirmed by the additional small-scale work in 2009 (Fig. 2.2). However, it is possible that a shallow, undated, east–west aligned ditch identified in 2009 may define the southern limit to this part of the cemetery. The edges of the eastern part of the cemetery also appear to have been identified, except possibly in the north-east. Because the majority of both areas of the cemetery appear to have been explored, reliable observations can be made about their establishment, layout and development.

To undertake an assessment of the size of each part of the cemetery, and to make meaningful comparisons against other contemporary burial grounds, each has to be considered separately. In total 99 inhumation and the remains of a minimum of four cremation burials were found in the western part of the cemetery. A number of other contexts produced cremation-related material, and although it is uncertain whether these deposits derived from further burials, it is likely that the original total number of cremation burials was higher than four (see McKinley, Chapter 3). At Blacknall Field, Pewsey, 105 graves were excavated and it is thought that the majority of the site was investigated (Annable and Eagles 2010). Portway East is also believed to have been fully explored revealing the remains of 100 interments (Cook and Dacre 1985). Collingbourne, therefore, is directly comparable in terms of the number of burials, yet the western part of the cemetery covering an area of approximately 70 m (east to west) by 100 m (north to south) is notably larger than both Blacknall Field (40 m x 50 m) and Portway East (60 x 50 m). This is a result of the graves being relatively widely spaced, but it was also a consequence of the way that the cemetery was organised into two areas. The western part of the cemetery comprises a number of clusters of graves that can be interpreted as discrete plots where individual households buried their dead. The evidence is as follows: each plot contained the remains of individuals of different ages and both sexes and graves were added to each throughout the duration that the cemetery was in use. Orientation was also used to distinguish plots, although subtle variations in alignment are noted in most plots, for example C and E, which reflect a more complicated picture, perhaps indicating the existence of sub-plots that may have resulted from inter-household relationships between individual members. This is a common structuring principle for Anglo-Saxon cemeteries and has been identified in Wiltshire at Blacknall Field and Petersfinger; it also reflects the importance of kin in these communities (Stoodley 1999a, 135).

In the western part of the cemetery, six plots can be identified (A–F; Fig. 5.2). Plot A is roughly in the centre of the area and contains burial remains/graves of Phase I and II (Fig. 5.3). It has a number of undated burials, but does not contain any that are later than Phase II. Two adjacent graves (59 and 66) had burials superimposed (graves 60 and 65 respectively) on them, a similarity that supports the idea that the area belonged to related individuals, particularly as the later graves did not disturb the individuals in the earlier ones. Alternatively it may be evidence of burial taking place after the plot had gone out of use but, for whatever reason, it was not possible to dig fresh graves in previously undisturbed ground. Overall it is a small, possibly short-lived, plot.

The majority of the graves excavated in 1974 were found to the north-west of Plot A and form a distinct group (Plot B) that probably also includes graves 35–37 and 40–42. The earliest interment, with its applied brooches, was made in grave 23 (Phase I); burials were then added during the 6th century.

In 1974, three graves (15, 22 and 28) were found on the western edge of the site and are shown here within Plot B. They were separated from the main area by a distance of approximately 30 m. Grave 15 has a date centering on the 6th century. Perhaps the

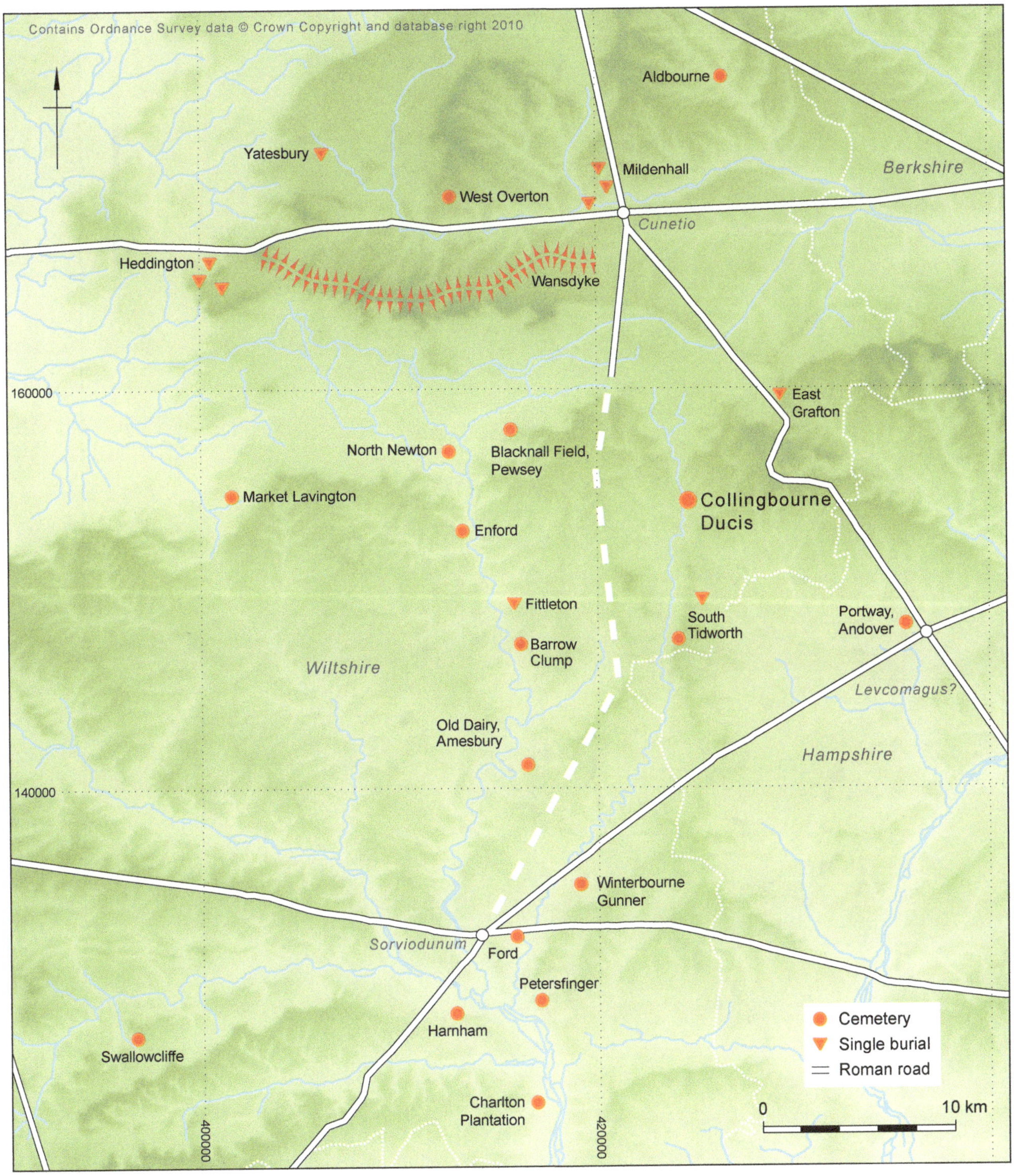

Figure 5.1 Locations of Wiltshire and Hampshire cemeteries discussed in text

group represents outliers of the cemetery, or alternatively the graves could be part of another burial ground to the north-west.

Plot C was established in the south of the western area and may have developed around the four-post mortuary structure 1268, which is probably one of the earliest features in this part of the cemetery. However, the lack of alignment of any of the graves either at right angles or parallel with it, or 'arrayed' towards it, suggests it was not a focus for the inhumation graves, one of which (grave 82) later cut it. The structure may have marked the establishment of this plot, possibly having been erected over the remains of a founder's (?redeposited) cremation burial. The earliest datable inhumations (Phase II), including grave 82, are in a row just to the south of the structure and demonstrate the careful laying out of the plot. Moreover, the juxtaposition of two weapon burials

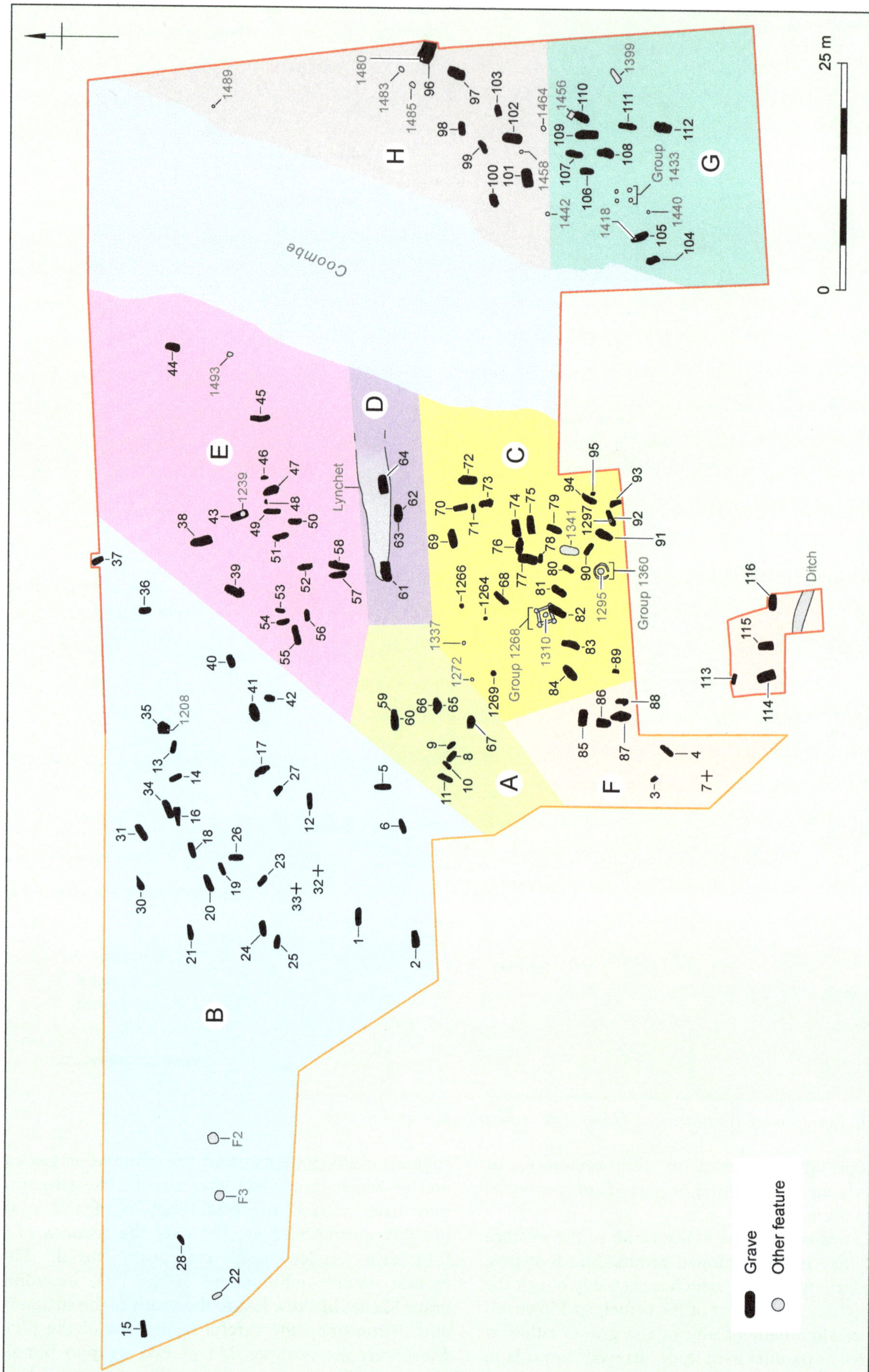

Figure 5.2 Cemetery plan: grave plots (A–H)

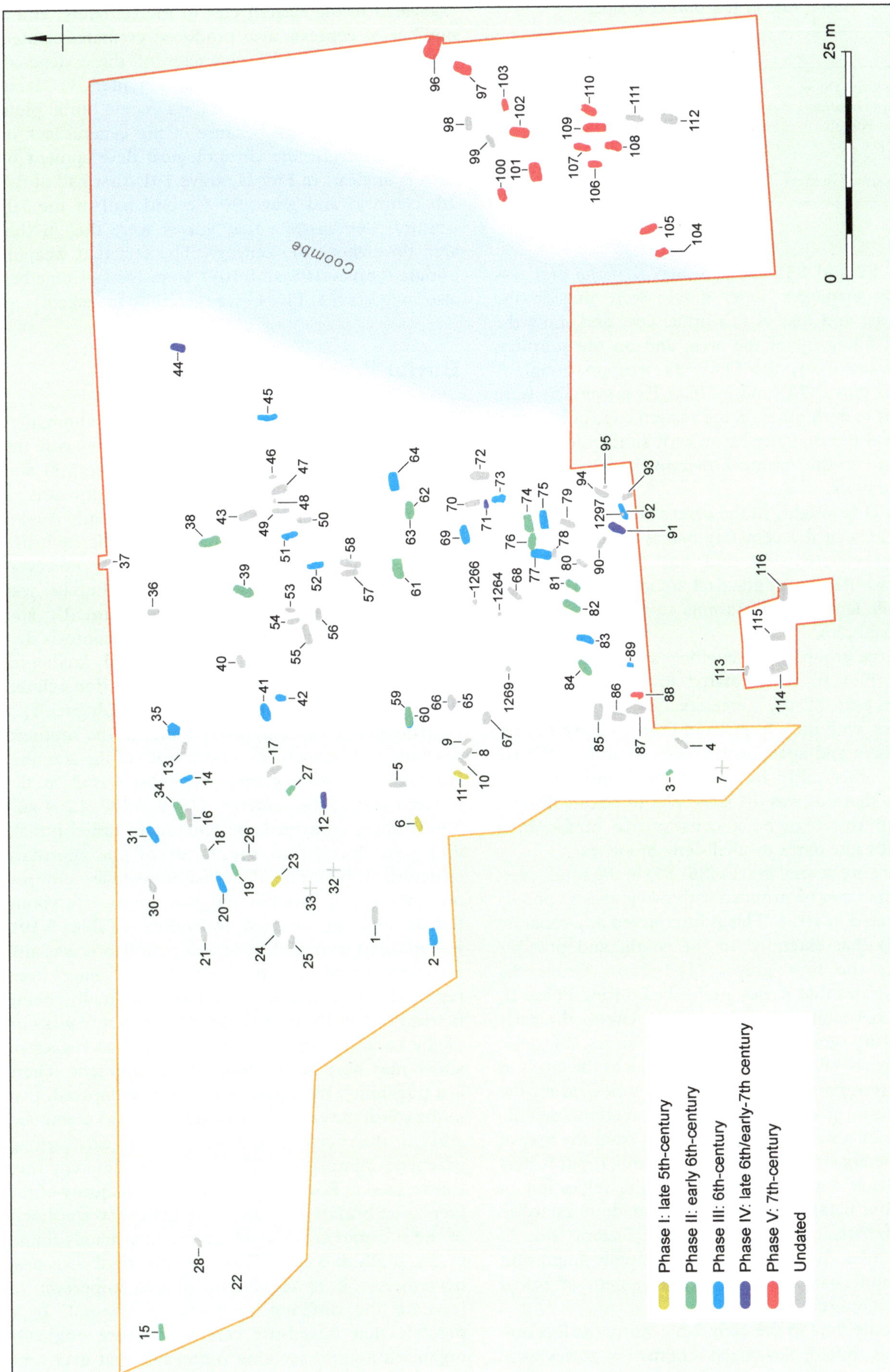

Figure 5.3 Cemetery plan: distribution by phase (based on grave goods)

Table 5.1 Burial rites in Wiltshire cemeteries

Cemetery	*Inhumations (no.)*	*Cremations (no.)*
Collingbourne Ducis	115	*c.* 4
Charlton Plantation	46	1
Harnham Hill	79	0
Petersfinger	71	0
Blacknall Field	105	4
Winterbourne Gunner	*c.* 95	0

(graves 82 and 83) also indicates that the plot was carefully managed. Later graves were dug to the north-east and east of this initial core and show the gradual filling up of the area, and on the southern edge is grave 91, the Phase IV weapon burial. A Phase II grave (74) and a Phase III grave (75) were adjacent to each other on the eastern edge of the area, and are either evidence for an early subdivision within the plot, or the eventual merging together of two separate plots.

Plot D is roughly in the centre of the eastern edge of this area of the cemetery and is distinguished by three graves (61, 62 and 64) that are aligned west–east. All except grave 64 are in Phase II, and all are adult females. This seems to represent another short-lived plot.

A large group of quite widely spaced inhumation graves (Plot E) was situated in the north of the western part of the cemetery. All the small-long brooches, with the exception of those in grave 62, are in this area and apart from graves 38 and 39 (Phase II), no other early burial can be identified. It is possible that this was the latest plot to be established, although this may be a consequence of ascribing artificially late dates to small-long brooches.

There are several graves (85–89) in the south-west corner that can be grouped with two graves (3 and 4) investigated in 1974. This is interpreted as a separate plot (F) that extended to the south, and possibly includes the four graves (113–116). Grave 3A demonstrates that it was established during Phase II, with burial taking place possibly as late as the early 7th century (grave 88 with a Type 4 knife).

Grave 44 (Phase IV, Plot E) is one of the latest in the western part of the cemetery. It was sited on the north-eastern edge of the area overlooking the coombe and was somewhat isolated from the rest of the cemetery. It may simply be an outlier, but it may be evidence for an early stage in the relocation of burial, but before the decision was made to establish a new burial area on the opposite (eastern) side of the coombe. It is, therefore, potentially important to an understanding of the development of burial at Collingbourne.

At some time in the early 7th century the location of burials shifted. Seventeen inhumation graves were excavated in the eastern part of the cemetery, and a number of contexts also produced cremated-related material, although the character of these deposits remains uncertain (McKinley, Chapter 3). It is possible to identify two spatially separate burial plots (G and H), although because of the general lack of datable artefacts, the chronological development of each is unclear. In Plot H, grave 101 (first half of the 7th century) and grave 96 (second half of the 7th century) demonstrate that graves were dug in this area throughout the century. The fact that weapon burials (graves 108 and 109) were located together also suggests that Plot G was carefully managed.

Burial Practice

The 1974 excavation only recovered inhumation burials. It was a finding that was in line with the evidence from other Wiltshire sites (Table 5.1) and strengthened the view that the county was a predominantly inhuming area during the early Anglo-Saxon period, indeed inhumation was the exclusive rite in some cemeteries. During 2007, however, evidence of at least four cremation burials was recovered (three urned and one unurned), and cremated bone was found in a further 24 contexts that 'represent the remains of formal and incidental deposits of pyre debris, and cremation-related deposits of uncertain form' (McKinley, Chapter 3).

Evidence of cremation was found in the southern portion of the cemetery on both sides of the coombe. All four cremation graves were discovered in the western part of the cemetery (1269, 1297, 1264 and 1266); three contained the remains of urned burials and were located to the north of the mortuary structure (1268). The identified individuals comprise one infant, one juvenile and two adults – a young female and an unsexed individual (Table 3.10). Redeposited cremated bone and pyre debris was also recovered from the area, which may have been reserved for cremation, perhaps originally being marked out by structure 1268. The structure was one of the earliest features in the area and as suggested above may have been a founder's monument. There is a possibility, but one which cannot be proved, that in the south the earliest burial tradition was cremation and to the north a correspondingly early group practiced inhumation. The zoning of different rites can be seen at Portway East where the majority of the cremation burials were discovered in the western part of the site, and at Alton where they are mainly found in the south and east. These are not rigid divisions; nevertheless it is clear that it was important to separate the different methods of disposal. It is possible that mixed-rite cemeteries were originally organised around separate zones, but that over time the division between the practices became less clear as graves encroached into the areas separating them.

Can Collingbourne be described as a true mixed-rite cemetery? According to Howard Williams (2002, 64, fn 76) this is a cemetery in which cremation accounts for between 15–85% of the total number of interments. Because of uncertainties surrounding the interpretation of many of the deposits (see McKinley, Chapter 3), it is difficult to gauge the overall prevalence of the practice. The total number of confidently identified cremation burials ranges from four to nine. The latter figure gives a proportion of just 8%, and on the basis of this Collingbourne cannot be considered a true mixed-rite cemetery. It therefore has more in common with the Wiltshire cemeteries as opposed to those from the neighbouring county of Hampshire (Table 5.2). It is possible, however, that its position close to a mixed-rite zone rendered it susceptible to these influences (see also McKinley, Chapter 3).

The cremation practices are similar to what is found elsewhere in the south of the country. In addition to ceramic urns, cremated remains were also placed directly into the ground (cremation burial 1297). Examples of the latter have been found at Portway East (40% were unurned) and at Alton (Evison 1988). Cremated remains were found in the fills of inhumation burials at Collingbourne and similar evidence was found at Portway East. The cremated material may have been deliberately placed during the closing of the grave, perhaps evidence that a relationship had existed between the two individuals, or was being created through this action (see McKinley, Chapter 3). The burnt timber in grave 77 may have come from a pyre and could also be evidence of a link between the inhumed and the individual who had been cremated on that structure. The notion is strengthened by the fact that it lay on the edge of the main group of cremation graves.

Cremation was a minority rite, but it appears to have been a persistent aspect of the mortuary strategies adopted by the community. This is evidenced by the small number of deposits that were recovered from the later, eastern part of the cemetery. Although no formal cremation burials were found, the presence of placed deposits, for example in graves 96 and 105, indicates the continued importance of this rite in the mortuary strategies of the community. Moreover, this is the first evidence for cremation-related activity in 7th-century Wiltshire. The site can be placed alongside St Mary's Stadium, Southampton (Birbeck 2005, 11–13), Weston Colley, Micheldever (Fern and Stoodley 2004), and Apple Down, West Sussex (Down and Welch 1990, 108) as part of a small, but significant, corpus of evidence for the continued importance of this practice into the 7th century.

Table 5.2 Cremation and inhumation rites in Hampshire mixed-rite cemeteries

Cemetery	*Proportion cremation vs inhumation (%)*
Alton	45/55
Portway East	55/45
Worthy Park	27/73

Other Aspects of Burial Practice

Grave Construction and Embellishment

A potentially important topic is the shape and size of a grave and the presence of any associated structure. These are variables that may have been determined by social or cultural values, for example the greater effort invested in the construction of a grave may be a measure of that individual's, or their family's, standing in their community (Tainter 1975).

The average length and width of an adult grave at Collingbourne was 2.02 m and 0.87 m respectively. The figures are similar to the data from contemporary Wiltshire cemeteries, especially Blacknall Field (Table 5.3). Comparison of grave depth is not possible because of the differential survival of topsoil between sites; it is only a useful form of analysis within individual cemeteries, especially comparing depth against other variables, such as burial wealth (Sherlock and Welch 1992, 91). However, at Collingbourne no correlation exists between the depth to which a grave was dug and whether the burial included grave goods or not (based on the adult burials in the western part of the cemetery), and both record an average depth of 0.26 m.

Several graves stand out as being larger than the average, such as grave 61 with a length of 2.31 m and a depth of 1.13 m, but none are especially commodious. The opposite situation is occasionally found, for example grave 92 in which the body appears to have been put into a grave that was too small. Perhaps in these cases the grave was not

Table 5.3 Grave dimensions at Collingbourne Ducis (figure in brackets = all years) and comparable sites

Cemetery	*Length (m)*	*Width (m)*	*Depth (m)*
Collingbourne (west & east)	2.02 (1.96)	0.87 (0.83)	0.28 (0.32)
Collingbourne (west)	1.98 (1.92)	0.84 (0.80)	0.27 (0.33)
Collingbourne (east)	2.14	0.97	0.31
Petersfinger	1.92	0.73	0.46
Blacknall Field	2.02	0.89	0.26

Table 5.4 Grave dimensions from 7th-century cemeteries (sites selected on basis of available data)

	Average length (m)	*Average width (m)*	*Average depth (m)*
Aldbourne	1.92 (18)	0.79 (18)	0.22 (18)
Bargates	2.13 (13)	0.35 (12)	0.33 (13)
Winnall II	2.05 (29)	0.41 (29)	0.40 (32)

intended for the occupant, or the individual was unworthy of the effort that was required to create an adequately sized grave, though the grave goods suggest this was not the case here.

Grave size is a variable that may have been determined by the occupant's sex (Stoodley 1999a, 67). The analysis revealed, however, that this is not the case at Collingbourne: in the western part of the cemetery, the average length of graves containing male remains is 1.88 m, compared to 1.92 m for females. A more detailed analysis of the data revealed that males buried with weapons had longer graves (average 2.06 m) than those without (average 1.83 m). Most of the weapon graves contained spears and it was probably the need to accommodate this weapon that resulted in a longer grave. It is intriguing that the graves of females are on average longer than those containing males without weapons. If expenditure on the grave is linked to status, then this finding has implications for an understanding of female status in the community.

By the 7th century the size of the grave had increased (see Table 5.3: Collingbourne (east)). This is a phenomenon recognised in other late cemeteries (Table 5.4) and coincides with a reduction in the quantity of grave goods. The removal of portable wealth may have resulted in greater expenditure on the actual structure of the grave. It is well known that the 7th century witnessed a rise in the number of structural features (Hogarth 1973) and grave size may have been part of this development.

The majority of graves in the western part of the cemetery were of a sub-rectangular shape or sub-rectangular with one or both ends rounded. This is in contrast to Blacknall Field where there is a greater proportion of irregularly shaped graves, while the majority of graves in the late cemetery at Aldbourne were of an irregular sub-rectangular form. The general lack of commonality between the sites indicates that grave shape was determined by local preferences and the nature of the ground that was encountered. Yet on the whole, neat rectangular graves with square corners, as noted at Petersfinger, are rare in burial grounds sited over hard geologies, and the necessary investment of energy in order to create regularly shaped graves was not afforded priority.

Anglo-Saxon graves of the 5th and 6th centuries had relatively simple structural features, such as timber coffins, stone linings or a layer of some type of organic material on the floor of the grave. The evidence from Collingbourne is in agreement, with a few examples of flints around the grave edge and/or over the body. Grave 77 is an exception: during excavation it was found to have a burnt timber along the right hand side of the grave. As already discussed the timber may have come from a cremation pyre and could be evidence of a link between the inhumed and an individual who had been cremated at a similar time. Wiltshire has not produced any comparable examples, but at Berinsfield, Oxfordshire, burnt timber was found along both sides of G104 (Boyle *et al.* 1995, 121), and G125 had a block of burnt wood at its foot end. No definitive evidence for coffins was recovered at Collingbourne, although the remains of wood were identified on the upper surfaces of the shield boss and buckle in grave 83, which indicates the prior existence of a timber covering of some description.

A row of large flints lined the northern edge (left side) of grave 59 and they were also found in small quantities in several other graves, though some were probably incidental inclusions. At Portway East, Petersfinger and Winterbourne Gunner a number of burials had large flints lining the grave wall. This may have been simply to embellish the interior of the grave, or to strengthen the sides of the grave (Evison 1994, 28), although it seems unlikely that this would have been necessary on chalk. A different situation is provided by Collingbourne grave 10: the burial was covered by four large flints, and it was reported that when Collingbourne grave 1 was disturbed by workmen it also had a covering of large flints. This may have been a superstitious act to keep the spirit of the dead in the grave (Wilson 1992, 83). Or, it can be interpreted in a more positive light – evidence of extra investment in the grave, perhaps a small cairn (in the case of grave 1) to protect the deceased. When a small number of flints are found, for example the two associated with the individual in grave 78, it is difficult to know whether they were deliberate inclusions or had entered accidentally and it would be unwise to comment further. Stones continued to have a role in the 7th century, as the large flints associated with the burial in grave 110 demonstrate, though the disposition of these is not clear (not shown in Fig. 2.75).

A more sophisticated structure is represented by the bed on which the adult female in grave 96 was discovered. Bed burials comprise a rare and important group of mortuary features that date to the 7th century, and record a distribution that is centred on Wessex and the Cambridgeshire area, with several outliers (Speake 1989, 98–110). The practice may be related to coffin burial, but with an emphasis on the display of the deceased (Malim and Hines 1998, 268), the bed functioning as a type of bier. The evidence for the Collingbourne bed comes from a group of iron fittings, which can be divided into headboard stays, double cleats and eyelets/split spiked loops (see Watson, Chapter 4). Very little organic material was identified, although in keeping with other examples, it was made from planks of ash. It appears to have been a plain box bed with sides, held together with joints, which could be dismantled when the bed was moved. A pair of iron brackets that joined two planks of oak may have belonged to a separate grave cover. The bed burial at Coddenham, Suffolk had a timber cover with brackets that were possibly to help move it into position (Watson 2006, 26).

The reconstruction of the bed shows it with an upright headboard held in position with twisted metal headboard stays (see Fig. 4.2). These stays were fixed, which meant that the bed could not be easily dismantled. However, the examination of the metal fittings has revealed that the majority of them are damaged, suggesting that the bed was dismantled before being placed in the grave. At Coddenham, the bed had also been dismantled prior to burial, and at Edix Hill, Cambridgeshire it is suggested that the headboard had been broken to fit it in the grave (Malim and Hines 1998, 265). It is not clear why the Collingbourne bed had to be dismantled. The bed's dimensions have been estimated to be 1.5 m by 0.6 m while the grave cut measured 2.58 m by 1.56 m, thus it could have been easily accommodated. Furthermore, although the height of the bed (estimated to be between 0.45–0.50 m) may have been such that it necessitated the removal of the headboard, the original ground surface would have been greater than the 0.40 m depth recorded for the cut.

The nearest bed burial to Collingbourne was uncovered at Swallowcliffe Down, Wiltshire in 1966 (Speake 1989). It was a more sophisticated structure, although in common with the Collingbourne bed, it had a pair of twisted headboard stays. In addition, there are possible examples of bed burials from Roundway Down and Winklebury Hill, Wiltshire and Woodyates, Dorset (Speake 1989, 105–10). Because of the very small sample, it is not possible to say whether there is a particular type of Wessex bed. This stands in contrast to the examples in the Cambridge group which display certain similarities (Malim and Hines 1998, 207).

Beds are generally associated with rich burials, the combination of portable wealth and investment in the grave furniture indicating that the deceased was of some importance within their community. This is clearly the case at Swallowcliffe Down, while the finds from Roundway Down (if there was a bed) also confirm that it was a rich burial. It is therefore surprising that there were no (surviving) grave goods in Collingbourne grave 96. Yet the natural resources which went into the bed, the actual effort in its construction, plus the grave cover and the size of the cut, all indicate a person/family of some wealth and status. In common with Collingbourne, there are several examples that were also apparently otherwise unfurnished: Shudy Camps (Lethbridge 1936) and Cherry Hinton, Cambridgeshire, while from Wessex comes the possible bed burial at Winklebury Hill (Speake 1989, 105) – though the latter appears to have been robbed, which may explain the lack of grave goods. Despite the fact that the accompanied bed burials have been dated to the 7th century, it is possible that the examples with little or no wealth post-date them, perhaps being as late as the second quarter of the 8th century – a time when the practice of depositing grave goods had all but ceased (Geake 1997, 125). If the bed burial is related to the practice of coffin burial, then this would strengthen the notion because the latter were an important feature of mortuary practice in later Anglo-Saxon England.

Although no textiles have been preserved on the bed fittings from Collingbourne, it is possible that the burial included soft furnishings, such as covers or pillows, as has been inferred for Coddenham (Watson 2006, 26) and Edix Hill, grave 18 (Malim and Hines 1998, 266). Such furnishings, along with carvings and/or painted planks, would have increased the luxuriousness and richness of the burial and may have been a substitute for metal artefacts.

Cemetery Structures

Evidence of an external timber mortuary structure (group 1268) was found in the south of the western part of the cemetery. It was a square, ditched enclosure with a posthole at each corner and a central pit (see Fig. 2.1). The fill of the pit (1310) contained the partial remains of what may have been a redeposited urned burial along with some redeposited pyre debris (see McKinley, Chapter 3). The structure had been cut across its south-east corner by grave 82 (see Chapter 2), but a number of comparable examples can be cited (Table 5.5). At Alton, Hampshire, structure C7 (1.8 m by 1.8 m) is very similar in terms of size and morphology (Evison 1988, 34–6). At Butler's Field, Lechlade, Gloucestershire, there was a similar structure, although it was rectangular and enclosed two cremation burials; it was also cut across a corner by a later inhumation grave (Boyle *et al.* 1998, 38). At Apple Down, West Sussex, 31 four-post structures were identified, although only one had a ditched enclosure (Down and Welch 1990, 25–33). Examples are also known from the continental homelands of the Anglo-Saxons

Table 5.5 Comparison of four-post mortuary structures

Cemetery	*Structure no.*	*Postholes*	*Enclosure*	*Central cremation*	*Size*	*Date*
Collingbourne Ducis	Structure 1268	4	Y	?redeposited	2 m x 2 m	Late C5
Alton	C7	4	Y	1	1.8 x 1.8 m	Late C5–early 6C
Lechlade	Enclosure 12	Probably 4	Y	2	Approx. 2 x 1.5 m	Late C5–6C
Apple Down	32	4	Y	1	1.7 x 1.2 m	C5–C7

where they date from the early Roman period to the 8th century (Down and Welch 1990, 32–3). Similar mortuary structures are, however, known from Romano-British cremation cemeteries, especially at urban and military sites in southern England and Wales (Black 1986; Struck 2000; McKinley 2008b, 107, 188–9; Chapter 3). It is possible that the Anglo-Saxon structures represent a continuation of a Roman tradition, although the decline of cremation as a mortuary rite during the late Roman period in Britain weakens this notion. It seems safer to view the structures as an import – one that accompanied the re-introduction of cremation by Germanic settlers in the 5th century.

The accumulated evidence is remarkably consistent and indicates that a cremation deposit had been housed within a timber structure constructed of posts with planking or wattle and daub walls. It was set within shallow trenches and was possibly roofed. They are interpreted by both Evison (1988, 36) and Down and Welch (1990, 29) as small structures that contained the ashes of the dead around which acts of commemoration could take place. The evidence reflects a significant expenditure on materials and labour, possibly indicating that these individuals, or their families, enjoyed a higher than average standing in their community.

At Collingbourne, Alton and Apple Down small quantities of cremated bone were recovered from the postholes and gullies of the structures demonstrating that they had been refurbished. Moreover at Apple Down, cremated bone found its way – by accident or design – into the postholes during the renewal of several structures (Down and Welch 1990, 29), evidence perhaps that these features continued to have had an active role to play in mortuary activity. It may be correct to interpret the inhumation graves that cut through the Collingbourne and Lechlade examples in a similar way. Although the earlier structures were apparently redundant, they still seem to have retained enough significance to continue to attract burial.

A penannular gully with a central posthole (Group 1360) was investigated on the southern edge of the site in the western part of the cemetery. It lay about 5 m south-east of mortuary structure 1268 and was 2 m in diameter (see Figs 1.2 and 2.2). Penannular gullies have been found surrounding inhumation graves of the 7th century, especially in Kent (Hogarth 1973), though in Kent cremation burials, particularly of the 6th century and later, are very rare and there are no examples surrounded by ditches. However, at Portway East three annular ditches were found, two of which enclosed cremation-related deposits of probable 6th-century date (F2 and F3) and are of a similar size to structure 1360 (with diameters of 1.90 m and 2.20 m respectively). Monument 1360 produced only a tiny quantity (0.1 g) of cremated human bone, all from the ditch fill and possibly incidental, but the presence of a posthole may suggest that it was constructed as a cenotaph to an individual whose remains were unable to be interred in the cemetery. Alternatively it might have acted as a marker drawing attention to the group of graves in the southern part of the cemetery in a similar way to how the line of posts on the eastern edge of Portway East may have functioned (Stoodley 2007, 159).

Structure 1433 comprised four postholes that defined a rectangle 1.5 m long by 1.2 m wide on the southern edge of the eastern part of the cemetery (Fig. 1.2). At Apple Down many of the four-post structures had similar dimensions to Structure 1433 (Down and Welch 1990, 202–5) and although several did not produce a central cremation grave, it is argued that the evidence could have been destroyed (Down and Welch 1990, 25–6; McKinley, Chapter 3). Evidence of cremation-related activity was present in the eastern part of the cemetery, and it is plausible that Structure 1433 represents another mortuary house, though no cremated bone was present in the postholes defining this structure. Alternatively it may have been signalling the location of the graves around it, or because it had a peripheral location, the position of the cemetery within the wider landscape.

Orientation

In the following discussion the direction refers to the position of the head. A wide range of alignments exist (Table 5.6), although the majority are concentrated in an arc orientated from south-south-east to west, which is typical of an early Saxon cemetery. At Petersfinger, the principal orientations were either south or west, while at Blacknall Field most were aligned to the west, although there were a smaller number of southerly ones.

It is often difficult to understand why specific orientations were chosen, although it seems likely that man-made or natural features were used as general reference points. The former seems probable when graves were arranged in rows, for example at Winnall II, Hampshire, a boundary may have served as a reference point (Meaney and Hawkes 1970). At Burghfield, Berkshire, the majority of graves were influenced by the curve of the prehistoric earthwork that the cemetery clustered around (Butterworth and Lobb 1992). At Aldbourne (Wilts), it is probable that a natural feature was used; in this case the graves followed the line of the ridge on which the cemetery was sited (Stoodley *et al.* 2012). At Collingbourne it seems that at least some of the interments were aligned on the coombe running in a north-north-east to south-south-west direction; this applies especially to the graves in Plots C and G, but further to the north and west the local topography appears to have had less influence on orientation.

If the Collingbourne group is broken down by chronology the reasons become clearer. In the western part of the cemetery, although the majority was concentrated within an orientation range of 158° to 270°, a closer examination reveals some subtle patterning. In Plot B most individuals had been buried with their heads either to the west or west-south-west. In Plot E orientation is mainly to the south, while in Plot C the majority had their heads to the south-west. If, as suggested above, the various plots belonged to separate households, then it appears that each used a different alignment to help differentiate their graves, irrespective of age or sex. There are some exceptions: towards the centre of Plot C several graves had been orientated to the west (graves 74, 75 and 76), of which graves 74 and 76 belong to Phase II.

The bulk of the interments in the eastern part of the cemetery are aligned in a range from south to west. Yet again, subtle variation can be discerned: the graves in Plot H generally had their heads to the west, while the majority of those in Plot G were aligned to the south, south-south-west and south-south-east. It is observed that during the 7th-century orientation became standardised (Hyslop 1963; for a review see Boddington 1990, 179–82), a development which is seen as contrasting with the earlier period where a much greater degree of variation is observed (Stoodley 1999a, 64–5). For example, at Aldbourne, Wiltshire, the majority of the burials were orientated south-west, while at Winnall II, (Hampshire), most were to the west. Collingbourne demonstrates that this was not always the case and is similar to the late cemeteries of Monkton Deverill, Wiltshire (Rawlings 1995), Bargates, Dorset (Jarvis 1983) and Didcot, Oxfordshire (Boyle *et al.* 1995), where a standard orientation had not been followed. It seems that at Collingbourne, at least, orientation was still a method to distinguish the identity of separate plots.

Table 5.6 Summary of burial orientation at Collingbourne

Orientation (head first)	*2007/9 (% observable)*	*1974 (% observable)*	*Combined (% observable)*
Unobservable	4 (5%)	3 (9%)	7 (6%)
N–S	1 (1%)	0	1 (1%)
N(NE)–S(SW)	0	0	0
S(SE)–N(NW)	6 (7%)	6 (18%)	12 (10%)
S–N	20 (24%)	4 (12%)	24 (21%)
S(SW)–N(NE)	9 (11%)	5 (15%)	14 (12%)
SW–NE	9 (11%)	0	9 (8%)
W(SW)–E(NE)	12 (15%)	4 (12%)	16 (14%)
W–E	14 (17%)	11 (33%)	25 (21%)
W(NW)–E(SE)	4 (5%)	0	4 (4%)
N(NW)–S(SE)	3 (4%)	0	3 (3%)
Total	82	33	115

Nine burials had been made on an atypical alignment, with the head somewhere between north-north-west and east. Four of the burials were of young individuals, while two of the adults were over 45 years and the decision to use a rare alignment may have been determined to some extent by the individual's age. Grave 90 is worthy of further mention because it contained the only crouched burial, that of a *c.* 12–14 year old probable female. The grave was located on the southern edge of Plot C and had a different alignment to the other graves (Fig. 5.2). The position in which the individual had been placed, in conjunction with the grave's orientation, was being used to mark this out as different to the other members of the plot. Grave 90 is similar to G1 at Market Lavington, Wiltshire which occupied an isolated location but contained a prone female with her head to the north-east (Stoodley 2006b, 176). At both Collingbourne and Market Lavington a suite of practices, that included orientation, was used to mark certain individuals out. Non-standard orientations were still being chosen in the 7th century as graves 104 and 105 (heads to the north-north-west) make clear. One of these is a subadult possible female (grave 104), while the other is an adult female over 45 years of age (grave 105), and both had been sited close together on the south-western edge of the cemetery.

Multiple Burial

In 1974 two graves containing the remains of two or more burials, some *in situ* and others disturbed and redeposited, were investigated. Grave 4 contained a

Table 5.7 Burial position at Petersfinger and Pewsey (numbers)

	Extended supine	Flexed	On one side	Crouched	Prone
Petersfinger	49	2	6	5	0
Blacknall Field	69	19	1	7	0

contemporary burial of an adult male overlying a subadult, while a very disturbed deposit (grave 3) produced remains from three individuals, although the character of the interment is unknown. The low incidence of multiple burial is typical of the period, and a national study of the practice has found that the majority of examples involve an adult female and child, or two adults of differing sex (Stoodley 2002). In both situations a kin-based relationship may have existed, although it is possible that an already prepared grave provided an opportunity to bury unrelated community members who had died at similar times (Stoodley 2002, 120–1).

Burial Position

It was possible to discern the position of 96 of the burials made at Collingbourne (including some of the data from 1974) (Fig. 5.4). In common with almost all early Anglo-Saxon cemeteries the majority (64/67%) had been laid out in an extended supine position (Tables 5.7–8). The position was associated with both sexes and individuals of any age, although adult males were the most likely group to have been treated in this manner (23/82%; adult females: 25/64%). Women and younger individuals demonstrate more variability, which is at odds with that found elsewhere. For example, at Blacknall Field, equal numbers of males and females were laid extended and supine; the majority of other positions were taken by younger individuals. In a very general sense this variation can be interpreted as a way of distinguishing between certain individuals. But more specific reasons why such variation occurred will probably never be known. For example, why at Collingbourne were the 4–7 year old in grave 53 and the 5–7 year old in grave 89 both flexed on the right side, while the 12–14 year old in grave 90 was crouched on the left.

Table 5.8 Burial position at Collingbourne Ducis (numbers in brackets = 1974 excavations)

	Male	Female	Non-adult	Total
Extended supine	16 (7)	19 (6)	11 (5)	46 (64)
Flexed supine	3	3 (1)	1 (1)	7 (9)
On one side	1	9 (1)	8 (2)	18 (21) (right: 8; left: 8)
Crouched	–	–	1	1
Prone	(1)	–	–	(1)

A particularly interesting burial is the prone male from grave 11 excavated in 1974. This is the rarest position, both in Wiltshire and nationally (Stoodley 1999a, fig. 43; Wilson 1992, 80–2), and because it tends to be associated with a lack of burial wealth and occasionally the maltreatment of the interred, it is seen as having negative connotations (Harman *et al.* 1981, 164). It seems that certain people were being singled out, either because of something they did, or that they were subject to, and the fact that Market Lavington G1, a prone adult female, was separate to the rest of the cemetery underlines this. The Collingbourne burial is different, however. This male had a Roman disc brooch, possibly fastening a cloak in a classical fashion, and his grave was incorporated into the main part of the cemetery. Because prone burial was also practiced in the Roman period (Philpott 1991, 71–2), it is possible that the individual was signalling his allegiance to a non-Germanic cultural tradition through both position and costume.

If the Collingbourne burials are divided by chronology it is found that 40% (n=53) of the burials in the western part of the cemetery were extended supine (all years), but this rises to 81% (n=14) in the eastern part of the cemetery, demonstrating that more constraint controlled this aspect of burial in the later phase/s.

Social Structure and Community Identity

Burial rites are a product of the living and therefore have the potential to comment on the structure of the society that produced them. Both areas of the cemetery at Collingbourne can be described as community burial grounds: it was where the rural agriculturally-based settlement that was located a short distance away (Pine 2001, and see below) interred their dead during a period of over 200 years. In this section several social identities that were key to the way early Anglo-Saxon society was structured are discussed. It should be cautioned, however, that burial ritual is a medium through which the social practices of the living are channelled. They are actively constructed and may not provide a mirror image of that society, rather an indirect idealised version may result (Härke 1997).

Gender and Age

The analysis of early Anglo-Saxon burials has revealed that gender was an important structuring

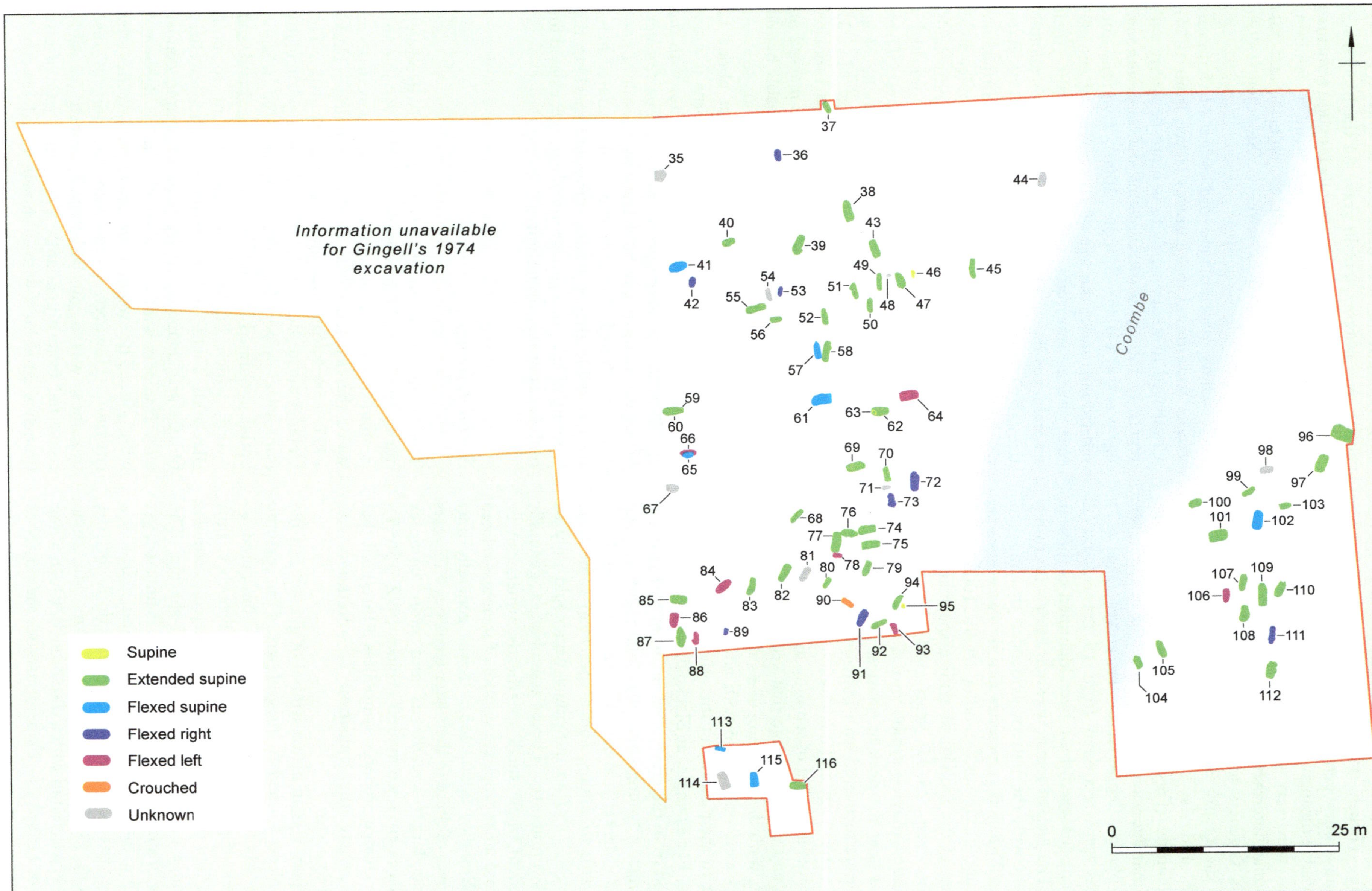

Figure 5.4 Cemetery plan: burial positions

principle for all communities in the 5th and 6th centuries (Brush 1993; Stoodley 1999a). The signalling of one's gender was afforded priority, being highly visible through the provisioning of grave goods: weapons were very strongly associated with males, while female interments are typified by an abundance of dress fasteners and items of jewellery. A strict gender dichotomy is found in Wiltshire (Stoodley 1999b) and is confirmed by the work at Collingbourne (Figs 5.5 and 5.6), which has also shown that age was a significant factor in the nature of the objects deposited in the graves (Fig. 5.7). Weapons were recovered from 15 graves, and all except one (unsexed) have been identified as those of males. The lack of female weapon burials is entirely consistent with the pattern evidenced in almost all early Anglo-Saxon cemeteries and no cases have yet been found in Wessex (Stoodley 1999b, 100).

Three of the individuals with a spear and shield were between 25–35 years old, and such a combination may be symbolic of a status related to age, that is at the peak of physical fitness. Both the swords were recovered with individuals judged to be over 45 years of age and it is possible that this wealthy artefact was a symbol of seniority and the status that old age and the knowledge that accumulated with it brought. With the exception of a subadult (grave 15), weapons were only found with adults and this is in contrast to the majority of the other Wiltshire burial grounds. For example, at Blacknall Field a spear was recovered from the grave of an infant of 3–4 years, at Petersfinger a 'young child' was found with a spear, while at Market Lavington weapons were being placed with subadults, and a spearhead came from the grave (27) of an individual who could only be aged as immature. These assemblages generally consisted of single small spearheads, which can be considered an appropriate symbol of their age-related status (Stoodley 2000, 465). It was generally only from graves of those in their later teens (ie, >15 years old) that larger spearheads and more complex assemblages are encountered (Härke 1992, 156–7), and this change probably symbolises a threshold that marked where the transition to adulthood was deemed to occur.

Jewellery was an active symbol of gender, but the various pieces formed an integral part of the costume and the whole ensemble has to be considered as expressive of gender identity. Single brooches, pins and less than three beads are not restricted to females and cannot be interpreted as gender-specific. The presence of single brooches with males is unusual, yet it is found throughout the country and indicates a minority rite amongst certain sections of the population (Stoodley 1999a, 34). An older male (grave 84) was found with a disc brooch, which along with grave 11 (see above), demonstrates the existence of this practice at Collingbourne. In grave 11 it was acting as a fastener, but in grave 84 the brooch was discovered by the lower leg and its function remains a mystery. No male was found with a feminine assemblage, which although an unusual and rare practice, does occur elsewhere (Stoodley 1999a, 76–7).

Jewellery assemblages indicative of feminine gender were found in 22 graves (seven from 1974). Compared to weapons, there is more flexibility with regard to the age associations of jewellery, although age was still a factor (Stoodley 2000). Two immature individuals under the age of 10 (graves 42 and 89) had been interred with jewellery, but their assemblages did not include brooches. For example, the *c.* 5–7 year old in grave 89 had a small necklace. Similar age-related patterning is found throughout the county. At Blacknall Field, for example, small bead necklaces were found with young individuals; there, grave 35 – that of a *c.* 2–2.5 year old, had a collection of four beads on the upper chest. These modest assemblages were probably symbolic of an age-related feminine status. From the age of *c.* 12 years, individuals were eligible for pairs of brooches and longer strings of beads. This change marked an important age-related threshold, one probably bound up with biological maturity (Stoodley 2000, 465). At Blacknall Field this is found to occur at about 12 years (Stoodley 2010), but at Collingbourne it is not witnessed until the late teens and coincides with the age at which weapons were interred. For females, biological maturity can be delayed as a result of poor nutrition, though this cannot be demonstrated here. It is possible that a similar threshold marking the 'coming of age', or a similar rite of passage, existed for both sexes in this community.

Social Hierarchy

The quantity and quality of grave goods deposited during the 5th and 6th centuries is highly variable and is often interpreted as signifying differences in social status that existed *within* local communities (Härke 1997, 138–9; Sherlock and Welch 1992, 102). The Collingbourne burials do not exhibit a particularly impressive range of wealth, however. No weapon burial contained the full 'set' of spear, shield and sword, which marks it out as different to both Blacknall Field and Petersfinger. The jewellery burials are characterised by pairs of simple copper alloy fasteners with only a small number decorated with gilt. The woman in grave 92 typifies the situation. However, along with her pair of disc brooches, was a gilt bell-shaped brooch (possibly converted from a pendant). The simple pair of disc brooches combined with a showier third brooch is

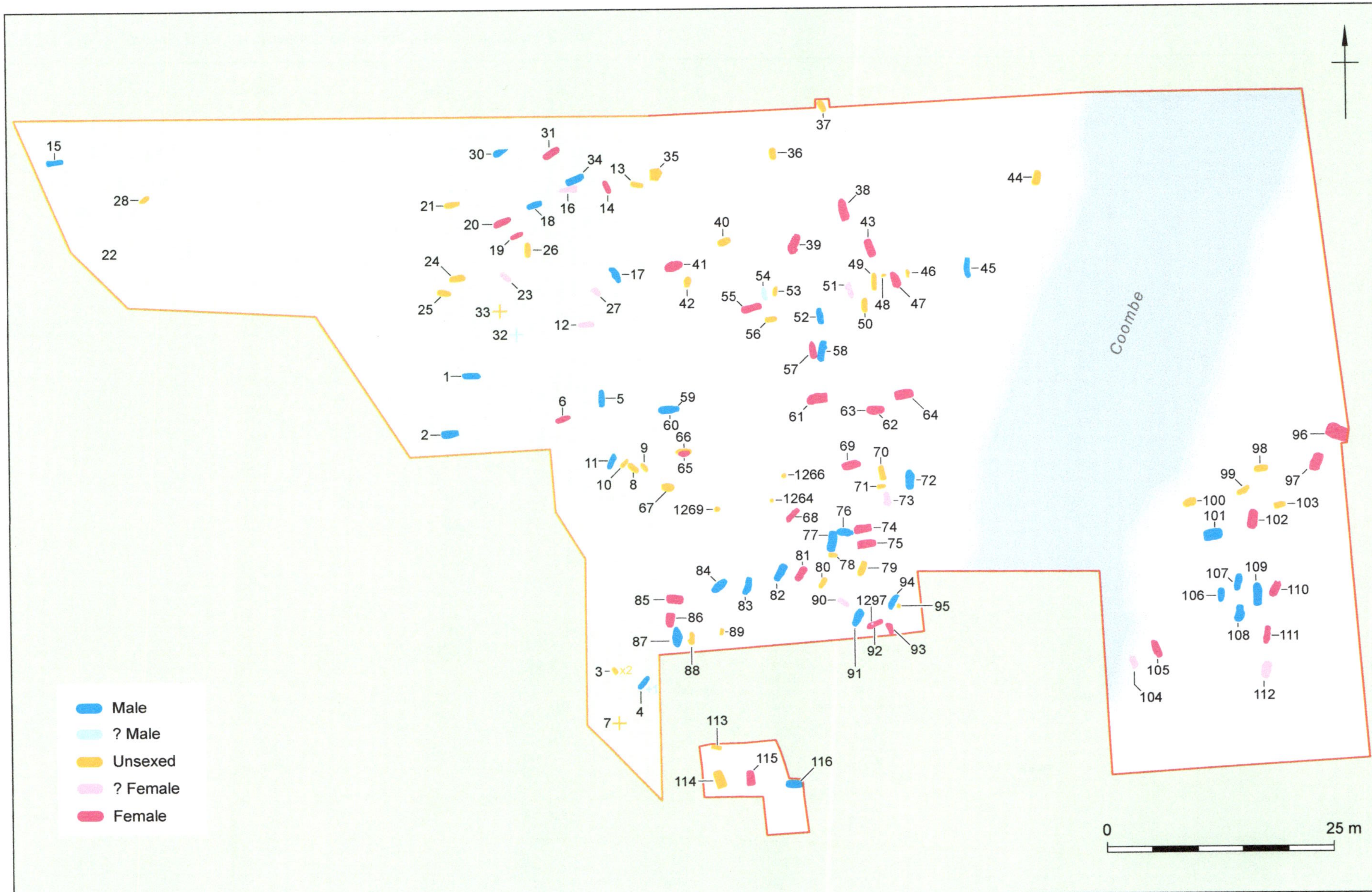

Figure 5.5 Cemetery plan: distribution by sex

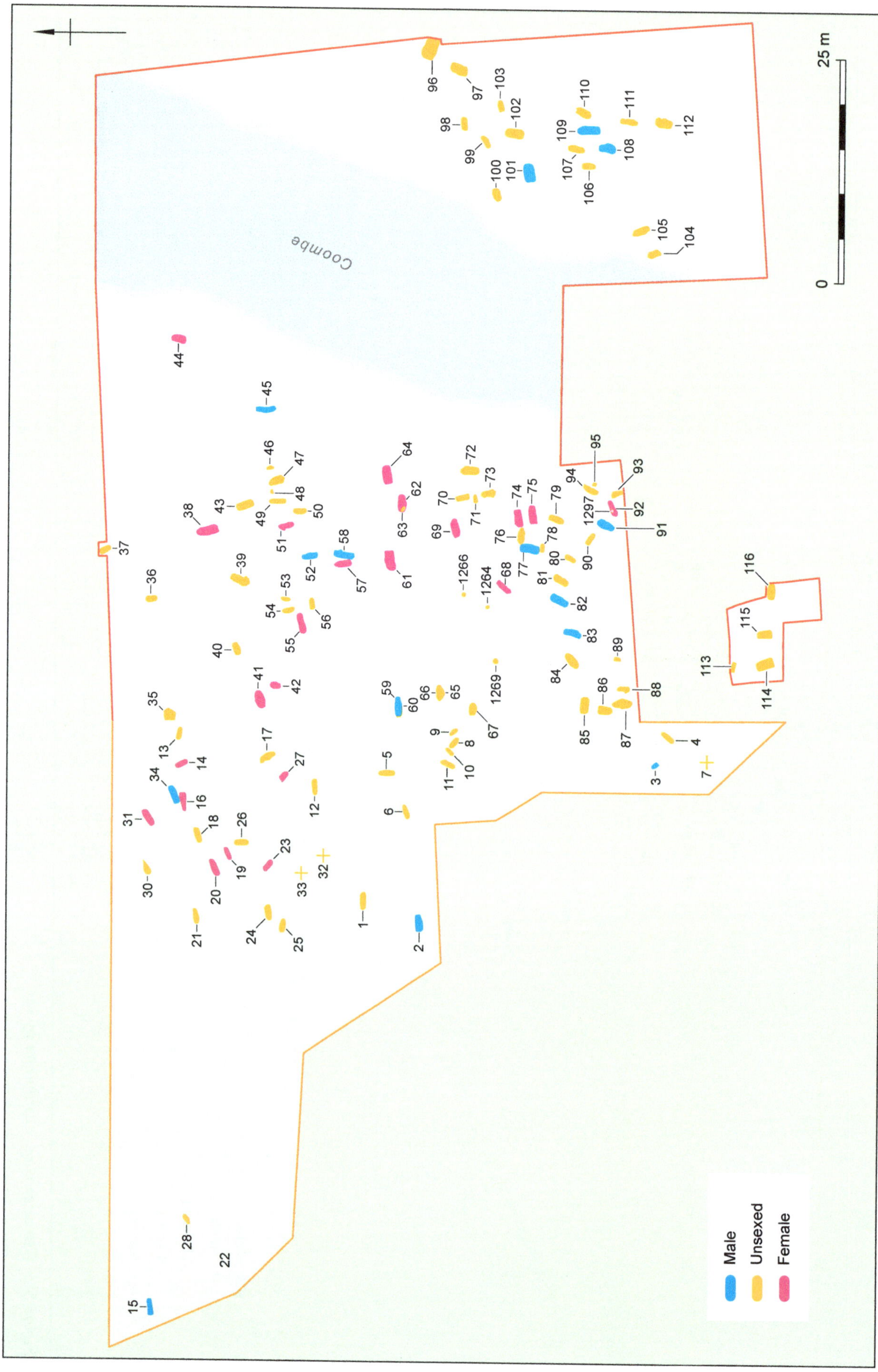

Figure 5.6 Cemetery plan: distribution by gender (based on grave goods)

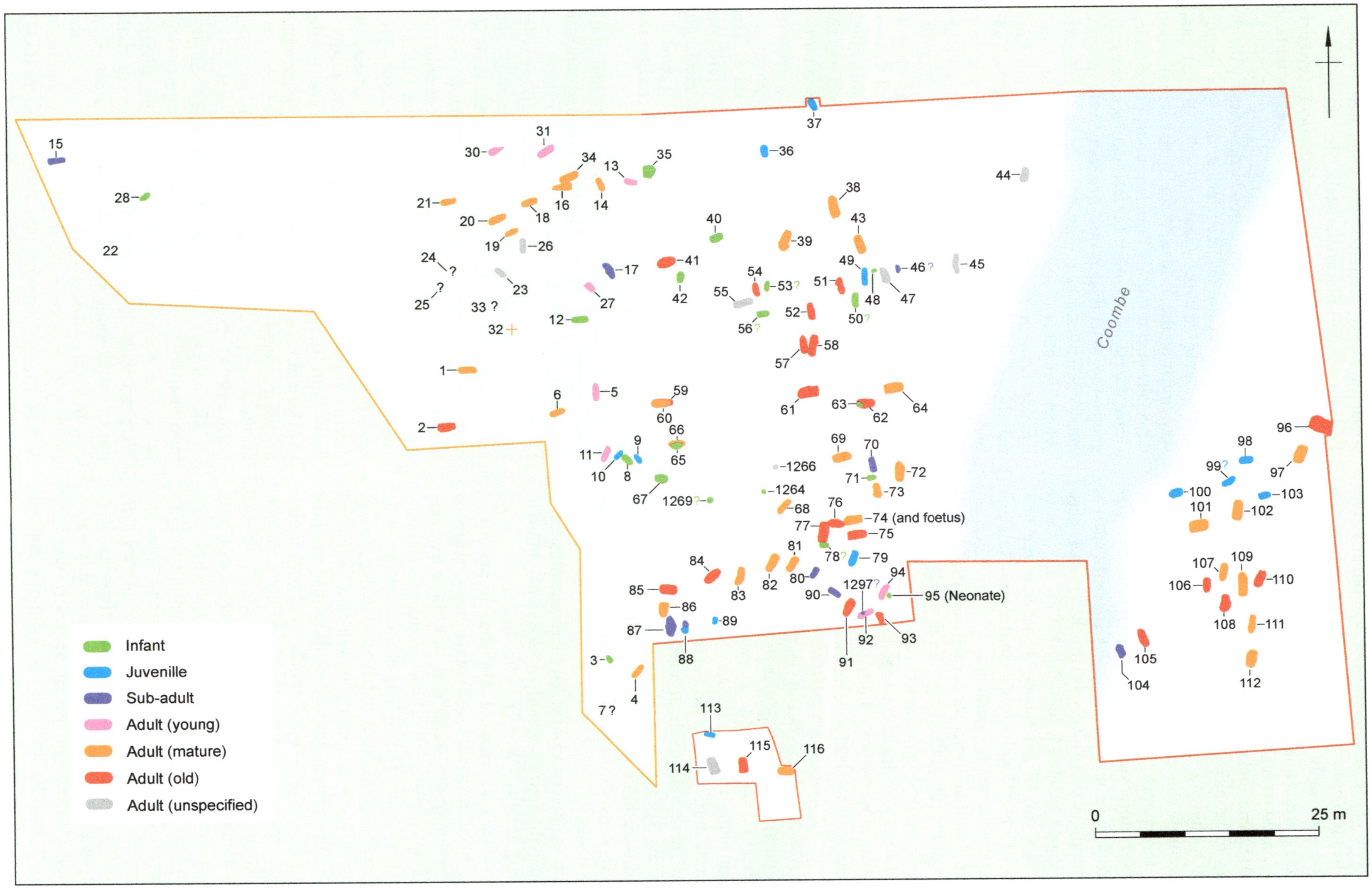

Figure 5.7 Cemetery plan: distribution by age

reminiscent of the assemblages that combined a great square-headed brooch with a pair of more modest fasteners, such as Blacknall Field G21 (with saucer brooches). Great square-headed brooches are likely to have belonged to high-ranking females (Hines 1997, 294–301) who belonged to families of sufficient standing to acquire such wealth. Did the woman in grave 92 enjoy a similarly high rank within the Collingbourne community, but without the necessary means to acquire such finery she was forced to improvise? Moreover, there is a general lack of objects considered to be indicative of greater wealth, such as metal-bound wooden vessels (buckets) and glass vessels (Cook 2004, 44; Stoodley 1999a, 33). Grave 69 with its pair of gilt saucer brooches is the only example of a burial with a bucket and it is notable that it is a relatively simple example.

With a limited range of wealth on display it is difficult to identify different grades that might reflect a vertically ranked community. According to Härke (1992, 150–53) males with weapons enjoyed a higher status than those without. Furthermore it is possible that males with a pair of weapons, such as a spear and shield, ranked above those interred with only a single spear (Alcock 1981), but it is difficult to know how to interpret the individuals in graves 52 and 59 who had a shield and a sword respectively. Although single weapons, both are wealthy, especially the sword, and it would probably be erroneous to consider these individuals in similar terms to those with single spears. In addition, grave 59 had a lining of large flints along one edge of the grave and this extra expenditure may indicate a higher than average status.

Given the diversity of the jewellery assemblages, it is particularly hard to identify evidence for different grades of wealth. Women who had a range of jewellery, such as pairs of brooches (especially if gilded), bead necklaces and other accoutrements, may have enjoyed a status that was above average. For example, grave 38 which produced, amongst other items, a pair of small-long brooches, and a large collection of beads that included 69 of amber, one of carnelian and one of quartz, as well as a chatelaine complex. The aforementioned adult woman in grave 69 with a pair of gilt saucer brooches and bucket may also have enjoyed a similar status, and the same can be said about the woman in grave 92.

It is notable that the majority of males with two weapon types and females with gilt brooches were found in Plot C, which may indicate that this was the pre-eminent household in the community; one that had been able to dispose of a higher level of wealth on the death of a household member. However, it is probably wisest to conclude that overall this was a community, which in burial at least, was not particularly wealthy and did not exhibit a marked social hierarchy, certainly not compared to either Petersfinger or Blacknall Field. In terms of the modest assemblages of weapons and jewellery deposited with the dead, Collingbourne has more in common with Portway East.

The quantity of grave goods deposited with the dead is found to decline during the 7th century (Boddington 1990; Geake 1997, 84–5) and consequently the evidence for social stratification, especially in community burial grounds, becomes less clear. Where 7th-century burials had included grave goods the assemblages are generally very modest: many individuals had only a knife and/or buckle. Where jewellery occurs, it is found to be much simpler than in the preceding century, consisting mainly of pins and necklets (Geake 1997, 85). Weapon burials are also rare. The evidence from Collingbourne is generally in agreement, although grave 101 with a spear and shield and grave 96 with a bed are exceptions. If burial wealth was still a measure of status, then it may be correct to interpret them as leading members of the 7th-century community. Both occur in Plot H, perhaps indicating that this was the paramount household in the late phase/s. Bed burials are usually associated with a range of wealthy artefacts, and that at Swallowcliffe Down provides a particularly good example (Speake 1989). The absence of any other grave goods in the Collingbourne example may be chronological (see above), or alternatively it may indicate that a generally low level of disposable wealth also characterised the 7th-century community.

At the same time that grave goods were disappearing from the community burial grounds, a new group of wealthy burials appear on the scene. Examples are often in isolated locations that command impressive view-sheds (Semple 2003) and are usually associated with earthworks, such as prehistoric barrows (Semple 2003; Williams 1997). Wiltshire has produced a relatively large number of this class, for example the barrows at Ford (Musty 1969) and Swallowcliffe Down (Speake 1989). This is a development that marks a major change in mortuary strategy and is believed to have resulted from both deep and widespread changes to the structure of society. These burials can be interpreted as evidence for a process of stratification that was part of the emergence of large Anglo-Saxon kingdoms (Arnold 1997, 201–10).

The new elite used portable wealth, monumentality and topography to signify and symbolise their newfound standing in society. Weapons were now primarily a signifier of male status, rather than a general symbol of masculinity and this can explain their general absence in the community cemeteries of the time. For example, at Aldbourne only one weapon was recovered (G34) and Monkton Deverill produced no examples. However, at Collingbourne, the eastern part of the cemetery produced three weapon burials (graves 101, 108 and 109), which argues for the existence of local elites and a continuation of the traditional ways of symbolising this status in death.

Wealthy assemblages of jewellery have also been found in barrows, for example at Swallowcliffe Down, and Geake (2002, 147) has shown how the women of the 7th century were more likely to be interred with gender-specific grave goods than men. For example, in the Wessex burial grounds of Winnall II and Didcot (Boyle *et al.* 1995), jewellery is present in modest quantities. The female in Collingbourne grave 110 is the only example in the 7th-century phase with jewellery, and the invisibility of women is something the cemetery has in common with Aldbourne and Monkton Deverill. In contrast to other areas in southern England, it seems that it was no longer important to express femininity at the community level and the change to the way women were buried may reflect a concomitant reduction in their status (Stoodley 1999a, 103–6).

Community and Household Identity

Each early Anglo-Saxon cemetery is different. In some cases it is the way the graves are arranged and their orientation, in others it is the types of grave goods with the dead and the manner in which they were deposited, or perhaps the way the cadaver had been laid in the grave (Pader 1980). The differences between cemeteries that are relatively close can be striking (Fisher 1988; Lucy 2000; Pader 1980) and can be viewed as one of the ways in which communities could express an identity. Burial would have been a public affair under the jurisdiction of individual communities and households (Halsall 1996), and a funeral provided the opportunity to reinforce this identity by transmitting it to a wider audience. As already discussed, Collingbourne differs to its neighbours, in particular by the wider range of brooch types that it had compared to both Petersfinger and Market Lavington – a distinction that may be indicative of a community founded upon a greater cultural diversity, and one that thus formed a key element of their local identity.

A closer examination of the data reveals a more complex situation: differences in burial practice existed between individual plots. For example, as already described, there are subtle variations in grave orientation between each plot; also, the majority of small-long brooches and pins were found in Plots B and E in the northern area of the western part of the cemetery, while most of the rarer types of burial positions were found in Plot C in the centre. This variation possibly derived from individual households which used the occasion of the funeral to articulate, perhaps to re-assert, in a visual manner, the identity of their household and kin.

Collingbourne Ducis in the Wider Landscape

The cemetery was located at *c.* 140 m OD on the north slope of a dry valley and 200 m east of the River Bourne. The ground drops away to the south affording views across the lower lying land of the valley and also to the confluence of the Bourne and its tributary. This place was specifically chosen and it can be suggested that the following factors determined its location: proximity to routeways, and the inter-visibility between these, the settlement(s) and the cemetery.

It is notable that the cemetery was not sited on the upper slopes of the valley, rather it was on the third river terrace. This would have rendered it visible, not only to people in the valley but also to those passing along the Bourne. It can be argued that the position had been carefully selected so as to draw attention, perhaps to direct people for ceremonies of interment and remembrance (Williams 1997, 25). The cemetery functioned as a topographic marker in a landscape that had been carefully manipulated in order to facilitate social contact.

The inter-visibility of the burial ground and its view-shed thus provides insights into how Collingbourne may have been encountered in more general terms by the people who inhabited the area and travelled the land. The engagement with burial sites at particular points may have served to integrate the ancestors into the fabric and routine of daily life. This seems to be the case at Overton Hill, West Overton, Wiltshire, where a small group of early Saxon burials were interred in several barrows of Roman and Bronze Age date (Eagles 1986; Semple 2003). The barrows were located on downland close to where two major routes intersected – the Roman road from Bath to Mildenhall and the Ridgeway (Fig. 5.1), and the decision to place the Anglo-Saxon dead in these barrows must have been intentional and influenced by factors other than the ready availability of a pre-existing monument.

In fact a considerable number of Wiltshire's Anglo-Saxon burials and cemeteries have a direct association with a prehistoric monument. It was a practice that could take place in the 6th century, for example at Barrow Clump (Stoodley forthcoming), but was more prevalent in the 7th. At Collingbourne there are no known prehistoric barrows in the immediate vicinity of the cemetery, which implies that its position was made sufficiently obvious by its location close to the valley bottom and possibly also by the above-ground structures on the southern edge of both the western and eastern parts of the cemetery.

Collingbourne has also produced evidence of a settlement. It was only partially investigated, and little is understood about its size and how it was organised, but the evidence does allow for a tentative examination of the relationship between the living and the dead. The settlement had been established in the valley bottom of the River Bourne approximately 150 m to the south-west of the cemetery (Pine 2001). The majority of the structural evidence dates to the later Saxon period, but one sunken-featured building was erected sometime in the 5th to 7th centuries and demonstrates that a close spatial association had existed between the living and their dead during the early Saxon period. A similar relationship is demonstrated in the Bourne Valley at Winterbourne Gunner (20 km to the south of Collingbourne), where pottery was recovered 400 m north of the cemetery close to the river (Eagles 2001, 206). At Petersfinger a pit containing Saxon pottery was discovered near the River Avon 800 m to the west of the cemetery. However, a different situation is provided by Market Lavington, where settlement and cemetery were adjacent (Williams and Newman 2006, 171–3).

The settlement would have been an important element within the landscape, its presence determining where the cemetery was sited. Lucy's (1998) work on the Anglo-Saxon cemeteries of East Yorkshire has shown that the changing spatial relationships between the settlements and the cemeteries have a chronological dimension and that by the 7th century the dead were being placed high up on the Yorkshire Wolds. This might indicate an increasing marginalisation of the ancestors (Lucy 1998, 99). However, when the community at Collingbourne shifted the focus of its burial ground in the 7th century it chose a spot just 30 m to the east on the opposite side of the coombe.

The reasons why communities chose to bury their dead in a new location are not fully understood, but it seems clear that one general explanation will not suffice (Boddington 1990). Social change that accompanied the emergence of kingdoms during the 7th century may have necessitated a break with the past and a desire by a community to disassociate itself from the ancestors. At the same time religious change and the conversion to Christianity may have required that the dead were interred in a new non-pagan resting place (Faull 1976, 233). Changes to the landscape and how the land was organised could also have played a role and is likely to explain why the distance between early and late cemeteries varied, for example at both Portway (Stoodley 2006a) and Winnall (Meaney and Hawkes 1970) relatively large distances separated the burial grounds.

Whatever factor(s) was responsible, it was sufficiently strong to result in the use of a new location, but it did not separate the two burial grounds by any great distance. Burial shifted in an easterly direction along the terrace; it was not sited further up-slope away from the settlement. The inter-visibility of the cemetery and settlement must still have been an important consideration in the creation of the mortuary landscape, with the short distance between the two intended to reinforce the relationship between the living and the dead and to enable ancestor worship and rituals of remembrance (Williams 2006). Moreover, that the settlement had not moved very far by the later Saxon period indicates that the dead still exerted a powerful influence over the living, their settlement patterns and the organisation of the landscape.

Appendix 1
Catalogue by Grave of all Material Examined and Analysed for Mineral-preserved Organics (MPO)

by Elizabeth McCormick

Grave No.	*Object No.*	*Material*	*Object type*	*MPO*	*Textile*	*Comments/observations*
35	33	Iron	Knife	?	N	Possible area of horn on tang, not enough to verify
35	32	Iron	Pin	N	N	–
37	68	Iron	Knife/ dagger	Y	Y	Horn on tang, extends 2 mm onto blade. Areas of mineral-replaced textile on the blade (from adjacent clothing as knife found on body), abraded
38	217	Iron	Knife	Y	N	Horn on tang. Copper alloy cover around top of tang and blade shoulder
38	219	Iron	Knife	N	N	No MPO, only a part of the blade survives
38	49	Copper alloy	Brooch	?	?	Possible minute areas of highly abraded MPO on back around pin fulcrum. Mineral-replaced textile on associated find ON 237 suggests it is the brooch pin of ON 49
38	51	Copper alloy	Brooch	–	Y	Mineral-replaced textile fibres around pin fulcrum, highly abraded
38	214	Copper alloy	Brooch	?	?	Possible MPO on back plate around catch
38	216	Iron	Buckle/ hinge	–	Y	Small area mineral-replaced textile, abraded/deteriorated. Object may be part of a hinge rather than a buckle
38	50	Copper alloy	Toilet implements	–	Y	Longer of the implements is a scraper, identity of the shorter implement unknown. Spangle may have originally been attached to the single suspension ring. MPO on scraper's suspension ring, abraded, likely to be textile. Mineral-replaced textile on single suspension ring and spangle, abraded. Associated pieces consist of thin layer of abraded mineral-replaced textile, corrosion and soil. Found on upper chest
38	64	Copper alloy	Scraper	N	N	Object identified as a scraper on suspension ring. Found between legs
38	220	Iron	Latchlifters	N	N	Object identified as latchlifters. No MPO
38	63	Copper alloy	Uncertain	N	N	Object could be a knife covering, possibly from knife ON 219. Very similar to copper alloy fitting found on knife ON 217, which is also from grave 38
38	65	Copper alloy	Uncertain	N	N	–
38	213	Copper alloy	Suspension ring	N	N	Object identified as a suspension ring rather than a finger-ring as twisted with a small hole
38	218	Copper alloy	Fragment	–	Y	Consists of copper alloy, iron corrosion, and MR textile fibres; possibly catch plate of brooch ON 214
38	215	Iron/ copper alloy	Latchlifters	N	N	Too large to be toilet implements; object identified as latchlifters. Includes a copper alloy ring and implement, with a group of iron implements and possible iron ring. The pieces are grouped closely together indicating that they were contained within a bag. No MPO to verify
38	212	Iron	Uncertain	N	N	Corroded iron lump, possibly two pieces twisted together. Found at the side of body/hip with a group of beads (group 62). No MPO
38	237	Iron	Uncertain/ brooch pin	–	Y	Mineral-replaced textile preserved in iron corrosion, abraded. Likely to be iron pin and textile from brooch ON 49, which it was found associated with

Grave No.	Object No.	Material	Object type	MPO	Textile	Comments/observations
39	47	Copper alloy	Brooch	–	Y	Mineral-replaced textile across back, highly deteriorated
39	48	Copper alloy	Cosmetic brush	Y	N	Object identified as cosmetic brush, with suspension ring and spangle. Iron core inside bundle of coarse mineral-replaced fibres, tied together with finer, extant fibres. Coarser fibres horse or hog – identified using SEM; irregular waved crenate scale pattern, close margins. Finer fibres plant – identified using SEM and FTIR. Treatment: brush cover mechanically cleaned
39	78	Copper alloy	Toilet implements	(Y)	N	Scoop and two picks on a suspension ring. No MPO on object. Associated piece is bone
39	205	Copper alloy	Fragment	N	N	–
39	204	Iron	Ring	(Y)	Y	Areas of mineral-replaced textile across ring, abraded, features obscured by corrosion. Found on upper chest so textile could be from clothing or remains of a purse. Human bone from body adhered to ring
39	206	Iron	Uncertain	–	Y	Identified as three objects; two would have been implements suspended from rings, the other was a mount. MPO across all, obvious as mineral-replaced textile on a few areas of each object, features obscured by corrosion
40	53	Iron	Knife	Y	N	Horn on tang, extends 2 mm onto blade, where a raised line in the corrosion also verifies the extent of the handle originally. Areas of leather on the blade shoulder and along the blade back, compacted featureless powder
40	52	Iron	Buckle	–	Y	Impression of a couple of threads, adjacent area may be abraded mineral-replaced textile
40	54	Iron	Pursemount	?	?	Object identified as a pursemount. Half has been left un-cleaned; possible evidence of MPO beneath
41	67	Copper alloy	Brooch	–	Y	Mineral-replaced textile across back, details obscured by solidified layer of iron corrosion and clay
41	72	Copper alloy	Brooch	(Y)	Y	Mineral-replaced textile around pin fulcrum, details obscured by solidified layer of iron corrosion and clay; 2/2 twill, spin obscured, not enough remains to do thread count. Area of human bone/tissue on top of textile from placement on body's shoulder
42	39	Iron	Knife	Y	N	Horn covers tang
42	38	Copper alloy	Ring	N	N	Object identified as suspension ring
42	40	Iron	Latchlifter	–	Y	MPO across latchlifter and suspension ring, obvious as mineral-replaced textile in few places, abraded
42	224	Copper alloy	Ring	–	?	Possible MPO, if so mineral-replaced textile
43	96	Iron	Knife	Y	N	Horn on tang, grey in appearance as covered in calcite. Prominent raised line in corrosion 5 mm onto blade denotes the original extent of the handle
43	95	Iron	Belt fitting/ buckle	N	N	Object identified as buckle. No MPO
44	402	Iron	Knife	Y	N	Horn on tang
44	291	Copper alloy	Uncertain	N	N	–
45	89	Iron	Knife	Y	N	Horn on tang
45	77	Iron	Spearhead	Y	N	Mineral-replaced wood in detached shaft end, small amount in head of shaft. Ash, mature timber – identified using optical microscopy; ring porous (bands of vessels relating to seasonal growth)

Grave No.	Object No.	Material	Object type	MPO	Textile	Comments/observations
47	84	Iron	Brooch	–	?	Possible areas of MPO, highly abraded
47	86	Iron	Buckle	N	N	–
47	80	Iron	Toilet set	–	Y	Object identified as a toilet set, including a scoop, probable picks, and possibly a scraper. Mineral-replaced textile fibres, deteriorated
49	87	Iron	Knife	?	N	Possible MPO remains on tang. Iron rivet on tang near to blade shoulder would have helped attach the handle
51	29	Iron	Knife	Y	N	Possible evidence of horn on tang, very deteriorated. Leather on detached blade pieces, compact featureless powder. 'Pelt blade piece'; hair impressions visible in surface, identified as pig using SEM
51	2	Copper alloy	Brooch	–	Y	Mineral-replaced textile around pin fulcrum, fibres full of iron corrosion; can only superficially identify as tabby. Mineral-replaced fibres on catch.
51	26	Copper alloy	Brooch	–	Y	Small area of mineral-replaced fibres below pin fulcrum, badly deteriorated. Rest of area around fulcrum may also be MPO – too deteriorated/abraded to see any distinguishing features
51	55	Iron	Buckle	Y	Y	Leather on buckle plate, identified as pig. Few areas of mineral-replaced textile on reverse of buckle plate, some Z type threads evident
51	31	Iron	Uncertain/ brooch pin	–	?	Found underneath brooch ON 26, could be remains of iron pin. Possibly some mineral-replaced textile
52	44	Iron	Knife	Y	N	Small areas of horn on tang, abraded
52	1	Iron	Shield boss	–	Y	Mineral-replaced textile on boss fragments and grip; tabby weave, ZZ spin, thread count 20x12 over 10 mm^2. SEM identified as plant fibres
52	405	Iron	Spearhead	Y	N	Found amongst fragments of shield boss ON 1, but identified as a broken spearhead socket and a separate object. Mineral-preserved wood in shaft. Possibly ash – identified using optical microscopy; ring porous
53	46	Iron	Buckle	–	?	Possible MPO on pin and on buckle where pin attaches, if so it is highly abraded mineral-replaced textile
54	34	Iron	Knife	Y	N	Horn covers tang, extends 2 mm onto blade
54	35	Iron	Mount	?	?	MPO front and back, too indistinct to identify. Single attachment at back means object is likely to be a decorative mount rather than a brooch
54	41	Iron	Uncertain	N	N	Object is either a purse mount or firesteel
55	43	Iron	Knife	Y	Y	Horn covers tang. Few fibres of mineral-replaced textile on associated pieces, abraded
57	73	Copper alloy	Brooch	–	Y	Costume jewellery; packing material between front and back plate, front plate gilded. Coloured glass piece (blue) would have originally been set in the centre of the front plate. Mineral-replaced textile on back plate, deteriorated
57	74	Copper alloy	Brooch	–	?	Same as ON 73. Coloured glass (red) at centre. Possible MPO on back plate and in detached catch, deteriorated
57	S5115	Copper alloy	Brooch	(Y)	?	Possible abraded MPO on iron pin. Tissue on catch; likely to be human. Catch may belong to ON 73 or ON 74. Some of the fragments are gilded
57	S5128	Copper alloy	R. arm brooch	–	?	Possible mineral-replaced threads on two pieces. Some of the fragments are gilded. ON 5128 may belong to ON 73 or ON 74
57	75	Iron	Pin	N	N	–

Grave No.	*Object No.*	*Material*	*Object type*	*MPO*	*Textile*	*Comments/observations*
58	71	Iron	Knife	Y	N	Area of horn on tang
58	70	Iron	Buckle	Y	Y	Leather on inner buckle plate surfaces, identified as pig. Mineral-replaced textile on reverse of buckle and back plate; tabby tablet weave at edge of 2/1 twill, thread count 13x13 over 10 mm^2, ZZ spin. Mineral-replaced textile on outer surface of front buckle plate, abraded. Possible carry strap, eg, for knife ON 71
58	69	Iron	Spearhead	Y	N	Mineral-preserved wood survives length of shaft. Ash, mature timber – identified using optical microscopy; ring porous
59	18	Iron	Knife	Y	Y	Horn on tang up to blade shoulder. Mineral-replaced textile strip on blade; 2/2 twill, ZZ spin, thread count 14x14 over 10 mm^2. Leather on blade tip and underneath textile strip, abraded
59	16	Copper alloy	Buckle	–	Y	Small areas of abraded mineral-replaced textile around iron pin
59	17	Copper alloy	Tweezers	N	N	Found at waist adjacent to buckle ON 16, likely suspended from the belt
59	25	Copper alloy	Clasp	–	Y	Plates fit together. Mineral-replaced textile on inner surfaces of both plates, obscured by clay. Area of textile covered in copper corrosion on front of one of the plates also. Possible carry strap fastener for sword ON 15, but this cannot be ascertained as positioning in grave is unclear
59	15	Iron	Sword	Y	N	Horn across hilt; orientation different on lower guard, grip and upper guard showing the handle was made in three parts. Areas of wood on the blade, but no evidence of hair/fleece. Wood is willow/poplar, identified using SEM; uniseriate rays, simple perforation plates, diffuse porous. Treatment: end of tang re-adhered
61	12	Iron	Knife/ dagger	–	Y	Mineral-replaced textile on blade beneath calcite layer, small area revealed, highly abraded
61	8	Copper alloy	Brooch (veil ring?)	N	N	No MPO. Object placement at side of skull suggests it is a veil ring. Similar but different to ON 14
61	14	Copper alloy	Brooch (veil ring?)	N	N	No MPO. Object placement at side of skull suggests it is a veil ring. Similar but different to ON 8
61	10	Copper alloy	Brooch	–	Y	Mineral-replaced textile on front of brooch; 2/1 twill, ZZ spin, thread count 10x10 over 10 mm^2. Mineral-replaced textile across back, details obscured by solidified layer of iron corrosion and clay. Found at sternum
61	11	Copper alloy	Brooch	–	Y	Small areas of mineral-replaced textile on back, deteriorated. Pair to ON 10 but found at lower left ribcage
61	13	Copper alloy	Pick	N	N	Object identified as pick on suspension ring
62	21	Iron	Knife	?	?	No visible MPO. Band on blade has been left un-cleaned; may be evidence of MPO beneath *cf.* ON 12
62	19	Copper alloy	Brooch	–	Y	Mineral-replaced textile on back, deteriorated/abraded. Some Z type threads evident
62	20	Copper alloy	Brooch	–	Y	Mineral-replaced textile on back around both pin fulcrum and catch, highly abraded
62	24	Copper alloy	Brooch catch	N	N	Object identified as a catch, probably from brooch ON 19. No MPO; inside catch is iron corrosion and pin only
62	22	Iron, Copper alloy	Buckle	?	Y	Object identified as buckle and plate. Buckle and back plate are iron. Front plate and buckle inlays are copper alloy. Possible leather on inner surface of back plate, abraded. Impression of a few mineral-replaced threads on top edge of back plate. Associated pieces are deteriorated mineral-replaced textile

Grave No.	Object No.	Material	Object type	MPO	Textile	Comments/observations
64	5	Copper alloy	Brooch	–	Y	Small areas of mineral-replaced textile around pin fulcrum, some Z type threads evident; animal, possibly wool – sheep suggested by SEM; possible mosaic scales with smooth margins. A possible braid edge is visible on top of the pin fulcrum; plant – identified using SEM
64	6	Copper alloy	Brooch	–	Y	Mineral-replaced textile across back, obscured by solidified layer of iron corrosion and clay. Small defined area at edge can be superficially identified as tabby, with Z type threads evident; plant – identified using SEM
64	9	Iron	Uncertain/ buckle plate	N	N	Object likely to be buckle plate. Possible MPO
64	230	Copper alloy	Fitting	–	?	Possible mineral-replaced textile on attachment
64	201	Copper alloy	Coin	N	N	Hole in coin
64	202	Copper alloy	Coin	N	N	Hole in coin, same size as that in ON 201
64	200	Iron	Pin	–	?	Possible MPO, if so abraded mineral-preserved textile, obscured by clay
66	123	Iron	Knife	(Y)	N	Bone from the interned body
67	138	Iron	Knife	Y	N	Horn on tang
68	116	Iron	Knife	N	N	–
68	117	Iron	Buckle	–	Y	Area of very abraded mineral-replaced textile, can only see definition of a few fibres
69	177	Iron	Knife	Y	N	Small areas of horn on tang, highly abraded, 3.5 mm onto blade
69	189	Iron	Knife	–	Y	Just blade remains. Mineral-replaced textile both sides of blade; twill, too deteriorated to identify further
69	280	Iron	Knife	Y	N	Horn on tang, abraded
69	163	Copper alloy	Brooch	(Y)	Y	Mineral-replaced textile around pin fulcrum, abraded, few Z type threads evident. Cream area on top of textile is a human skin surface cast
69	164	Copper alloy	Brooch	–	Y	Mineral-replaced textile around pin fulcrum, obscured by solidified layer of iron corrosion and clay. Mineral-replaced threads also on catch; animal, possibly sheep – suggested by SEM but too deteriorated to confirm. Associated pieces are mineral-replaced textile covered in clay. One piece consists of twisted threads, probably a bead cord or tablet weave border, ZZ spin, thread count 14x6 over 10 mm^2.
69	168	Copper alloy	Toilet implement	N	N	Scoop twisted along its length, two picks and a suspension ring. Found on the upper chest; may have been hanging from around the neck or between the two saucer brooches ON 163 and 164. No MPO
69	169	Copper alloy	Binding	Y	N	MPO around some rim rivets, too little to identify further, would expect to be wood. Length of rim rivet 4 mm, length of base rivet 15 mm
70	187	Iron	Knife	N	N	No MPO, only a part of the blade survives
70	188	Iron	Buckle	N	N	–
71	196	Iron	Knife	?	?	No visible MPO. Band on blade has been left un-cleaned; maybe evidence of MPO beneath *cf.* ON 12
72	197	Iron	Knife	N	N	
74	175	Iron	Knife	?	?	Possible area of mineral-replaced textile fibres on blade, possible rest of un-cleaned area is also textile *cf.* ON 12
74	170	Copper alloy	Brooch	–	?	Possible mineral-replaced fibres around pin fulcrum
74	173	Copper alloy	Brooch	–	Y	Mineral-replaced textile on detached pin fulcrum, highly abraded. Mineral-replaced thread on detached catch; plant – identified using SEM

Grave No.	*Object No.*	*Material*	*Object type*	*MPO*	*Textile*	*Comments/observations*
75	166	Copper alloy	Brooch	–	Y	Possible MPO on back plate, deteriorated. Mineral-replaced textile on detached catch
75	167	Copper alloy	Brooch	–	Y	Mineral-replaced textile attached to back plate around catch, deteriorated. Wool fibres – identified as sheep using SEM; mosaic scales, smooth margins and varied cross-sections
75	181	Iron	Buckle	N	N	–
76	263	Iron	Knife	N	N	–
76	264	Iron	Buckle	–	Y	Area of mineral-replaced textile on reverse of buckle plate, deteriorated, abraded. Associated pieces are deteriorated textile
76	198	Iron	Stud	N	N	Half cleaned, no visible MPO
77	190	Iron	Knife	Y	N	Horn covers tang, extends 3 mm onto blade
77	180	Iron	Buckle	N	N	No MPO. Buckle may be part of carry strap for shield ON 178 or a belt fastener
77	178	Iron	Shield boss	Y	Y	Wood on boss flange, reverse of grip, and studs. SEM identified as lime; spiral thickening, multiseriate rays. Leather on stud. Leather carry strap wound round grip, 16 mm wide. Textile on outer side of grip; 2/1 twill, ZZ spin, thread count 12x8 over 10 mm^2. Boss found on body; textile is from clothing. SEM shows fibres to be animal, probably sheep; irregular waved mosaic, varied cross-sections
77	179	Iron	Spearhead	Y	N	Mineral-preserved wood in shaft. Hazel, sapling wood – preliminary identified as hazel/alder using optical microscopy; diffuse porous, radial vessel chains, and uniseriate rays – SEM confirmed as hazel; short scaliriform perforation plates, aggregate ray. Sapling as rays arranged towards the centre
79	136	Iron	Knife	Y	N	Horn covers tip of tang, extends around it
80	184	Iron	Buckle	–	Y	Small area mineral-replaced textile, abraded. No pin to buckle so may have had a textile rather than leather strap, not enough MPO to verify
81	120	Iron	Knife	Y	N	Horn on tang beneath the calcite, where the tang has been cleaned impressions in the magnetite are evidence of horn
81	115	Copper alloy	Brooch	(Y)	Y	Mineral-replaced textile across back, details obscured by solidified layer of iron corrosion and clay. Human tissue on top of textile
81	121	Iron	Buckle	–	Y	Area of mineral-replaced textile, abraded
81	113	Iron	Pin	Y	?	MPO, too deteriorated to identify
82	124	Iron	Knife	Y	N	Horn on tang, appears grey in places due to calcite
82	106	Iron	Shield boss	Y	N	Wood on boss flange and studs. SEM identified as lime; spiral thickening, multiseriate rays. Leather on boss flange. Human tooth due to placement of boss on face
82	107	Iron	Spearhead	Y	N	Mineral-preserved wood within shaft. Ash – identified using optical microscopy; ring porous
83	118	Iron	Knife	Y	N	Few areas of horn on tang. Raised line in corrosion 4 mm onto blade denotes the original extent of the handle
83	103	Iron	Buckle and buckle plate	Y	Y	Object identified as buckle and buckle plate. Mineral-replaced textile on buckle top, badly deteriorated. Wood on buckle, evidence of a grave covering; *cf.* ON 102
83	102	Iron	Shield boss	Y	N	Leather and wood on boss flange. Grip inserted into front of shield board and bound in strips of leather 5–7 mm wide. One rivet on flange has copper alloy washer. Wood on front of boss relates to a grave covering, probably oak; ring porous, tyloses
83	101	Iron	Spearhead	Y	N	Small amount of mineral-preserved wood in shaft. Possibly ash; there may be bands of double vessels, but high amount of corrosion in pores and limited amount of wood make identification difficult

Grave No.	Object No.	Material	Object type	MPO	Textile	Comments/observations
84	137	Copper alloy	Brooch	N	N	–
85	93	Iron	Knife	?	N	Possible small area of horn on end of tang
85	91	Iron	Buckle	?	?	Possible MPO, accretions highly abraded so difficult to ascertain
85	94	Iron	Pin	N	N	–
85	92	Iron	Ring	–	Y	Object identified as a purse ring, with six separate items, likely to be the contents. Mineral-replaced textile on ring and contents, abraded. Ring is too small for a hand to pass inside it; the ring probably passed over the top of the pouch to hold the textile around the contents
85	235	Copper alloy	Uncertain	N	N	Found associated with ON 92. Object likely to be a fitting from the purse of which ON 92 is the ring; the small width of the gap indicates it was mounted on leather, such as a purse strap. No MPO to verify
87	97	Iron	Knife	Y	N	Horn covers tang, extends 7mm onto blade. Possible areas of leather on the blade, but highly abraded; thin powdery layer only
88	133	Iron	Knife	Y	N	Horn covers tang and blade shoulder, extends 11 mm onto blade. Iron rivet to secure handle. Possible highly abraded leather on blade
88	130	Iron	Buckle	?	Y	No MPO on buckle. Possible leather on inner sides of buckle plates, abraded. Mineral-replaced textile across reverse of back plate, features unclear
89	239	Copper alloy	Coin	–	?	Possible area of mineral-replaced textile, not enough survives to ascertain. Found with 1 amber and 9 glass beads (group 141)
91	128	Iron	Knife 'dagger' / seax	Y	N	Horn covers tang. Large blade; 175 mm long, 27 mm wide so may be better defined as a seax rather than a knife
91	127	Iron	Nail	N	N	–
91	125	Iron	Spearhead	Y	N	Mineral-preserved wood in shaft. Ash – identified using optical microscopy; ring porous
91	126	Iron	Ferrule	Y	N	Object identified as ferrule of spear ON 125; found at other end of grave, confirmed by same wood species inside both shafts. Ash, mature timber – identified using optical microscopy; ring porous
92	135	Copper alloy	Brooch	(Y)	Y	Mineral-replaced textile across back, details obscured by solidified layer of iron corrosion and clay, some Z type threads evident, no further identification possible. 2-ply thread, extant fibres, between mineral-replaced textile and brooch back; plant – identified using SEM, confirmed by FTIR. Human tissue on top of textile
92	222	Copper alloy	Brooch	(Y)	Y	Pair to ON135. Small pieces of mineral-replaced textile on front. Mineral-replaced textile across back, badly deteriorated, can see some Z type threads. Plied thread, extant fibres, between mineral-replaced textile and brooch back; *cf.* ON 135. Human bone on top of textile
92	221	Copper alloy	Brooch	–	Y	Object identified as cloak brooch. Small areas of textile on front; plant – identified using SEM, confirmed by FTIR. Mineral-replaced textile across back; 2/2 twill, ZZ spin, thread count 14x14 over 10 mm^2, animal – identified using SEM. Front gilded
92	223	Textile and residue	Textile and residue	(Y)	Y	Textile pieces, deteriorated, some Z type threads evident. Mineral-replaced thread; wool fibres – identified as sheep using SEM; mosaic scales, smooth margins and varied cross-sections. Extant thread obscured by corrosion, no identification possible. Residue result of decomposing human tissue
92	142	Copper alloy	Finger-ring	N	N	–

Grave No.	*Object No.*	*Material*	*Object type*	*MPO*	*Textile*	*Comments/observations*
93	161	Iron	Knife	Y	N	Small amount of horn on tip of tang. No obvious blade shoulder to knife
93	132	Iron	Uncertain	N	N	Object identified as a mount. Hole at each end for a rivet, small width, 2 mm max. indicates it was mounted on leather. Possibly a purse mount *cf.* ON 165
93	165	Copper alloy	Uncertain	N	N	Object identified as possible purse mount. Found near to ON 132, and similar dimensions (1 mm gap at closed end, 2 mm at open end) indicating it was also mounted on leather; could both be mounts from a purse
94	195	Iron	Knife	Y	N	Horn on blade shoulder, extends 4 mm onto blade. Recessed line runs the length of the blade, 3 mm in from the blade back edge and less than 1 mm wide; evidence of an inlay, none of which remains
96	349	Copper alloy	Coin	N	N	–
96	348	Copper alloy	Uncertain	N	N	–
97	285	Iron	Knife	N	N	–
100	287	Iron	Knife	Y	N	Horn on tang, more defined near tip
101	282	Iron	Knife	Y	Y	Horn on tang
101	281	Iron	Buckle	–	Y	Mineral-replaced textile across reverse of buckle and back plate, highly abraded and obscured by corrosion
101	268	Iron	Shield boss	Y	Y	Wood on boss flange; diffuse porous, solitary pores, uniseriate rays. SEM confirmed as willow/poplar; uniseriate rays, simple perforation plates. Leather on boss flange and inside of grip. Central section of grip wrapped with plied thread
101	276	Iron	Spearhead	Y	N	Mineral-replaced wood in shaft, covered in calcite deposits. Willow/poplar, identified using SEM; uniseriate rays, simple perforation plates, large crossfield pits
102	272	Iron	Knife	N	N	No MPO, only a part of the blade survives
103	277	Iron	Knife	?	N	Possible MPO at end of tang, if so horn likely
104	252	Iron	Knife	Y	N	Horn on tang, fine layer, highly abraded
104	256	Iron	Nail	?	?	Half has been left un-cleaned; possible evidence of MPO beneath
106	257	Iron	Knife	N	N	–
106	253	Iron, Copper alloy	Buckle	Y	Y	No MPO on buckle. Buckle and back plate are iron. Front plate is copper alloy. Leather on inner sides of plates, abraded. Mineral-replaced textile on outer sides of plates; area on front plate visible as tabby, ZZ spin, not enough to count threads. Tabby also visible on one associated piece
107	271	Iron	Knife	Y	N	Horn on tang, highly abraded. Prominent raised line in corrosion 1 mm onto blade denotes the original extent of the handle
107	270	Iron, Copper alloy	Buckle	?	–	Iron buckle, Copper alloy rivets. Possible small amount of leather remains between plates, accretions abraded so difficult to ascertain. Treatment: plate pieces re-adhered
108	260	Iron	Knife	Y	N	Horn covers tang
108	261	Iron	Buckle	–	?	Possible small area of mineral-replaced textile, abraded
108	199	Iron	Spearhead	Y	N	Very small amount of mineral-preserved wood survives, on inner walls of shaft. SEM revealed fungal growth, vessels full of corrosion; too degraded to identify other than uniseriate rays which indicate alder/hazel or willow/poplar
109	275	Iron	Nail	?	?	Half has been left un-cleaned; possible evidence of MPO beneath
109	279	Iron	Spearhead	Y	N	Mineral-preserved wood in shaft, covered in calcite deposits and abraded. Too deteriorated to identify

Grave No.	Object No.	Material	Object type	MPO	Textile	Comments/observations
110	266	Iron	Knife	N	N	–
110	267	Copper alloy	Buckle	N	N	–
110	269	Copper alloy	Pin: garment fastener	N	N	Found vertically on the upper right chest of a female it is likely that this pin is a garment fastener. No MPO
Colluvial deposit in coombe	140	Copper alloy, glass, gold	Brooch	Y	N	Setting to central garnet is possibly bone or shell. Stones identified as garnets using XRF; almandine variety. Gold foils behind triangular garnets. Front of brooch is gilded. Base metal has a high silver content
n/a	7	Iron	Strip	N	N	–
Posthole	262	Iron	Strip	?	?	Areas have been left un-cleaned; possible evidence of MPO beneath
Subsoil	153	Iron	Fitting	N	N	–
Subsoil	242	Iron	Uncertain	N	N	–
Subsoil	243	Iron	Cleat	N	N	–
Subsoil	150	Iron	Nail	Y	N	Large nail, MPO on shaft
Subsoil	149	Copper alloy	Key	N	N	–
Subsoil	111	Iron	Spearhead	Y	N	Mineral-preserved wood in shaft. Ash – identified using both optical microscopy; ring porous, and SEM; multiseriate rays, no spiral thickening
Subsoil	112	Iron	Spearhead	Y	N	Mineral-preserved wood in detached shaft end and head of shaft, abraded, breakage recent. Object identified as a hunting/throwing spear due to its size. Iron rivet across inside of shaft to hold wood in place. Wood possibly willow/poplar – suggested by SEM; uniseriate rays, simple perforation plates
Subsoil	146	Iron	Stud	N	N	–
Subsoil	229	Iron	Wire	N	N	–

Appendix 2
X-ray Fluorescence (XRF) Analysis of the Metalwork

by Elizabeth McCormick

X-ray fluorescence (XRF) analysis was used to identify the composition of copper alloys, any surface coatings such as gilding and tinning, and manufacturing techniques such as the use of solders. XRF analysis was carried out on all of the copper alloy finds (see below), with the exception of four brooches (ONs 73, 74, 166 and 167) and a knife fitting (on ON 217) which required further remedial conservation and were sent back to Wiltshire Council Conservation Service before there was an opportunity to undertake XRF analysis.

Analysis was carried out using an EDAX-EAGLE II spectrometer at 40kV and 300mA in a non-vacuum atmosphere, for a live time of 50 seconds. A vacuum was used for the garnets and bone/shell setting on brooch ON 140 in order to pick up the lighter elements which were expected in these cases. Rather than focus analysis on one spot on the object, which could give a biased result, the whole surface was analysed to give an average, more representative result.

XRF analyses the surface of an object and ideally requires a completely flat surface, meaning that the results given for archaeological material should be regarded as qualitative rather than quantitative. This is because on archaeological objects the surface is corroded and only approximately reflects the base metal, and according to the specific burial conditions the composition of the remaining metal may also differ somewhat from that at manufacture due to differential leaching of the component elements (Peacock 2007, 32). Therefore the amounts of components can be compared relative to each other qualitatively, but quoting precise percentages of each based on the analysis would be misleading.

Grave	*ON*	*Object Type*	*Area Analysed*	*Elements detected **	*Alloy type*	*Other features*
38	49	Brooch	Front	Cu, Sn, Pb	Leaded bronze	–
38	51	Brooch	Front	Cu, Sn, Pb	Leaded bronze	–
38	214	Brooch	Front/Back	Cu, Sn, Zn, Pb	Leaded gunmetal	–
38	213	Suspension ring	Ring	Cu, Sn, Zn, Pb	Leaded gunmetal	–
38	218	Fragment	Not Analysed – too much iron corrosion and soil			
38	215	Latchlifters	Implement	Cu, Sn, Zn, Pb	Leaded gunmetal	–
			Ring	Cu, Sn, Zn, Pb		
38	63	Uncertain	–	Cu, Sn, Zn, Pb	Leaded gunmetal	–
38	65	Uncertain	–	Cu, Sn, Zn, Pb	Leaded gunmetal	–
38	50	Toilet implement	Scraper	Cu, Sn, Zn, Pb	Leaded gunmetal	–
			Scraper ring	Cu, Sn, Zn, Pb		
			Implement	Cu, Sn, Zn, Pb		
			Implement ring	Cu, Sn, Zn, Pb		
			Spangle	Cu, Sn, Zn, Pb		
			Ring	Cu, Sn, Zn, Pb		
38	64	Tweezers	Tweezers	Cu, Sn, Zn, Pb	Leaded gunmetal	–
			Ring	Cu, Sn, Zn, Pb		
38	217	Knife fitting	Not analysed – object sent back before analysis			
39	47	Brooch	Front	Cu, Sn, Zn, Pb	Leaded gunmetal	–
39	48	Cosmetic brush	Tubing	Cu, Sn, Zn, Pb	Leaded gunmetal	Tip of tubing tinned.
			Ring	Cu, Sn, Zn, Pb		Tin solder along tubing
			Spangle	Cu, Sn, Zn, Pb		join edges
39	205	Fragment	Not analysed – too much corrosion and soil			
39	78	Toilet implement	Scoop	Cu, Sn, Zn, Pb	Leaded gunmetal	–
			Pick	Cu, Sn, Zn, Pb		
			Pick 2	Cu, Sn, Zn, Pb		
			Ring	Cu, Sn, Zn, Pb		
41	67	Brooch	Front	Cu, Sn, Zn, Pb	Leaded gunmetal	–
41	72	Brooch	Front	Cu, Sn, Zn, Pb	Leaded gunmetal	–

Grave	*ON*	*Object Type*	*Area Analysed*	*Elements detected **	*Alloy type*	*Other features*
42	224	Ring	Ring	Cu, Sn, Pb	Leaded bronze	–
42	38	Ring	Ring	Cu, Sn, Zn, Pb	Leaded gunmetal	–
44	291	Uncertain		Cu, Sn, Zn, Pb	Leaded gunmetal	
51	2	Brooch	Front	Cu, Sn, Zn, Pb	Leaded gunmetal	Surface was tinned
51	26	Brooch	Front	Cu, Sn, Zn, Pb	Leaded gunmetal	
57	73	Brooch	Not analysed – object sent back before analysis			
57	74	Brooch	Not analysed – object sent back before analysis			
57	S5115	Brooch; catch and fragments	Catch	Cu, Sn, Zn, Pb	Leaded gunmetal	Tin solder on catch. Mercury gilded (fragments)
57	S5128	Brooch	Brooch	Cu, Sn, Pb	Leaded bronze	Mercury gilded
59	16	Buckle	Front	Cu, Sn, Zn, Pb	Leaded gunmetal	–
59	17	Tweezers	Tweezers	Cu, Sn, Zn, Pb	Leaded gunmetal	–
59	25	Clasp	Plate 1 Plate 2	Cu, Sn, Zn, Pb Cu, Sn, Zn, Pb	Leaded gunmetal	–
61	8	Brooch	Ring	Cu, Sn, Zn, Pb	Leaded gunmetal	–
61	14	Brooch	Ring	Cu, Sn, Pb	Leaded bronze	–
61	10	Brooch	Front Central stub	Cu, Sn, Zn, Pb Cu, Sn, Pb	Leaded gunmetal	Surface probably tinned. Tin solder on central stub; may be evidence of a broken attachment.
61	11	Brooch	Front Central stub	Cu, Sn, Zn, Pb Cu, Sn, Pb	Leaded gunmetal	Surface probably tinned. Tin solder on central stub; may be evidence of a broken attachment
61	13	Pin	Pin Ring	Cu, Sn, Zn, Pb Cu, Sn, Zn, Pb	Leaded gunmetal	–
62	19	Brooch	Front	Cu, Sn, Zn, Pb	Leaded gunmetal	Tin/lead solder on catch
62	20	Brooch	Front	Cu, Sn, Zn, Pb	Leaded gunmetal	Tin/lead solder on catch
62	24	Catch	Catch	Cu, Sn, Zn, Pb	Leaded gunmetal	Tin solder on catch. Alloy type confirms ON 24 is probably from ON 19
62	22	Buckle	Buckle Plate Buckle Inlays	Cu, Sn, Zn, Pb Cu, Sn, Zn, Pb	Leaded gunmetal	–
64	5	Brooch	Front Front dull grey areas	Cu, Sn, Pb Cu, Sn, Pb	Leaded bronze	Surface was tinned
64	6	Brooch	Front Front and back dull grey areas	Cu, Sn, Pb Cu, Sn, Pb	Leaded bronze	Surface was tinned
64	201	Coin	Front/Back	Cu, Sn, Pb	Leaded bronze	–
64	202	Coin	Front/Back	Cu, Sn, Pb	Leaded bronze	–
64	230	Fitting	Fitting	Cu, Zn, Pb	Leaded brass	–
69	163	Brooch	Front	Cu, Sn, Zn, Pb	Leaded gunmetal	Mercury gilded. Gild is predominantly gold, with silver
69	164	Brooch	Front	Cu, Sn, Zn, Pb	Leaded gunmetal	Mercury gilded. Gild is predominantly gold, with silver
69	169	Binding	Rim Fittings Base	Cu, Sn, Zn, Pb Cu, Sn, Zn, Pb Cu, Sn, Zn, Pb	Leaded gunmetal	Evidence the fittings, base, and rivets were tinned
69	168	Toilet implement	Scoop Pick 1 (longer) Pick 2 Ring	Cu, Sn, Zn, Pb Cu, Sn, Zn, Pb Cu, Sn, Zn, Pb Cu, Sn, Zn, Pb	Leaded gunmetal	–

Grave	*ON*	*Object Type*	*Area Analysed*	*Elements detected **	*Alloy type*	*Other features*
74	170	Brooch	Front	Cu, Sn, Pb	Leaded bronze	Tin solder on catch
			Catch	Cu, Sn, Pb		
74	173	Brooch	Front	Cu, Sn, Zn, Pb	Leaded gunmetal	Tin solder on catch
75	166	Brooch	Not Analysed – object sent back before analysis			
75	167	Brooch	Not Analysed – object sent back before analysis			
81	115	Brooch	Front	Cu, Sn, Zn, Pb	Leaded gunmetal	–
84	137	Brooch	Front	Cu, Sn, Zn, Pb	Leaded gunmetal	–
85	235	Uncertain	Less corroded pieces	Cu, Sn, Pb	Leaded bronze	–
89	239	Coin	Front/Back	Cu, Sn, Pb	Leaded bronze	–
92	135	Brooch	Front	Cu, Sn, Pb	Leaded bronze	Identical composition to ON 222
92	222	Brooch	Front	Cu, Sn, Pb	Leaded bronze	Identical composition to ON 135
92	221	Brooch	Front	Cu, Sn, Pb	Leaded bronze	Mercury gilded
92	142	Finger-ring	Ring	Cu, Sn, Zn, Pb	Leaded gunmetal	–
93	165	Uncertain	Front/Back	Cu, Sn, Zn, Pb	Leaded gunmetal	–
96	348	Uncertain		Cu, Sn, Pb	Leaded bronze	–
106	253	Buckle	Buckle Plate	Cu, Sn, Zn, Pb	Leaded gunmetal	–
107	270	Buckle	Studs	Cu, Sn, Zn, Pb	Leaded gunmetal	–
110	267	Buckle	Loop	Cu, Sn, Zn, Pb	Leaded gunmetal	–
			Pin	Cu, Sn, Zn, Pb		
			Plate	Cu, Sn, Zn, Pb		
110	269	Pin	Pin	Cu, Sn, Zn, Pb	Leaded gunmetal	–
Colluvial deposit in coombe	140	Brooch	Front/Back	Cu, Ag, Sn, Zn, Pb	High silver content	Mercury gilded
			Garnets	Mg, Al, Si, (Ca), (Ti), (Cr), (Mn), Fe		Garnets: almandine variety
			Setting	P, Ca		Setting: shell (or bone)
Subsoil	149	Key	Key	Cu, Sn, Zn, Pb	Leaded gunmetal	–

* Elements present in relatively high levels (except copper in copper alloys) are underlined
S = from soil sample

Bibliography

Adams, J.C., 1987 *Outline of Fractures*, London, Churchill Livingstone

Akerman, J.Y., 1855a 'An account of excavations in an Anglo-Saxon burial ground at Harnham Hill, near Salisbury', *Archaeologia* 35, 259–78

Akerman, J.Y., 1855b 'Note on some further discoveries in the Anglo-Saxon burial ground at Harnham Hill, near Salisbury', *Archaeologia* 35, 475–9

Alcock, L., 1981 'Quantity or quality: the Anglian graves of Bernicia', in Evison, V.I. (ed.), *Angles, Saxons and Jutes. (Essays presented to J.N.L. Myers)*, Oxford, 168–83

Allen, M., 2005 'Radiocarbon dating', in Birbeck *et al.* 2005, 11–13

Anderson, T. and Andrews, J., 1997 'The human bones', in Parfitt, K. and Brugmann, B., *The Anglo Saxon Cemetery on Mill Hill, Deal, Kent*, London, Soc. Med. Archaeol. Monog. 14, Appendix II, 214–39

Annable, F.K. and Eagles, B.N., 2010 *The Anglo-Saxon cemetery at Blacknall Field, Pewsey, Wiltshire*, London, English Heritage

AOC Archaeology Group, 2009 *Report on the human bones from the London Transport Museum*, unpublished client report

Applebaum, S., 1954 'The agriculture of the British Early Iron Age as exemplified at Figheldean Down, Wiltshire', *Proc. Prehist. Soc.* 20, 103–14

Arnold, C.J., 1982 *The Anglo-Saxon Cemeteries of the Isle of Wight*, London, British Museum

Arnold, C.J., 1997 *An Archaeology of the Early Anglo-Saxon Kingdoms*, 2nd edition, London, Routledge

Aufderheide, A.C. and Rodríguez-Martín, C., 1998 *The Cambridge Encyclopaedia of Human Palaeopathology*, Cambridge, Univ. Press

Avent, R., 1975 *Anglo-Saxon Disc and Composite Brooches*, Oxford: Brit. Archaeol. Rep. Brit. Ser. 11

Baggs A.P., Freeman J., Smith C., Stevenson J.H. and Williamson, E., 1999, 'Collingbourne Kingston', in Crowley, D.A. (ed.), *A History of the County of Wiltshire: Volume 16: Kinwardstone Hundred*, 126–39; accessed at http://www.british-history.ac.uk/report.aspx?compid=23044 February 2009

Bass, W.M., 1987 *Human Osteology*, Columbia, Missouri Archaeological Society

Bayley, J., 2003 'The cremations', in Hawkes and Grainger 2003, 188–9

Bayliss, A., Hines, J., Høilund Nielsen, K., McCormac, G., and Scull, C., 2013 *Anglo-Saxon Graves and Grave Goods of the 6th and 7th Centuries AD: a chronological framework*, Leeds, Soc. Med. Archaeol. Monog. 33

Beek, G.C. van, 1983 *Dental Morphology: an illustrated guide*, Bristol, Wright PSG

Bergman, R.A., 1998 *Anatomy Atlases: illustrated encyclopaedia of anatomical variation*, www.anatomyatlases.org

Berry, A.C. and Berry, R.J., 1967 'Epigenetic variation in the human cranium', *J. Anatomy* 101(2), 261–379

Birbeck, V., with Smith, R.J.C., Andrews, P. and Stoodley, N., 2005 *The Origins of mid-Saxon Southampton: excavations at the Friends Provident St Mary's Stadium, 1998–2000*, Salisbury, Wessex Archaeol. Rep. 20

Blakelock, E., 2011 *The Early Medieval Cutting Edge of Technology: an archaeometallurgical, technological and social study of the manufacture and use of Anglo-Saxon and Viking iron knives, and their contribution to the early medieval iron economy*, unpubl. PhD thesis, Bradford Univ.

Blakelock, E. and McDonnell, G., 2007 'A review of the metallographic analysis of early medieval knives', *Historical Metallurgy* 41(1), 40–56

Black, E.W., 1986 'Romano-British burials customs and religious beliefs in south-east England', *Arch. J.* 143, 201–239

Boddington, A., 1990 'Models of burial, settlement and worship: The final phase reviewed', in Southworth, E. (ed.), *Anglo-Saxon Cemeteries: a reappraisal*, Stroud, Alan Sutton, 177–99

Böhner K 1958 *Die Fränkischen Altertümer des Trierer Landes*, Germanische Denkmäler der Völkerwanderungszeit ser B, 1, 1 and 2, Berlin

Bond, J.M., 1993 'Cremated animal bone', in Timby, J., 'Sancton I Anglo-Saxon cemetery: Excavations carried out between 1976 and 1980', *Arch. J.* 150, 300–8

Bond, J.M., 1994 'The cremated animal bone', in McKinley 1994, 121–35

Bond, J.M. and Worley, F.L., 2006 'Companions in death: The roles of animals in Anglo-Saxon and Viking cremation rituals in Britain', in Gowland,

R. and Knüsel, C. (eds), *Social Archaeology of Funerary Remains*, Oxford, Oxbow Books, 89–98

Bonney, D., 1979 'Early boundaries and estates in southern England', in Sawyer, P., (ed.), *English Medieval Settlement*, London, Arnold

Boulle, E., 2001 'Osteological features associated with ankle hyperdorsiflexion', *Internat. J. Osteoarchaeol.* 11 (5), 345–9

Boyle, A., Dodd, A., Miles, D. and Mudd, A., 1995 *Two Oxfordshire Anglo-Saxon cemeteries: Berinsfield and Didcot*, Thames Valley Landscape Monographs 8, Oxford, Oxford Archaeological Unit

Boyle, A., Jennings, D., Miles, D. and Palmer, S., 1998 *The Anglo-Saxon Cemetery at Butler's Field, Lechlade, Gloucestershire*, Thames Valley Landscape Monographs 10, Oxford, Oxford Archaeological Unit

Boylston, A., 2012 'Human remains', in Stoodley *et al.* 2012, 63–71

Brothwell, D. R., 1972 *Digging Up Bones*, London, British Museum (Nat. Hist.)

Brothwell, D.R. and Zakrzewski, S., 2004 'Metric and non-metric studies of archaeological human remains', in Brickley, M. and McKinley, J.I. (eds), *Guidelines to the Standards for Recording Human Remains*, Brit. Assoc. Biological Anthropol. Osteoarchaeol. and Inst. Fld Archaeol. 24–30

Brown, G., Field, D., and McOmish, D. (eds), 2006 *The Avebury Landscape: aspects of the field archaeology of the Marlborough Downs*, Oxford, Oxbow Books

Brugmann, B., 2004 *Glass Beads from Early Anglo-Saxon Graves*, Oxford, Oxbow Books

Brush, K., 1993 *Adorning the Dead: The social significance of early Anglo-Saxon funerary dress in England (fifth to seventh centuries AD)*, unpubl. PhD thesis, Univ. Cambridge

Buckwalter, J.A., 1995 'Aging and degeneration of the human intervertebral disc', *Spine* 20, 1307–14

Buikstra, J.E. and Ubelaker, D.H., 1994 *Standards for Data Collection from Human Skeletal Remains*, Arkansas Archaeol. Survey Res. Ser. 44

Butterfield, B.G. and Meylan, B.A., 1980 *Three-dimensional Structure of Wood: an ultrastructural approach*, London and New York, Chapman and Hall

Butterworth, C.A. and Lobb, S.J., 1992 *Excavations in the Burghfield Area, Berkshire. Developments in the Bronze Age and Saxon Landscapes*, Salisbury, Wessex Archaeol. Rep. 1

Cameron, A., 1988 'Cremation: a report on additional material', in Evison 1988, 466–7

Cameron, E., 2000 *Sheaths and Scabbards in England AD 400–1100*, Brit. Archaeol. Rep. Brit. Ser. 301, Oxford, Archaeopress

Carver, M.O.H., 1986 'Anglo-Saxon objectives at Sutton Hoo 1985', *Anglo-Saxon England* 15, Cambridge, Univ. Press, 139–52

Castleden, R., 1992, *Neolithic Britain: new Stone Age sites of England, Scotland and Wales*, Routledge

Cleal, R.M.J., Walker, K.E., and Montague, R., 1995, *Stonehenge in its Landscape: Twentieth-century excavations*, London, English Heritage Archaeol. Rep. 10

Cook, A.M. and Dacre, M.W., 1985 *Excavations at Portway, Andover 1973–1975*, Oxford, Oxford Univ. Comm. Archaeol. Monog. 4

Cook, J.M., 2004 *Early Anglo-Saxon Buckets: a corpus of alloy and iron-bound stave-built vessels* (ed. B Brugmann), Oxford, Oxford Univ. School Archaeol. Monog. 60

Cosack, E., 1983 *Das sachsische Graberfeld bei Liebenau*, Teil 1, Gebr. Mann Verlag. Berlin

Cronyn, J., 1990 *The Elements of Archaeological Conservation*, London, Routledge

Davies, S.M., 1985 'The excavation of an Anglo-Saxon cemetery (and some prehistoric pits) at Charlton Plantation, near Downton', *Wilts Archaeol. Natur. Hist. Mag.* 79, 109–54

Dias, G. and Tayles, N., 1997 '"Abscess Cavity" – a misnomer', *Int. J. Osteoarchaeol.* 7, 548–54

Dickinson, T.M., 1976 *The Anglo-Saxon Burial Sites of the Upper Thames Region, and their Bearing on the History of Wessex,* circa *AD 400–700*, unpubl. D.Phil thesis, Univ. Oxford

Dickinson, T.M., 1979 'On the origin and chronology of the early Anglo-Saxon disc brooch', in Hawkes, S., Brown, D. and Campbell, J., *Anglo-Saxon Studies in Archaeology and History* 1, Brit. Archaeol. Rep. Brit Ser. 72, Oxford, 39–80

Dickinson, T.M., 1993 'Early Saxon saucer brooches – a preliminary overview', *Anglo-Saxon Studies in Archaeology and History* 6, Oxford, 11–44

Dickinson, T.M. and Härke, H., 1992 *Early Anglo-Saxon Shields*, London, Antiq. Soc. London/ *Archaeologia* 110, 31–70

Down, A. and Welch, M., 1990 *Chichester Excavations 7: Apple Down and the Mardens*, Chichester District Council

Eagles, B.N., 1986 'Pagan Anglo-Saxon burials at West Overton', *Wilts Archaeol. Natur. Hist. Mag.* 80, 103–19

Eagles, B., 1994 'The archaeological evidence for settlement in the fifth to seventh centuries AD', in Aston, M. and Lewis, C. (eds), *The Medieval Landscape of Wessex*, Oxford, Oxbow Books, 13–32

Eagles, B., 2001 'Anglo-Saxon presence and culture in Wiltshire *c.* AD 450–*c.* 675', in Ellis, P. (ed.), *Roman Wiltshire and After: Papers in honour of Ken*

Annable, Devizes, Wilts Archaeol. Natur. Hist. Soc., 199–235

Edlin, H.L., 1949 *Woodland Crafts in Britain. An Account of the Traditional Uses of Trees and Timbers in the British Countryside*, London, Batsford

Egging Dinwiddy, K. and Schuster, J., 2009 'Thanet's longest excavation: Archaeological investigations along the route of the Weatherlees–Margate–Broadstairs wastewater pipeline', in Andrews, P., Egging Dinwiddy, K., Ellis, C., Hutcheson, A.,. Philpotts, C., Powell, A.B. and Schuster, J., *Kentish Sites and Sites of Kent: a miscellany of four archaeological excavations*, Salisbury, Wessex Archaeol. Rep. 24

Egging Dinwiddy, K. 2011 'An Anglo-Saxon cemetery at Twyford, near Winchester', *Proc. Hants Fld Club Archaeol. Soc.* 66, 75–126

Eiken, O. and Jonsson, K., 1980 'Carpal Bone Cysts', *Scandinavian J. Plastic and Reconstructive Surgery and Hand Surgery* 14 (3), 285–90

Ehara, S., El-Khoury, G.Y. and Bergman, R.A., 1988 'The accessory sacroiliac joint: a common anatomical variant', *American J. Roentgenology* 150, 857–9

Ekwall, E., 1991 *The Concise Oxford Dictionary of English Place-names,* Oxford, Univ. Press

Evison, V.I., 1977 'Supporting-arm and equal-arm brooches in England, *Studien zur Sachsenforschung,* 127–47

Evison, V.I., 1987 *Dover: Buckland Anglo-Saxon Cemetery*, London, Hist. Build. Monum. Comm. England Archaeol. Rep. 3

Evison, V.I., 1988 *An Anglo-Saxon Cemetery at Alton, Hampshire*, Gloucester, Hants Fld Club Monog. 4

Evison, V.I., 1994 *An Anglo-Saxon Cemetery at Great Chesterford, Essex*, London, Counc. Brit. Arch. Res. Rep. 91

Faull, M., 1976 'The location and relationship of the Sancton (Humberside North) Anglo-Saxon cemeteries', *Archaeol J.* 56, 227–33

Farronato, G., Garagiola, U., Carletti, V., Cressoni, P. and Bellintani, C., 2010 'Psoriatic arthritis: temporomandibular joint involvement as the first articular phenomenon', *Quintessence Int.* 41(5), 395–8.

Fell, V. and Starley, D., 1999 *A Technological Study of Ferrous Blades from the Anglo-Saxon Cemeteries at Boss Hall and St Stephen's Lane – Buttermarket, Ipswich, Suffolk*, Portsmouth, Ancient Monuments Laboratory report 18/99

Fern, C. and Stoodley, N., 2004 *The Early Anglo-Saxon Cemetery at Weston Colley, Micheldever, Hampshire: an interim report on excavations and fieldwork undertaken in 2004*, Privately published

Fielden, K., 1978 'The skeletal material', in Gingell 1978, 62

Finnegan, M., 1978 'Non-metric variations of the infracranial skeleton', *J. Anatomy* 125 (1), 23–37

Fisher, G., 1988. 'Style and sociopolitical organisation: a preliminary study from early Anglo-Saxon England', in Driscoll, S.T. and Niecke, M.R. (eds), *Power and Politics in Early Medieval Britain and Ireland*, Edinburgh, Univ. Press, 128–44

Fitzpatrick, A.P and Morris, E.L (eds), *The Iron Age in Wessex: recent work*, Association Française D'Etude de L'Age de Fer/Wessex Archaeology

Fulford, M.G., Powell, A.B., Entwistle R. and Raymond F., 2006 *Iron Age and Romano-British Settlements and Landscapes of Salisbury Plain*, Salisbury, Wessex Archaeol. Rep. 20

Gale, R. and Cutler, D., 2000 *Plants in Archaeology*, Westbury and Royal Botanic Gardens, Kew

Geake, H., 1997 *The Use of Grave-goods in Conversion-period England,* c. *600–*c. *850*, Oxford, Brit. Archaeol. Rep. Brit. Ser. 261

Geake, H., 2002 'Persistent problems in the study of Conversion-Period burials in England, in Lucy, S. and Reynolds, A. (eds), *Burial in Early Medieval England and Wales*, Soc. Medieval. Archaeol. Monog. 17, 144–55

Gejvall, N.G., 1981 'Determination of burnt bones from prehistoric graves', *OSSA Letters* 2, 1–13

Geological Survey of Great Britain (England and Wales) (GSGB) sheet 283, 1:50,000

Gingell, C.J. 1978 'The excavation of an early Anglo-Saxon cemetery at Collingbourne Ducis, Wiltshire', *Wilts Archaeol. Natur. Hist. Mag.* 70/71 (1975–76), 61–98

Guido, M., 1978 'The beads', in Gingell 1978, 66–7

Halsall, G., 1996 'Female status and power in early Merovingian central Austrasia: The burial evidence', *Early Medieval Europe* 5, 1–24

Harding, P. and Stoodley, N., forthcoming 'Excavations at the Old Dairy, London Road, Amesbury', *Wilts Archaeol. Natur. Hist. Mag.*

Härke, H., 1989a 'Early Saxon weapon burials: Frequencies, distributions and weapon combinations', in Hawkes, S.C. (ed.), *Weapons and Warfare in Anglo-Saxon England*, Oxford, Oxford Univ. Comm. Archaeol. Monog. 21, 49–61

Härke, H., 1989b 'Knives in early Saxon burials: blade length and age at death', *Medieval Archaeol.* 33, 144–8

Härke, H., 1992 'Changing symbols in a changing society', in Carver, M. (ed.), *England in the Age of Sutton Hoo*, Woodbridge, Boydell Press, 149–65

Härke, H., 1997 'Early Anglo-Saxon social structure', in Hines, J. (ed.), *The Anglo-Saxons: towards an ethnography*, Woodbridge, Boydell Press, 125–70

Harman, M., 1998 'The human remains', in Boyle *et al.* 1998, 43–52

Harman, M., Molleson, T. and Price, J.L., 1981 'Burials, bodies and beheadings in Romano-British and Anglo-Saxon cemeteries, *Bull. Brit. Mus. Natur. Hist. (Geol.)* 35 (3), 145–88

Havelková, P. and Villotte, S., 2007 'Enthesopathies: test of the reproducibility of the new scoring system based on current medical data', *Slovenská Antropológia* 10, 51–7

Hawkes, S.C. and Grainger, G., 2003 *The Anglo-Saxon Cemetery at Worthy Park, Kingsworthy, near Winchester, Hampshire,* Oxford Univ. School Archaeol. Monog. 59

Henderson, J., 1985 'The human remains', in Cook and Dacre 1985, 61–7

Hiatt, B., 1969 'Cremation in Aboriginal Australia', *Mankind* 7(2), 104–20

Hills, C. and Lucy, S., 2013 *Spong Hill IX: Chronology and Synthesis,* McDonald Institute for Archaeology

Hillson, S.W., 1986 *Teeth,* Cambridge, Univ. Press

Hines, J., 1997 *A New Corpus of Anglo-Saxon Great Square-headed Brooches,* Woodbridge, Boydell Press

Hirst, S., 2000 'An approach to the study of Anglo-Saxon glass beads', in Price, J. (ed.), *Glass in Britain and Ireland AD 350–1100,* Brit. Mus. Occas. Paper 127, 121–9

Hirst, S and Clarke, D., 2009 'Body bearers, containers and covers', in *Excavations at Mucking: volume 3, the Anglo-Saxon cemeteries; excavations by Tom and Margaret Jones,* Museum of London Archaeology, London, 468–78

Hoffman, M., 1983 'Beds and bedclothes in medieval Norway', in Harte, N.B. and Ponting, K.G., *Cloth and Clothing in Medieval Europe,* London, 351–67

Hogarth, A.C., 1973 'Stuctural features in Anglo-Saxon graves', *Archaeol. J.* 130, 104–19

Holden, J.L., Phakley, P.P. and Clement, J.G., 1995a 'Scanning electron microscope observations of incinerated human femoral bone: a case study', *Forensic Sci. Internat.* 74, 17–28

Holden, J.L., Phakley, P.P. and Clement, J.G., 1995b 'Scanning electron microscope observations of heat-treated human bone', *Forensic Sci. Internat.* 74, 29–45

Hunt, D.R. and Bullen, L., 2007 'The frequency of os acromiale in the Robert J. Terry Collection', *Internat. J. Osteoarchaeol.* 17, 309–17

Hyslop, M., 1963 'Two Anglo-Saxon cemeteries at Chamberlain's Barn, Leighton Buzzard, Bedfordshire', *Archaeol. J.* 120 (1963), 161–200

Jarvis, K.S., 1983 *Excavations in Christchurch 1969–1980,* Dorchester, Dorset Natur. Hist. Archaeol. Soc. Monog. 5

Katzenberg, M.A. and Saunders, S.R., 2008 *Biological Anthropology of the Human Skeleton,* Hoboken, New Jersey

Kennet District Council (KDC) 2002 *Collingbourne Ducis Conservation Area Statement,* Planning Services

Knocker, G.M., 1956 'Early burials and an Anglo-Saxon cemetery at Snell's Corner, near Horndean, Hampshire', *Proc. Hants Fld Club Archaeol. Soc.* 19, 117–71

Lawson, A.J., 2000 *Potterne 1982–5: animal husbandry in later prehistoric Wiltshire,* Salisbury, Wessex Archaeol. Rep. 17

Leeds, E.T., 1913 *The Archaeology of the Anglo-Saxon Settlements,* Oxford, Clarendon Press

Leeds, E.T., 1945 'The distribution of the Angles and Saxons archaeologically considered', *Archaeologia* 91, 1–106

Leeds, E.T. and Shortt, H. de S., 1953 *An Anglo-Saxon Cemetery at Petersfinger, near Salisbury, Wiltshire,* Salisbury, South Wiltshire and Blackmore Museum

Leney, L. and Casteel, R.W., 1975 'Simplified procedure for examining charcoal specimens for identification', *J. Archaeol. Sci.* 2, 53–159

Lethbridge, T.C., 1936 'A cemetery at Shudy Camps, Cambridgeshire', *Cambridge Antiq. Soc., Quarto Publications, new series* V, 9–12

Lewis, M.E., 2007 *The Bioarchaeology of Children: perspectives from biological and forensic anthropology,* Cambridge, Univ. Press

Lewis, M.E., 2010 'Life and death in a civitas capital: metabolic disease and trauma in the children from late Roman Dorchester, Dorset', *American Journal of Physical Anthropology* 142, 405–16

Lewis, M.E.. and Roberts, C., 1997 'Growing pains: the interpretation of stress indicators', *Int J Osteoarchaeol.* 7, 581–6

Lucy, S., 1998 *The Early Anglo-Saxon Cemeteries of East Yorkshire: an analysis and re-interpretation,* Oxford, Brit. Archaeol. Rep. Brit. Ser. 272

Lucy, S. 2000 *The Anglo-Saxon Way of Death: burial rites in early England,* Stroud, Sutton Publishing

Lucy, S. and Reynolds, A., 2002 'Burial in early medieval England and Wales: past, present and future', in Lucy, S. and Reynolds, A. (eds), *Burial in Early Medieval England and Wales,* Leeds, Soc. Med. Archaeol. Monog. 17, 1–23.

MacGregor, A. and Bolick, E., 1993 *A Summary Catalogue of the Anglo-Saxon Collections (non-ferrous metals),* Oxford, Brit. Archaeol. Rep. Brit. Ser. 230

Magnus, B., 1999 'Monsters and birds of prey. Some reflections on form and style of the Migration period', *Anglo-Saxon Stud. Archaeol. Hist.* 10, 161–72

Major, N.M. and Helms, C.A., 2000 'Sacral Stress Fractures in Long-Distance Runners', *American J. Roentgenology* 174, 727–9

Malim, T. and Hines, J., 1998 *The Anglo-Saxon Cemetery at Edix Hill (Barrington A), Cambridgeshire,* York, Counc. Brit. Archaeol. Res. Rep. 112, 261–8

Marzinzik, S., 2003 *Early Anglo-Saxon Belt Buckles (late fifth to early eighth centuries AD)*, Oxford, Brit. Archaeol. Rep. Brit. Ser. 357

Mays, S., 1998 *The Archaeology of Human Bones*, London, Routledge

Mays, S. and Taylor, G.M., 2003 'A first prehistoric case of tuberculosis from Britain', *Internat. J. Osteoarchaeol.* 13, 189–96

McCormick, E. and Watson, J., 2010 *Collingbourne Ducis, Wiltshire: Examination and analysis of the metalwork from the Anglo-Saxon cemetery*, English Heritage Res. Dept. Rep. Ser. 9/2010, Portsmouth, English Heritage

McDonnell, G., 1992 'Metallography of the Coppergate knives', in Ottaway, P. (ed.), *Anglo-Scandinavian Ironwork from 16–22 Coppergate*, The archaeology of York 17/6, London, York Archaeological Trust, 591–99

McDonnell, G., Fell, V. and Andrews, P., 1991 The *Typology of Saxon Knives from Hamwih*, London, Ancient Monuments Laboratory report 96/91

McKinley, J.I., 1993a 'Bone fragment size and weights of bone from modern British cremations and its implications for the interpretation of archaeological cremations', *Int. J. Osteoarchaeol.* 3, 283–7

McKinley, J.I., 1993b 'Cremated Bone', in Timby, J., 'Sancton I Anglo-Saxon Cemetery Excavations carried out between 1976 and 1980', *Archaeol. J.* 150, 287–99

McKinley, J.I., 1994 *The Anglo-Saxon Cemetery at Spong Hill, North Elmham. Part VIII: the cremations*, Gressenhall, E. Anglian Archaeol. 69

McKinley, J.I., 1997 'The cremated human bone from burial and cremation-related contexts', in Fitzpatrick, A.P., *Archaeological Excavations on the Route of the A27 Westhampnett Bypass, West Sussex, 1992: volume 2*, Salisbury, Wessex Archaeol. Rep. 12, 55–72

McKinley, J.I., 2000a 'The analysis of cremated bone', in Cox, M. and Mays, S. (eds), *Human Osteology*, London, Greenwich Medical Media, 403–21

McKinley, J.I., 2000b 'Phoenix rising; aspects of cremation in Roman Britain', in Millett, M., Pearce, J. and Struck, M. (eds), *Burial, Society and Context in the Roman World*, Oxford, Oxbow Books, 38–44

McKinley, J.I., 2000c 'Putting cremated human remains in context', in Roskams, S. (ed.), *Interpreting Stratigraphy: site evaluation, recording procedures and stratigraphic analysis*, Oxford, Brit. Archaeol. Rep. Int. Ser. 910, 135–40

McKinley, J.I., 2003 'The Early Saxon cemetery at Park Lane, Croydon', *Surrey Archaeol. Collect.* 90, 1–116

McKinley, J.I., 2004a 'Compiling a skeletal inventory: cremated human bone', in Brickley, M. and McKinley, J.I. (eds.), *Guidelines to the Standards for Recording Human Remains*, Brit. Assoc. Biological Anthropol. and Osteoarchaeol. and Inst. Field Archaeol., 9–12

McKinley, J.I., 2004b 'The human remains and aspects of pyre technology and cremation rituals', in Cool, H.E.M., *The Roman Cemetery at Brougham, Cumbria, Excavations 1966–67*, Britannia Monog. 21, 283–309

McKinley, J.I., 2004c 'Archaeological Investigations at The Bostle, Bronze Age and Anglo-Saxon Barrow Cemeteries, Balsdean, East Sussex, 1997', *Sussex Archaeol. Collect.* 142, 25–44

McKinley, J.I., 2005 'Cremated human remains' and 'Skeletal human remains', in Birbeck *et al.* 2005, 17–22, 47–52 and 107–10

McKinley, J.I., 2006a 'Human bone: Scheme-wide overview, Channel Tunnel Rail Link (CTRL) Section 1', specialist report series, York, Archaeology Data Service (ADS)

McKinley, J.I., 2006b 'Cremation … the cheap option?', in Gowland, R. and Knüsel, C. (eds), *Social Archaeology of Funerary Remains*, Oxford, Oxbow Books, 81–99

McKinley, J.I., 2008a 'In the heat of the pyre: efficiency of oxidation in Romano-British cremations – did it really matter?', in Schmidt, C.W and Symes, S.A (eds), *The Analysis of Burned Human Remains*, Oxford, Elsevier, 163–83

McKinley, J.I., 2008b 'Ryknield Street, Wall (Site 12)', in Powell, A.B., Booth, P., Fitzpatrick, A.P. and Crockett, A.D, *The Archaeology of the M6 Toll 2000–2003*, Oxford/Salisbury, Oxford Wessex Archaeol. Monog. 2, 87–190

McKinley, J.I., 2009a 'The human remains', in Egging Dinwiddy, K., *A Late Roman Cemetery at Little Keep, Dorchester, Dorset*, Wessex Archaeology online publication, http://www.wessexarch.co.uk/reports/64913/little-keep-dorchester, 11–35

McKinley, J.I., 2009b 'Human bone', in P. Andrews, 'West Thurrock: late prehistoric settlement, Roman burials and the medieval manor house. Channel Tunnel Rail Link Excavations 2002', *Trans Essex Soc. Archaeol. and Hist.* 40, 20–32

McKinley, J.I., 2009c The human bone from the Anglo-Saxon mixed-rite cemetery at Ringlemere, Kent, unpublished report for the British Museum

McKinley, J.I., 2010 Cherry Lodge Farm, Shrewton, Wiltshire (72100). Human bone publication report, Wessex Archaeology unpublished client report

McKinley, J.I., 2014 'Cremated human bone and mortuary rite', in N. Cooke and A. Mudd, *A46 Nottinghamshire: the archaeology of the Newark to Widmerpool improvement scheme, 2009*, Cotswold Archaeology Monograph 7/Wessex Archaeology Monograph 34, Cotswold Wessex Archaeology, Cirencester/Salisbury, 316–24

McKinley, J.I., forthcoming "How did it go?" ... putting the process back into cremation', in Pearce, J. (ed.), *Death as a Process*, Oxford, Oxbow

McKinley, J.I. and Bond, J.M., 1993 'Cremated animal bone: summary discussion', in Timby, J., 'Sancton I Anglo-Saxon cemetery: Excavations carried out between 1976 and 1980', *Archaeol. J.* 150, 308–9

McOmish, D., Field, D. and Brown, G., 2002 *The Field Archaeology of the Salisbury Plain Training Area*, Swindon, English Heritage

McOmish, D., Field, D. and Brown, G., 2010 'The Bronze Age and Early Iron Age midden site at East Chisenbury, Wiltshire', *Wilts Archaeol. Natur. Hist. Mag.* 103, 35–101

McParland, L.C., Collinson, M.E., Scott, A.C., Campbell, G. and Veal, R., 2010 'Is vitrification in charcoal a result of high temperature burning of wood?' *J. Archaeol. Sci.* 37, 2679–87

Meaney, A.L. and Hawkes, S.C., 1970 *Two Anglo-Saxon Cemeteries at Winnall, Winchester, Hampshire*, London, Soc. Medieval Archaeol. Monog. 4

Menghin, W., 1983 *Das Schwert im frühen Mittelalter*, Stuttgart, Theiss

Mills, A., 1991 *The Popular Dictionary of English Place-names*, Parragon Book Service (after Oxford University Press)

Molleson, T.I., 1993 'The human remains', in Farwell, D.E. and Molleson, T.I., *Excavations at Poundbury 1966–80. Volume II: the cemeteries*, Dorset Natur. Hist Archaeol. Soc. Monog. 11

Murphy, P., 1994, 'The carbonised plant remains from the cremations', in McKinley 1994, appendix II (microfiche)

Musty, J., 1969 'The excavation of two barrows, one of Saxon date, at Ford, Laverstock, near Salisbury', *Antiq. J.* 49, 98–117

Musty, J. and Stratton, J.E.D., 1964 'A Saxon cemetery at Winterbourne Gunner, near Salisbury', *Wilts Archaeol. Natur. Hist. Mag.* 59, 86–109

Myres, J.N.L., 1977, *A Corpus of Anglo-Saxon Pottery of the Pagan Period*, Cambridge, Univ. Press

Neville, B.W., Damm, D., Allen, C. and Bouquot, J., 2002 *Oral and Maxillofacial Pathology*, 2nd edition, London, Saunders

Nielsen-Marsh, C., Gernaey, A., Turner-Walker, G., Hedges, R., Pike, A. and Collins, M., 2000 'The chemical degradation of bone', in Cox, M. and Mays, S. (eds), *Human Osteology in Archaeology and Forensic Science*, London, GMM, 439–54

Oestigaard, T., 1999 'Cremations as transformations: when the dual cultural hypothesis was cremated and carried away in urns', *European Jour. Archaeol.* 2(3), 345–64

Ogden, A.R., 2005 *Identifying and Scoring Periodontal Disease in Skeletal Material*, Biological Anthropol. Research Centre, Univ. Bradford

Ogden, A.R., 2007 'Advances in the palaeopathology of the teeth and jaws', in Mays, S. and Pinhasi, R. (eds), *Human Palaeopathology: new directions in diagnosis and interpretation*, Chichester, John Wiley, 283–307

Ortner, D.J. and Putschar, W.G.J., 1985 *Identification of Pathological Conditions in Human Skeletal Remains*, Washington, Smithsonian Institution Press

Pader, E.J. 1980 'Material symbolism and social relations in mortuary studies', in Rahtz, P., Dickinson, T. and Watts, L. (eds), *Anglo-Saxon Cemeteries 1979. The Fourth Anglo-Saxon Symposium at Oxford*, Oxford, Brit. Archaeol. Rep. Brit. Ser. 82, 143–59

Peacock, Z., 2007 *Barrow Clump, Figheldean, Wiltshire; investigative conservation of Anglo-Saxon metalwork: archaeological conservation report*, English Heritage Res. Dept. Rep. Ser. 88/2007, Portsmouth, English Heritage

Penn, K., 2011 *The Anglo-Saxon Cemetery at Shrublands Hall Quarry, Coddenham, Suffolk*, E. Anglian Archaeol. 139

Philpott, R., 1991 *Burial Practices in Roman Britain. A Survey of Grave Treatment and Furnishings AD 43 – 410*, Oxford, Brit. Archaeol. Rep. Brit. Ser. 219

Pine, J., 2001 'The excavation of a Saxon settlement at Cadley Road, Collingbourne Ducis, Wiltshire', *Wilts Archaeol. Natur. Hist. Mag.* 94, 88–117

Pleiner, R., 2006 *Iron in Archaeology: early European blacksmiths*, Praha, Archaeologický Ústav Avěr

Powers, R., 1988 'Cremations', in Evison 1988, 464–6

Powers, N., 2008 'Cremated human remains', in Ennis, T., *An Early Saxon Cemetery at Rayleigh, Essex: excavations at the former Park School*, E. Anglian Archaeol. 127, 46–50

Prior, J. and Alvin, K.L., 1983 'Structural changes on charring woods of *Dictostachys* and *Salix* from southern Africa, *Internat. Assoc. Wood Anatomists Bull.* 4 (4), 197–206

Rawlings, M., 1995 'Archaeological sites along the Wiltshire section of the Codford–Ilchester water pipeline', *Wilts Archeol. Natur. Hist. Mag.* 88, 26–49

Richards, J., 1991 *Stonehenge Environs Project*, London, English Heritage Archaeol. Rep.

Roberts, C. and Cox, M., 2003 *Health and Disease in Britain from Prehistory to the Present Day*, Stroud, Sutton

Roberts, C. and Manchester, K., 1997 *The Archaeology of Disease*, Stroud, Sutton

Roberts, C. and Manchester, K., 2005 *The Archaeology of Disease,* 3rd edition, Cornell Univ. Press

Roberts C. and McKinley J.I., 2003 'Review of trepanations in British antiquity focusing on funerary context to explain their occurrence', in Arnott, R., Finger, S. and Smith, C.U.M., *Trepanation, History-Discovery-Theory*, Abingdon, Swets and Zeitlinger

Rogers, J. and Waldron, T., 1995 A *Field Guide to Joint Disease in Archaeology*, Chichester, Wiley

Ross, S., 1991 *Dress Pins from Anglo-Saxon England: their production and typo-chronological development*, unpubl. D.Phil thesis, Univ. Oxford

Salter, R.B., 1999 *Textbook of Disorders and Injuries of the Musculoskeletal System: an introduction of orthopaedics, fractures and joint injuries, rheumatology, metabolic bone disease, and rehabilitation*, 3rd edition, Baltimore

Samuels, L.E., 1999 *Light Microscopy of Carbon Steels*, Ohio, ASM.

Scheuer, L. and Black, S., 2000 *Developmental Juvenile Osteology*, London, Academic Press

Schwartz, J.H., 1995 *Skeleton Keys: an introduction to human skeletal morphology, development, and analysis*, Oxford, Univ. Press

Schweingruber, F.H., 1990 *Microscopic Wood Anatomy,* 3rd edition, Birmensdorf, Swiss Federal Institute for Forest, Snow and Landscape Research

Semple, S., 2003 'Burials and political boundaries in the Avebury region, north Wiltshire', *Anglo-Saxon Studies in Archaeology and History* 12, 72–91

Sherlock, S. and Welch, M. 1992 *An Anglo-Saxon Cemetery at Norton, Cleveland*, York, Counc. Brit. Archaeol. Res. Rep. 82

Sjovold, T., 1969 *The Oseberg Find and other Viking Ship Finds* (trs. M.F. Sjovold), Universitetets Oldsakamling

Soames J.V. and Southam S.R., 2005 *Oral Pathology*, 4th edition, Oxford, Univ. Press

Sobajima, S., Kim, J.S., Gilbertson, L.G. and Kang, J.D., 2004 'Gene therapy for degenerative disc disease', *Gene Therapy* 11, 390–401

Speake, G., 1989 *A Saxon Bed Burial on Swallowcliffe Down*, English Heritage Archaeol. Rep. 10

Stace, C., 1997 *New Flora of the British Isles,* 2nd edition, Cambridge, Univ. Press

Starley, D., 1996 *A Technological Study of Knives and Spearheads from the Excavations at Mucking, Essex*, Portsmouth, Ancient Monuments Laboratory report 37/96

Stedman, M. and Stoodley, N., 2000 'Eight early Anglo-Saxon metalwork pieces from the central Meon Valley, Hampshire', *Proc. Hants Fld Club Archaeol. Soc.* 55, 133–41

Stirland, A.J., 2005 *The Men of the Mary Rose: raising the dead*, Stroud, Sutton

Stoodley, N., 1999a *The Spindle and the Spear: a critical enquiry into the construction and meaning of gender in the early Anglo-Saxon burial rite*, Oxford, Brit. Archaeol. Rep. Brit. Ser. 288

Stoodley, N., 1999b 'Burials rites, gender and the creation of kingdoms: the evidence from seventh century Wessex', Oxford, *Anglo-Saxon Stud. Archaeol. Hist.* 10, 99–107

Stoodley, N., 2000 'From the cradle to the grave: Age organisation and the early Anglo-Saxon burial rite', *World Archaeol.* 31 (3), 456–72

Stoodley, N., 2002 'Multiple burials, multiple meanings? Interpreting the early Anglo-Saxon multiple interment', in Lucy, S. and Reynolds, A. (eds), *Burial in early medieval England*, Leeds, Soc. Med. Archaeol. Monog. 17, 103–21

Stoodley, N., 2006a 'Changing burial practice in seventh-century Hampshire: The Anglo-Saxon cemetery at Portway West, Andover', *Proc. Hants Fld Club Archaeol. Soc.* 61, 63–80

Stoodley, N., 2006b 'The cemetery', in Williams and Newman 2006, 173–9

Stoodley, N., 2007 'New perspectives on cemetery location in the seventh century AD: The example of Portway, Andover', Oxford, *Anglo-Saxon Stud. Archaeol. Hist.* 14, 154–62

Stoodley, N., 2010 'The social structure of the Anglo-Saxon cemetery', in Annable and Eagles 2010, 87–100

Stoodley forthcoming Barrow Clump, Figheldean, Wiltshire

Stoodley, N., Boylston, A. and McKinley, J.I., 2012 'An Early Anglo-Saxon cemetery at Aldbourne, Wiltshire', *Wilts Archaeol. Natur. Hist. Mag.* 105, 58–96

Stratascan, 2006 Geophysical Survey Report, Collingbourne Ducis, Wiltshire, unpublished report

Struck, M., 2000 'High Status burials in Roman Britain (first–third century AD) – potential interpretation', in Millett, M., Pearce, J. and Struck, M. (eds), *Burial, Society and Context in the Roman World*, Oxford, Oxbow Books, 85–96

Stuckert, C., 2010 'The human remains', in Annable and Eagles 2010, 111–38

Swanton, M.J, 1973 *The Spearheads of the Anglo-Saxon Settlements*, London, Roy. Archaeol. Inst.

Tainter, J.A., 1975 'Social inference and mortuary practices; An experiment in numerical classification', *World Archaeol.* 7, 1–15

Taylor, G.M., Young, D.B. and Mays, S. 2005 'Genotypic analysis of the earliest known prehistoric case of tuberculosis in Britain, *J. Clinical Microbiol.* 43 (5), 2236–40

Thomas, N., 2005 *Snail Down, Wiltshire: the Bronze Age barrow cemetery and related earthworks, in the parishes of Collingbourne Ducis and Collingbourne Kingston. Excavations 1953, 1955 and 1957*, Wilts Archaeol. Natur. Hist. Soc./English Heritage Monog. 3

Trotter, M. and Gleser, G.C., 1952 'Estimation of stature from long bones of American whites and Negroes', *American J. Physical Anthropol.* 10(4), 463–514

Trotter, M. and Gleser, G.C., 1958 'A re-evaluation of estimation of stature based on measurements of stature taken during life and of long bones after death,' *American J. Physical Anthropol.* 16 (1), 79–123

Tubb, P.C., 2011 'Late Bronze Age/Early Iron Age transition sites in the Vale of Pewsey: the East Chisenbury midden in its regional context', *Wilts Archaeol. Natur. Hist. Mag.* 104, 44–61

Tylecote, R.F. and Gilmour, B.J.J., 1986 *The Metallography of Early Ferrous Edge Tools and Edged Weapons,* Oxford, Brit. Archaeol. Rep. Brit. Ser. 155

Underwood, R., 1999 *Anglo-Saxon Weapons and Warfare,* Stroud, Tempus

Walker, P., Bathurst, R., Richman, R., Gjerdrum, T. and Andrushko, V., 2009 'The causes of porotic hyperostosis and *cribra orbitalia*: a reappraisal of the iron-deficiency-anaemia hypothesis', *American J. Physical Anthropol.* 139, 109–25

Walton Rogers, P., 2007 *Cloth and Clothing in Early Anglo-Saxon England AD 450–700,* York, Counc. Brit. Archaeol. Res. Rep. 145

Ward, C.V, Mays, S., Child, S. and Latimer, B., 2010 'Lumbar vertebral morphology and isthmic spondylosis in a British medieval population', *American J. Physical Anthropol.* 141, 273–80

Watson, J., 2006 *The Examination and Reconstruction of an Anglo-Saxon Bed Burial from Smythes Corner (Shrublands Quarry), Coddenham, Suffolk,* English Heritage Res. Dept. Rep. Ser. 60/2006, Portsmouth, English Heritage

Watson, J., 2009 'Swords: Hilts and scabbards' and 'Spears: Organic evidence', in Hirst and Clark 2009, 569–71

Welch, M.G., 1992 *Anglo-Saxon England,* London, English Heritage

Wells, C., Grainger, G., Denston, B. and Hawkes, S.C., 2003 'The inhumations and cremations', in Hawkes and Grainger 2003, 153–87

Wessex Archaeology 2006 *Land to the rear of 106–108 Cadley Road, Collingbourne Ducis, Wiltshire. Assessment of results of an archaeological evaluation and watching brief,* unpublished client report ref. 62670.02

Wessex Archaeology 2008 *Land to the rear of 106–108 Cadley Road, Collingbourne Ducis, Wiltshire: Assessment report on archaeological excavation and proposals for post-excavation analysis and publication,* unpublished client report ref: 62671.03

Wessex Archaeology, 2009a *106 Cadley Road, Collingbourne Ducis, Wiltshire: Archaeological watching brief report,* unpublished client report ref. 71830.01

Wessex Archaeology, 2009b. *Roxanna, Cadley Road, Collingbourne Ducis, Wiltshire: Archaeological watching brief report,* unpublished client report ref: 71750.01

Wessex Archaeology 2013 *An Early Bronze Age Barrow and Anglo-Saxon cemetery at Barrow Clump, Figheldean, Wiltshire: interim assessment report* on the 2012 Operation Nightingale excavation, unpublished report ref: 83570.01, available online at: http://www.wessexarch.co.uk/system/files/BarrowClump2012.pdf#sthash.NqHgJRFa.dpuf

Williams, H., 1997 'Ancient landscapes and the dead: The re-use of prehistoric and Roman monuments in early Anglo-Saxon burial sites, *Med. Arch.* 41, 1–32

Williams, H., 2002 '"Remains of Pagan Saxondum"? – The study of Anglo-Saxon cremation rites', in Lucy, S. and Reynolds, A. (eds), *Burial in Early Medieval England,* Leeds, Soc. Med. Archaeol. Monog. 17, 47–71

Williams, H., 2004 'Death warmed up. The agency of bodies and bones in Early Anglo-Saxon cremation rites, *J. Material Culture* 9 (3), 263–91

Williams, H., 2006 *Death and Memory in Early Medieval Britain,* Cambridge, Univ. Press

Williams, P. and Newman, R., 2006 *Market Lavington, Wiltshire: an Anglo-Saxon cemetery and settlement,* Salisbury, Wessex Archaeol. Rep. 19

Wilson, D.M., 1992 *Anglo-Saxon Paganism,* London, Routledge

Wood, M., 1986 Domesday: *A search for the roots of England,* London, BBC books

Lightning Source UK Ltd.
Milton Keynes UK
UKOW07f0228260516

274983UK00005B/15/P